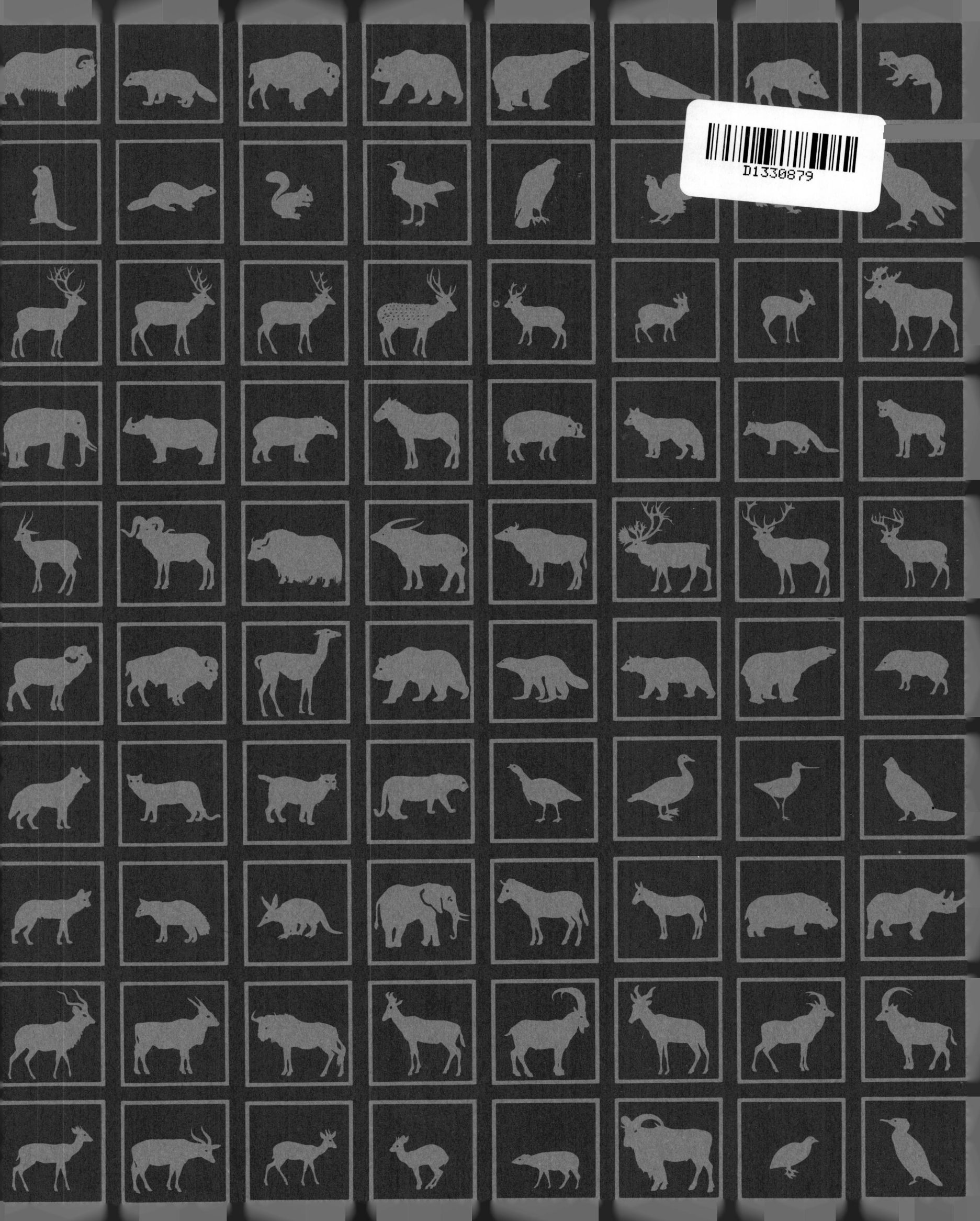

The Book of Hunting

Conception and editorial direction:
Ruth Bucher

Graphic conception and design:
Hans Kammermann

Technical advisor:
Ernst Schäfer

English-language editor:
Norman Gelb

Text:
X. Ammann, Ruth Bucher, C. Hettier de Boislambert, Hartmut Jungius, Augustin Krämer, Fred Kurt, Walther Niedl, Karl Salzle, Ernst Schäfer

Introduction:
Norman Gelb

Animal drawings:
Walter Linsenmaier

English translation:
Maureen Oberli-Turner

PADDINGTON PRESS LTD

NEW YORK & LONDON

The Book of Hunting

Library of Congress Cataloging in Publication Data

Main entry under title:
The Book of hunting.

Translation of Das Buch der Jagd.
Includes index.
1. Hunting. 2. Game and game-birds. 3. Wildlife
conservation. I. Bucher, Ruth, 1911-
SK33.B88113   799.2   77-5031
ISBN 0-448-22185-3

IN THE UNITED STATES
PADDINGTON PRESS LTD.
Distributed by
GROSSET & DUNLAP

IN THE UNITED KINGDOM
PADDINGTON PRESS LTD.

IN CANADA
Published by
McCLELLAND & STEWART LTD.

IN AUSTRALIA
Distributed by
ANGUS & ROBERTSON PTY. LTD.

IN SOUTHERN AFRICA
Distributed by
ERNEST STANTON (Publishers) (Pty.) LTD.

Introduction

Hunting is man's most venerable calling, pursuit and profession. Older than civilization, older than agriculture, it is as old as mankind itself.

Hunting is a world of its own. It is a realm in which the hunter probes the elusive, timeless mysteries of the man–animal confrontation. It is a region in which he tests his skills, rates his reflexes and proves himself against a range of personal and objective yardsticks. Hunting is a vast domain, measured by many moods and methods: by caliber and cunning, patience and pride, by alertness and often by agony over the squandering of our natural heritage.

This book, a panoramic image of the world of hunting, is dedicated to hunters and nature lovers everywhere. They will find in these pages the enchantment which has drawn man the hunter into the woods and the fields since he first walked the Earth. The hunter who ventures out in search of game these days may be better armed and more warmly clothed than his prehistoric forebears. But he is going through the same spiritual motions. The bond between him and the animal he hunts is the same. And, though we have come a long way since the days of primitive *Homo sapiens*, many of his basic hunting methods—stalking, lying in wait, trapping—are the same as well.

It is commonly believed that man developed his skills as a hunter because of his superior brain power. But, in fact, it may have been just the other way round. In his book *The Hunting Hypothesis* Robert Ardrey suggests that man evolved from his ape-like ancestors and developed a larger, more intricate brain *because* he was a hunter, unable to match the strength and speed of the animals he hunted. What were his teeth compared to the tusks of a wild hog? How could his agility match that of a big cat? Where were his claws? To compensate for these comparative physical shortcomings, man evolved a superior brain—still his proudest distinction. To survive, he had to develop the capacity to devise ways for outwitting and overwhelming his prey. He had to invent effective weapons. He had to form bands of hunters to outmatch animals which would otherwise have escaped, leaving him without a meal.

That was the genesis of human communities. Those earliest concerted hunting expeditions, with primitive humans functioning as a team, were the origins of what was gradually to develop over enormous spans of time into the towns and metropolises of today. Remarkable as it may seem, Chicago, London, Paris, Peking—all cities of the world—actually have their remote roots in a group of cavemen banding together for the first time to bring down a mammoth elephant for dinner!

Those early hunters—the forebears of all hunters in history—depended on the animals they pursued or trapped to nourish and sustain them. Inevitably, they formed religious-mystical links with the animal world without which they could not have existed. In many cases, they worshipped the animals they hunted. These served as intermediaries between themselves and the dark, inscrutable forces which they believed governed their often harsh environments and their often disagreeable climates. Prehistoric cave drawings testify to the attention and implicit tribute paid to mammoths, bison, deer and other game animals by the world's first artists, men who probably held semi-priestly rank in their communities.

About 11,000 years ago our ancestors discovered, probably somewhere in the Middle East, that crops could be cultivated. They discovered that if those crops were properly tended, they would be able to feed themselves and their families (and, later, their communities) on a regular basis. Until this birth of agriculture, humans had always sustained themselves through hunting, fishing and gathering edible wild plants. But the advent of agriculture had little immediate effect on hunting habits. It spread slowly around the world and much time passed before tending the fields was a common activity in human settlements. But, even after agriculture had become a standard part of human life, hunting remained a major source of food. When the hunting was bad, people went hungry in many places. When it was good, it was time for rejoicing. Animal gods and goddesses were invoked to influence the forces affecting mankind's well-being. Right through early history, these animal deities played an important role in man's spiritual evolution. As often as not, the animal gods were deified representatives of commonly hunted species. Such was the bond between man and his prey that this audacious choice of victim-as-god struck the hunter as neither inappropriate nor ironic.

Even when civilization had progressed far enough for game to be no longer essential for survival hunting continued to be widely practiced. Charles Dickens explained: "There is a passion for hunting something deeply implanted in the human breast." This very real "passion" extended across various aspects of hunting—the thrill of stalking, the pleasure of tramping through forest or across meadow or of scanning the horizons of jungle-ringed savannah on a sun-baked morning, and the excitement of aiming at and hitting the target.

It is impossible, however, to define accurately the source of man's hunting enthusiasm now that, in most cases, he no longer *must* hunt to survive. But it is an obsession and an instinct which transcends the categories and classes into which humans divide themselves. Hunters come from all walks of life. For some, it may be the refreshing "return to nature" sought by so many city dwellers. For other people, it is the ancient lure of the encounter between man and his prey, between victor and victim. Then there is the challenge of the hunt, the test of skill through which the hunter puts himself each time. There are those who relish handling fine weapons. For others, alas, it is merely the antlers they will bring back to hang on the wall of the den, or the bear skin to drape across the floor in front of the fire.

There is, however, no justification or excuse for random, senseless slaughter of animals today. There are too many endangered species, too many breeds on the brink of extinction. Responsible hunters, cherishing the animals they hunt, value the rules and regulations imposed by the community to keep those animals from disappearing from the face of the Earth. It is a problem which our primitive ancestors, comparatively few in number and armed only with clubs, throwing sticks, spears and arrows, did not have to contemplate. But the increasing intrusion of human settlement into areas once exclusively the domain of game animals and the development of modern hunting weapons have changed all that. The American bison has barely been saved from extinction. The polar bear is now in serious danger. The World Wildlife Fund has compiled a list of thirty-six species and sixty-four sub-species of mammals that have died out altogether since about 1600, as well as dozens of species of birds. It is obvious that the animal kingdom must be protected or there will be few animals to see and even fewer to hunt. It is a prospect which responsible hunters everywhere are coming increasingly to recognize.

That is one of the many dimensions of the world of hunting with which the following pages deal in depth. This book embraces all facets of hunting and the animal world to which hunting is related. Richly punctuated with some of the most extraordinary animal photographs ever published, this book covers, among other subjects: the history of hunting, the animal kingdom, the religious-mystical implications of the man–animal confrontation, hunters and their weapons, hunting methods, animal conservation and biology. This book brings to life the thrill and adventure of hunting and the wonders of our natural heritage.

The primeval phenomenon of the hunt, the ceaseless struggle for survival, as old as life itself; animals hunting and being hunted in turn, the weaker and less nimble succumbing to the stronger and more agile. The big cats, the most perfect beasts of prey, evolved over thousands of generations. Just as prehistoric tigers tracked down giant deer during the Stone Age, lions hunt zebra on the great African plains today. It is usually the lioness which goes in for the kill.

A moment of truth in the great drama of life. Mortal terror and the cry of death. With bared teeth, a fleeing baboon faces its deadly enemy, the leopard, for the last time. Its fate is sealed; its anguished shrieks and maneuverings are in vain. But sometimes a troop of baboons, uttering fierce battle cries, will move in to attack, regardless of danger, to save one of their own.

"Is man an ape or an angel?" the nineteenth-century British prime minister Benjamin Disraeli asked, and concluded: "I . . . am on the side of the angels." Alas, he was wrong. Since Disraeli's times, the controversy over human origins kindled by Darwin's theory of evolution has been neatly resolved. Overwhelming and conclusive evidence has led to general acceptance that man's ancestor was an ape, probably of a species which ascended to historic oblivion, fading out in the shadow of the human it became. There is no longer any doubt about a link. A profusion of behavioral similarities confirms a common ape-man heritage, though not always to everyone's satisfaction. When, in South Africa's Makapan caves, Raymond Dart found the remains of ancient baboons with broken skulls alongside the bones of antelopes, and suggested that they had been attacked by larger apes which had used the bones as weapons, he was met with incredulity. Dart's contention that non-human primates could hunt with weapons other than those with which they were naturally endowed was dismissed as absurd. However, Jane Goodall, who studied the behavior of chimpanzees in the wild over an extended period of time, observed that they did indeed use sticks and branches as weapons and levers and that they were capable of killing young baboons and bush pigs with carefully aimed stones. They also used twigs to "fish" termites from termite mounds and could manipulate leaves as spoons. Despite these skills, the gap between ape and man remains vast. The development of the human brain was more significant than man's purely physical evolution. Modern man's brain weighs between thirty-six and fifty-two ounces; the chimpanzee's weighs only about fourteen ounces. The implications of this difference are enormous. They account for man's attainment of an upright posture, speech and technological skills. His ability to create sophisticated weapons made him nature's supreme hunter. The invention of the bow and arrow was a turning point in history. Comparison between the prehistoric wall painting, above, and the photograph of the Bororo-Peul hunter from Brazil, left, reveals not only how long ago the bow and arrow were perfected but also that the development of weapons mirrors the development of general technological aptitudes of peoples.

The Essence of Hunting

There is no intention here to trace the history of hunting from its primeval origins to the present day. Man's ingenuity when faced with beasts of prey, superior in strength, speed and instinct, will be recounted in the following pages. But to attempt a detailed record would inevitably be hopelessly monotonous. Prehistoric man devised all the basic forms of hunting known to mankind. His descendants merely perfected existing techniques—hunting with lances, spears, harpoons, lassos, slings, boomerangs and bows and arrows; extricating prey from caves and lairs; trapping it with snares and nets; stalking it with animal masks and other forms of camouflage; stampeding game over steep cliffs, as did the buffalo-hunting Indians of America's Great Plains, or toward previously positioned hunters. Those methods are—or were—common to so many peoples around the world that it would be pointless to describe them over and over again, with only the settings different. Instead, in the following pages, the vast kaleidoscope of hunting will be examined and illuminated by extracting and exploring its highlights. Here are the ways of the hunter and of his prey. Here also are related cultural phenomena—for example, religious practice, magic and ritual as defined in the confrontation between man the hunter and the animal he hunts, and as recorded in photographs, some of which are published here for the first time.

Left: Archers and cattle. Prehistoric drawings, Jabbaren, Tassili, in the Sahara.

Hunting, Magic and Art before the Dawn of History

The artistic pursuits of mankind have always reached to the heart of things. They have always reflected whatever has been thought most crucial to human existence and most basic to the human spirit. It is, therefore, no surprise that hunting is one of the earliest and most widespread themes of mankind's aesthetic imagination. A rich legacy of primitive art testifies to the exalted position occupied by hunting in the pattern of even prehistoric human endeavor.

It is still there for all to see. Painted or engraved on stone, out in the open or deep within sunless caverns, in many parts of the world, these renderings reveal what the primitive hunter saw, or thought he saw, when meeting the challenge of the chase and the kill.

The cave drawings of northern Spain and southern France are particularly well known around the world, by virtue of excellent illustrations in books on prehistoric art. The primordial graffiti in the cave of Lascaux, which has been called the Sistine Chapel of Prehistory, are almost as famous as more recent masterpieces of art. There is, however, an important distinction. Stone Age artists had

no predecessors. Unlike their successors, whose works fill our museums, they learned from no one. They were the innovators, the curtain raisers. What they did opened an era. A purely aesthetic assessment of their work, therefore, does not suffice. Nor is it possible to determine if it was only the joy of creation which impelled men, in the closing phase of the last great Ice Age, to decorate the walls of their caves, or stones outside, with images of animals—with panoramas of deer, wild horses, primitive cattle, mammoths, bisons, troglodytic bears, wild boars, ibexes and other creatures which roamed the world. It is clear, however, that their artistic motives were enhanced and perhaps transformed by an impersonal, obsessive, probably religious desire to cover their cave walls or nearby outcroppings with hosts of animal tableaux.

Did prehistoric hunters hope to rob the animals of their strength and magnify their own by capturing the essences of their prey on stone with ocher, feldspar, charcoal and whatever other useful drawing substances were within reach? Or did they hope to

induce the herds of wild animals they hunted to multiply through ritual magic invoked by their own artistic involvement? Was it luck they were after, or power? Or both? How much of it was a tribute to a deity of the animals, a god to whom Stone Age man prayed, a god he feared, a god he sought to please and appease?

Any suggestion that their art was mere decoration can be dismissed by contemplating the enormous effort that went into it. Many images were drawn or etched deep within caves, far from natural light. Fires had to be built and sustained while the caveman artist got on with his work. The paintings at Font-de-Gaume are 215 feet from the cave entrance, and in Niaux the cave paintings are more than a quarter of a mile in. Even with the help of flashlights and torches, it is not always easy to locate some of them today. They were often concealed in hidden corners and niches. It seems obvious that they were not intended exclusively as aesthetic objects to be admired and acclaimed. Much more must have been involved.

Intriguingly, the hunter himself is often only incidental to these

images. In the caves of northern Spain and southern France particularly, the emphasis is almost exclusively on the animals, with only grudging artistic attention paid to the humans whose prey they had become. This emphasis is, however, not evident in the famous, exquisite rock drawings and engravings of the Tassili plateau in the Sahara. There, the portrayals are on open rock faces or under overhanging rock formations. Rather than concentrating on the prey, or even on hunting, the Tassili images cover a formidable range of human activity, with hunting an essential but not exclusive focus.

Right: Detail from a fresco in the Great Hall in Lascaux, also known as the Hall of the Bull.

Cave drawings from eastern Spain, between 10,000 and 2000 B.C. The vigor of the figures is characteristic of the art of this region and is in contrast to the still-life approach of much prehistoric art.

The Cult of the Bear

Discoveries within the last few decades that prehistoric man had lived and formed stable communities in the alpine regions of Switzerland caused a stir in archaeological circles. It had been believed that such altitudes could only have supported human life long after the last great Ice Age, when more agreeable climates would have been conducive to settlement.

Surprise that primitive man was much more adaptable than had been believed was compounded by a further remarkable finding. Trappings of a comparatively sophisticated hunting culture were unearthed in the innermost recesses of the alpine caves in which those prehistoric humans lived. Evidence accumulated and soon it became evident that they had venerated bears which, it seemed, they had also hunted. With what appears to have been loving piety, skulls and bones of bears were carefully placed in stone enclosures, in niche-like indentations in cave walls, along the walls in slab-protected chambers and on rock ledges. In each case, the bones seem to have been handled with such care and devotion that they have been preserved in remarkably good condition for more than 120,000 years. This suggests distinct religious motivation.

It also suggests very strongly that there existed a primitive alpine hunting and sacrificial bear cult. The existence of similar cults in various other primitive communities, in some cases persisting to the present day, makes this conclusion particularly intriguing.

Bear cults have been so varied, and their nuances so numerous, that a study of them could prove exhaustive. Wherever the bear existed as an animal to be hunted—among Siberian tribes, for example—it also played an important role in the religious practices of the tribes involved. It was usually either the object of divine worship or figured as a messenger from the gods. Sometimes it was worshipped as an ancestor who had donned a bearskin and only seemed to be a bear.

A strikingly distinctive bear cult was that of the Ainu, a people from northern Asia whose surviving descendants now live mostly on the island of Sakhalin. The Ainu believed in a hierarchy of spiritual beings, at the head of which was a supreme god. This god was, however, so exalted and inaccessible to mere humans that he could never be addressed directly. Extremely pious, the Ainu surrounded themselves with sacred objects within their homes and often on exterior walls as well. Most intriguing of these objects were the *inoa*—sacrificial staffs or wands—which were planted in the ground in series (as shown in picture 4 at the right). The *inoa* were regarded as mediators between man and the deities, and were important components of sacrificial ceremonies, serving as exalted messengers—as, indeed, did the bear. Speeches in praise of the bear were made at festive banquets. Prior to ritual sacrifice, appeals for forgiveness and mercy were directed at the animal.

It was considered especially important for the Ainu to capture a bear cub alive during their ritual bear hunt. This cub would be carefully raised and was often suckled by an Ainu woman. When it was grown—two or three years old—a great bear festival would be arranged. In the opening ceremony a respected member of the tribe would approach the bear, sit down before its wooden cage and inform it that it was now about to be sent home to its ancestors. While the tribal dignitary pleaded for the bear's forgiveness, its human foster-mother would weep copiously. The animal would then be taken from its enclosure and led by ropes to the place of sacrifice where it would be strangled between two sections of a tree-trunk split down the middle.

Japanese paintings and drawings provide much detailed information about these and related ceremonies. One shows a dead bear spread out on a mat. Behind it, swords are displayed and a number of *inoa* protrude from the ground. In front of the bear there are sacrificial offerings—cakes in a lacquered dish and sake bowls on pedestals.

In the evening a feast was held in which the bear was ceremoniously consumed, and washed down with substantial amounts of sake. For the feast, a wooden hut known as the "bear chapel" was erected on the edge of the village. Its walls were of wickerwork, stretched between posts and covered with a canopy-like roof of boughs and leafed branches. The front of the hut was left open to afford a good view of the bear. The animal's head, together with part of its skin, was attached to a screen, with its eyes fixed on the revelers.

1

3

Japanese scroll. Scenes relate to the bear cult of the Ainu on southern Sakhalin Island, 19th century.

1 Sacrificial bear in its cage. Women took part in these bear festivities, although they had little to do in most other Ainu religious rites.

2 Bear being led by ropes to the place of sacrifice.

3 Wake of dignitaries for the sacrificed bear.

4 Honoring the bear. Sacrificial offerings on display.

2

4

Cultures of Ancient America

Many things are obscured by the passage of time, but no shroud of mystery covers the ways of hunting in ancient Peru, even in the period before that country was conquered by record-keeping Spanish adventurers in the sixteenth century. The Chimu, whose civilization was to be absorbed by the Inca Empire (which was in turn to be crushed by the Spaniards), were prolific designers of decorative pottery, enormous amounts of which they buried with their dead. Of many shapes and sizes, these vessels, with their descriptive scenes of everyday Chimu life and of Chimu legends, tell us much more, and in much greater detail, than could a library of written documents. This is life captured in simple picture form, and a comprehensive idea of the hunting customs of this ancient people can be formulated from their ceramic illustrations.

Portrayals of fox-hunting scenes are particularly impressive. The fox was considered sacred, a devotion which is probably best exhibited by the bronze knob of a Chimu ceremonial staff. The knob bears concentric rings with bells attached and is enclosed by the images of four foxes up on their hind legs performing a graceful dance. This ritual staff, dating back to around A.D. 1200, was found at Chanchan, the Chimu capital.

Their apparently exalted religious status did not save foxes from being hunted by the Chimu. A surviving illustration provides the proof—across a landscape of sandy hills, indicated by a wavy line (and by cacti not included in the detail produced here), two hunters are shown pursuing foxes. Their elegant attire indicates aristocratic standing. Their weapons are reed spears and a woven sling and throwing sticks. Many richly decorated throwing sticks have been found in Chimu tombs.

Deer hunting was probably also popular. Several pictures indicating as much, like those above, have been found on excavated pottery. The Chimu were unfamiliar with the laws of perspective. Depth of field was indicated by series of stripes superimposed on each other. Hunters and their game thus seem suspended over a large net which is knotted to stakes projecting diagonally from the ground. The attire and adornment of the deer hunters are as opulent as those of the men who hunted foxes. Unlike fishing and seal hunting, which

were undertaken by more simply clad hunters, it appears that deer hunting was the preserve of the nobler classes.

According to the early Chimu, it was not only man who was a dedicated hunter, but gods and demons. The preference was, apparently, for fish and bird hunting. Pictures illustrating such pursuits are common in painting on unearthed pottery. An example is an image of the great snaketail god, who is seen grasping a wildly protesting cormorant by the neck before dispatching it with an ax. These illustrations indicate the significance of hunting in ancient Peru. Although they stem from a time when hunting had already ceased to be the main source of sustenance for the people involved, they reveal that the hunt had become a popular sport and pastime.

Most of the relics of hunting in the Aztec civilization of Mexico come from a later period, when the Aztec culture was in the process of being brutally obliterated by the Spanish *conquistadores*.

An illustrated map, drawn around 1550 by Aztec artists at the command of Spanish overseers, shows the sea teeming with fish and water birds and the land profusely populated with deer, hare and fowl—all of them eminently huntable game. The weapons shown in the map are bows and arrows and nets. It is likely that Aztec peasants went hunting to enrich their scanty diet or to earn money by selling their catch.

The Aztec domain, between the lakes of high valleys, offered far too little scope for intensive agriculture. Nevertheless, even though fish and fowl played an important role in providing sufficient nourishment, hunting became more than an economic necessity for the Aztecs. Members of their aristocracy, personally untroubled by such questions, hunted only for pleasure on their enormous estates, in splendid parks and on the open range, all rich in game birds. One historian says, "When Montezuma wanted to be diverted, he had twenty-five of his leading nobles summoned together and went with them to one of his palaces, in the district known today as Tacubaya. He then went into the palace garden alone and amused himself by shooting at birds with a pea-shooter." Even the Spaniards allowed the Aztec emperor, who was an enthusiastic hunter, this simple

pleasure when he was their prisoner in this capital city of Tenochtitlán. Under observation, he was even permitted to hunt deer, hare and rabbit in the surrounding region.

The Aztecs were also fond of *battue* hunts, in which animals were driven toward hunters by beaters deployed to beat the underbrush and woods and thus frighten the prey into stampeding. Such hunts were especially organized in Quecholi, the fourteenth month of the Aztec calendar, which was dedicated to the war god, Uitzilipochtli, and to Mixcoatl, the god of

Vessel and painting. Classical Maya period, probably A.D. 650–750.

hunting. "On the tenth day of the month, all the hunters of Mexico and Tlateloco met on the wooded slopes of the mountain Zacatepetl and spent the night there in bowers. At daybreak, they formed themselves into a long line, 'like a rope made of a single strand,' and drove deer, coyotes and rabbits down into the valley, where they picked them off." Anyone who killed a roebuck or a coyote received a present from the emperor, who also invited all the participants to a post-hunt feast. In the evening, the hunters returned to their homes in the cities with the heads of their prey as trophies.

Hunting developed into a ceremonial occasion as well as a nobleman's sport among the Aztecs. But for the Chichimec, a nomadic

people of the plains of northern Mexico from whom the Aztecs may have sprung, hunting had been primarily an important source of food. Aztec priests retained Mixcoatl, the Chichimec god of hunting, singling him out for particular veneration and establishing him well up in their pantheon of deities. Although the ancient Chichimec weapon, the bow and arrow, had already lost its crucial importance to spears and axes by the time the Aztecs established their formidable empire on the Mexican plateau in the fourteenth and fif-

and Huichol Indians of Mexico still revere the morning star as the great hunter, the first to have taught the gods how to shoot with bow and arrow. These tribes believe too that this deity also appears sometimes as a huge deer—an omen, they say, of luck in hunting.

In ancient American art there is no end of surprises in the intricate profusion of symbolic elements with which the gods come equipped, and in often enigmatic mythological happenings. The deer has penetrated the mythology of the whole primitive world with its magical

holding a bundle of bamboo sticks in his left hand blows on a large shell trumpet. On the right, a deer is trapped by two men armed with spears—the one on the left blows on a shell trumpet; the one on the right grasps the antlers above the deer's head. The animal wears a blanket decorated with death symbols in the form of crossed bones. A vulture hovers over the deer, apparently ready to pounce on its remains.

To interpret this scene it is necessary to take into account the fact that many life and death

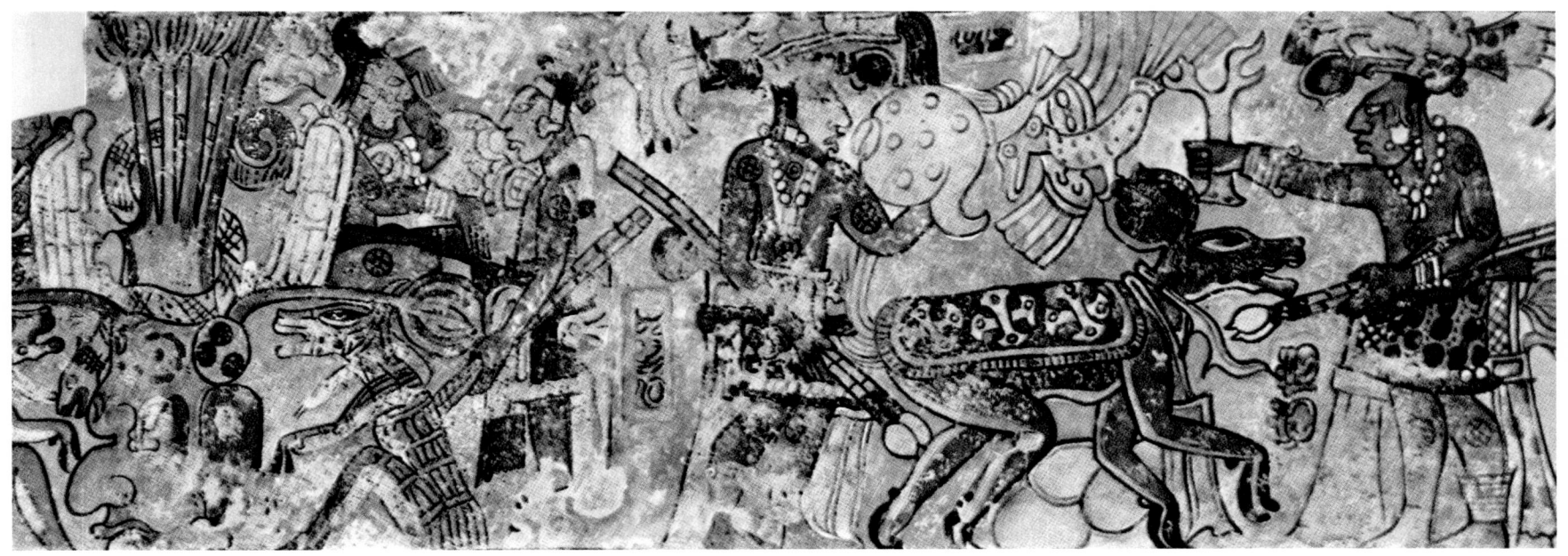

teenth centuries, it now became, along with the net hunting bag, the symbol of the hunting god.

Mixcoatl was also regarded as the ancestral deity of the Chichimec. His sacred pavilion was transferred to the Aztec capital as a tribute to a deity the Aztecs had adopted, as a discrete concession to the Chichimec and as a memorial to the god of those the Aztecs considered their ancestors. This "temple" was a reproduction of their ancestral flatlands, adorned with artificial rocks and thorny plants, particularly cacti and agaves for verisimilitude. A ceremonial hunt was organized on this miniature landscape every year.

The morning star was revered as the Aztec "god of the darting rays." In mythology it figured as guardian and hunter. In the course of cultural evolution its identity was virtually fused with that of Mixcoatl. Today the Cora

overtones, sometimes threatening, at other times a symbol of fertility, tranquillity and friendship. But it was in ancient Mexico that the deer played its most powerful symbolic role, partly through mystery and enigma. Having no system of phonetic spelling, the Aztecs were obliged to express their profound and intricate religious beliefs and experiences by means of pictures. The large number of pictorial images representing abstract concepts, none of them accompanied by written explanation, makes it no easy task to gain insight into the reality of the time.

The reproduction shown here of a decorative panorama on a colorful Mayan receptacle portrays a religious event in which the deer plays a central role. To the left is a tree growing out of a human head. A snake is coiled around the branches, in which men sit. Two fauns sit beneath the tree. In the middle, a man

symbols were associated with deer. The annual development and casting off of antlers, for example, was reminiscent of the rhythms of nature in the course of the seasons. The scene, inscribed on pottery believed buried in the tomb of a priest of aristocratic standing, was probably meant to symbolize growth and decline. To the left, the sprouting tree and snake coiled in its branches represent growth and periodic renewal. To the right, the deer, cornered by hunters, wearing death symbols and watched over by an impatient vulture, represents a fate of obvious inevitability.

Animal Symbolism and Hunting in Ancient China

Early in its history, ancient China freed itself of the restrictions of an exclusively hunting culture and a way of life to match. It developed an agricultural economy which profoundly and fundamentally altered its social and spiritual structure. The way opened for the evolution of a highly developed civilization, the first recorded flowering of which occurred during the Shang Dynasty, around 1500 B.C.

Royal graves of the period were already conceived as palatial subterranean tombs and came equipped with rich collections of accessories. Aside from bone carvings, ceramics and gold jewelry, sacred bronzes interred with the remains of high-born personages are of social interest. Although they had little to do with hunting, they provide an insight into the commanding spiritual role played by animals of the plains and forests, despite the fact that agriculture and cattle breeding had long since prevailed over hunting as the chief source of food.

Bronze vessels which are now considered priceless were still often cast in the form of wild animals. They were often embellished with elaborate ornamentation, consisting largely of abstract animal figures and resembling a kind of demons' playground. These figures are sometimes so obscure and/or grotesque that providing an explanation of these remarkable animal realms and of the mysterious symbolism they reflect is sheer guesswork. The artists, and probably those for whom the works were executed, must have been well-nigh obsessed with this nightmare world. Variations on the same disturbing theme would not otherwise have been so repeatedly devised.

Without doubt, we would be less perplexed by these convoluted products of extravagant imagi-

nations if they included at least a few representations of domestic animals. But this never happens. Instead of sheep, we see the more exotic argali of the mountain slopes. Man's oldest friend, the dog, is ignored. The ox, so prominent a feature of agricultural society, is also missing. The pig, a sacrificial animal in ancient China as well as a provider of meat, is similarly absent from the art of the period.

Nor is the plant life to be found in these portrayals; not even images of corn or rice are displayed on these bizarre sacred bronzes, although symbols of such staples are evident in the art of virtually every other civilization in the world—in that of the Demeter fertility cult of the ancient Greeks, for example, and in the art of the Aztec corn goddess.

It is reasonable to conclude that this civilization built on farmers and peasants—and the Shang Dynasty was certainly that—was probing after deeper significance when it took its mystical symbols from the world of the wild, sometimes imaginary animals, entirely overlooking its own day-to-day experience. This assumption is underscored by an almost manic preference for the tiger as the subject for artistic representation. It appears repeatedly in the figurative and ornamental art of the period.

To seek after underlying motives, it is necessary to examine the status of the tiger among Siberian peoples to the north of China, many of whom retained much of their earlier patterns of behavior and belief up to relatively recent times, and from whom the early Chinese appear to have absorbed a body of myth and tradition. These peoples were resourceful hunters, compelled by the harsh climate of their region to perfect their hunting skills, particularly with regard to whatever big

game was available. Such traditions invariably give birth to legend and myth about venerated animals which symbolize the animal kingdom upon which a hunting community subsisted.

Existing remnants of early art objects of these northeast Asian tribes show that the tiger was never portrayed as an enemy. It was always depicted as a beneficent creature. Its image radiates

the power to heal. Parts of the animal were used as amulets. Its claws, for example, served as protection against the evil eye. Its skin rendered the evil intentions of others powerless and pacified those with wicked designs. To possess toe bones of the tiger's forepaws was a guarantee of success in all undertakings. Dried tiger-eyes offered insight into things which normally remained hidden from human gaze.

According to legend, these Siberian tribesmen never shot at tigers. If one encountered a tiger on his travels, he would respectfully change course. If he met one while out hunting, he would cast aside his weapons, bow low and say, "O Ancient One, give me success in the hunt and lead the animals I seek toward my weapon."

The Manchurian-Tungusic peoples not only revered the tiger as a deity, they also sacrificed part of their prey to it. Even skin hunters among them declined to hunt the tiger and the animal was for a long time assiduously protected from Russian and Chinese peoples who migrated to the region and who felt differently about tigers. Fear by hunters that they might kill a tiger by mistake or in self-defense is said recurringly to have induced a standard nightmare in which an

elegantly clad, white-haired old man appeared and moaned, "Why did you kill my son? You should not have crossed his path. You should not have chosen the road he took. You should not have raised your eyes to him and when you chanced to see him in the distance, you should have knelt before him." Such dreams and subsequent confessions to the tribe's tiger clan became rituals. The "transgressor" was obliged to provide a sacrificial ceremonial feast to purge his fear and imagined guilt.

This taboo on killing was not restricted to the tiger. It also included any animal which had been wounded or even chased by a tiger. If it was discovered that an animal killed by a hunter had been fleeing from a tiger, the hunter would renounce all claim to it. There was a ritual for this as well. The hunter would appeal to the divine spirit, explaining, "Great One, this animal belongs to you. It was not I who killed it; it was you."

Not only was the tiger spared, it was helped when it was in trouble. A legend tells of a hunter who once heard a tiger roaring fearfully. Approaching carefully, he saw that a giant snake had coiled itself around the animal. He drew his hunting knife and cut the tiger free of the snake's embrace, earning the animal's gratitude and spiritual protection.

Interestingly, Siberian hunters believed tigers also helped them when they were in danger, and would even bring them food to save them from starvation when they ran out of supplies and were cut off by harsh weather conditions.

There is a legend of a hunter who, with his wife and child, rowed up a winding stream into a forest to go hunting. As they left the boat, a storm suddenly blew up and tore it from its mooring, leaving them stranded without food or weapons. Such was their predicament that death seemed inevitable. But they prayed to the tiger. "Our Father, don't you see that we are dying of hunger? Bring us something to eat." A moment later, there was a noise in the underbrush and a tiger appeared with a deer in its mouth. It dropped its prey at the feet of the stranded family, commanded them to eat and withdrew again into the forest.

It is remarkable that the ancient Chinese clung to hunting traditions and legends for so long a time after they had moved into other stages of social development. But

sacred beliefs have an exceptionally tenacious quality; man has repeatedly shown that he endows them with new meanings and trappings if circumstances require, rather than relinquishing them altogether. The tenacity of the tiger cult is displayed in an ancient Chinese bronze vessel for sacrificial wine, decorated with what is obviously a symbolic scene. It shows a tiger holding a man between its forepaws. The animal's upper jaw is suspended like a protective arch above the

man's head. The tiger appears to be gazing into the distance. Its powerful teeth give it a demonic appearance.

Chinese thinking has always been based on clearly defined dualism. The *yang* concept expresses the bright, masculine principle. *Yin* represents the dark, feminine aspect. For example, the sun is the symbol of *yang* and the moon symbolizes *yin*. Oracular inscriptions show that the tiger was considered a feminine deity, and

thus was deemed a dark, receptive and fertile element in the drama of life. The animal was assigned a crucial function—as an earthbound spirit, it was a guardian of life. Thus, on the sacred bronze, the man in the mouth of the tiger is the animal's ward, its friend rather than its victim. This is borne out by the serenity and confidence on the man's face. There is in fact wide leeway for interpretation of the details of the intricately wrought decoration, but it all appears to lead back to security in life and death.

Therein lies at least part of the explanation of why the tiger and other beasts of prey retained their position as friends, guardians and helpers of man in the Shang spectrum of belief. The agricultural civilization, inheriting elements of belief from its hunting predecessors, inherited the tiger cult as well. The animal was wrapped in a new symbolism, that of Earth itself, and was worshipped as the protective deity of the most important source of sustenance and the principal occupation for man at the time—agriculture.

It is not surprising that this agricultural people needed no new symbols; the old ones were conveniently available and capable of being readily transformed. This is a dramatic example of how the spiritual culture of the early hunters, persisting through later periods though modified by new interpretations, was capable of influencing even much more highly developed civilizations. Although peoples whose existence was based exclusively on hunting never succeeded in evolving highly developed cultures, partly because they were always nomadic, their religious concepts and ethical perceptions were often impressive and profound, and should not be underestimated.

Hunting lost its dominant position as agricultural cultures developed. But it would be a mistake to conclude therefore that hunting ceased to be practiced with enthusiasm and dedication. Farmers and artisans of the countryside and towns considered hunting an enjoyable pastime as well as a means for supplementing their often limited diets. Hunting also became the sport of the ruling classes.

That is the way it developed in the Shang kingdom. The ruler lived in his palace, the largest complex of buildings in the land, where the business of state was carried out and the important decisions were taken. It was also the starting-off point for the king's hunting expeditions. There is evidence that Shang rulers were dedicated hunters who tracked

Panoramic hunt in the presence of the Emperor and his court. Horizontal scroll, painted on silk in color and black ink, mounted on silk brocade. About 1700.

This scroll depicts a royal hunt which, in China, was not the common occurence it was in Europe, Egypt, Assyria, Persia and Japan. The scroll, complemented by another which shows camp activity after the hunt, is very rare and may even be unique.

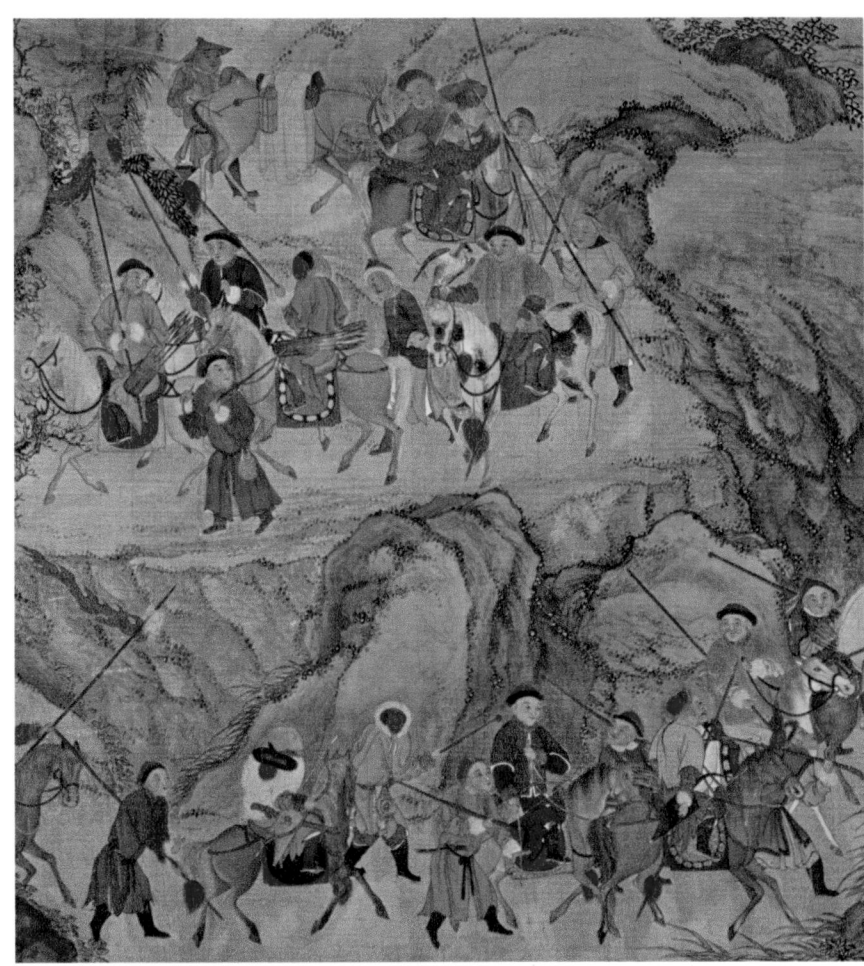

deer and boar in nearby mountains: relics tell of soothsayers being consulted for a forecast of the potentate's hunting prospects. If a successful hunt bore out a soothsayer's prediction, he was handsomely rewarded. Customs related to hunting were sustained in China for centuries, as can be seen in these two sections of a picture, probably drawn around A.D. 1700.

The picture-story deals with a hunt organized by the famous Manchu emperor Kang-hi (1662–1722). The impressive hunting display must have been reminiscent of practices in the region from which Manchu conquerors of the Chinese had come. They had originally lived as hunters and cattle-breeders on the Sungari River in northeastern Asia. The illustrations show finely bred horses—more than two hundred of them in a single scene! It also shows skillful riders, who seem completely at home on horseback, and the exuberant joy of the hunt is an artistic testament to a wild, free past.

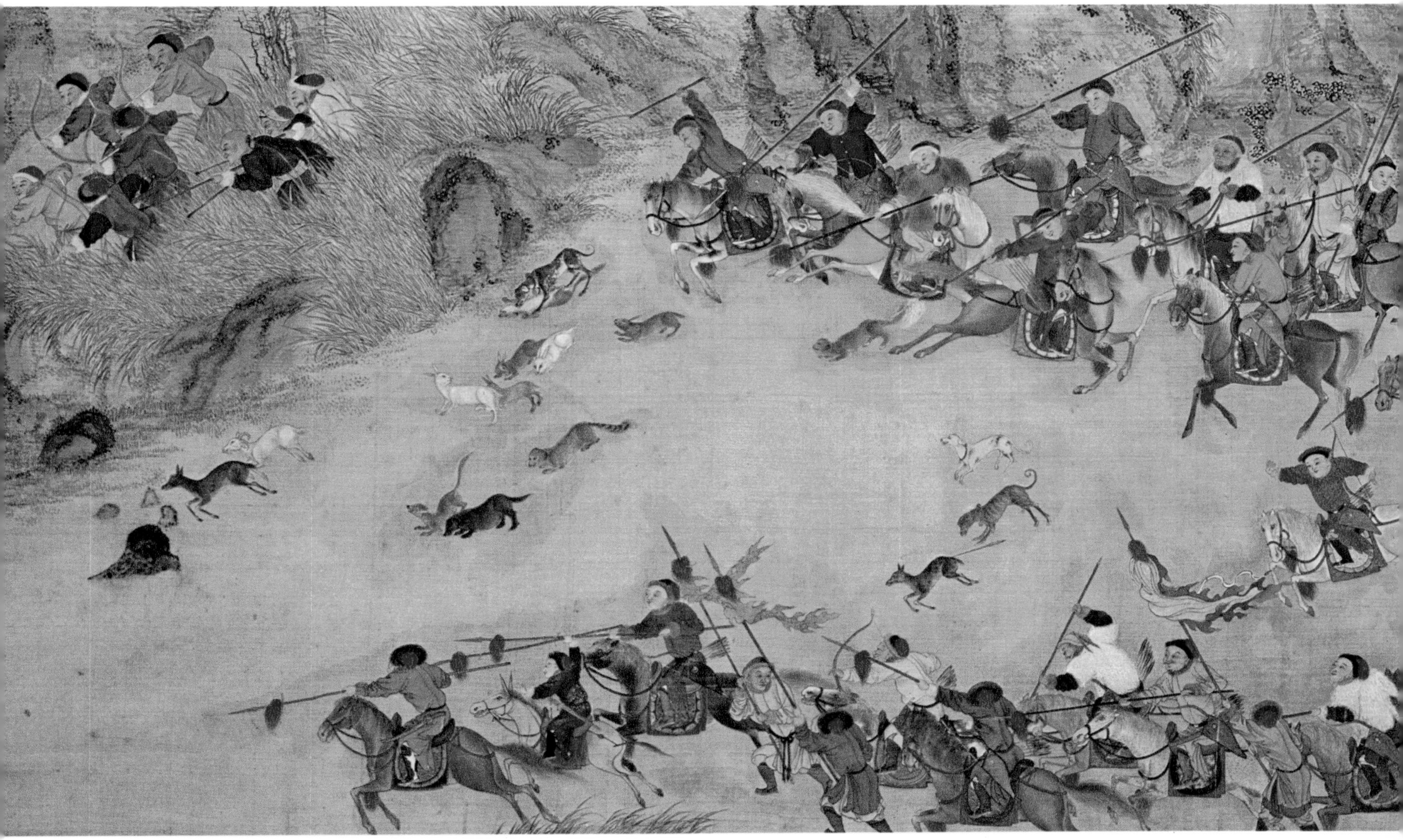

Hunting in the Land of the Pharaohs

Remnants and relics of ancient Egyptian civilization, which have come to light through extensive excavation, make it possible to establish with certainty that the Egyptians at the time of the Pharaohs were very much involved with hunting and fishing. In addition to tell-tale weapons, carved images of animals which were commonly hunted have been found in tombs—Barbary sheep, ibexes, hartebeests, hippopotamuses, elephants, fish and various birds. A further pointer to the existence of a definite hunting culture in ancient Egypt is the fact that dogs were often buried with their masters.

Various animal images of deities reveal a particularly close bond between man and game. Many of the findings date back to primitive cultures which laid the foundation of the spiritual world of the later, highly developed Egyptian civilization and of its forms of expression.

Ancient Egypt was exceptionally rich in game. Ibex lived in herds in the mountains. Many species of antelope roamed the dunes of the desert. Deer, ostrich and giraffe were by no means rare and leopards and lions provided sufficient challenge for those tempted by more dangerous hunting.

Desert hunting was practiced as a sport by the Egyptian aristocracy and notably by the pharaohs. A great many pictures and carvings bear witness to this pastime. Things were made comparatively easy for *battue* hunters, those who were assisted by beaters who panicked the animals into the desired direction. The hunting area was roped off with strong net-like obstructions. The game was then virtually delivered into the hands of the hunters by the beaters who came armed with sticks and ropes to frighten the animals. A hunter was required only to shoot arrow after arrow while some servants collected the kill and others replenished his supply.

Nearly all the Egyptian pharaohs were dedicated hunters. It is said that Thutmose III killed 120 elephants on a single "hunt." Even peaceable Amenophis III had his wild-bull hunts in the Nile Delta region immortalized on stone. He also boasted that he had killed 102 "wild-eyed lions" with his own hands during the first decade of his reign. Ramses III commemorated his game hunts on the outer walls of the temple of Medinet Habu. There is

no shortage of evidence testifying to the enthusiasm for hunting manifested by the kings of ancient Egypt.

Particularly popular were water-bird hunts with throwing sticks as weapons. These were, however, exclusively a privilege of the aristocracy. More risky hunting, of hippopotamus for example, was left to noblemen's retainers who hunted them from boats. A harpoon was used, the shaft of which detached itself from the point when it struck home. If the wounded hippopotamus tried to dive, the hunter cut the rope to keep his boat from capsizing. The animal was bound to rise to the surface again to breathe, whereupon it was once more harpooned. Thus weakened by repeated wounds, it could be lassoed and dragged to land.

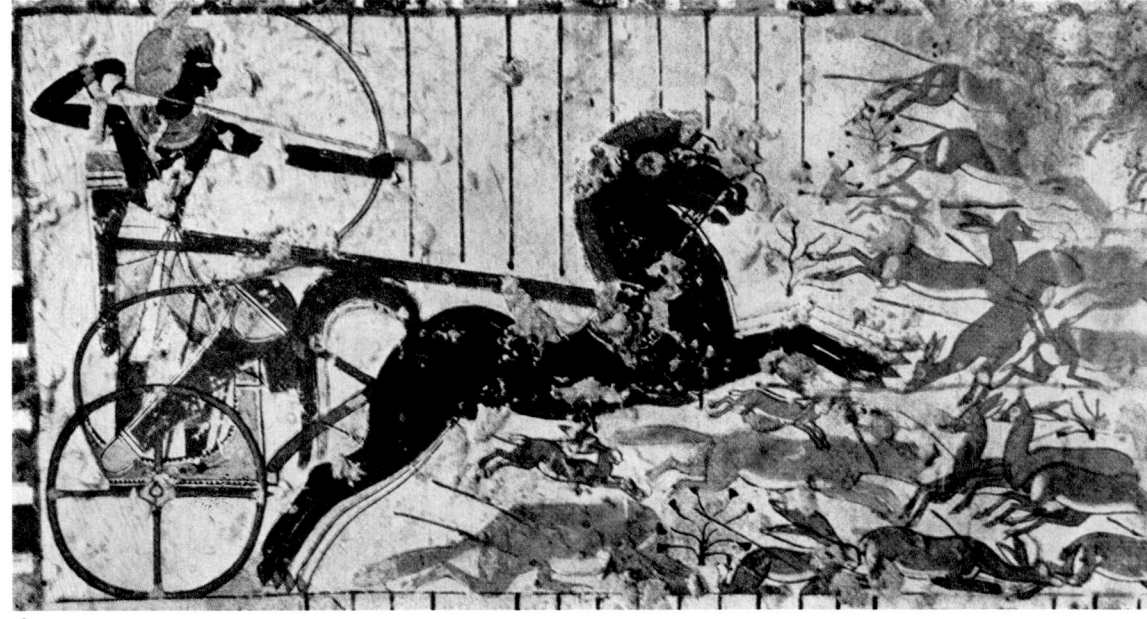

3

4

The Royal Hunt in Assyria

Left: Dog-keeper with a mastiff. These powerful dogs were used to hunt big game. Detail from a relief from Ashurbanipal's Nineveh palace.

Right: Deer hunting with nets in a game reserve. The animals are pictured in profile, their antlers front-view. Probably fallow deer. Assyrian relief, 7th century B.C.

Ashurbanipal was a great and powerful king who ruled over Assyria in the seventh century B.C. No doubt his stonemasons were aware of the delicacy of their task when they were commanded to carve images of the king out hunting, to serve as decoration for the royal palace at Nineveh. Ashurbanipal, last of the great Assyrian kings, wanted not only to immortalize his victories as a warrior, but also to be known forever as the greatest hunter of his time. With these magnificent relief images, the king impressed his name on the memory of man with greater and more lasting impact than he did with even his military feats.

With these imposing plaques the bold, imperturbable royal conqueror of lions provided posterity with visions of astonishing narrative power. The king's hunting mastiffs strain at their leashes. The lions are dangerously agitated, having been kept in their cages without food for days. Furiously angry, they wait impatiently for the trap-door to be raised and the cage to be opened. In all the portrayals, the king is ready, unflappably awaiting the animals' attack. On horseback, in his chariot, or even on foot, he enters combat supremely confident of victory. Sometimes he is armed with bow and arrow; sometimes with sword or lance. The lions, further angered by the mastiffs and their keepers, leap at their tormentors. And when one of the bloodthirsty creatures attacks the king's horse, its rider coolly runs it through with a spear. Finally, there is nothing to see but dying lions, their death agonies eloquently portrayed.

The almost godlike glorification of the king, incessantly repeated in these stone plaques, can, however, arouse a degree of distaste, particularly among those who might feel that hunting should not be trivialized into a form of ritual slaughter. Nevertheless, it would be a mistake to underrate the magnificence of the artistic accomplishment or the significance of the tale it has to tell.

There was a great abundance of lions in Assyria. The heroic legendary companions Gilgamesh and Enkidu recounted how they had hunted lions together and King Tiglath-pileser I—who ruled over Assyria about 400 years before Ashurbanipal—is said to have slain almost a thousand of them.

A variety of other creatures was energetically hunted by the Assyrians, including some animals which have since become extinct in the region or whose numbers have been greatly depleted. Among them are the wild bull, a cousin of the European bison, which roamed the not easily accessible mountainous regions. Elephants were probably also hunted in Assyria, at least during its early period, as was the now completely extinct wild ass, known for its legendary speed. The wild ass probably inhabited the lowlands of Assyria, alongside gazelles. Judging from numerous surviving stone carvings, it was a favorite challenge to the hunter's skill.

In the hieroglyphics of the Sumerian civilization, hunting was expressed by a sign consisting of two adjoining squares which symbolized an enclosed space and meant "surrounded." It appears from this that hunting in that part of the world was originally undertaken with nets or with strategically dug pits.

The Babylonian *Gilgamesh* epic indicates that such hunting procedures were, in fact, widely employed. It describes how a hunter complains that the wild man-saint Enkidu, who ate herbs with gazelles and shared animals' waterholes, constantly spoiled his hunting: "He filled in the pits which I had dug. He tore away my nets. He freed the game I was about to claim and commanded me to stop hunting."

Assyrian hunters believed they could increase their hunting by establishing close links with the animal world. Undoubtedly, the domestication of the horse was a major development. It was far easier to overtake and kill game from horseback than on foot. Even greater advantage derived from horse-drawn carriages which provided hunters with elevated positions and greater safety from animal attack, as well as speed.

The Greek historian Herodotus refers to the dog as the hunter's friend and helper. He notes that a Persian governor in Babylon owned "so many dogs that four large villages were allotted the task of providing food for them." Existing images indicate that these dogs were the same powerful breed of Molossian mastiffs which were portrayed on the stone reliefs of Ashurbanipal's palace.

The Hunt of the Indian Prince

Below: A moment of danger. Hunters try to kill a tiger which has turned on their elephant with slashing claws and sharp teeth. 18th-century Indian miniature from the Alwar Museum.

Right: A wounded boar falls to the ground. The hunter is about to administer the death-blow. 18th-century Indian miniature. Bikauer private collection.

Below right: Mounted huntresses overtake gazelles. 18th-century Indian miniature. Jaipur private collection.

The magnificent courts of the Indian maharajahs were maintained well into the nineteenth century, and some even later. As a consequence, a wealth of paintings and other illustrations, covering a period of more than 350 years, has survived to offer a precise picture of the history of the regal hunt in India. Pomp and splendor, extravagant costumes and richly decorated harnesses distinguish these images which, in tradition, are generally characterized by vigorous and dramatic action.

Over the ages, a particular animal of prey has tended to emerge as the center of focus of each hunting culture. In Siberia, it was the bear. In parts of Africa, it was the leopard; in the Middle East, the lion. In India, it was undeniably the tiger. There are innumerable portrayals of encounters with tigers, partly because the maharajahs wanted to leave a permanent record of their personal courage. Hunting antelope, deer and other more timid animals was much less a feature of hunting-related art in India than it was elsewhere. Aside from wall paintings and miniatures, some wonderfully expressive sculpture has been preserved, as well as decorated seals and coins, all confirming the passion for risky hunting displayed by the Indian princes.

An impressive series of sculptures on pillars in the temple of Madura shows how the princely hunters pursued tigers on horseback. Splendidly harnessed horses rear up before the attacking animals as their riders take aim with lances. Servants accompanying the hunt on foot crouch nearby, apparently without fear or anxiety, as if absolutely confident of their masters' skill and certain of the animals' fate.

Tigers were also hunted on foot. The maharajah strode forth in chain-mail armor and a helmet decorated with feathers, and carrying a round shield in one hand and a dagger in the other. His attacking arm was thickly bandaged to protect it against bites and scratches. Sometimes his weapon was a moderately long sword welded to an iron glove which reached to his elbow. Helmet and shield were usually made of magnificently molded iron, sometimes inlaid with gold, and decorated with scenes of court life. In some cases, they were contrived of ornamented elephant or rhinoceros skins.

The most popular form of tiger hunting, and the most expensive, was the *battue* hunt with elephants. A massive caravan, with extravagantly harnessed and ornamented elephants and horses, which drew the excited admiration of the populace, moved slowly, elegantly, through the countryside to the jungle. The maharajah and his guests made camp in a jungle clearing, where scores of tents were erected and where every comfort and convenience available at the time was provided. The camp resembled a transplanted palace, replete with a host of servants, jugglers, dancers and musicians.

A special corner of the clearing was for the elephants which served as mounts for the maharajah, his guests and his retinue, and the maharani and her ladies-in-waiting, as well as for the beater elephants which patrolled the hunting area to drive game toward the weapons of the hunters. Generally on these occasions the hunted animals included rhinoceroses, tigers, leopards and wild oxen—deer and boar were not specific targets. Such lavish hunting expeditions have long since disappeared.

At one time, their devotion to hunting often led maharajahs to set aside a portion of their land as a game preserve to which only they and their guests had access.

But the English colonizers of India showed little respect for the enormous herds of game which the maharajahs had husbanded. In particular, they depleted the number of tigers, that most beautiful and majestic of animals, to a catastrophic degree.

The modern weapons the English brought with them also led to the demise of another traditional form of hunting in India which had required great courage and skill— the pursuit of deer and, especially, boar. Indian hunters on horseback were armed only with lances to challenge this kind of game. They had to ride extremely carefully so as not to wound their hunting hounds which pursued the prey at full gallop. At the same time, they had to remain continually alert for attack from enraged boars which were easily capable of bringing down their horses. With the advent of modern firearms, such hunting was deemed obsolete and, whatever its former attractions, was no longer practiced.

Hunting in Ancient Persia

Surviving remnants of the ancient mysterious culture of Luristan, which is believed to have reached its peak between 1500 and 1200 B.C., suggests that it was obsessed with the animal kingdom. Images of animals appear on all sorts of relics excavated from the ruins of Luristan. Virtually all were of beasts of prey, which indicates that hunting must have played a central role in the everyday life and religion of this lost kingdom.

Among the most spectacular remains of Luristan are intricately engraved funerary bronzes discovered in tombs, one of the most impressive of which shows an archer seated in a hunting carriage drawn by a panther. A fine gray-green patina enhances the beauty of the object. The theme of an archer in a war chariot is, in fact, borrowed from the culture of nearby Mesopotamia. But Luristan was unique in its cultural expression; its artists put their own distinctive touches to their work. Instead of the by then traditional horse drawing the chariot, the panther is there, with its larger-than-life dimensions, its gaping mouth, its monstrous fangs and its protruding tongue—truly a fabulous beast, worthy of the royal tombs of Luristan and conveying a picture of close cultural links with hunting.

For obvious reasons, the further we move into historical times, the more abundant are archeological discoveries. The vast quantity of rediscovered antiquities would have enabled us to reconstruct a picture of hunting practices over the course of time, even if surviving written accounts had not been handed down.

An arc of history extends to embrace the various peoples who have been dominant or influential in shaping Persian culture over the centuries—the Assyrians, the Achaemenids, the Parthians, the Sassanians—all of whom left impressively descriptive works of art. Their styles were, however, not derived from their Luristani predecessors. Powerful Sassa-

nian rulers, for example, acquired not only their elephants and *mahouts* from India, but also their court artists. Indeed, a distinct court art characterized the Sassanian era, particularly after their victory over the Parthians in 224 B.C. They created a mighty Persian kingdom and their courtly art can be compared to that which flourished much later in France under Louis XIV. Like that of France, it was graced with an enchanting baroque style of great splendor and majesty.

The chased silver bowls are particularly renowned, embellished as they are with images of kings engaged in hunting various animals with bow and arrow, sword and spear. Many of the bowls also bear elegant likenesses of lions, panthers, bears, boars, deer, gazelles, buffalo, bulls, argali bucks and wild geese.

Reliefs in the Taq i Bostan caves, which date from the fifth century A.D., appear to give a detailed picture of the royal hunt. The king, followed by his wives, is shown riding into an arena under the royal symbol of the umbrellas and is greeted by a fanfare from female musicians. Two or three elephants, ridden by *mahouts*, usher a jostling herd of fallow deer through a gateway into a wattle-fence enclosure. The deer are flanked by mounted royal

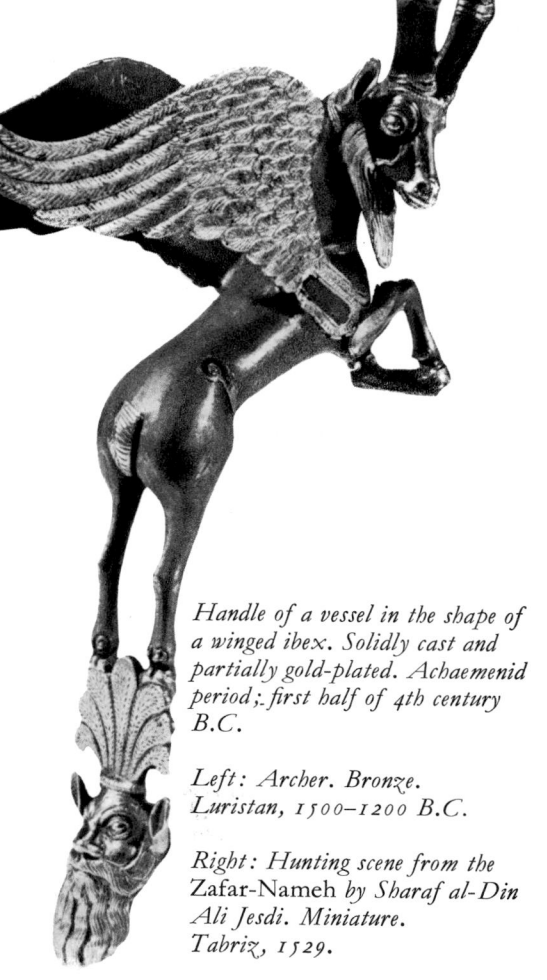

Handle of a vessel in the shape of a winged ibex. Solidly cast and partially gold-plated. Achaemenid period; first half of 4th century B.C.

Left: Archer. Bronze. Luristan, 1500–1200 B.C.

Right: Hunting scene from the Zafar-Nameh by Sharaf al-Din Ali Jesdi. Miniature. Tabriz, 1529.

attendants to keep them from breaking free and to ensure that the king, galloping in their midst, enjoys an untroubled hunt. He alone is privileged to kill the game.

An abundance of old Persian hunting scenes is also offered by a wealth of extant miniatures. The illustration on the right is the *Zafar-Nameh*, taken from the tales of Timur, the great Mongol conqueror of the fourteenth century. In his conquests, Timur traversed Persia and the Caucasus. Hunting at the time was undertaken on horseback or on foot, with bow and arrow, lance, sword or dagger. The prey included lions, tigers, ibex, deer and hare. The scene at the top left of the picture is typical of Persian art—above the elephant, taking no part in the scene as a whole, is a snarling cheetah. The dark head of a grotesque unicorn peers threateningly from behind rocks and appears to watch the proceedings below disapprovingly. This strange creature appears time and time again, in various forms, in Persian art, both in hunting scenes like this one and in heroic battles against mythical monsters. In the battle scenes, the unicorn is often transformed into a dragon, assuming the identity of a mysterious demon.

Sassanian silver bowl, depicting King Khosru II out hunting. Partially gold-plated. From the collection of the Emirs of Badakhasham, 6–7th centuries A.D.

African Pageantry

Left: A hunter, armed with bow and arrow, carrying a slain antelope over his shoulders. Unlike most of the royal art of Benin, this work is in no way naturalistic. From the lower Niger region.

Below: A hunter, possibly from the Bini tribe, takes aim at an ibis perched on the branch of a tree. Benin. The work of the "master of the leopard hunt."

Few of the civilizations which have risen and fallen on the continent of Africa can compare, in grandeur and sophistication, with that of the kingdom of Benin. It flourished in what is now part of Nigeria from the fourteenth to the seventeenth centuries. Its symbol was the leopard.

A beast of prey was used as a royal emblem generally only where mighty rulers, revered as gods, reigned with unqualified authority. Benin, like ancient Egypt, offers a classic example of the development of such a symbol. In Benin, the leopard was the sign of the

Oba, the monarch to whom even human sacrifices were made, and it was as significant in the symbolism of the kingdom as was the lion in ancient Egypt.

The royal art collections and palace ceremonies bear witness to the leopard's role in Benin. There were leopards of carved ivory, leopard-shaped bowls for ritual hand-washing, bronze plates engraved with superb leopard heads, and much else besides in a similar vein. The plate shown here clearly indicates that the animal was a symbol of power even when it was being hunted. It was pictured with majestic dimensions compared with the small-

Left: Portuguese soldier with crossbow and feathered arrows. He wears on his belt a hook for stretching his bowstring. Bronze. Benin, about 1600.

Below: Leopard hunt portrayed on a bronze plate. An overhead view of the vegetation; the leopards are in profile; the Portuguese hunters in half-profile. They carry fuse-operated rifles and hunting swords. Benin. Probably the most important work of the "master of the leopard hunt."

ish, wretched figures of hunters, whose authority stems only from the weapons they wield.

The oba kept live leopards as a sign of his nobility and power. He himself was addressed as "leopard of the house." Real house leopards were, however, not to be confused with jungle leopards. Living or dead, all captured leopards had to be delivered to the oba and a hunter who had killed one was interrogated by a high official and was obliged to repeat seven times that he had killed a jungle leopard and not one of those from the palace. A simple

mistake in choice of words could have cost him his head.

The oba Ohen is shown on a bronze plate clutching a pair of leopards by their tails, illustrating his absolute might through his humbling of these dangerous beasts. His feet are portrayed in the shape of a fish tail. According to legend this formidable ruler was transformed into the sea god Olokun after becoming lame.

Greece and Rome

The roots of the Western world are intertwined with myths and legends of hunting. The enchanting images of, for example, Artemis of ancient Greece and Diana of ancient Rome, the virginal goddesses of hunting, are inextricably associated with classical antiquity. Armed with bows and arrows and accompanied by frolicking nymphs, they are usually envisioned wandering through their native forests, which were otherwise the haunt of a vast array of prey. There are also the tales of Hercules and his heroic encounters with wild animals, his triumphant tangle with the Nemean lion, which had an impenetrable pelt, and with a fire-breathing bull; his victory over man-eating mares and his capture of a golden-horned hind. There is the legend of Atalanta, who was suckled by a bear and grew up to be a famous huntress, pledged to chastity but falling passionately in love despite herself.

Legends, however, tend to conflict with reality. Hunting in classical antiquity was not often pursued along romantic or heroic lines— no more than it is today. There were no hunting laws or seasonal restrictions. A hunter went after down-to-earth game and was unlikely to encounter a nymph or a golden-

Above: Dish portraying the legendary Calydonian boar hunt. The work of vase-painters Glaukytes and Archikles. From Vulchi, about 540 B.C.

Below: Detail on the blade of a dagger, inlaid with gold, silver and black niello. From a grave in Mycenae. About 1550 B.C.

horned hind in the forest. But, unlike procedures which prevailed in many subsequent early European civilizations, the right to hunt was not linked to ownership of land. It was not the exclusive privilege of the aristocracy. It did not depend on social rank, season or region and it did not matter whether the land on which the hunting took place belonged to someone else, the state or no one at all. Nor were there restrictions on the right to kill or

capture wild animals. Wild game was deemed to be ownerless until caught, even down to bees which, strangely enough, were considered huntable animals. Whoever killed an animal became its rightful owner, even if the place where the killing took place was fenced in. It was firmly believed that the number of animals of prey was inexhaustible and hunting went on relentlessly, even through animal breeding seasons.

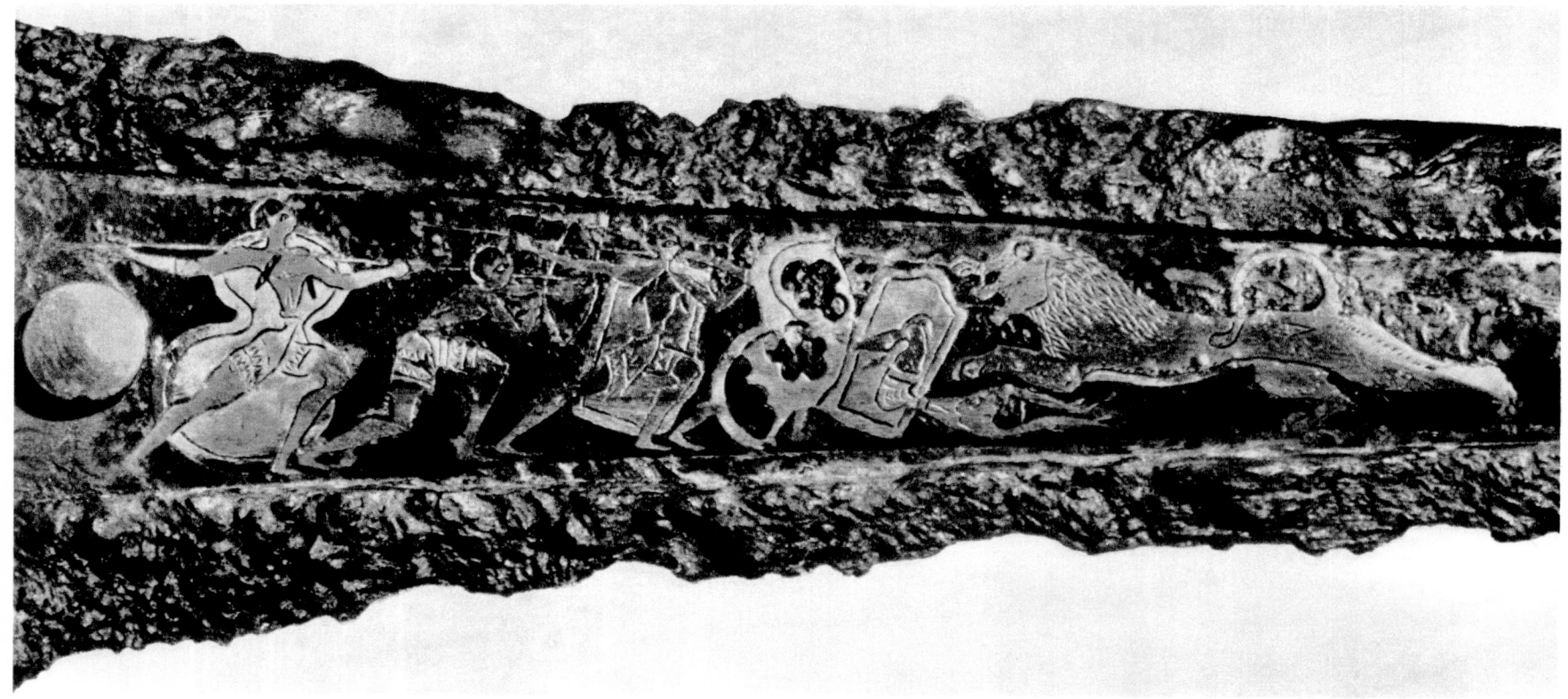

1 2 3 4

Hunters either went out alone—when, for example, seeking solitary concealment in the underbrush—or in groups—as when boar hunting. Hunting in classical antiquity, as in other times, was divided into two primary categories: for sport and for edible game. Various methods were employed to hunt such carnivorous animals as lions, leopards, lynxes and bears. A deep, circular pit might be dug around a column of earth on which a goat was tethered to a stake. The top of the pit would be concealed. Attracted by the goat's terrified bleating, an animal predator, attempting some hunting of its own, would crash into the pit from which it was then unable to escape. Less risky, and frowned upon by more sporting hunters, was the use of poisoned meat as bait to dispatch the hunted animals. More risky, and at times even reckless, was attempting on horseback, and often at nightfall, to separate beasts of prey from their herds to kill them.

Hunting lions, which were to become extinct in Greece, always assumed the character of a dangerous struggle. Pictures and epic poems describe in great detail the dangerous nature of encounters with lions. It was considered out of the question for a lion hunter, even a valiant Greek warrior, to venture out alone on the hunt; the pursuit of

5

lions was always a group project. The blade of
a dagger, ornately decorated with inlaid
detail, found in a grave at the remains of a
palace in Mycenae, is particularly instructive in
the ways of the classical lion hunt. It shows
five men in full battle dress in an encounter
with three powerful lions, two of which
are already in flight. The third animal is seen
attacking the hunters, one of whom is stretched
out on the ground. All but one of the men are
equipped with man-sized shields, covered
with animal hide. These shields were worn
hanging from straps around the hunters'
shoulders to leave their hands free to manipulate their heavy lances.

With regard to edible game, the first move
was to track down the animals' lairs or hiding
places. If, for example, hunters discovered a
herd of deer, they would drive them out of the
underbrush into previously laid nets and then
kill them with arrows or spears, or stampede
them onto spears already fixed diagonally
into position. Red deer were sometimes caught
by traps laid along their known paths. As for
wild boar, the hunters used nets into which
they drove their prey, which were then
bombarded with stones and spears and set
upon by hunting dogs. If a boar managed to
slip away from the net, hunters went after it
with spears and swords. Portrayals of this
theme, frozen in art and minus the bedlam
that must have accompanied it, are provided
by stately images of the legendary Calydonian
boar hunt, after the goddess Artemis had
sent a wild boar to ravage a kingdom which
had not offered her sufficient sacrifice. Sarco-
phagi in the Lateran Museum in Rome record
this legendary picture-story.

Hunting before spectators was another
tradition of classical antiquity. The center
of this grotesque pastime, the so-called
venationes, was Rome itself, where the Circus
Maximus was the favored arena. It was there
that Roman emperors arrived with much
fanfare and ceremony to observe the cruel and
bloody spectacle. The carriages of the emperors were radiant with ivory or, as during the
time of Aurelian (A.D. 270–275), embellished
with silver and golden wheels. Six horses, in
single file, drew the carriage, though in some
cases it was a team of four deer instead. Under
the cruel and extravagant Emperor Caligula
(A.D. 37–41), the hunt procession consisted of

a hundred carriages, each drawn by four horses except for two bringing up the rear, one hitched to four camels and the other to four elephants.

The festivities began with fights between animals in which drunken elephants and teased lions, bears, rhinoceroses, tigers, leopards and hyenas were set upon each other, sometimes by the hundred. Then came the actual "hunt" in which hunters from far and wide participated. They were offered the opportunity to kill a wide variety of game including, aside from the aforementioned, buffalo, crocodiles, giraffes, zebras, wild boar and ostriches, without the normal inconveniences of actually going out looking for them.

The late Roman era left behind a unique document about hunting procedures at the time. It is in the form of magnificent mosaics discovered at the Villa Erculia in Piazza Armerina in Sicily. Dating back to the third or perhaps the fourth century, they display hunting practices and customs in glowing colors. The so-called "Big Hunt" is a grandiose but simply defined artistic composition. The "Small Hunt" is a kaleidoscope of hunting as practiced by Roman aristocrats. The constituent images present so vivid an impression of the ways of the hunter in late Roman times that they need no description. Of particular interest, however, is the ceremonial sacrifice to Diana, virgin goddess of the hunt. As impatient horses stamp restlessly, two servants carry a wild boar to the place of sacrifice on a pole. A bearded hunter, clearly well pleased with himself, adds a hare to the sacrifical ceremony. As was frequently the case throughout history, cult ritual and culinary displays coincided after the hunt. Religious ceremonies evidently stimulated Roman appetites. The serene post-hunt scene is the focal point of the whole mosaic.

Celts and Teutons

Left: Small carriage model in bronze, with rider, dog and boar. Celto-Iberian, from Merida, Spain, c. 4th century B.C.

Right: The boar god of Euffigneix (Haute-Marne, France). Limestone statue, likely to have been copied from wooden idols. Probably pre-Roman.

Below: Cernunnos, the deer god, wearing a cap with antlers. He holds a torque in his right hand; a snake with a ram's head in his left hand. From a silver cauldron, Gundestrup, Aland Islands. About the time of Christ.

Celtic civilization straddles the line between the Stone Age and historic times. Many vestiges of the Celtic era manifest a legacy of prehistoric imagery, molded by more recent influences. From the regions of the Helvetii, a Celtic tribe in what is now Switzerland, there comes, for example, a bronze statue of a female figure, the goddess Artio, leaning gently backwards. Near her is a tree and under its branches a bear approaches. In her left hand, the goddess holds flowers and fruit; in her right hand, a dish. It is reasonable to assume that there was a symbolic link between the bear and the goddess, partly from the serenity of the scene and partly from the fact that her name derived from the Celtic word

artos which means bear. Needless to say, Artio was revered by Celtic hunters as their patron goddess.

A connection can be established with the Greek legend of Callisto who was turned into a bear (the origin of the Great Bear constellation) by the great goddess Hera because Callisto was loved by Zeus. Another legend suggests instead that Zeus turned Callisto into a bear to protect her from Hera's jealousy. Still another version has it that, since the servants of Artemis, the goddess of hunting, sometimes took the form of bears, the Callisto legend may refer to Artemis herself. The fact that the grave of Callisto is located in Triko-lonoi in Arcadia, on a hill where a temple of

Artemis stands, is said to support this last legend.

Another of Artio's relations in the Celtic realm was Arduina, goddess of wild boars, who is portrayed on a bronze relic found in the Ardennes. She, too, appears to confirm the theory that huntable animals were placed under the protection of female goddesses to save them from extinction. Epona, the horse goddess, an embodiment of the Mother Goddess, is another example. She was revered first and foremost by Celts dedicated to the art and profession of horse-breeding. All these cults indicate distinct hunting cultures, as does the Celts' widespread use of iron weapons, their mastery of horseback riding and the

Right: Celtic figure of a boar. Bronze. Probably part of a helmet. Found in Liechtenstein with many sacrificial offerings. The figure is less than two inches high.

Below: Procession of warriors from Torslunda, Aland. The helmets are embellished with figures of boars. Stamped bronze.

Below: Bear-killer from Torslunda. Stamped bronze. Ornamentation for helmets and sword sheaths.

settlement of many Celtic groups in non-cultivable highland and wooded regions.

The Teutons had a long history as farming peoples. But hunting has always also been a major source of their food supply. Together with fishing, it was, in addition, a stimulus to commerce and trade. Baskets, nets and hooks were used to catch river trout and salmon. The sea yielded up herring and cod which were landed from rowing and sail boats. Astonishingly prosperous communities sprang up near regions known for good fishing and bird-catching. Further north, there was seal hunting with clubs and whaling with harpoons.

A number of different archaeological sources indicate that deer and moose hunting were most popular in northern Teutonic regions. Along one of the northernmost Norwegian fjords, where high, steep rock outcroppings rise from the sea, engravings of deer—hundreds of them—have been scratched onto stone, about thirty feet up. In a series extending for miles, they face westward to the open sea.

A few centuries ago this region swarmed with deer and local farmers hunted them. They did so by the most wasteful and perhaps the cruellest method, driving them over cliffs onto the rocks below, and then descending to kill off those which had survived the fall. No doubt the pictures scratched on the rocks refer to this practice. It is possible that the engravings were part of a hunting ritual associated with placing a spell on the game and making them susceptible to the shouts and clamor that would send them panicking to

their deaths. Similar spell-casting is evident in animal images on rock found in Bohuslan in Sweden.

The Teutons were, however, also aware of the inherent beauty of a wild animal. Such a sentiment is reflected in the moving lament of Sigrun from the ancient song of Helgi:

And Helgi rose among the heroes
Like the mighty deer in the morning dew
Lifting its antlers high above all others
Their shining tips against the radiant sky.

For the Teutons, the poetic transfiguration of animals plays an important role in mythology. The bear, against which men could test

and prove their strength, and often the most sought-after prey, was frequently in legend transformed into something else. The bear-killer from Torslunda, pictured here, is one of the rare examples of a naturalistic theme in Teutonic art. Examples of animal symbolism are more common, in various art forms. An ancient Norse poem tells how the spirit of a hero enters into battle in the shape of a mighty bear while his body remains behind, asleep. Nor is the lowly boar neglected. The god Freyr galloped across the sky on the "gold-bristled" boar Gullinborsti, bringing light as only the sun itself could.

43

Chronicler of Medieval Hunting

Count Gaston de Foix (1331–1391), feudal lord of the northern slopes of the Pyrenees, also known as *Phoebus* ("the radiant one") because of his blond curls and good looks, was a warrior and a politician as well as one of the most daring hunters to stalk the pages of history. His famous work, *Traité de la Chasse*, begins with the declaration, "I have enjoyed three things most of all in my life—weapons, love and hunting." He devoted his book to the last of these three, considering hunting the one skill of which he was a true master. Indeed, his writing bears witness to a knowledge and understanding so fundamental that it served as the model for many subsequent books on hunting.

The high regard still extended to Gaston Phoebus's work can be attributed not only to his classic descriptions of medieval hunting but also to the enchanting miniatures which accompany the text. The finest of the forty miniatures which have survived the ravages of time were probably fashioned at the scriptorium of Bedford around 1405. Compared with earlier examples, they were executed in an almost naturalistic style, though the backdrop—as was often the case in images of saints at the time—was painted as a carpet-like patterned plane.

It is unlikely that Gaston Phoebus commissioned these pictures; they were completed several years after his death. But he was rich

enough to indulge in such a luxury. His own wealth, supplemented by that of his wife, who was the daughter of the King of Navarre, could have provided him with virtually anything he wanted at the time. In his castle at Orthez, he kept six hundred of the finest hunting horses and huge packs of hounds trained to track down deer, bear and boar.

The weapons which figured most prominently in Gaston Phoebus's writings are javelins, hunting spears and tridents, the last of which were used primarily for otter hunting. Long and short bows and crossbows were also popular among hunters in the region at the time. Like Emperor Maximilian, another devotee of the art of hunting, Phoebus provided his readers with excellent instructions on the use of weapons. Of the boar spear, he wrote: "As soon as the point of the spear enters the body of the boar, the shaft should be firmly clamped against the hunter's armpit and thrust forward as strongly as possible, without letting go for an instant. Should the boar prove to be stronger than the hunter, he should twist from one side to the other, never letting go of the spear, until God comes to his rescue or assistance comes from some other source." Gaston Phoebus described how he was often thrown to the ground by enraged boars and how his horse was gored to death beneath him. He also noted that he witnessed the death of many hunters and their servants in confrontations with wild game. He was not exaggerating—his own brother was killed in a fight with a bear and his grandfather was killed during a deer hunt.

Though he himself did not suffer a similar fate, Gaston Phoebus's death was part of his hunting life. He died, at the age of sixty, while returning with his attendants from a bear hunt.

Miniatures from Traité de la Chasse *by Gaston de Foix. About 1405.*

The Animal as a Sacred Symbol

Long before recorded history, man was cloaking animals in myth and regarding them as symbols and embodiments of supernatural power. When and how it began is impossible to say. We can only speculate on the degree to which animal symbols and "spirits" influenced both the early human world and man's consciousness.

The oldest evidence of the existence of man in Europe is the remains of a lower jaw, probably dating from an interglacial period over half a million years ago. This human fossil has become known as *Homo heidelbergensis*. The region in which it was found was also discovered to have been rich in fauna which co-existed with early man. It has yielded the remains of

kind by making them available. Very likely, the subsequent veneration of deer as a harbinger of prosperity and peace derived from this apparent act of goodwill on its part.

The continuous process of casting off and renewing antlers was, however, probably also regarded as a symbol of death and renewal, a theme inherent in all of nature and one of which primitive man, dependent on nature, must have been particularly conscious. No doubt, early man was also fascinated by developments which were seemingly contrary to natural law. For example, abnormally colored animals have always been objects of wonder, and often of fear and horror as well. In cultures where the color white is

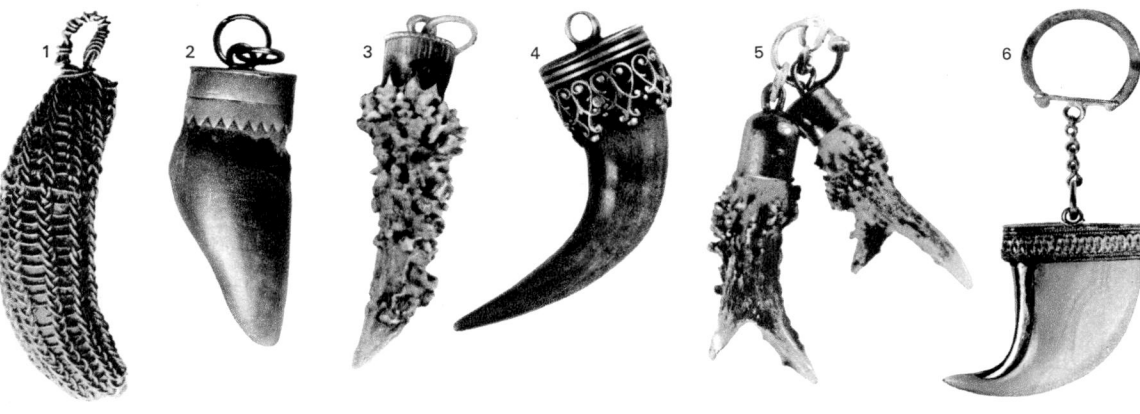

moose, red deer, roe deer, European bison, primitive horses, elephants, hippopotamuses, rhinoceroses, bears, cave-dwelling lions, panthers, lynx and saber tooth tigers. Pitted against such creatures, prehistoric man must have been keenly aware of his inferiority in strength and speed. Yet he was dependent upon them for his food and from the very beginning he realized that a fair measure of the good things of this world came from the animal kingdom.

Inevitably, he looked upon their naturally endowed weapons as symbols of their superior power which, when acquired and perhaps worn by him, would bestow greater might than he otherwise possessed. Deer captured the imagination of primitive hunters with their antlers. The annual process of shedding and renewing antlers seemed to have magical significance. Man found the discarded antlers extremely useful for fashioning tools and weapons and deer were considered to have made a deliberately friendly gesture to man-

regarded as having divine overtones and as being a symbol of good luck, the killing of a white chamois, which was regarded as a god in animal form, could have led to the execution of the hunter. Great symbolic significance was also attached to a white deer, which was said to free those it visited from hardship and want and, more specifically, to lead hunters to concealed fresh water springs.

Animal amulets still have some significance today, more so in some places than in others, with an element of superstition definitely underlying what often seems a purely decorative motif. Whether consciously or otherwise, the human imagination continues to regard animals with a measure of sanctity.

1 Tiger's tooth amulet in a wire net. Northern Thailand. 20th century.

2 Deer's hoof, mounted in silver. Alpine. 19th century.

3 Part of first antlers of a young roebuck, mounted in silver. Alpine. 18th century.

4 Part of first antlers of a young chamois, mounted in silver. Alpine. 16th century.

5 Part of first antlers of a young roebuck, mounted in silver. Alpine. 19th century.

6 Lion's claw pendant, mounted in gold. A hunting trophy and child's amulet. Somalia. Modern.

7 Bezoar shaped as a tree with a boar at its foot. German. End of 15th century. Bezoars, small balls of hair and vegetable fiber often found in the digestive organs of animals, were once used as antidotes for poison and as medicine against plague.

Patron Saints of Hunting

Anyone seeking to trace the origins of Christian animal symbolism, as it is expressed in the history and legends of hunting, has a wonderfully rich selection of source material at his disposal. A host of animal images are portrayed in medieval churches. Lions, deer, bears, rams, hares and ermine were, traditionally, symbols of Christ to the builders of those magnificent edifices, as well as to the people and clergy of the period. The red fox, on the other hand, signified the devil and hell.

St. Hubert has been the patron saint of hunting since at least the tenth century. Traditional "Hubert Hunts" are still held in his honor in parts of Europe. But Christian animal symbolism pre-dates St. Hubert's emergence as the guardian of hunters or hunters' luck.

It goes back at least as far as St. Eustace, who lived in the second century A.D. and who, before his conversion, was Placitus, commander-in-chief of the Roman army of Emperor Trajan. Jacobus de Voragine wrote of him: "One day, Placitus set out into the woods on horseback, as he often did. In the forest, he saw several deer, one of which was more stately than the others. The other deer scattered. Only the distinctive one stayed, moving majestically toward a nearby rockface.

There Placitus saw Our Lord Jesus Christ standing between its antlers. The deer turned to him and said: 'Placitus, why do you hunt me? You should know that I am Christ, the true Son of God. And I love you because you are charitable. Believe in me and be baptized.' With those words, the deer disappeared."

There are some impressive artistic portrayals of this legend. Antonio Pisanello (1397–1451) painted the scene in oils. Dürer did an etching of it. Several Baroque artists brought the legend to life on canvas and on church walls. Where St. Eustace is not specifically identified in these portrayals, the artist's intention could have been to venerate St. Hubert instead. He is, for example, portrayed above the portal of the chapel of Amboise Castle in France and in paintings by such masters as Lucas Cranach and Jan Breughel.

Hubert was, at the beginning of the eighth century, bishop of the then thriving town of Lüttich in Germany. He apparently was a vain, pleasure-loving man until—like Eustace—he had a miraculous vision in the forest. "A deer appeared before him," a biographer-clergyman was later to write, "bearing the sign of the Holy Cross between its antlers. He heard a voice saying: 'If you do not believe in the Lord, you will go to hell.' Startled, Hubert, who had been on horseback, dismounted and fell to his knees in prayer." From that moment on, he changed his ways.

Hubert died in 727. First buried in Lüttich, his body was later transferred to the Andain Monastery in the Ardennes—today known as St. Hubert's Abbey—which hunters visit to pay tribute to their patron saint. According to the Hubert legend, his golden key had healing powers; his name was invoked particularly to cure rabies. St. Hubert's feast day falls on November 3, the day on which he was canonized in 1744. In his honor, the deer-stalking season was regularly suspended on that day in parts of Europe.

In fact, not all that much is known about Hubert the man. The only source of specific information is the *Vita Sancti Huberti*, a brief biography written by a monk seventeen years after his death. It neither mentions that he had been a hunter nor contains any description of anything else that might link him to hunting, though several references are made to miracles he performed. It seems likely, therefore, that the earlier Eustace hunting legend was inherited by Hubert. It is possible that hunting thereby acquired a patron saint who may himself never have been a hunter.

Below: The legend of Hubert. Relief over the portal of the Hubert Chapel in Amboise Castle on the Loire in France. The chapel was built by King Charles VIII at the end of the 15th century.

Falconry

The origins of falconry are lost in the shadows of history. It is believed likely, however, that it was first practiced by Asiatic horsemen who, accompanied by their magnificent hounds, roamed endless steppes in search of both sustenance and sport. In the western world, falconry can be traced far back in time, but it did not reach its peak of popularity until the Crusades when Christian knights, intrigued by its practice in the Middle East, brought it back with them to their own countries, where it quickly became the height of courtly fashion.

Emperors and kings, dignitaries of the church, princes and aristocrats—all regarded the art of hunting with falcons on their wrists to be the noblest and most manly of pastimes. Their enthusiasm led to falconry becoming a status symbol among the upper strata of society in the late middle ages, a sport only

the unfashionable or impoverished could do without. The falcons were carried everywhere, even to church and to battle, so that they became living symbols not unlike those of eagle fetishes or of the uraeus serpent in the headdress of Egyptian pharaohs. To some degree, the falcon shared the rank of its master, its own noble status corresponding to that of its owner. The falcon was considered as invulnerable to social change as was nobility itself at the time. A feudal law early in the ninth century required that a vanquished knight be permitted to retain his falcon, as

well as his sword and his rank. It was customary for a bishop or prelate to have his favorite falcon in attendance when celebrating Mass; it was also common for nobles to place their birds on the altar during the service. It is, therefore, not surprising that the classic age of falconry is richly documented with highly descriptive writing about falcons and falconry.

Falconry reached its zenith in Europe at the time of the Hohenstaufen, German princes who established a dynasty of Holy Roman Emperors. One of the most celebrated of this line, Frederick II, who was famous both as a ruler and a warrior, was also admired as one of the most skillful falconers of his time. Frederick was also a dedicated and careful student of nature and produced a remarkable book, *De Arte Venandi Cum Avibus (On The Art of Hunting with Birds)*. Originally meant to be purely a textbook for falconers, it

delved much more deeply into its general subject and is still regarded as a useful study of the bird world. Frederick is known to have been an accomplished draughtsman and it is likely that the accompanying illustrations were his work as well.

The Iceland falcon and the gyrfalcon, both native to the far north, the saker falcon, and the blue-foot falcon from southern Russia and the Balkans were most widely used by European falconers. Among falcon prey were pheasants, wild duck, herons, grey partridges, crows, magpies and hares. The favorite victim

of falconers was the long-legged heron which was hunted to the accompaniment of trumpets and drums.

Whatever the prey, the occasion was highly ceremonial. First came the master of the falcon hunt. He was followed by musicians playing appropriate falconry music. Then came nobles and their guests, followed by falconers in pairs, each with a falcon perched on his gloved wrist. Boys carrying cages of hooded spare falcons brought up the rear. A master of the falcon hunt at a royal court might lead a hunt of fifty falconers, with some three hundred falcons at his disposal.

As soon as a soaring falcon swooped on its prey, drums and trumpets sounded out. When a falcon pounced upon an unfortunate heron and brought it to earth, falconers raced to the spot to reward it with bits of food. Knights would pluck the feathers from the dead heron's head and plant them in their headdresses. However, if the heron should be found to be only injured, it would be carefully nursed back to health. A silver ring would be placed round its right leg with the name of the master of the hunt and the place and date of its injury, and it would be set free. Thus a particularly unlucky heron could fall victim to falcons several times, as was the case with one such bird caught by Frederick August, king of Poland and elector of Saxony in 1751. He himself had caught the heron his falcon brought down ten years earlier and it had also been caught by the Sultan of Turkey seven years after that. The heron's leg was banded for a third time and it was again set free.

Elaborate falcon hunts continued to be held in the royal courts of Europe until well into the eighteenth century. An interesting footnote to history: Austrian and Prussian dignitaries and generals met at a falcon hunt in 1763 to seal the peace agreement which ended the war between their countries. It was a prelude to the emergence of Prussia as a major power and set the stage for the development of modern Germany.

The Imperial Hunter

Right: Hunting deer with bow and arrow. Miniature from The Secret Book of Hunting, *written by Emperor Maximilian I. Details of the picture probably drawn to the emperor's specifications. There is a marked medieval atmosphere to the scene. Particularly characteristic of the period is the placing of the various phases of the hunt on different levels. The picture is best examined top toward bottom.*

Below: Hunting scenes from the Theuerdank.

Fowl hunting on horseback with bow and arrow.

Lifting a chamois from a rock sanctuary with a spear 9 to 12 feet long.

Boar hunting on horseback. The hunter's legs are protected.

"When God created man, He gave him power over fish, birds and all wild beasts. This is God's promise, that no one need forfeit his life or his health to those creatures." The medieval treatise, the *Sachsenspiegel* (1234), from which this quotation is taken, established the rules which governed hunting in the Holy Roman Empire until the fouteenth century— poaching was punished only by fines; physical punishment was rarely invoked. Around 1500, however, during the reign of Emperor Maximilian I, rigid aristocratic control over disposal of hunting rights was established. Princely power and the unrestrained pursuit of pleasure established privileges for the highly placed, encroachments upon which were often punished with extreme cruelty.

Maximilian, whose ability as a hunter and knowledge of hunting were justifiably acclaimed, wrote extensively about the sport. In one of his books, *The Secret Book of Hunting*, he offered the following advice to his successor: "... take great joy in hunting. But be well-advised to be accompanied by your secretary and your counsellors so that they can cope with ordinary people who might approach you, something better handled out in the field than indoors." This imperial desire to foster association with the common folk far from the royal court tempered imperial and aristocratic privilege. It was said that

Maximilian himself lived up to the advice he tendered to his successor. But his actions often belied his intentions. He totally ignored any damage to the crops and property of others resulting from his hunting pursuits. He jealously and autocratically guarded the imperial right to hunt where, when and how he wished.

But contravention of forestry and hunting rules by others was severely punished. Even clergymen were not exempt from imperial wrath in the case of transgressions. In fact, Maximilian issued a proclamation specifically concerning monks in which it was said: "those encountered by the Chief Forester engaged in hunting are to be arrested and held until they swear to report to the Lord Chamberlain. Should they continue in the pursuit of hunting and should they again be arrested, the Chief Forester is commanded to divest them of their clerical cloaks which will be sent to the Imperial Court."

In 1514, an imperial mandate was issued to all the emperor's subjects forbidding them to set foot in his hunting preserves while carrying rifles, pistols or other firearms. As late as 1518, Maximilian instructed his chief forester to guard his forests and the wild game therein with the greatest vigilance. No one was to be allowed to hunt deer, bear, chamois, heron, duck or hare in the imperial hunting

grounds. Neither prelates, lords nor noblemen were exempt from this decree. A contemporary report casts light on the emperor's view of forestry and hunting laws: "The Emperor, who has reserved all deer and boar for his own hunt, has commanded that all persons taking exception to this decree should bring charges against him to which he is prepared to offer suitable reply. This effectively ended all complaints."

The damage done to farmers' property by protected wild game, and even more to the principle that all wild animals, birds and fish are common property, led to numerous violations of what had become imperial privilege. But not until after Maximilian's death in 1519 was hunting again practiced by all and sundry in the lands over which he had reigned. Game had multiplied enormously and, no longer burdened by restrictions, hunters engaged in a veritable massacre. Some of Maximilian's successors tried to redress the balance but, with each new ruler framing new hunting rules, more often than not the end product was an absence of foresight, a lack of understanding, and confusion.

The Chase

Well into the seventeenth century, the most popular form of organized hunting in Europe was coursing. This involved the use of hounds, not yet trained to respond to animal scents, catching sight of the prey and running it down.

Coursing animals required that the hounds be faster than the animals they pursued, because they invariably gave up the chase when they lost sight of the game. It was indiscriminate hunting and, if the prey was exceedingly fleet of foot, it was also futile.

The shortcomings of coursing were obvious and they led to the introduction of a more discriminating chase in which hounds were trained to pick up and follow the scent of certain animals—in Germany, generally deer and boar; in France and England, fox and hare as well. This form of hunting differed from its predecessor in that the aim was not to kill as many animals as possible, but to hunt and chase specific game. The hound was often slower than the animal it pursued. But it was able to follow its trail over extended and often rough terrain, which sometimes made things difficult, even dangerous, for hunters and their horses.

Johann Elias Ridinger (1698–1767) was probably the most noteworthy chronicler of hunting in his day. These seven scenes are taken from a series of sixteen of his engravings of the chase.

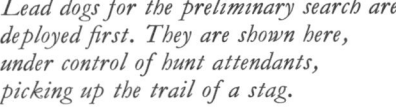

Lead dogs for the preliminary search are deployed first. They are shown here, under control of hunt attendants, picking up the trail of a stag.

Tracked down, the stag is frightened out of its hiding place by the lead dogs. This picture shows the stag in full flight through a dense forest, pursued by the lead dogs. Hunters seek to accelerate the stag's flight with shouts, cracking of whips and sounding of horns before giving it over to pursuit by the pack of hounds.

The chase is now on in earnest, with the terrified stag pursued by hunters and a large pack of hounds.

The stag is overtaken by the hounds. Exhausted, it tries to defend itself, sometimes wounding or even killing some of the dogs. They are, in turn, driven to attack their prey by shouts, whips and horns.

The stag, on the ground, is attacked by the hounds. At this stage, one of the hunters administers the coup de grace.

A variation on the same scene. The tendons of the stag's hind legs are cut. With the animal incapacitated and all danger past, a hunter stands by to administer the coup de grace.

The ceremony which formally marked the end of the chase. The hunter displays the stag's head to the hounds. The link with primitive ritual is obvious.

53

Pomp and Pageantry

In the seventeenth and eighteenth centuries, hunting was often transformed in Europe into a splendorous royal festivity. To the extent that it thereby increased in pomp and pageantry, it lost its human dimension and poetic overtones. The master of the hunt and his guests were interested only in shooting vast quantities of game which, for their convenience, were confined to narrow enclosures and denied any chance of escape. Great care was taken with the design of contrived "hunting grounds" and with the extravagant fittings of the canopy and platform from which hunters would shoot at helpless game and where they would also partake of an Epicurean banquet.

The so-called water hunt was particularly popular. If no natural lake was available, an artificial pond was created regardless of cost. The engraving shown here commemorates a typical royal water hunt of the period, held in 1748 at Leonberg in southern Germany. To produce a measure of surprise, an effort was made to force the animals—800 deer and wild boar—to run an unpredictable course within the enclosure before coming into the line of fire of the assembled hunters. As is seen in the picture, two huge wooden galleries were erected on either side of the outlet. A mighty triumphal gate stood in the center. This splendid construction was the stage for a cruel and bloody spectacle.

With drums rattling and trumpets blaring, the royal master of the hunt and his guests took their positions on a raised platform, sufficiently elegant and well-shaded to be worthy of their exalted stations. When they were in place, the animals would be released from their cages and permitted to rush wildly, in search of escape, toward a lake-front hedge which concealed a sudden drop into the water. Their targets in sight, the noble ladies and gentlemen opened fire from their elevated positions. Hundreds of slaughtered animals were later dragged ashore by barges.

It was the ultimately impossible extravagance, coinciding with anti-aristocratic ideals disseminated by the French Revolution, which finally brought these luxurious displays to a halt. By the middle of the nineteenth century, they had become a thing of the past.

The Old Order Changes

Left: The Kranichstein hunting lodge near Darmstadt, Germany, forms a backdrop for the hunt. Oil painting by Georg Adam Eger, 1755. The hunted deer was driven into the pond and then shot. In the foreground is Count Ludwig VIII of Hessen-Darmstadt.

Below: The Kranichstein hunting lodge, today a museum of hunting.

The countless old pictures of princely European deer and boar hunting scenes, with stately hunting lodges in the background, radiate a mood of complacency and unconcern—a climate of contentment few expected to end as abruptly as it did. Little significance was attached to the possibility that one day those charming idylls, which were exclusively the province of the aristocracy, would arouse enough hostility in others and would become so expensive to

ing to be poetical and probably never grasping the macabre overtones of the allegory on human life he suggested. Gracian, reflecting the view of the aristocracy, was convinced that human qualities could only be properly developed by the nobility which, he believed, was uniquely privileged to claim goodness, intelligence, humanity and related virtues. Whatever transpired amongst the lower orders had little significance. The palace was inhabited by true man;

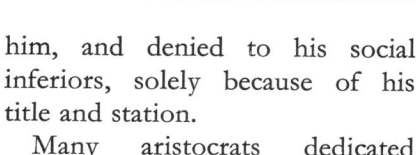

maintain that they would vanish from the stage. The grand, luxurious hunting pastime of the Old World was made possible by small armies of peasants, who often served without any recompense whatever and often under wretched conditions.

Looking back, it seems remarkable that the princes and lords who were charged with maintaining an orderly society could have been blind enough to dig their own graves so relentlessly. "Beasts and man may be compared to wildernesses and palaces," the Spanish writer Baltasar Gracian contended in the mid-seventeenth century, mean-

the wilderness (which meant anywhere outside the palace and its environs) was the habitat of lesser creatures, incapable of conscious thought or virtue. Gracian's thesis was not his alone; a number of other writers and thinkers espoused similar theories at the time. Social rank was for them all-important. It was accepted as natural that aristocrats should lead a life of pleasure, untroubled by concerns which bothered lesser mortals. The slightest challenge to this scheme of things could be punished with the utmost severity. The least important of petty princes could lay claim to privileges reserved for

him, and denied to his social inferiors, solely because of his title and station.

Many aristocrats dedicated themselves wholeheartedly to the art and sport of hunting simply to overcome the tedium of lives devoted exclusively to the pursuit of pleasure and petty distractions, occasionally interrupted by participation, at a safe distance, in war. Hunting, which could be practiced the year round, became a key part of the program of amusements and, in the process, widened the rift between "palace" and "wilderness." The peasantry, which carried the heaviest burden in prepar-

ing and maintaining the pageantry that was an essential part of aristocratic hunting, played finally no inconsiderable role in the upheavals which brought the aristocracy tumbling down from its position of privilege and power. Social equality was still to exist only as an idea. But the ways of hunting were to be altered beyond recognition.

At the beginning of the nineteenth century organized hunting was still largely the prerogative of the upper social stratum, but no longer could aristocrats recruit legions of unpaid peasants to transform their hunts into elabo-

Right: Bird's eye view of Chambord Castle. Originally planned as a hunting lodge, it later became a symbol of sovereignty of Francis I of France.

Below: Louis XIV hunting at Chambord. Etching by Jean Le Pautre, 1617–1682.

rate festivals. Furthermore, edicts and rules governing hunting, which had originated earlier but which had never been enforced to any serious extent, were now supplemented by up-to-date laws and regulations for which at least an effort at enforcement was made. These included prohibitions on more brutal forms of hunting. Secularization of church-owned estates, unification of various dukedoms and rationalization of government administration effectively

reduced the previously confusing number and variety of hunting regulations to more manageable proportions.

In the nineteenth century hunting became a pastime for the middle classes, flexing their social muscle as aristocratic privilege declined. The kind of outlay required for the luxurious hunting spectacles of the previous century was no longer available for the purpose. Expenditure on hunting, both in money and man-power, declined. Reputable commoners, with new-found wealth at their disposal, were able to buy or lease hunting rights from those gentry

who still retained them by law. These tenants were held responsible for preserving the hunting grounds in good condition, for respecting close seasons and seeing that others did the same, and for restricting the kill to reasonable numbers. Compensation by them for damage caused by game to private property was made compulsory. The value of agriculture and forests was rising; it followed that the population of game in fields and woods had to be reduced. At the same time, the democratic ideas spread by the French Revolution and other subsequent upheavals gave the peasantry an

awareness of its potential power and it seemed unwise to irritate peasants through over-protection of game which damaged their land or possessions.

In 1848, a year of revolutions in Europe, hunting conditions were basically altered and various rules and regulations simply vanished from the books. The undermining of state authority gave peasants the opportunity, which they seized, to hunt indiscriminately and, in the process, deplete herds of wild game. Their new freedom took a heavy toll. Some species virtually became extinct. The peasant rampage had been anticipated by some estate owners who, knowing what was to come, did more than their share of over-hunting as well. To make matters worse, the generation of hunters which succeeded the changes brought in by the 1848 upheavals had little idea of the moral obligations which should be part of the hunting code.

The result was that, to a large extent, an understanding of the finer points of hunting and true knowledge of wild game tended to reside with the relatively few remaining interested aristocrats, dreaming of a lost world, and with forestry officials. It was from their ranks that an effort to rationalize the methods of hunting and to enforce hunting restrictions

emerged. We are also in debt to them for descriptive accounts of hunting practices and procedures, many of which are still authoritative today.

A code was thus formulated which has, in the intervening time, altered little. Then, as now, the basic aim was to give the hunter a sense of duty and proportion, help him best use his skills and talents and protect game from senseless slaughter. Hunting—so long considered a privilege of noblemen—began to develop again as the province of all who chose to be hunters.

Except for the objects illustrated
on pages 65, 68 and 69 (bottom), which
are in the Bavarian National Museum,
all items shown in this section are in the
German Hunting Museum in Munich.
Aside from their significance in the
history of hunting weapons—they
represent extraordinary achievements in
European weapon-making—they have
been selected because pictures of them have
so far appeared only in museum
publications and, therefore, do not
duplicate illustrations in other recently
published studies of weapons.

Above: A wheel-lock harquebus,
about 1630. The entire stock is richly
ornamented in the tschinke manner with
figures and patterns of inlaid bone and
mother-of-pearl.

Below: Wheel-lock with inside wheel by
Simon Ewerth of Augsburg, Germany,
about 1740. The dial automatically
registered the number of firings.

Hunting Weapons

In feudal times, hunting weapons, especially guns, were status symbols—and to some extent they still are. The nobility decorated the finest rooms of their chateaus and lodges with their implements of hunting and of war. Experts and scholars have examined them closely to assess their elaborate workmanship and finely-wrought mechanisms. The gunsmiths of the period were artists—master engravers, unexcelled woodcarvers, wizards with gold and silver ornamentation. Theirs was a highly respected craft, the products of which, magnificent in design, served man's enigmatic wish to rule over other men and over animals. Modern hunting weapons—produced with highly developed industrial manufacturing techniques—are usually, though not always, superior in performance. However, they rarely match the elegance and beauty of their predecessors.

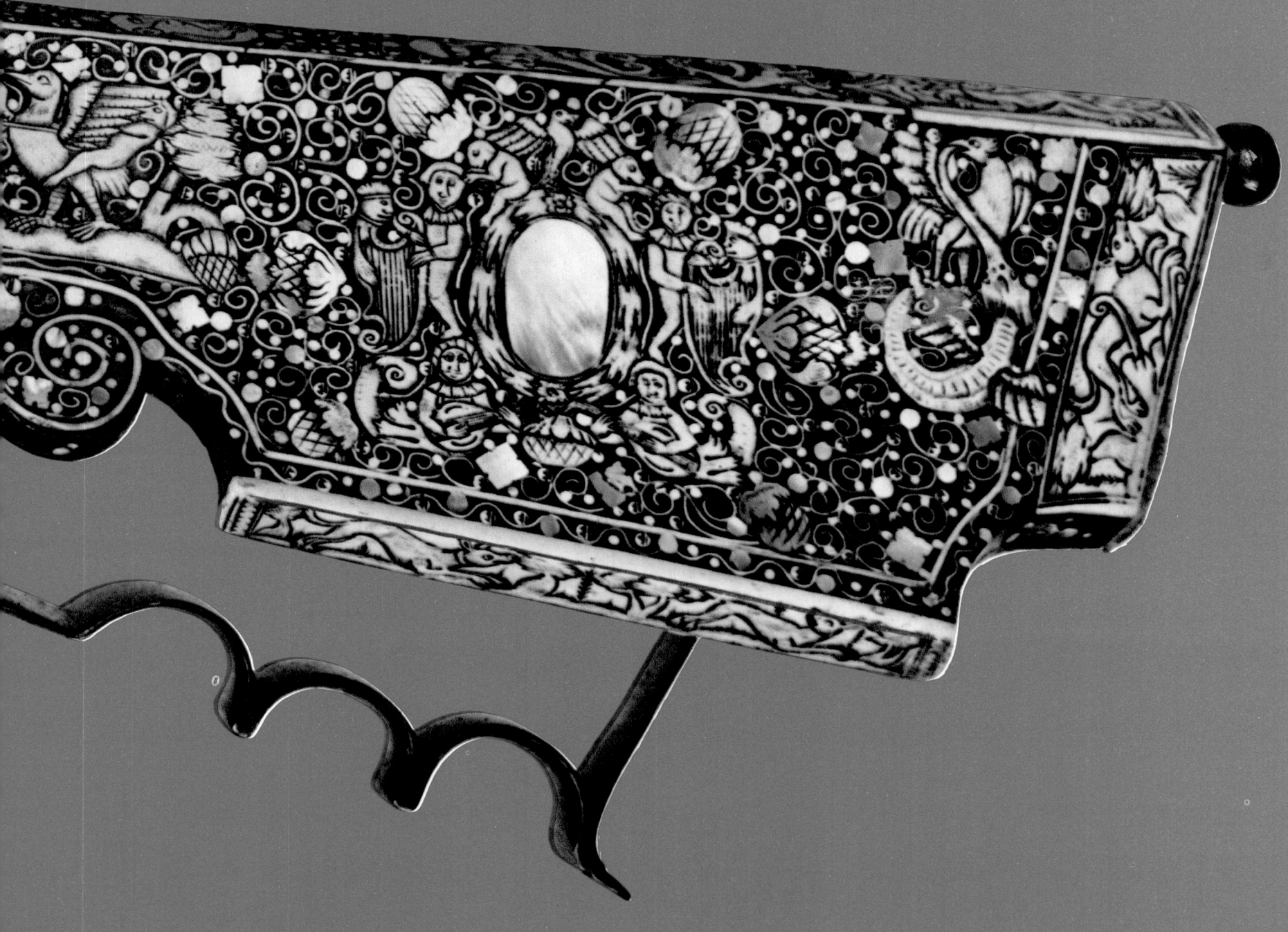

Hunting Spears

Left: Copper engravings by Stradanus:
Wolf hunt, boar chase and bear chase.
Stradanus was probably the most
prodigious translator of hunting into art
in the second half of the 17th century.
He vividly depicts the use of hunting
spears and swords.

The bear spear and boar spear, which were the most important and useful weapons for a hunter on foot hunting bear and wild boar, differed only in the strength of their blades. These blades were forged in one piece and, of necessity, were fashioned with sturdy central ribs and razor-sharp points. A shaft of very solid hardwood, not cut from a larger piece but grown to the required length, was inserted into a round or square blade socket. To keep the spear-thrusting hand from slipping, a narrow leather strip in spiral or lattice form, or embellished with knots or studs, was wound around the shaft. A particularly characteristic trimming of the boar spear was the cross-bar below the blade—either a rigid piece of iron, two to seven inches long and affixed at right angles to the shaft, or a strip of bone, antler or wood attached to a thong. This device prevented the blade from penetrating too deeply into the body of the animal and also helped the hunter hold off animals which charged into his spear.

The chamois spear is an especially interesting weapon, probably invented in the sixteenth century by Emperor Maximilian I. Illustrations of it feature in hunting books of the period. The chamois spear consisted of a shaft, between nine and twelve feet long, topped by a specially contrived socket knife with which to "lift out" chamois brought to bay in mountain niches by hunting dogs. In one of his books, Maximilian himself offers expert instructions on how to handle, care for and store these weapons. They require special cases for storage. "Furthermore, see that two good shafts are brought along on the hunt, a long

one and one medium sized. The shorter shaft should be two and a half arm spans long and the longer should be four arm spans long. They should be equally strong throughout and made of naturally grown, not cut, wood so that they will not bend. They should have good, well-tempered socket knives."

In the arms collection of Tratzberg Castle near Jenbach in Germany there are still three chamois spears from the time of Maximilian. It is possible that he used them himself because it was from there that he set out to hunt in the

Achen valley and surrounding region.

The emperor was keenly aware of the dangers of hunting and offered firm advice, even on incidental details. "You should," he wrote, "always have a (steel) helmet carried for you in your hunting bag so that, when you walk over the mountains and the hounds set stones rolling, your head will be protected. And a good rope, as well."

Little is known about chamois hunting before Maximilian. It may be that he was the first to devote specialized attention to the sport.

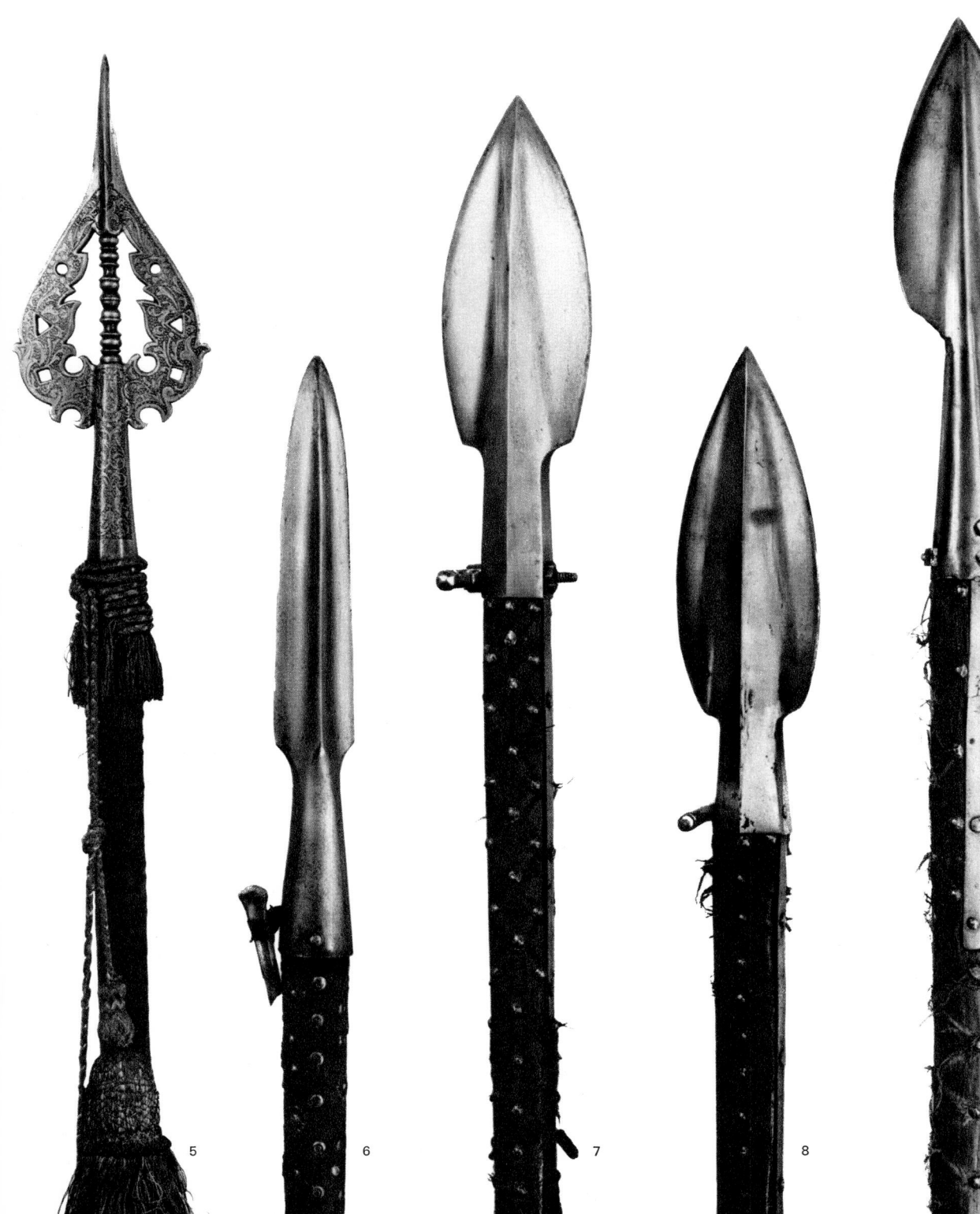

Hunting spears. 16th–18th century:

1   Boar spear with the initials A.R. on the staghorn toggle. From the armory of Frederick August, Elector of Saxony. 18th century.

2   Boar spear with the mark of its maker on the blade. 16th century.

3   Parade spear with etched and gilt blade. 17th century.

4   Hunting spear with escutcheoned monogram and coat of arms of the Elector of Saxony. From the Royal Trophy Room in Dresden. About 1700.

5   Parade spear with sculpted and ornamentally etched blade. 16th century.

6–9   Boar and bear spears. 17th century.

61

Hunting Swords

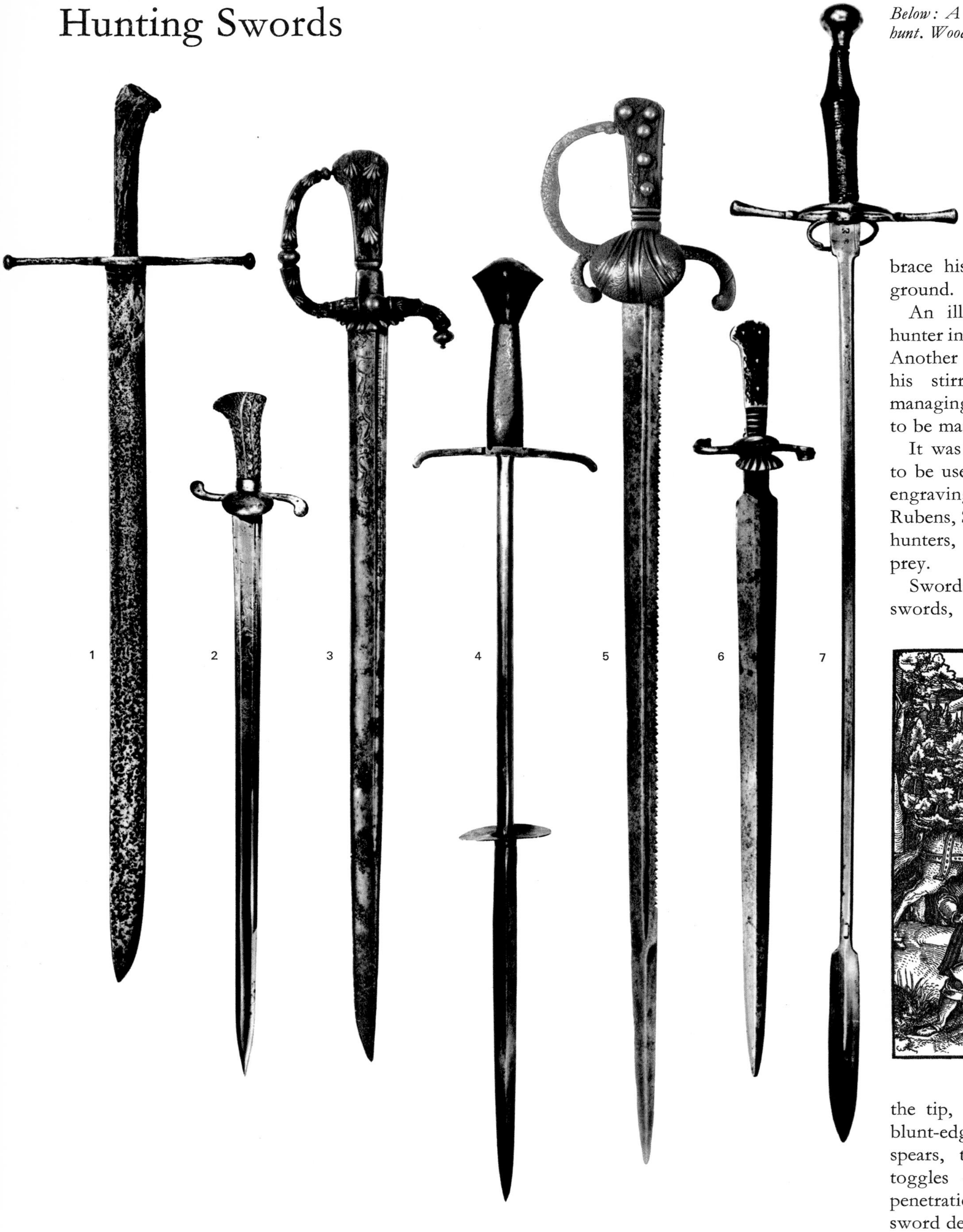

Below: A mounted hunter wields his sword on a stag hunt. Wood engraving by Hans Burgkmair.

brace his outstretched left foot against the ground.

An illustration in *Theuerdank* shows the hunter in that position, facing a charging boar. Another shows him with his foot caught in his stirrup while dismounting, but still managing to cope with the boar. His skill had to be matched by the quality of his weapon.

It was not uncommon for hunting swords to be used on horseback. A great number of engravings and paintings by such masters as Rubens, Snyders and Stradanus show mounted hunters, wielding swords, tangling with their prey.

Swordsmiths designed special boar-hunt swords, double-edged and widened toward

the tip, with most of the remaining length blunt-edged or rounded. Like boar and bear spears, these swords were equipped with toggles or cross-bars to govern depth of penetration, an important factor in hunting sword design.

Dissecting implements were often also taken along on the hunt and were considered indispensable for the well-equipped hunter who usually carried them on his belt. In addition to a heavy skinning knife, he usually had smaller knives, forks, an awl and a whetstone. These should not be confused with hunting cutlery used only at hunt dinners, which tended to be ceremonial affairs governed by strict ritual.

Hunting swords and sabers.

1 *Sword. 16th century.*

2 *Saber. About 1650.*

3 *Saber with decorated blade. 1659.*

4 *Boar sword with adjustable shield. 18th century.*

5 *Saber with saw-back blade. About 1650.*

6 *Sword. 16th century.*

7 *Boar sword made by swordsmith Wolfgang Stantler of Solingen, Germany. 16th century.*

Slashing at onrushing wild boars or bears, no matter how vigorously, could do them little harm. Hunting swords were, therefore, mainly designed to be used as thrusting weapons. The idea was to confront game brought to bay by the hounds, or already wounded, and to permit the enraged animal to run into the sword: the hunter would dismount, bend his right knee, support the sword firmly held with both hands against it, and

Crossbows

Medieval knights, true to their codes of chivalry, strongly objected to the introduction of the crossbow as a weapon of combat. Dismissing it as treacherous and dishonorable, they condescended to using it only for hunting. Though it had been known in Roman times, the crossbow did not come into common usage until the late Middle Ages. But even then, it was considered by many to be too cumbersome for anything except perhaps shooting contests, as well as cowardly and unmanly if used against humans. Feelings about it ran so high that it was actually outlawed by a Church council early in the twelfth century, a ruling confirmed by a subsequent synod which ordained that it could be used only against infidels. Clergymen were forbidden to engage in any "religious dealings with marauding bands or mercenaries, with crossbow men and similar blood-thirsty men." Townsmen, however, often ignored this prohibition and, under siege circumstances, found the crossbow an excellent weapon of defense. But at the battle of Crecy (1346), English longbowmen so decisively overwhelmed Genoese crossbowmen employed by the French that the weapon became obsolete.

Much later, after firearms were in wide use, the crossbow enjoyed a revival of popularity as a hunting weapon because of its accuracy and penetration power. It was also silent and did not scare off the prey.

Originally the bow was made of wood; then of horn strips glued together and covered with parchment, bast or birch bark. Later, it was made of steel which gave it greater firing range but introduced the danger of the bow cracking in severe frost. Emperor Maximilian I, that intrepid hunter, advised: "To begin with, always have several cases—for your hunting sword, gun, horn crossbow and steel bow. That is to say, the horn crossbow is for use in winter because of the frost; the steel bow in summer. However, the steel bow may be used in winter too if it is not too cold!"

For some designs, a hunter's strength was not enough to manipulate the bow which was, instead, drawn by a device called a German cog-and-ratchet winder. An English winder, a form of miniature pulley, was also sometimes employed.

Various kinds of crossbow arrows were required for hunting the various kinds of game.

A sharply pointed bolt was used for most ground game, a forked arrow for chamois, and a blunt bolt for eagles and most other winged game. A proficient hunter could count on hitting his target at a distance of up to two hundred paces.

Another variety of crossbow, the arbalest, later came into use for hunting. The bows of this lighter version could be drawn by hand—a little hook was used for the purpose. The projectiles were arrows, stones or clay bullets. The small missiles were fired from a pouch woven to the bowstring. Considerable skill was required for accuracy.

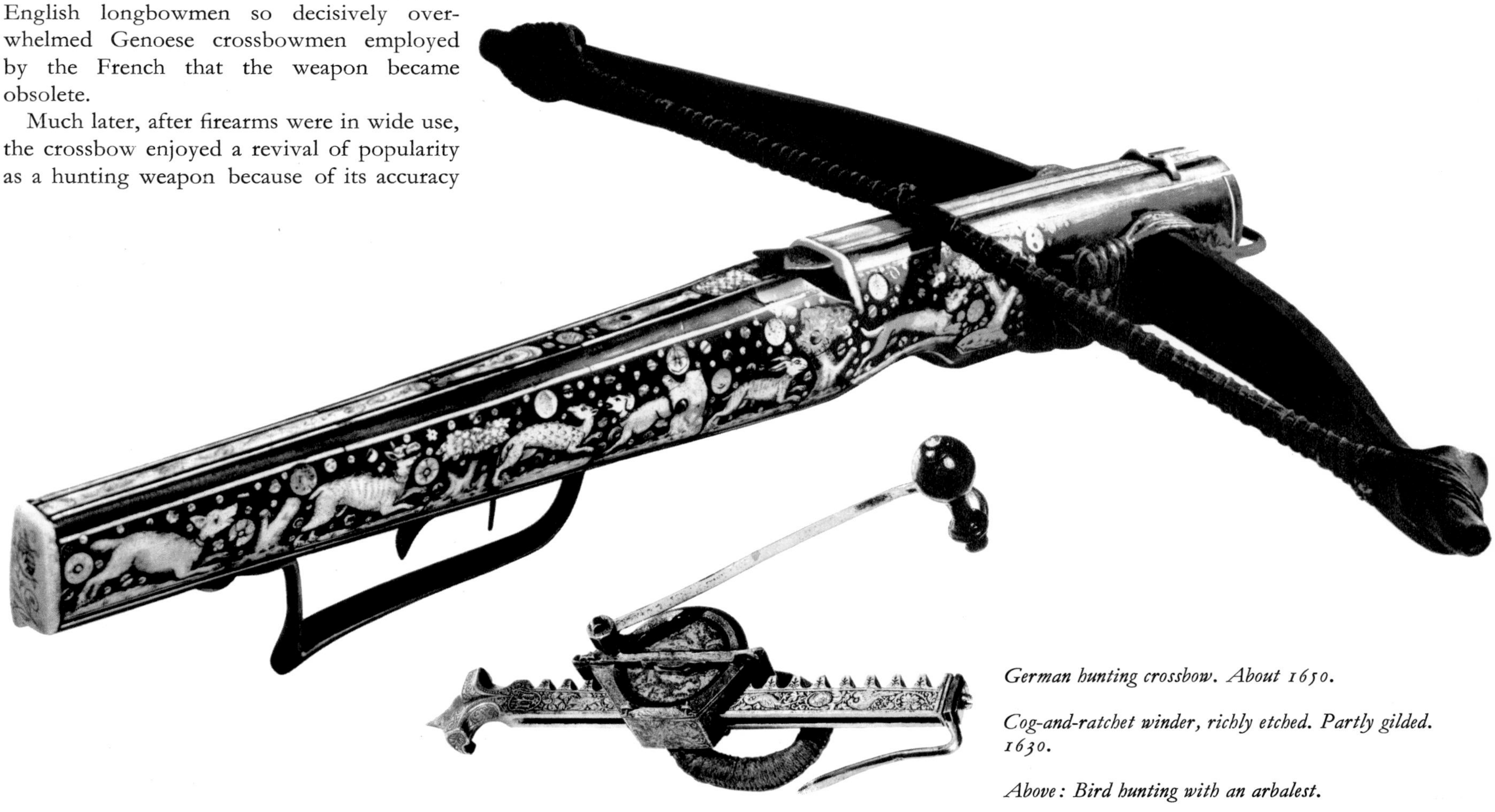

German hunting crossbow. About 1650.

Cog-and-ratchet winder, richly etched. Partly gilded. 1630.

Above: Bird hunting with an arbalest.

The First Handguns

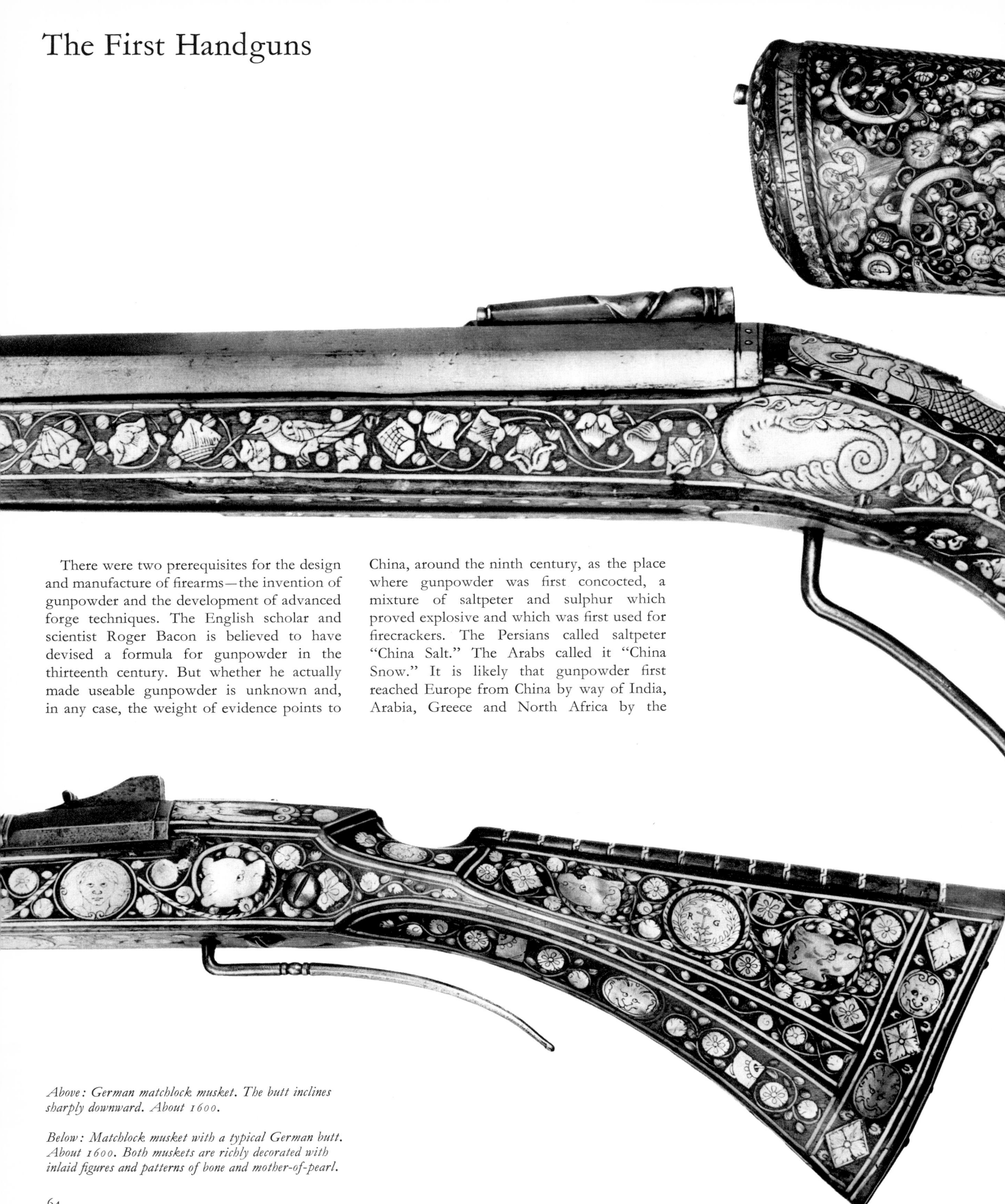

There were two prerequisites for the design and manufacture of firearms—the invention of gunpowder and the development of advanced forge techniques. The English scholar and scientist Roger Bacon is believed to have devised a formula for gunpowder in the thirteenth century. But whether he actually made useable gunpowder is unknown and, in any case, the weight of evidence points to China, around the ninth century, as the place where gunpowder was first concocted, a mixture of saltpeter and sulphur which proved explosive and which was first used for firecrackers. The Persians called saltpeter "China Salt." The Arabs called it "China Snow." It is likely that gunpowder first reached Europe from China by way of India, Arabia, Greece and North Africa by the

Above: German matchlock musket. The butt inclines sharply downward. About 1600.

Below: Matchlock musket with a typical German butt. About 1600. Both muskets are richly decorated with inlaid figures and patterns of bone and mother-of-pearl.

German matchlock rifle. 1582. The stock is
completely embellished with engraved bone inlay.
Hunting scenes and fabled animals are shown along with
biblical, mythological and profane scenes.

fourteenth century. It was, by then, composed of saltpeter, charcoal and sulphur and was to remain the only important explosive in use until the invention of nitroglycerin more than five hundred years later.

The first handguns were primitive miniature cannon which appeared in the fourteenth century. They were ungainly instruments which soldiers fired by holding a flame to a touch-hole. These cumbersome weapons, for which no measure of accuracy whatever could be claimed, sometimes went by the name of "fire tubes" or "boxes."

So imperfect an instrument inevitably lent itself to persistent efforts at improvement. The late fifteenth century saw the development of the harquebus which, for balance, was supported on a staff stuck into the ground, and of the matchlock which was ignited by a smouldering "match," a kind of fuse which had been soaked in a slow-burning inflammable solution and then dried.

Loading, firing and reloading was such a clumsy operation and so time-consuming, and accuracy was still so limited, that these weapons remained, for the most part, less effective than the bow or the crossbow. "Gunners" on battlefields often had to be chaperoned by pikemen to give them protection and time to reload before being overrun by the enemy. Whatever success these primitive guns had resulted from the fear they instilled through noise and sulphur smoke. This partly explains the victories of heavily outnumbered Spanish *conquistadores* over the Aztecs and the Incas in the newly discovered Americas.

Because of its inefficiency, the powder gun was not employed for hunting until well into the sixteenth century. Within a hundred years, however, progress had been swift enough for it to supersede the bow and the crossbow as the primary hunting weapons, although the matchlock, gradually made more effective, really became important only as a military handgun.

As gunsmiths improved "match" ignition through mechanical ingenuity, accuracy in aiming underwent improvement also. A cock was connected to the trigger, fixing tinder in a clamp and pressing the tinder onto the pan. The desired contact between primer and powder charge was thus achieved and a person handling the weapon was no longer required to keep an eye on both target and ignition. The door to modern weaponry had been opened.

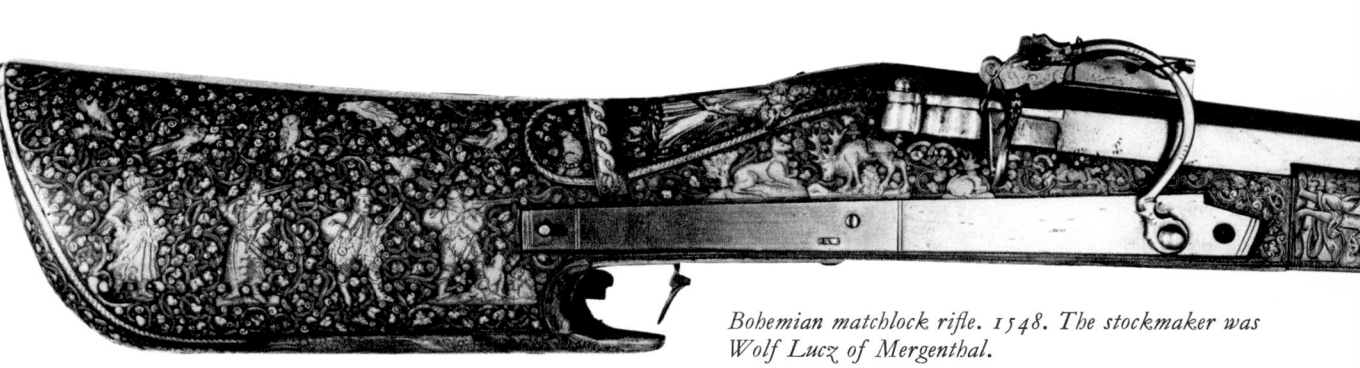

Bohemian matchlock rifle. 1548. The stockmaker was
Wolf Lucz of Mergenthal.

The Wheel-lock

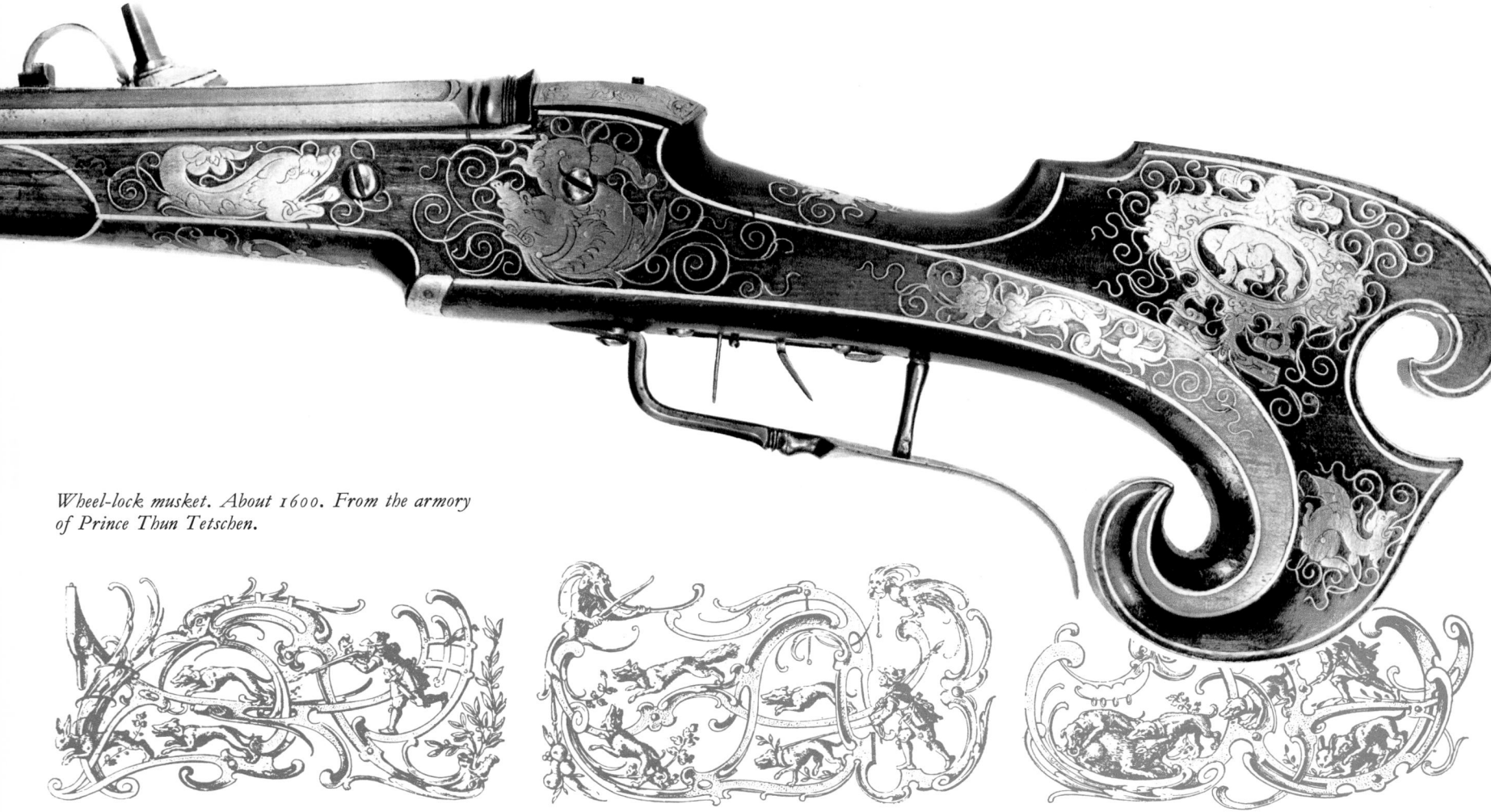

The wheel-lock, which was invented early in the sixteenth century, soon superseded the matchlock. Its mechanism was far more complicated but on the other hand it offered greater accuracy and was easier to use. The design was far from ideal, but it eliminated the need to keep a smoldering match handy. The new device was not completely trusted in its early days, however, and a match was often kept in reserve in case the apparatus failed to function properly.

The wheel of the wheel-lock was spring-loaded and it had a rutted edge which rubbed against a flint, thereby striking sparks. The sparks ignited priming powder which, in turn, triggered the main charge through the touch-hole. Unlike the matchlock, the wheel-lock could be carried loaded and ready for instant use.

The wheel-lock was expensive to produce, requiring the exertions of many master craftsmen, some of whom, like locksmiths, had not

Wheel-lock, richly decorated with patterns and figures. Second half of 17th century.

been traditionally associated with gun-making. In addition, some of the doubts aroused earlier by the introduction of the "unchivalrous" crossbow were revived and extended to the newly devised implement. Emperor Maximilian I, "the last of the knights," personally forbade the manufacture of the new weapon. Not until after his death

were handguns widely fitted with wheel-locks. The oldest such weapons still in existence are stored in the old Madrid armory of Maximilian's successor as Holy Roman Emperor, Charles V.

Although prohibitive manufacturing costs and complicated handling procedures ruled out the use of wheel-locks for military pur-

Wheel-lock musket. About 1600. From the armory of Prince Thun Tetschen.

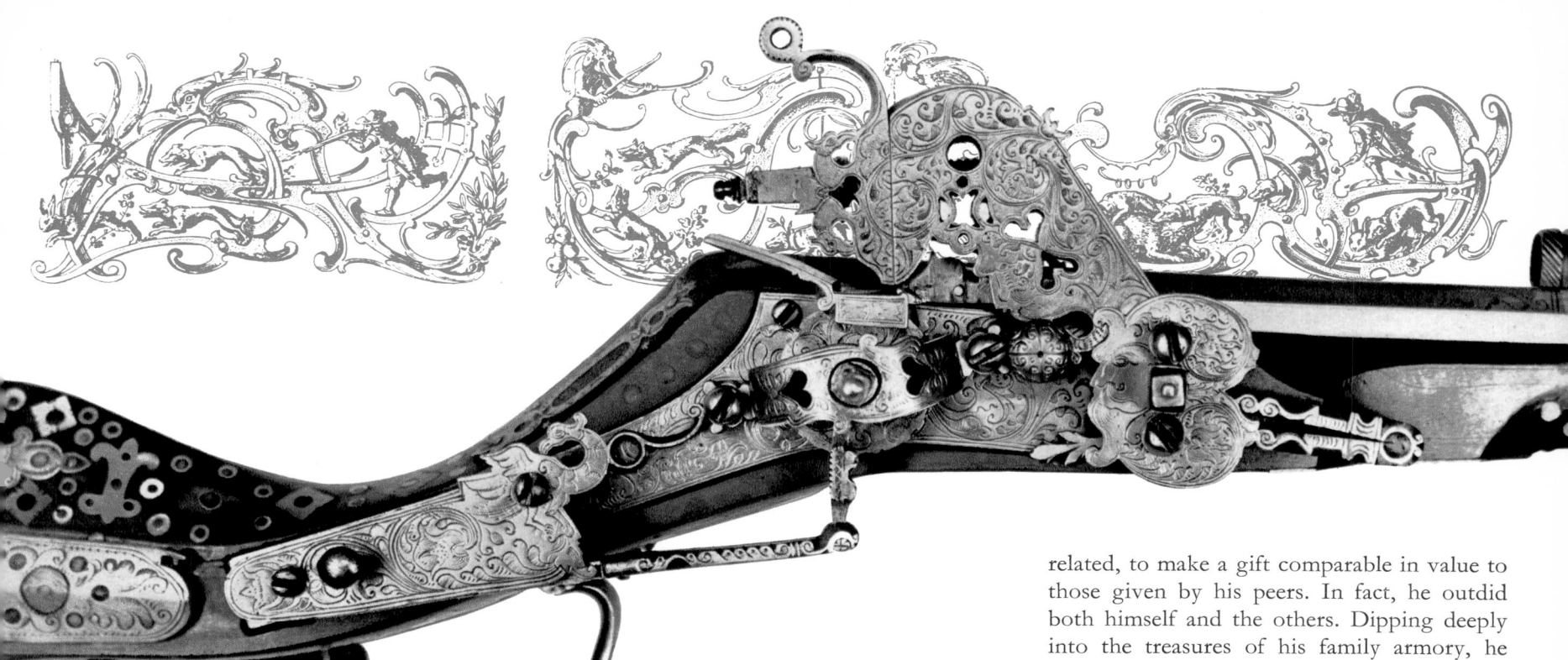

poses, the weapon enjoyed considerable popularity among hunters. This remained true even after it had been superseded by more advanced handguns.

Master craftsmen, increasingly united in privileged guilds, found weapon-making a lucrative vein of activity. Many a royal household employed its own gunmaker, stockmaker, steel engraver and goldsmith. Their masterpieces today grace many museums.

For many dedicated hunters, no price was too high to pay for so splendid a weapon and great value was attached to its artistic design. Princes sought to outdo each other in possessing precious pieces; they drew enormous pride and pleasure from magnificent household armories which they were able to display to guests. Richly decorated showpieces were sometimes given as lavish gifts.

The high regard in which beautifully, expensively made weapons were held among the aristocracy of Europe was demonstrated in an incident involving Maximilian of Bavaria, a seventeenth-century princeling not particularly known for his generosity. He was required, on the occasion of the marriage of two aristocrats to whom he was distantly related, to make a gift comparable in value to those given by his peers. In fact, he outdid both himself and the others. Dipping deeply into the treasures of his family armory, he produced the so-called *Turin Hunting Ornament* (these treasures, like rare stamps today, had reputations and special names of their own.) The pride of the master steel-engraver, Daniel Sadeler of Munich, it made a stunning present. It consisted of a wheel-lock musket, a wheel spanner and two powder flasks. The stock of the weapon had been made by Adam Vischer, whose pieces are distinguished by meticulous workmanship and a particularly colorful effect produced from blended materials—gold, silver, mother-of-pearl, copper and multi-colored bone inlay. Such a gift was enough to earn the otherwise obscure Maximilian a footnote in history.

Above: Wheel-lock tschinke, *a light birding rifle. About 1620. From the armory of Prince Thun Tetschen.*

Below: Wheel-lock. Ansbach. 1719.

Wheel-lock and game bag.
Maximilian I, Elector of Bavaria
(1597–1651).

When Maximilian ascended to power
in Bavaria, the craft of weapon-making
had reached its high point in the city
of Munich, his capital. Highly artistic
steel-engraving and masterly stockmaking
earned international renown for the
weapons produced there at the time.
This is one of those weapons, together with
its matching game bag, even the
engraved clasp of which is a work of art.
The stock was definitely the work of
Hieronymus Borstorffer, but who can
be credited with the steel engraving
remains an open question. Both Daniel
Sadeler and his student and successor,
Caspar Spaet, have been suggested.
Both were notable Munich engravers.
The wheel-lock was probably made
between 1630 and 1637. On the lock,
amidst foliate scrollwork, a hunter aims
his gun at a stag pursued by a dog. The
ground has been roughened and gilded,
heightening the pictorial effect. The
octagonal barrel is similarly decorated.

German leather hunting bag, with silk embroidery on its front showing stags against a pastoral background. 17th century.

Wheel-lock made by Johann Michael Maucher of Swabia. 1671. The six wheel-locks of this extraordinary stockmaker and woodcarver from southern Germany are among the most precious exhibits in the Bavarian National Museum. Maucher was famous for his wood-and-ivory relief work. But there was little consistency in his pictorial imagery. Scenes of Greek mythology alternated with scenes from the Bible. On the lock, the legendary Greek hunter Actaeon is harassed by his dogs, while on the butt there is a magnificent portrayal of St. George locked in combat with the dragon. The princess he has just rescued is on the left; her castle is on the right.

The Flintlock

The forerunner of the flintlock was the snaphance, a device of Scandinavian origin from which the flintlock itself was developed early in the seventeenth century. It then remained virtually unchanged for two hundred years until improved priming substances made such developments as the percussion-lock possible.

The flintlock mechanism was simple. A spring released by pressing the trigger activated the hammer which housed a flint which struck a metal plate above the priming-pan. This produced sparks to ignite the priming powder and thus to touch off the charge.

By employing sets of up to twenty-four guns, which could be immediately reloaded by gun-loaders, an early form of saturation firing could be achieved. But this rapid fire was not, at first, used for military purposes. Batteries of often superbly worked weapons were used for hunting in a fashion which arouses nothing but distaste today. The prey was cornered and literally shot to pieces by teams of hunters firing from safe vantage points.

A study of classic hunting weapons should not neglect eighteenth-century pistols which were fired by hunters on horseback. Pairs of flintlock pistols were part of the paraphernalia of the well-equipped hunter of the period, who was also wont to carry a shotgun and a pair of rifles on his hunting excursions. Unfortunately, these sets were split up when old armories were closed down during the past few decades—with, for example, some collectors buying only the pistols while others acquired the matching guns. There seems

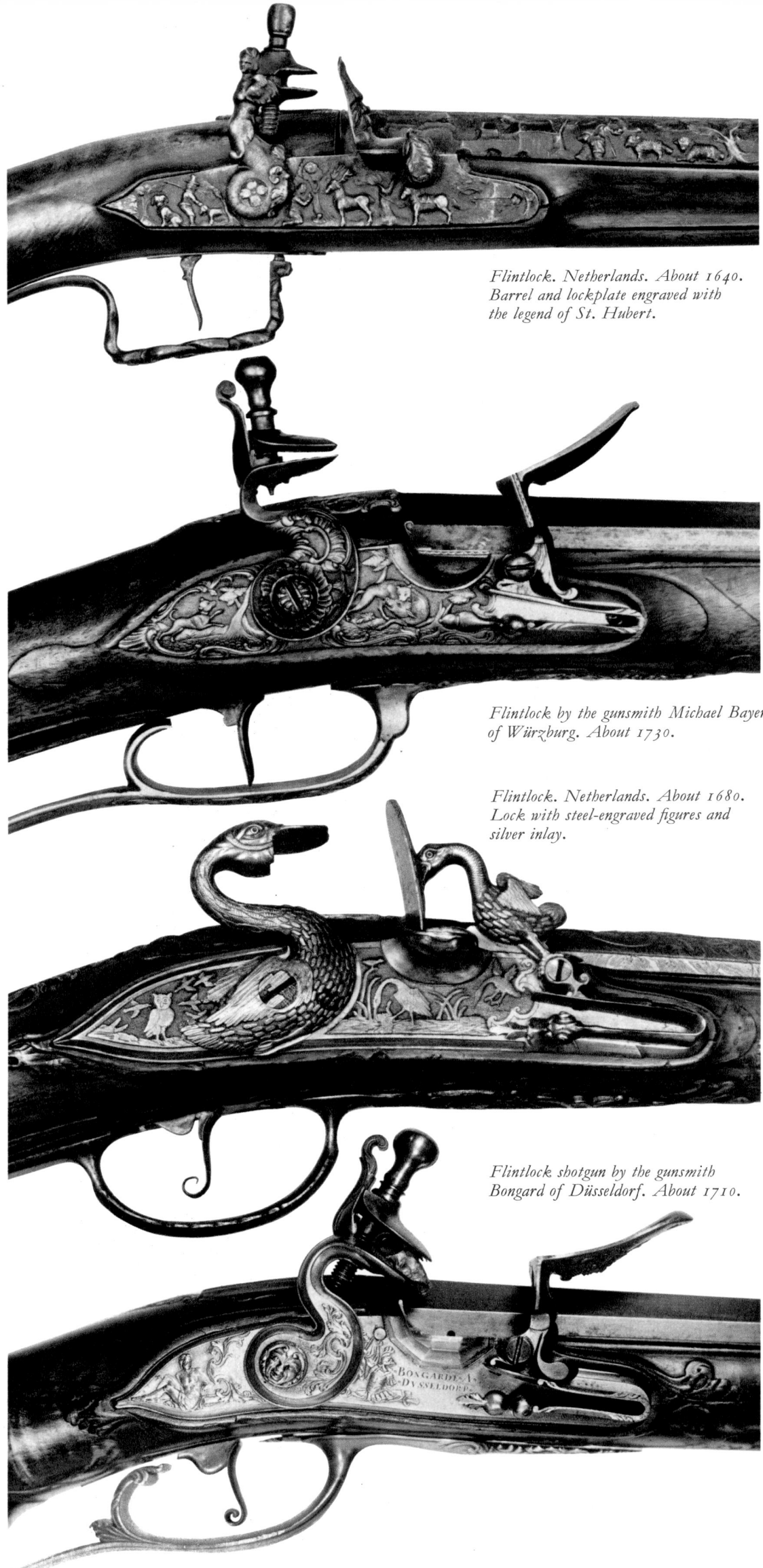

Flintlock. Netherlands. About 1640. Barrel and lockplate engraved with the legend of St. Hubert.

Flintlock by the gunsmith Michael Bayer of Würzburg. About 1730.

Flintlock. Netherlands. About 1680. Lock with steel-engraved figures and silver inlay.

Flintlock shotgun by the gunsmith Bongard of Düsseldorf. About 1710.

little hope of reuniting these often stunning sets of weapons.

Old hunting weapons remain important objects in our cultural history. Their value is increased if they can be identified by original make and owner. The weapon so identified does not, of course, become more magnificent. But it takes on added enchantment if it is known that, for instance, the hapless French queen Marie Antoinette or perhaps a German emperor went hunting with it. It then becomes a piece of history and also retains something of the personality of its former owner, lending the weapon a significance beyond that which its appearance conveys.

The German Hunting Museum in Munich owns a flintlock manufactured by the master gunmaker Pfeuffer around 1810. On the neck of the bolt are carved the initials of Friedrich Wilhelm Karl, the first King of Württemberg. The stock is decorated with elegantly engraved bone inlay. At the side of the lock, a hunter is depicted near a tree, aiming at a rabbit or fleeing wild boar. On the other side is a cluster of does and a stag chased by dogs. There is much foliated scrollwork. The gun has significance aside from its maker, owner and beauty. It calls to mind the famous festival of Diana at Bebenhausen, southern Germany, in 1812, the last of the old lavish and elaborate royal hunt spectacles.

Above: Snaphance double-lock. Brescia. About 1670.

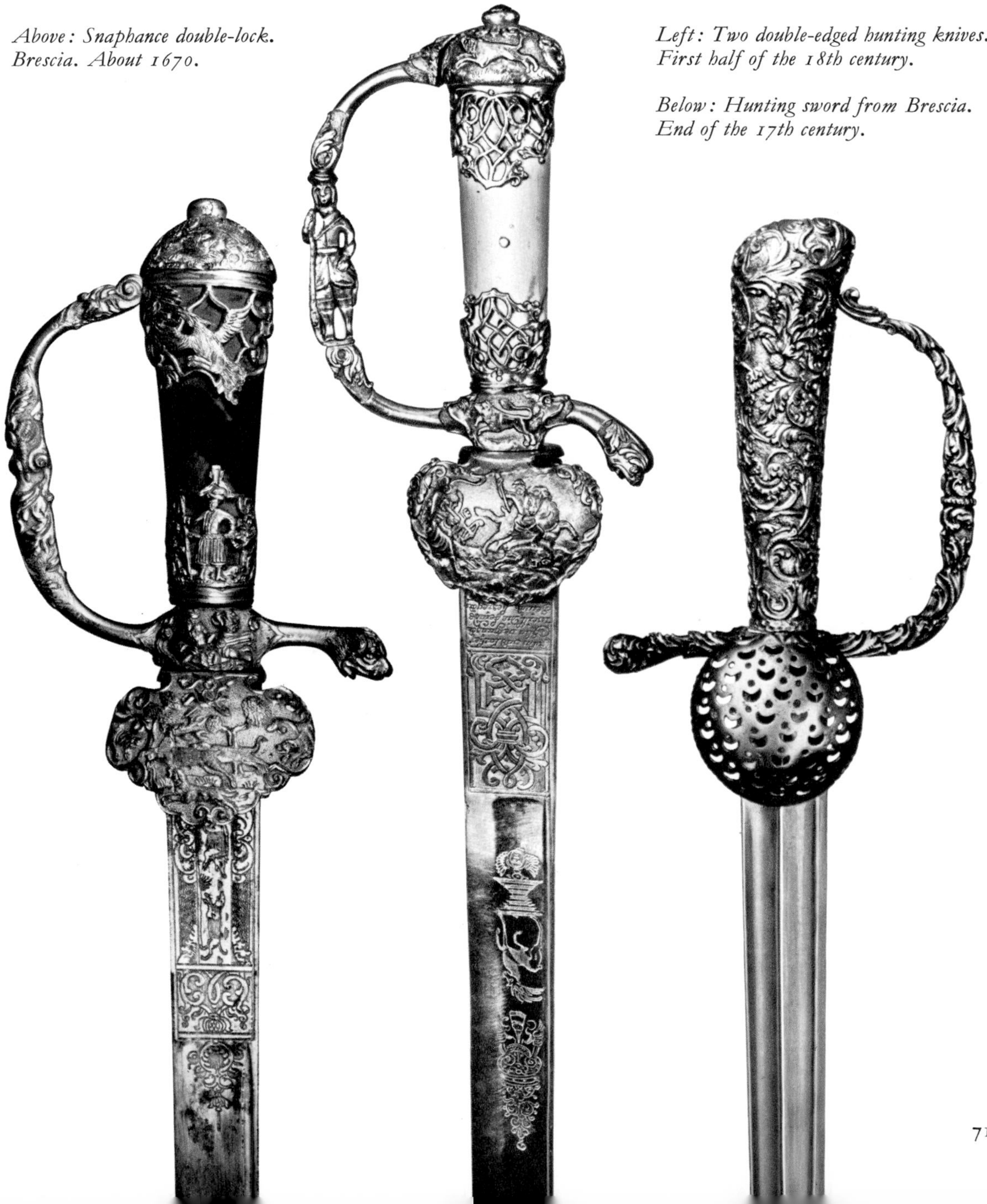

Left: Two double-edged hunting knives. First half of the 18th century.

Below: Hunting sword from Brescia. End of the 17th century.

71

In bygone days, a natural bond linked man and animals. Wild game provided much of man's sustenance, while prevailing customs and hunting methods generally prevented senseless killing. But later, mankind embarked on a path which led to the total destruction of some species and endangered the continued existence of others. Hunting was no longer essential to the perpetuation of the human race. It had become a sport and a pastime and all too often featured unrestrained, callous slaughter. Today, man is concerned with preserving his own species. It is no exaggeration to say that human survival is intimately entwined with what remains of the natural linkage between man and wild life. The true hunter is profoundly aware of his obligations not to engage in senseless animal slaughter and to prevent the further extinction and endangering of animal species. The true hunter is more keenly aware of the crucial importance of hunting regulations and animal conservation than people who have never lifted a hunting gun. The following pages are designed neither as a catalogue of trophies nor a guide for armed trophy hunters, but as a contribution to a deeper understanding of the magnificent animal world.

Origin of the Species

The Earth is about four and a half billion years old. But it was not until three billion years ago that chemical interactions which had been going on since the dawn of Earth-time finally produced living matter, in the form of simple cells which could multiply and grow. Evolution is a protracted process and it took another two and a half billion years for higher forms of life to begin to develop—about 500 million years ago.

Living things are given a stark choice. They adapt to prevailing environmental conditions or they do not survive. Over the course of time, the Earth's environment has been repeatedly subjected to upheaval and drastic change. The evolution of living things, therefore, has often been erratic. Unable to adapt, various species died out altogether. Others, basically more suited to survival, have barely changed over the ages.

The evolution of life on this planet began with invertebrates which lived in water. These were to include sponges, molluscs, jellyfish and crabs. Giant insects, some of which have been found fossilized in stratified coal veins, can also be traced back to primeval invertebrates.

Vertebrates, back-boned creatures of which primitive fish were the earliest species, first came into existence over 400 million years ago. These fish were the forebears of, among other animals, such amphibians as salamanders and newts which were, in turn, succeeded up the evolutionary tree by reptiles and, many millions of years later, by warm-blooded animals. The earliest mammals, comparatively small creatures, were at first unable to compete with reptiles for mastery of the land. Not until the Tertiary Period, about 65 million years ago, after the dynasty of giant reptiles had proved

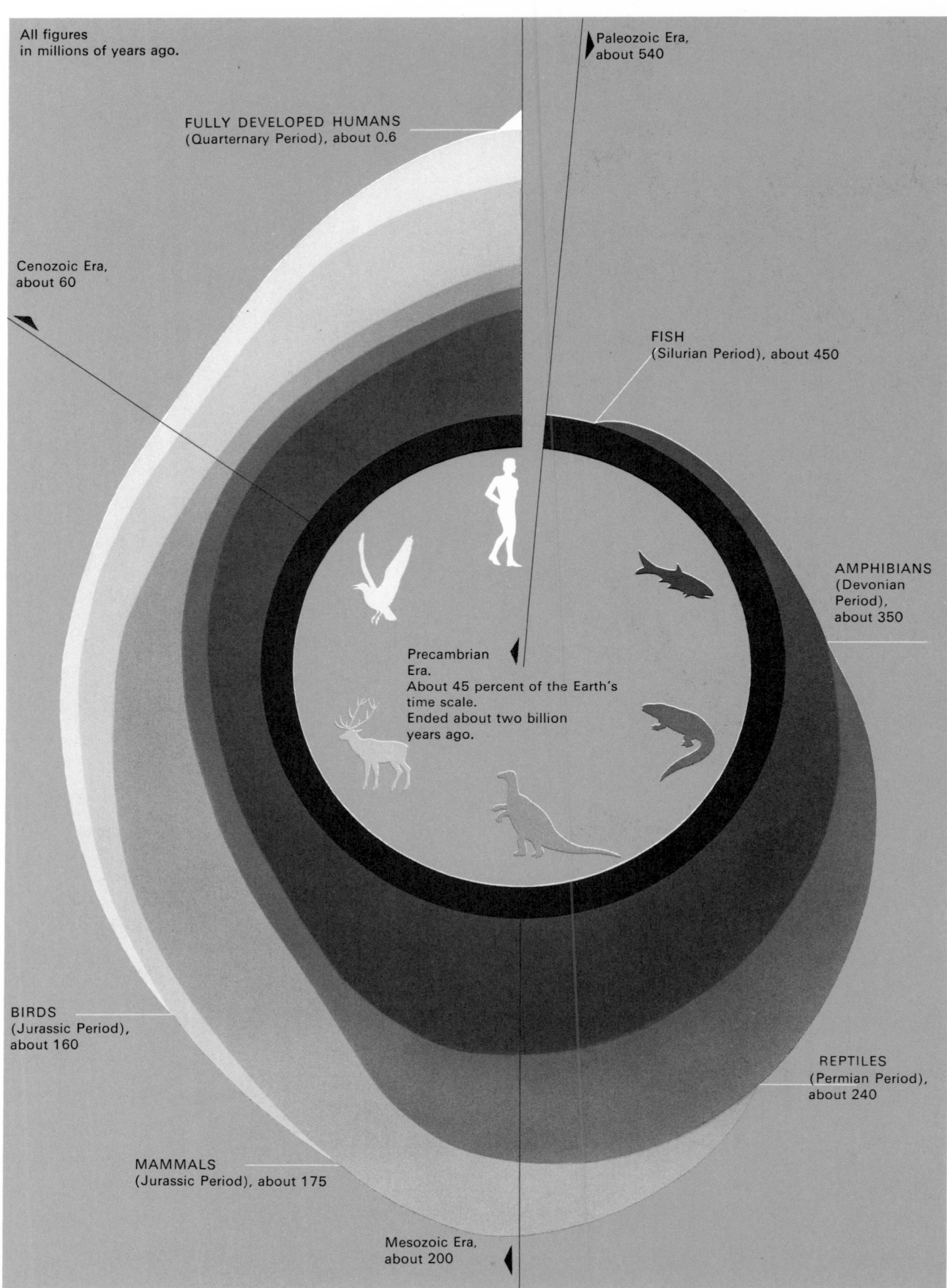

All figures in millions of years ago.

Paleozoic Era, about 540

FULLY DEVELOPED HUMANS (Quarternary Period), about 0.6

Cenozoic Era, about 60

FISH (Silurian Period), about 450

AMPHIBIANS (Devonian Period), about 350

Precambrian Era. About 45 percent of the Earth's time scale. Ended about two billion years ago.

BIRDS (Jurassic Period), about 160

REPTILES (Permian Period), about 240

MAMMALS (Jurassic Period), about 175

Mesozoic Era, about 200

Left: The evolution of five kinds of vertebrate can be schematically outlined as a time-and-space spiral. Fish, amphibians and reptiles date back to the Silurian, Permian and Devonian periods. Birds and mammals, however, did not reach the peak of their development until comparatively recently, in the Cenozoic Era. The turbulent development of man was the most recent development of all, barely yesterday on the Earth's time-scale.

Below: The first "huntable" animals developed from the Tertiary Period onward. They are pictured here at the top of an evolutionary tree. Although the elephant and the rhinoceros are today found only in tropical Africa and Asia, the even-toed ungulates (deer, antelope, sheep and goat), the beasts of prey, (marten, bear, dog and cat), the lagomorphs (including rabbits) and rodents represent the main bulk of the game animals. Whales and apes are not hunted by true hunters. Most of the smaller animals, including the ant-eater and duck-billed platypus, do not count as huntable game, but kangaroos do.

unable to survive environmental change, did the turbulent evolutionary development of mammals begin in earnest.

Meantime, vast physical changes had transformed the face of the Earth. According to available evidence, the planet's entire landmass at one time was concentrated in a single super-continent called Pangaea which, following terrestrial cataclysms, was fractured into two smaller giant continents. These were Laurasia—which was later to splinter into North America and Eurasia—and Gondwanaland—which was to break up to form South America, Africa, Australia and Antarctica. Before enormous upheavals sent the continents drifting into roughly the positions they occupy today, there was free migration of animals across the Earth's contiguous land areas. This accounts for the discovery of fossils of related extinct species in regions which are now strikingly remote from each other. It accounts also for the survival of related species of, for example, deer, rabbit and wildcat in different parts of the world.

After the continents had split apart, evolution of animals on each continent took place in isolation and separate strains evolved. The early isolation of some continents accounts for their distinctive wildlife—kangaroos and platypuses in Australia; ant-eaters in South America. (The Central American landbridge for migration between North and South America is comparatively recent.)

Survival for the higher mammals often meant moving great distances to find food and tolerable climates. The impact of glacial advance on northern zones meant that many of Africa's large animals originated in Eurasia and were propelled southward by an ice age. Similarly, a land link between North America and northern Asia in glacial periods permitted animals to migrate from one to the other.

The evolutionary process led eventually to the emergence of the most highly developed of all mammals—man himself. He made his appearance in primitive form at least one million years ago, though the period is not easy to fix, depending as it does on the discovery of controversial "missing links." Despite higher intelligence and more intricate skills, as civilization developed mankind often indulged in needless destruction. It is a practice he has still not abandoned and one which has led to the tragic extinction of many animal species, denying all humans, and hunters in particular, a picture and knowledge of some magnificent creatures of the animal world which had survived everything but the arrival of mankind.

Apes · Whales · Lagomorphs and rodents · Beasts of prey · Even-toed ungulates · Uneven-toed ungulates · Elephants · Insect-eaters · Scaly ant-eaters · Ant-eaters · Marsupials · Higher mammals · Duck-billed platypus · Primitive mammals · Echidna · Primordial mammals

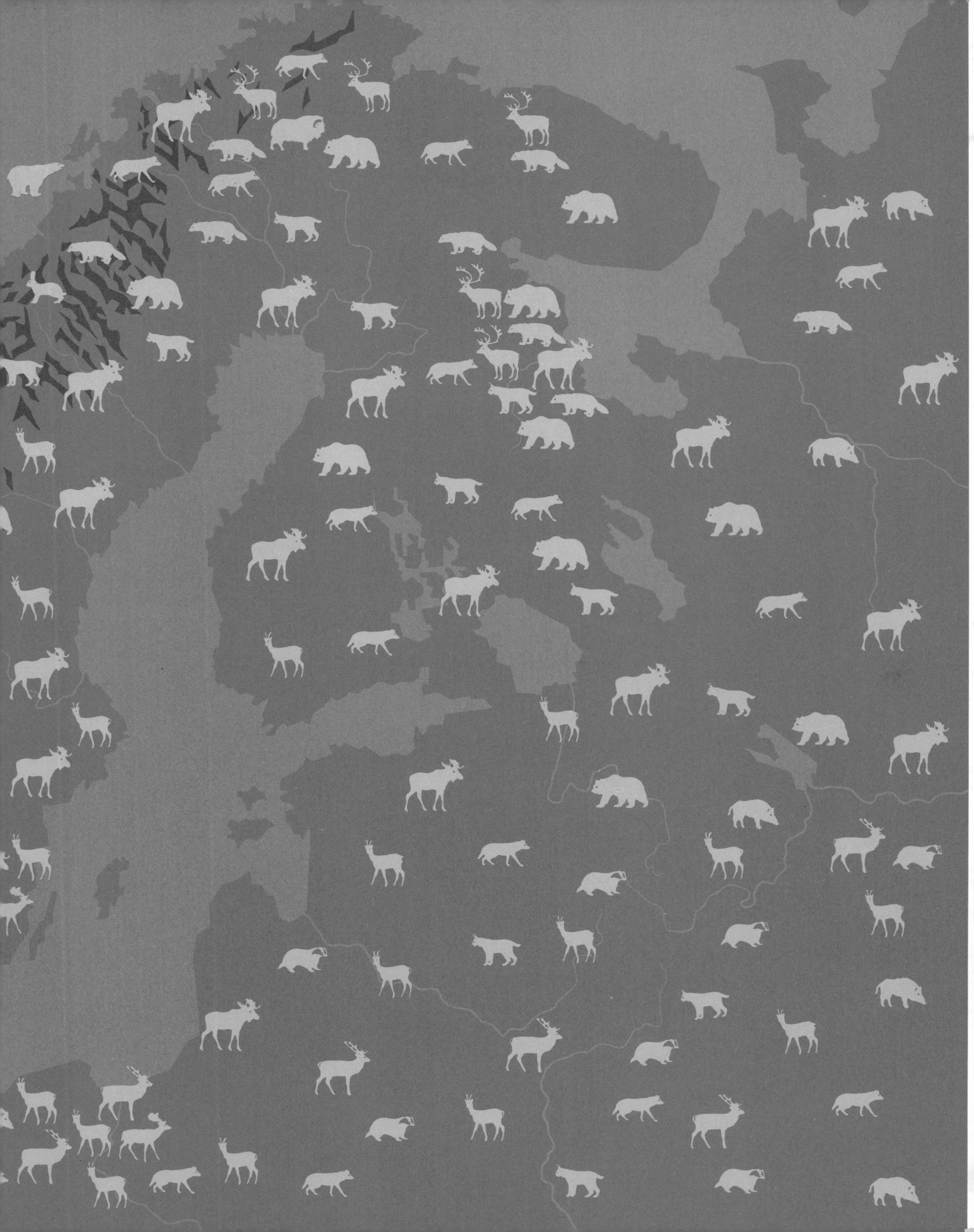

FALLOW DEER
Dama dama dama

Reintroduced into Europe from Asia Minor by the Romans. An extremely adaptable species of deer with remarkably sharp senses. Less destructive to vegetation than the red deer. Females comparatively tame; live in large herds. Adult males live in small, exclusive groups. Diurnal. Roam free over the entire continent. Probably the best-known deer bred in nature preserves.

MOUFLON
Ovis ammon musimon

The only extinct European wild sheep. Migrated to Mediterranean regions during the Ice Age. A few still found in Corsica and Sardinia. Introduced into several European countries in the nineteenth century. Extremely adaptable, remarkably sharp senses. Diurnal. Causes damage to vegetation when crossed with domestic sheep or where there is over-population.

EUROPEAN BISON
Bison bonasus

Closely related to North American bison. Now extinct in its natural habitat, it was once, like the aurochs, a creature of forests all over Europe. Survivors live in preserves of eastern Poland and the Soviet Union, notably in the Biaowiecza National Park. Also bred in various zoos. Strictly protected.

WILD BOAR
Sus scrofa

The boar is the oldest species of cloven-hoofed game in Europe. Extremely adaptable. Prefers large forest regions, usually sparsely wooded. Mainly nocturnal in regions inhabited by humans. Poor sight but excellent senses of smell and hearing. Omnivorous. Feeds largely on roots, fallen fruit, caterpillars and carrion.

ALPINE MARMOT
Marmota marmota

Lives in all alpine regions and in the Carpathian Mountains, on stony slopes about the treelines. Sun seeker. Constructs burrow of branches and twigs in which it also hibernates. Lays in a supply of hay. Gregarious. During feeding, one animal keeps watch and whistles to warn of approaching danger. Hunters call the male "bear" and the female "cat." The eagle is its natural prey.

HARE
Lepus europaeus

The commonest European species of small game. Originally an inhabitant of plains, it has considerably extended its habitat. Prefers civilized areas. Breeds mainly during dry periods; dampness often causes parasitic infection. Unlike the rabbit, the hare does not live in a burrow. The young animal is born fully developed. Dusk and night-time animal; nests by day.

BADGER
Meles meles

A plumpish relative of the marmot. Mainly active at dusk and at night. Sometimes shares its underground burrow with foxes. Hibernates intermittently, according to climate. Omnivorous. Lives on insects, snails, mice, birds' eggs (and is thus a menace to grouse), as well as berries, fallen fruit and carrion.

FOX
Vulpes vulpes

The commonest and most widespread animal of prey in the northern hemisphere. Extremely adaptable. Found from sea-level to the treeline, often in densely populated areas. Feeds on mice, berries, insects, fowl and small and young animals. Lives in underground burrow. Reproduces prolifically. The main carrier of rabies and, therefore, hunted intensively.

EUROPEAN POLECAT
Mustela putorius

Small, thick-set marten, native to all parts of Europe. Prefers to live close to the water. Main diet: mice, rats, frogs and insects. Paralyzes frogs with bites, to serve as preserved food. Discharges anal sacs when threatened and is thereby known for a disagreeable odor. The ferret, sometimes used for rabbit hunting, is a domesticated variety.

PINE MARTEN
Martes martes

Unlike the white-throated beach marten, which can extend its range to towns, the pine marten lives exclusively in densely wooded regions. Feeds mainly on rodents, especially squirrels. Hunts nocturnally. Plunders birds' nests; also eats berries and fruit. Extremely capable climber.

RED DEER
Cervus elaphus

Once found all over Europe, this species of large deer now lives in a few isolated districts of western Europe, especially between the Alps and the Carpathians. Unlike the fallow deer, it is extremely shy of man. Inhabits large wooded areas. The size, weight and number of tines of the antlers can be influenced by feeding conditions.

ROE
Capreolus capreolus

Agile, graceful Asiatic and European deer, the most widespread species of cloven-hoofed game in Europe. Once at home in sparse woodland and bush regions, now inhabits wider areas. Sharp rise in numbers due to extinction of its natural predators and effective conservation. Lives alone in summer; gregarious in winter.

MOOSE
Alces alces

Found all over northern hemisphere. Driven northward by warmer climate which followed the Ice Age. Thrives in marshy regions. Feeds on willows and water plants. Conservation in Scandinavia and the Soviet Union has resulted in a sharp increase in the formally declining population. Experimental farms in Soviet Union for domestication of moose.

REINDEER
Rangifer tarandus tarandus

Closely related to the caribou of North America and once found in large herds all over Europe, it migrated further and further northward after the Ice Age. Now found only in the northern reaches of Scandinavia where it has been domesticated, providing milk and meat. Both males and females grow branching antlers.

CHAMOIS
Rupicapra rupicapra

Hardy mountain antelope. Found in mountains of Europe and the Caucasus. Sedentary, adhering to definite haunts. Extremely sharp senses. Utters warning whistles when endangered. Summers over the treeline; winters just below. Related to similar species of Rocky Mountains and east Asian highlands.

ALPINE IBEX
Capra ibex ibex

An alpine species of wild goat, with close relatives found between the Caucasus and the Himalayas and from North Africa to Ethiopia. The Iberian ibex is a strikingly mutated species. Lives in herds. Highly adaptable. Once almost extinct in the Alps because of over-hunting, now found in preserves in Swiss and Italian highlands.

EUROPEAN BROWN BEAR
Ursus arctos

Largest dry-land wild beast in Europe. Now comparatively rare. Survivors found in the Pyrenees, Alps and Abruzzis; somewhat more prolific, and huntable, in eastern Europe, the Balkans and Scandinavia. Partial hibernator. Feeds mainly on plants, insects, snails, rodents, carrion and debilitated game. Sometimes attacks domestic animals.

WOLVERINE OR GLUTTON
Gulo gulo

Species of ferocious racoon found, like some species of bears, in north polar regions. A restless wanderer, it covers vast expanses of territory which it fiercely defends against rivals. Omnivorous, very powerful and, possessing strong jaws, can kill all types of game. But unless challenged prefers carrion.

WOLF
Canis lupus

Most prolific species of wild dog, ancestor of many breeds of domesticated dog. Found all over the northern hemisphere, almost exclusively in highland regions Hunts in packs. Pronounced hierarchical system. Function as a regulator of game increasingly recognized; reputation as an enemy of man increasingly questioned.

NORTHERN LYNX
Lynx lynx

Long-legged, medium-sized wildcat. Found all over northern hemisphere. Tufted ears, short tail, thickly haired paws, very sharp vision. Lives and hunts alone. Attempts made to reintroduce it to parts of western Europe where it has become extinct. Feeds on birds and mammals, including deer and reindeer.

Family Tree of the Deer

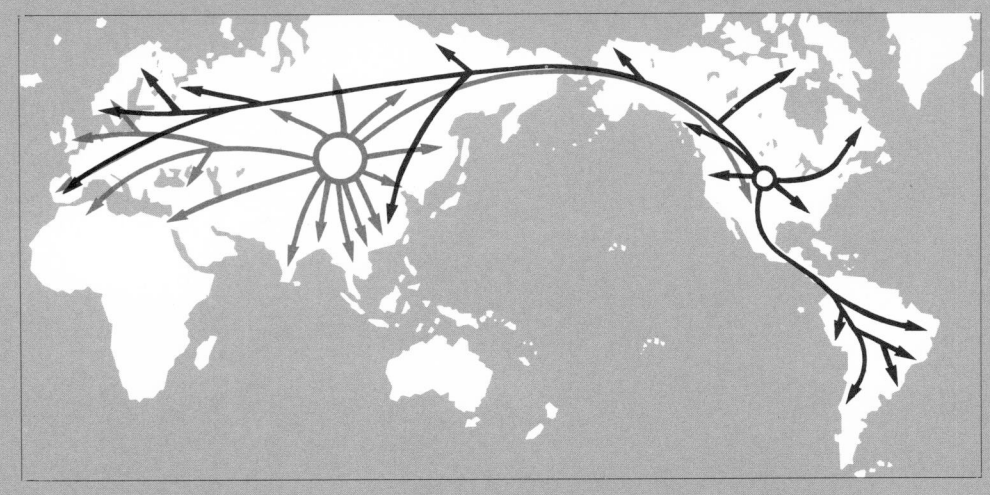

Red deer

Wapiti

Thorold's deer

Mule deer

White-tailed deer

Roe

Moose

Reindeer

Fallow deer

Père David's deer

Marsh deer

Eld's deer

Pampas deer

Chinese water

Barasingha

Indian sambar

Sika deer

Prong deer

Axis deer

Brocket

Muntjak

Hog deer

Pudu

Musk deer

Primitive deer

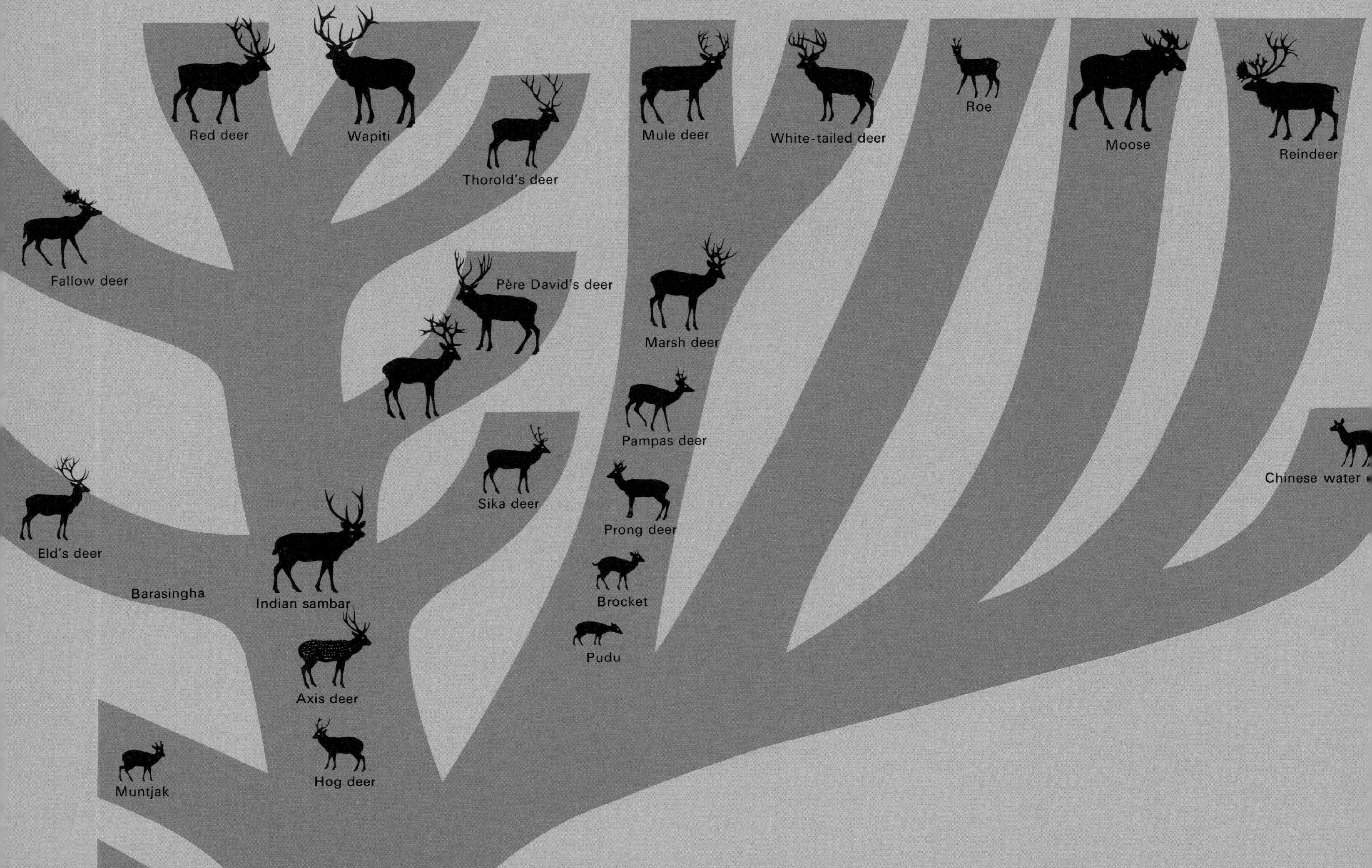

The ancestor of all the antler-bearing species was a primitive deer which grew only undeveloped knobs where antlers were to sprout. The evolution of the *true* deer originated with primitive even-toed ungulates some 30–50 million years ago when pygmy species, minus antlers, adapted to life in tropical forests. The next stage in development was the conquest of open country. Large, swift animals with extended backs and long limbs developed from such small, thickset jungle inhabitants as the muntjak and the musk deer. Adapting to life in the bush, they developed six-pointed antlers. (The hog deer, axis deer and sambar deer, still extant, bear some similarity to those prehistoric animals.) The evolutionary process took a sudden leap forward with the transference from the bush to the savannah, and deer with antlers with eight or more points, such as the sika, barasingha, Eld's deer and Père David's deer, appeared on the scene, as did species bearing palmated antlers, such as the fallow deer. The decisive development in today's antler-bearers, such as the moose, reindeer, red deer and wapiti, did not take place until the Ice Age.

From time immemorial, humans have hunted deer. Over thirty different species have provided important sources of food and trophies for man. Biological and ecological considerations make it essential for both hunter and conservationist to know something of how deer evolved.

The gradual development of all branches of the deer family has been largely dependent on the climatic conditions prevalent in their habitats. The body structure and form of antlers, as well as the animals' ways of life, were determined not only by the millions of years of development peculiar to each species, but also by environmental conditions. This explains the striking similarity of appearance and behavior between the old world primitive muntjak of tropical Asia and the South American brocket. These species are not related but are the result of parallel development determined by similar environmental conditions.

The chevrotain, which can still be found in Africa, is probably the most remarkable phenomenon among primitive deer. It is a living fossil among ruminants, having retained many of the same characteristics over fifty million years. The *chevrotin aquatique,* as this unique creature is known in French, flees from its enemies by diving and swimming. Its closest relative, the diminutive mouse deer, inhabits the tropical rain forests of southeast Asia—testifying to the existence of a landlink between the two continents some time in the distant past. Antlerless primitive deer today can be found only in central and eastern Asia—the mountain-dwelling musk deer and the water deer which lives in the rush thickets of eastern China. Although the two species are not related the bucks—which have tusk-like upper canine teeth up to five inches long—are practically identical in appearance. The musk deer is, incidentally, the only deer which, by virtue of its needle-sharp hoofs, can climb trees. The buck has a gland situated between its navel and reproductive organ which secretes a strong-smelling substance which is used in the manufacture of perfumes.

The oldest antler-bearing deer is the muntjak. It lived in Europe for millions of years but is today confined to southern and eastern Asia. This species bears short, forked horns on extended pedicles which are, however, not regularly renewed. The retention of the muntjak's primitive, backward-curving antlers can be attributed to its life in thick undergrowth. Its antlers have no significance as weapons; nor are they of hierarchical significance.

These primitive species of deer, which include the roe, inhabit relatively limited territory. With their curved backs, raised rumps and powerful back legs, they are ideally built to move easily through dense undergrowth. All have a sharp sense of smell and mark out their territory with glandular secretions which form invisible scent boundaries.

Deterioration of the climate in the Tertiary Period probably resulted in a separation of previously continuous forest areas. This emergence of distinct environments led ultimately to a universal alteration in the anatomy of almost all species of deer. Among the first to evolve were the "six-tined deer" adapted to the bush—the hog deer, axis deer and sambar deer. Development of the eight-tined sika and barasingha and many other multi-tined species took place later, as evolution proceeded on the lowlands and savannahs. The most highly developed, sometimes over-developed, antlers took shape during the Ice Age. The Irish giant deer bore antlers which, with branches well over eighteen feet from top to bottom, bordered on the biologically impossible and the species died out because of this over-specialization and the resulting inability to hold its own in the forests of the early Ice Age.

The last and highest branch of the deer family is represented by the wapiti and the red deer group. Its center of development was once again central Asia. It was from there that the red deer spread westward over the now submerged Bering isthmus into North America. The Tibetan Thorold's deer represents a strictly isolated Asian branch of this species. The first, at the time antlerless, red deer made their appearance in Europe in the first interglacial period. Antler-bearing red deer, adapted to open woodland, appeared during the second interglacial period, and marked the end of evolutionary development which had covered many millions of years.

From that point on, large deer species, including red deer and wapiti, began to

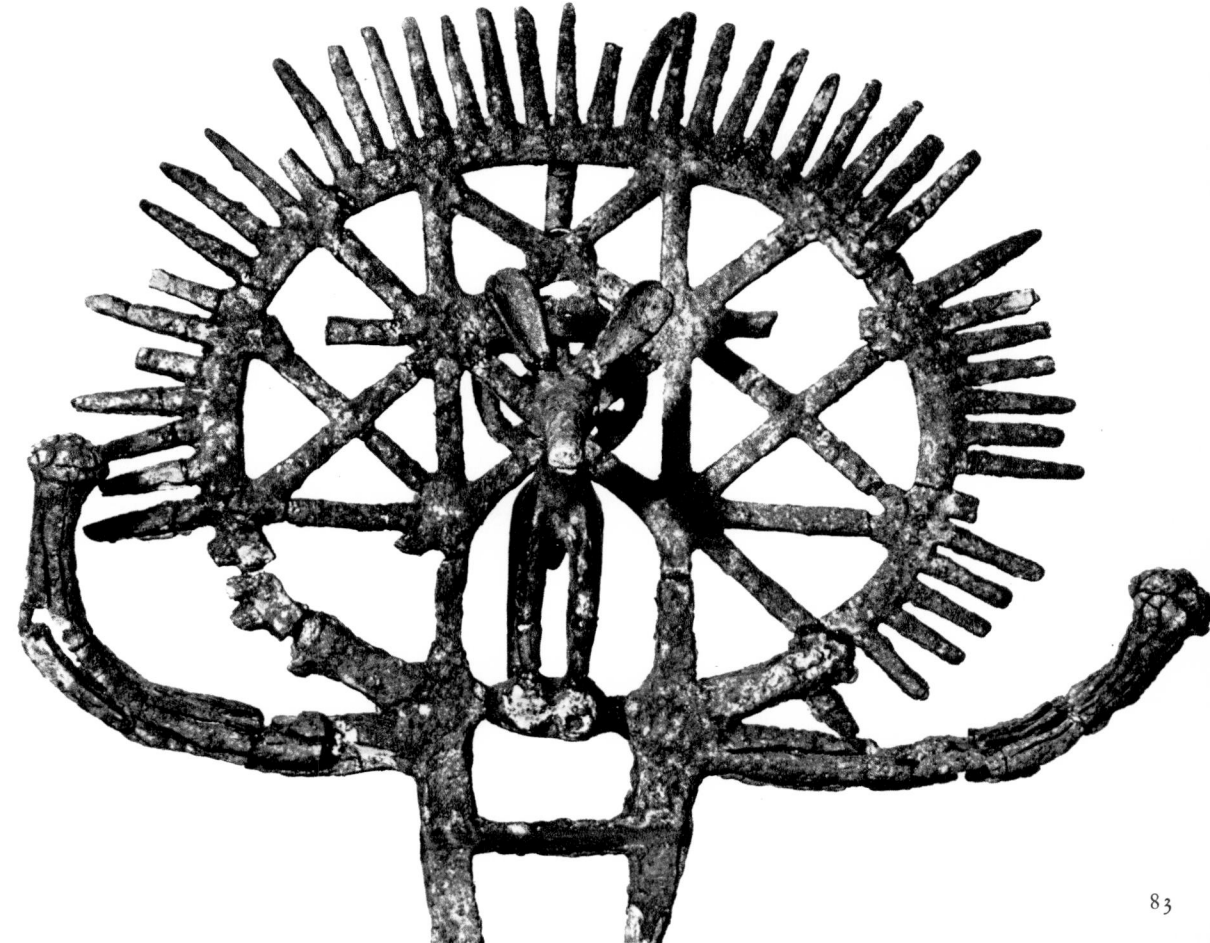

Deer of the Old World

Muntjak Hog deer Axis deer Barasingha Sambar Red deer

separate into numerous geographically isolated sub-species. Europe and the North African Atlas Mountains, which belong to the palearctic fauna region, are today inhabited by eight different breeds of red deer. Categorizing can be complicated. It should be noted that heavily-maned but smaller central and west European deer are already superseded in the Balkans by the maneless maral deer of the Caucasus, Crimea, Asia Minor and Iran.

In North Africa, the barbary deer has retreated to a small habitat in the Algerian–Tunisian border region. The Tyrrhenian red deer, a pygmy species which lives on the Mediterranean islands of Corsica and Sardinia, is also almost extinct today. Species related to the red deer, in Kashmir, Sikkim, eastern Tibet and western China, developed their own, easily distinguishable geographical breeds which, like their European counterparts, tend to be antler-bearing. But to the north of the Tibetan highlands, in central Asia, Tien Shan, Altai, Transbaikalia, northern Mongolia and eastern Siberia, "true" antlerless wapiti deer, belonging to the *Canadensis* group, make their appearance. These species form the bridge to the American wapiti which roams from British Columbia to the northern border of Mexico, along the Rocky Mountain highlands.

In the Tertiary Period, when the two American continents were joined together, the New World species of deer, which originated in the north, made their way southward. As a result, in addition to the evolution of the venado, pampas deer and white-tailed deer, a kind of reverse development took place in large forest areas, characterized by a decrease in body weight and a decline in antler development. Thus genuine pygmy deer—the pudu and the brocket, for example—evolved from more highly developed species.

The most important species of deer in North America were separated by glaciers into geographically isolated populations during the Ice Age. The east of the continent was inhabited by white-tailed or Virginia deer; the west by mule deer. The moose and caribou, which found a place in which to flourish in the Rocky Mountains, developed greatly during that period and spread over the entire northern hemisphere.

The longer the antlers of the deer the more important they become in determining the animal's social position in the herd and the outcome of ritualized fights between rivals during the rutting season.

The sequence of pictures of fighting deer shows, from top to bottom, the following scenario in combat between two apparently equally matched fallow deer: the two animals first make contact; the younger, darker-colored deer attacks; palmated antlers lock and the real test of strength begins; the fight ends with the retreat of the loser. (Pictured below.) The victorious animal escorts the coveted doe from the background.

Deer of the New World

Wapiti   Marsh deer   White-tailed deer   Mule deer   Guemal   Brocket

Antlers of the Red Deer

Red deer should be judged less by the general structure, strength or number of points of their antlers than by distinguishing physical characteristics at each stage of maturity. Aside from improvements to their environment and fodder, a good balance between the sexes, a supportable density of population and a regulated age-group structure, the most important single factor in general deer protection and care is allowing the well-proportioned, healthy stag to grow to maturity. It is absolutely essential that, though fawns should be meticulously culled, the middle age group should be protected as much as possible. Too many good antler-bearers are shot too young.

A red deer takes about five years to reach full maturity. Its first horns—hunters call them its first head—usually consist of

THE FIRST HEAD

At this age, a stag usually carries unforked antlers eight to sixteen inches long. Well-developed yearlings may sometimes already reveal the beginnings of a crown. Antlers are thus not completely reliable gauges of age, though obvious antler underdevelopment or early signs of flourishing are generally accurate indications of an animal's physical prospects. Year-old stags frequently stay with their mothers throughout the summer, not shedding their velvet until September. Their flesh is meager, their forms slender and long-legged. Their faces bear childlike expressions. Their heads are narrow and pointed. Their ears seem too long. The neck is slender and erect. There is a distinct joint between neck and blade.

THE YOUNG STAG

Young stags between the second and fourth head still bear obvious youthful characteristics. The neck becomes stronger, the mane longer, the bearing prouder. The rump develops a rectangular, well-proportioned aspect. The body weight is evenly distributed over all four legs. The line of the back has straightened; the bump at the point where the tail joins the body, typical of the yearling, has disappeared. Usually stags bear six-pointed antlers from the second head onward. Particularly vigorous specimens may already bear crowns. Fork-horns and uneven six-pointed antlers should be culled from the second head on. The antlers of young stags are usually, but not always, slender.

THE SEMI-MATURE STAG

So-called semi-mature stags are physically full grown from the fifth head onward. From this point on, all of the animal's surplus energy goes into the formation of its antlers. The sheer weight of the horns increases from year to year. Semi-mature stags shed their antlers four to six weeks before younger animals. The next head is thus usually fully developed by mid-summer. The stags shed their velvet in August. Formation of a crown generally takes place after the fifth year. The emphasis is on the upper portion of the antlers. Physically, the semi-mature stag already has a thick-set, sturdy appearance. The antlers are still held high even when the animal is in flight. Too many are, alas, shot before they can attain full maturity.

unforked antlers, with crowns of spikes very rare. The second head usually consists of six or eight tines. Particularly sturdy young deer may already boast antler crowns from their third to fifth head.

In most cases, culling must be carried out in the first five age groups. Semi-mature deer, between fifth and ninth head, often bear multi-tined antlers in which most of the tines spring from the upper part of the crown. In such cases, only extremely selective culling is justified.

Only between its tenth and fourteenth head does the red deer reach its full maturity. The approach of old age is usually noticeable after the age of twelve to fourteen years. The older a stag becomes, the lower is the position of the tines. Senile diminution of the antlers follows abruptly. Antlers of an aged deer can dwindle to unrecognizable proportions from one year to the next.

STURDY OLD STAG

This ten-year-old mature stag is an aristocrat among deer. The strong fourteen-pointer, with its well-formed double-crown still bears the entire weight of its antlers vertically, which indicates that the climax of antler formation has still not been reached. In the case of royal stags, this optimal point comes between twelve and fourteen years. Unfortunately, fine stags of this kind are considered fair game from ten years on. Typical characteristics of such stags are: the broad, rugged head; the dewlap mane; the powerful neck, horizontally carried; and strong forequarters. There is also a constant readiness for battle and the authority with which it keeps the herd of hinds together.

CULLING OF OLDER STAGS

Stags older than five years which show no distinct tendency to crown formation are subject to culling. A stag in the declining stage is distinguished by unmistakeable characteristics: its head has a foreshortened aspect; its maned neck is sturdy; its rump and forequarters are thick-set but its front legs tend to carry most of its weight. The above seven-to-nine-year-old stag bears long but thin and irregular antlers, typical of older animals suitable for culling. On the right, it carries a regular eight-tined antler with brow tine, middle tine and typical long fork; on the left, it carries a brow tine, a tray tine, a poorly developed middle tine and, on the rear-inclined point, the hint of an additional tine.

STAG PAST ITS PRIME

The entire body weight of a stag past its prime seems to have shifted to the forelegs and the stocky forequarters. The extremely thick-set appearance of the body makes the forelegs seem shorter. The croup falls away and the back legs have a completely underdeveloped appearance. The head is bull-like, the ears short, the underlip hangs down. Dewlap, neck and rump merge almost imperceptibly into each other. The stag pictured above has passed the climax of its antler development and is on the decline. The natural life expectancy of the red deer is sixteen years, twenty at the very most. In well-regulated deer preserves, old stags of this kind are likely to have been culled before reaching this stage of decline.

Crowning Pride

Antlers, those impressive hallmarks of the deer family, are justifiably regarded as one of the wonders of nature. The development of the red deer's antlers over a period of four to five months is an astonishing phenomenon, unmatched by any other animal. The antler can weigh up to twenty-five pounds and the apparent waste of bone substance can amount to up to thirty percent of the deer's skeleton weight.

Developing antlers are covered by a protective layer of cuticle equipped with a dense net of veins. This layer is discarded, through rubbing, after it has dried and the antlers have hardened at the end of their growth period, between the beginning of July and the end of August. Fully developed and thoroughly functional antlers are influenced by the condition and age of the animal. They are also crucially influenced by grazing conditions, because the animal's fodder is the source of calcium, phosphorus carbonate, protein and carbohydrate which form the nutritive basis essential for the growth of healthy antlers.

The antlers of the red deer, which are both unmistakable characteristics and fighting weapons, are composed of the frontal bone and the tines, the branches of the antlers. The value of the antlers is determined by size, strength and imposing appearance rather than by the number of tines. By simply flourishing its antlers, the well-endowed deer can often deter rivals from challenging its authority.

The evaluation of the antlers should be based exclusively on biological yardsticks rather than aesthetic criteria. Antlers are neither an end in themselves nor purely decorative bony structures. Their primary function for mankind today is to indicate whether the deer population is receiving all its needs for its healthy development and maintenance. A healthy live deer is more important to a serious hunter than dead antlers on his wall. He should, therefore, contribute to the maintenance of thriving, healthy deer in their habitats. Too often, hunters think of antlers exclusively as trophies and neglect the fact that deer, like all other animals, could become extinct.

The Roe and Its Antlers

When it comes to terminology, it is the same for the roe as it is with other deer—specialists tend to speak of antlers; hunters speak of horns. They refer, of course, to the same thing.

The normal head of a roebuck consists of three points on each antler, though there can be variations. According to the number of points, the hunter refers to, amont other things, forkhorns, six-pointers or eight-pointers, with the six-pointers most common. Variations in the horns of the roebuck are one of the animal's charms. They may be identical, twisted, bent or blunt, and their horn bone is often considerably ridged and beaded.

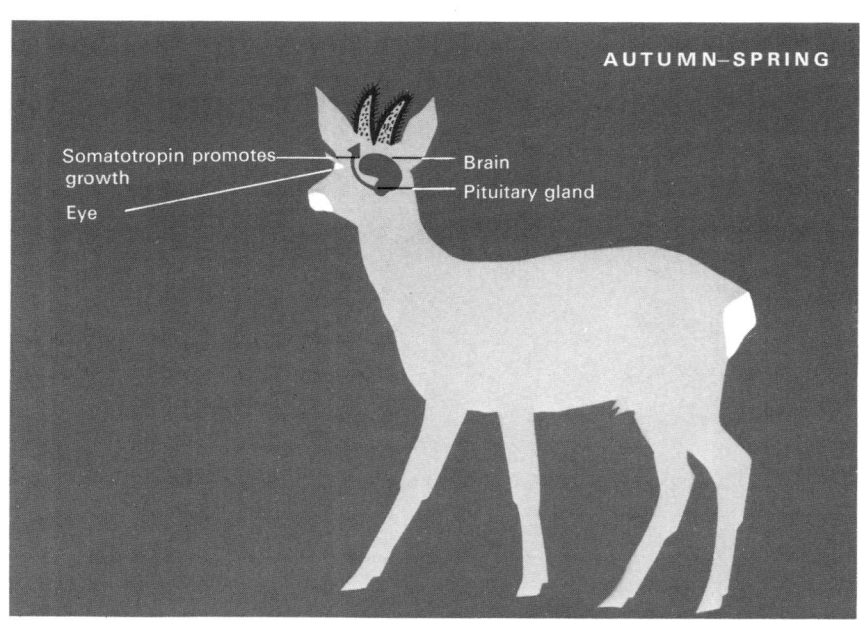

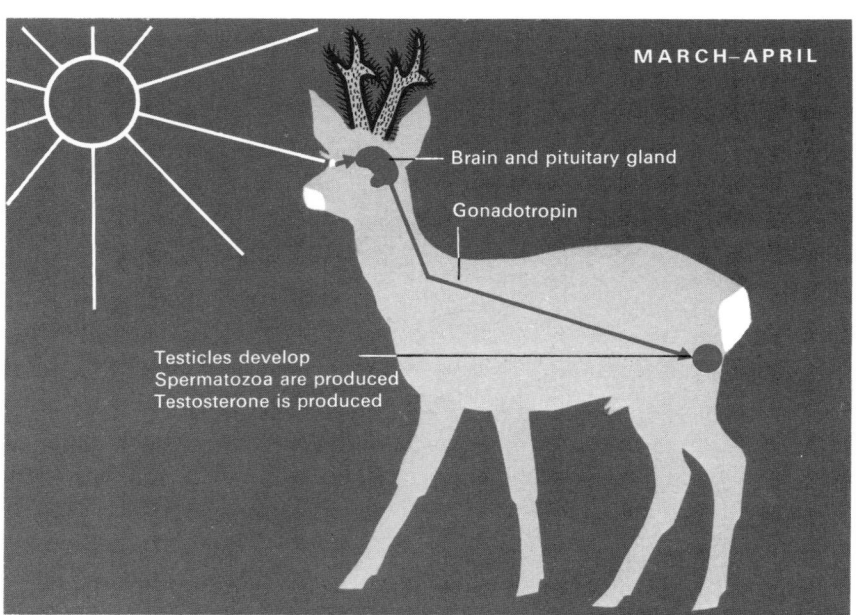

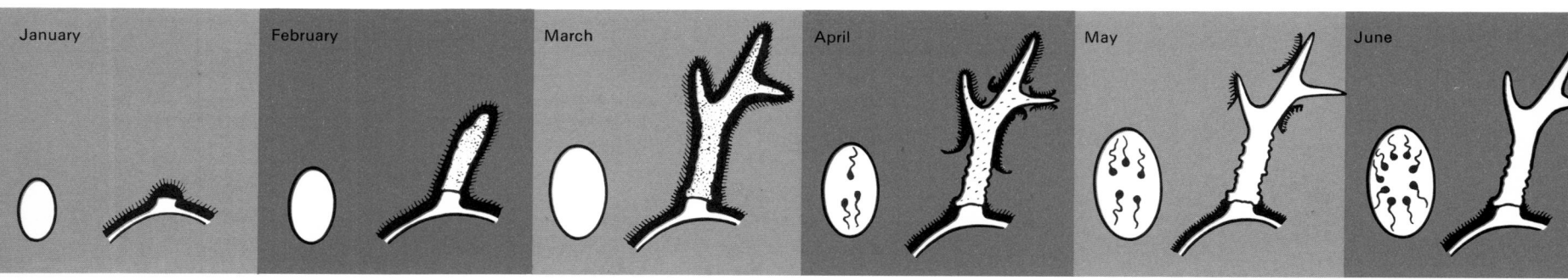

In winter, the hormone known as somatotropin promotes the growth of the roebuck's horns. The necessary nourishment is provided by the velvet; the antlers harden by degrees. Ossification begins at the base of the horns. The testicles are small and contain no spermatozoa.

Greater light intensity in springtime stimulates the pituitary gland to produce gonadotropin, a hormone which promotes the growth of the testicles and, thereby, the production of mature spermatozoa and the sex hormone, testosterone. Calcification and ossification of the horns begin.

In early summer, antler-growth ceases completely. The hardened horns and the dehydrated velvet die off. The buck sheds the velvet by rubbing its horns against trees and bushes. The dark brown coloration of the points is the result of the sap of the scraped trees.

The first horns begin to develop three to four months after the birth of the buck. The growth starts with two small, knob-like bumps covered by dark hairs. A few weeks later, usually in November or December, this first phase of development is completed. The strongest young bucks grow their first horns the same winter and shed them after only a few days or weeks. The horns of the weaker bucks, however, do not appear until the following spring.

Development of the antlers of the roebuck is remarkably rapid. Only twenty weeks pass between the shedding of the old horns and the shedding of the velvet of the new antlers. During the period of growth, the antlers are covered by this soft, furry sheath which is essential to their development. Contrary to prevailing belief, further development of the antlers does not follow naturally from their original sprouting from the skull; they are formed and nourished by the velvet cover which is permeated with blood vessels supplying the necessary nourishment for horn growth.

As soon as the antlers are fully developed, the velvet, having completed its function, is shed. The horns remain firmly anchored until the autumn, when they too are cast off.

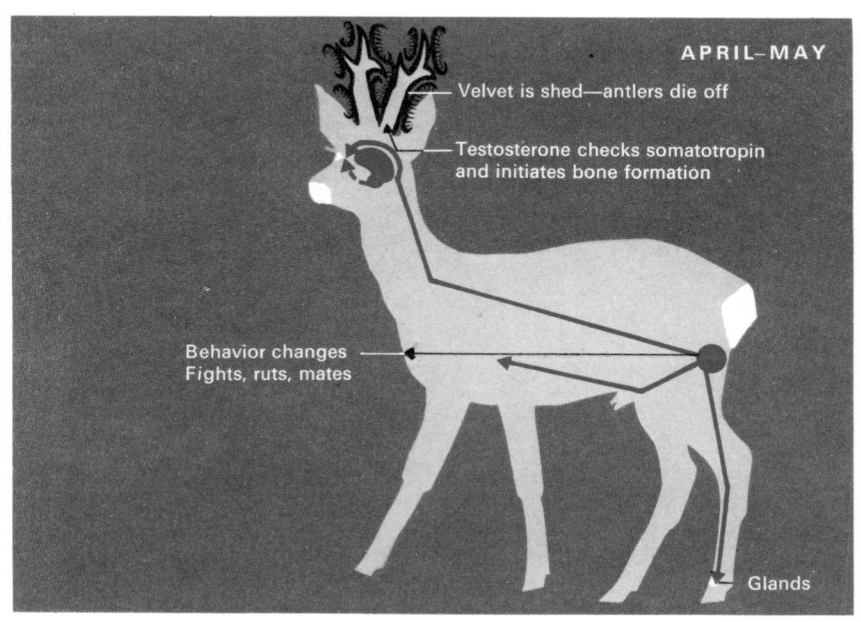

APRIL–MAY

Velvet is shed—antlers die off

Testosterone checks somatotropin and initiates bone formation

Behavior changes
Fights, ruts, mates

Glands

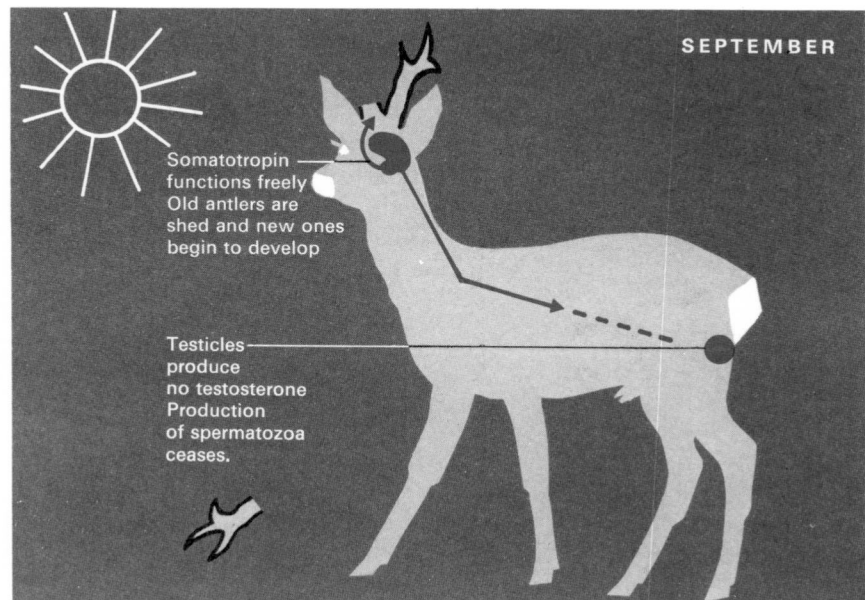

SEPTEMBER

Somatotropin functions freely
Old antlers are shed and new ones begin to develop

Testicles produce no testosterone
Production of spermatozoa ceases.

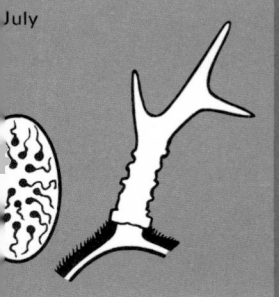 July

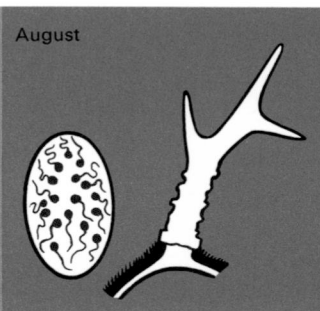 August

 September

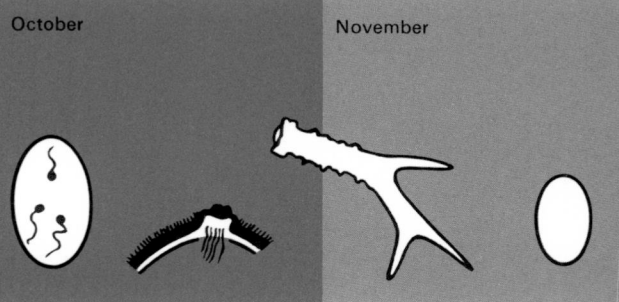 October November December

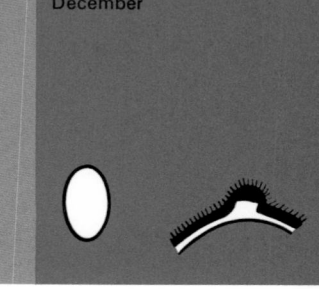

The testicles are now fully developed; rut begins. The antlers are seldom used as weapons for attack or defense in summer, but serve as instruments for marking out the buck's territory. The dead horns still remain firmly anchored.

In autumn, the secretion of gonadotropin by the pituitary gland gradually ceases. The testicles shrink; production of mature spermatozoa ceases; testosterone no longer dominates the somatotropin. Bone-destroying cells attack the base of the antlers which are then shed.

At the rim of the wound which results from loss of the antlers, a scab forms which accelerates the healing from within. As soon as the wound is closed, new velvet begins to form and new horns begin to develop.

Mutations

Black deer, known as melanists, are sometimes found among roe. The formation of their hair pigmentation is disturbed by mutation and instead of normal coloration a totally black coat develops. A population of black deer which was first recorded near Hanover, Germany, in the Middle Ages still survives in that region. White or dappled animals are extremely rare; the chances of survival for such conspicuous animals are limited. Their light-colored coats attract the attention of predators which can usually, however, only pursue their prey successfully when they themselves are suitably camouflaged in appearance. Albinos, which are more vulnerable to the hazards of sunlight and are weaker than normally colored deer, are also very rare. White piebalds, whose coats are punctuated with white patches, are, however, comparatively prolific.

Mother Nature has her moods and whims. Biological variations and deviations from the norm constantly appear in the animal kingdom, affecting virtually all creatures, including the roe. There exist, for example, roe deer with gleaming jet-black coats which, especially under winter gloss, seem like black silk velvet. Known as melanists, these animals are particularly prolific in northern Germany. As long ago as 1100, black deer were reported to be found near the city of Hanover and documents from the seventeenth century mention the existence of these comparatively rare animals elsewhere in western Europe. They began to expand their habitat shortly before the beginning of this century while gaining a stronger presence in their original home, where some eighty percent of all roe are black. In the area surrounding that original habitat, a survey taken in 1935 showed that black deer constituted between thirty and fifty percent of all roe. In districts further removed, melanists constitute less than five percent of the entire deer population.

Other variations include black roe with white or yellow marking on their posteriors. These have been detected primarily in the Osterburg district of Germany, although they have occasionally appeared in various other regions. They are known as "black-dappled." As with melanists, various grades of coloration exist among albino specimens. For example, entirely white does alternate with animals of varying degrees of dapple spotting. Aside from the few regions in which animals of biological variance have been placed under protection, melanists, albinos and dappled deer are rare. Although it is possible for such mutations to appear spontaneously, they have never yet—within recorded memory—increased to the extent that they threatened to supersede their normal-colored kin.

Conspicuous color variations among roe can be traced back to irregular changes in hereditary factors. Sometimes, however, other variations appear in which striking mutations cannot be attributed to heredity and which are not passed on to succeeding generations. Variations in the animals' hormone systems which lead to overgrowth and malformation of the antlers of the buck and to the development of antlers in the doe are often the result of injuries.

Wounds are sometimes inflicted to the testicles of roebucks during flight through thick undergrowth. Accidents of this kind are becoming increasingly frequent because of the spread of wire fences which prevent deer from entering areas being reforested. If the buck survives the injury, the damage to its sex glands often results in deviation in antler formation. Where testicles are injured shortly after birth, before the faun's first horns have begun to develop, the animal can remain hornless the rest of its life. When the testicles of a mature buck, which has already borne a succession of antlers, are injured the animal might shed its antlers immediately and begin at once to develop new ones. The growth would start normally, but instead of ceasing to grow when the time came for shedding the velvet, the development would continue until a large part of the forehead is covered; in extreme cases, the entire head. If the testicles of a buck in velvet are

Peruke buck: sickness or injury to the sex organs of the buck prevents normal hormone secretion. The process which determines the completion of antler development in the spring is thereby disturbed. The horns of castrated bucks continue to grow. The result, however, is not the standard crown of the normal roebuck, but irregular perukes, shown here, which neither harden nor shed their velvet.

Horned doe: the hormone secretions of mature does are sometimes disturbed with the result that they suddenly grow antlers, sometimes with velvet which the animal is able to shed. More often, however, horn-bearing does are hermaphrodites—animals which, though primarily female, bear both male and female characteristics. The doe in the photograph below clearly manifests a typical female external sex organ, as well as strong six-point antlers in

velvet. Hermaphrodites often occur when the mother doe carries twins of different sexes and the hormones of one embryo are absorbed by the body of the other.

injured the animal might not shed its antlers; the velvet might remain and the horn and velvet tissue might grow to abnormal proportions. In rare cases, castrated bucks have been known to retain their last antlers while new ones begin growing abnormally.

The enduring living antlers of the castrated buck retaining their velvet are known as perukes. The horns, growing remarkably rapidly, take various shapes. In the case of the "bishop's miter," for example, the velvet tissue grows so fast that, before long, skin-like tassles hang over the animal's eyes and cheeks. The "helmet peruke" consists mainly of horn tissue piled up to abnormal height.

Accidental castration of roe-bucks has provided a picture of how the hormone mechanism functions to regulate the cyclical change of antlers and the growth of horns. That the male sex organs and the sex hormone testosterone play an important role in this process is obvious from the fact that the rutting period coincides with the shedding of the velvet. Researchers, whose experiments have copied nature's accidents under controlled conditions, have examined the effect of castration on roebucks at various ages and in different seasons of year. They have also studied the effect of injected sex hormones on horn formation. Their experiments prove that the first antlers can only develop when the sex hormones take effect at the right moment. They also suggest that testosterone has an inhibiting influence on the antler growth of old bucks, ushering in the calcification and ossification process. Experiments in which the testicles of bucks bearing antlers in velvet were artificially stimulated to secrete larger quantities of testosterone, resulted in the immediate cessation of antler growth and the animal shedding its velvet and antlers.

Apart from reindeer, no female of the deer family normally grows antlers. But hunters have occasionally shot antler-bearing does, having mistaken them for bucks. Only recently have reasons for these mutations been discovered. The antlers, of varying lengths and shapes, result from various influences. They can be caused by injury or sickness of the frontal bones of the does or by hormonal imbalance.

Occasionally, however, antler-bearing does may be hermaphrodites, a phenomenon which sometimes also occurs in domestic cattle. The hermaphrodite characteristics take shape before birth and usually when there are twins.

Whereas most hoofed animals seldom bear twins, it is common among roe. The twins are often of different sexes. Sometimes the blood vessels which connect the developing embryos with the mother animal merge into each other, and the hormones of one embryo enter into the body of the other.

93

The Roe and Its Domain

Mid-April until end of June

1

End of June until end of August

2

4

5

6

Though many inhabitants of the animal world lay specific claim to territory and guard it, sometimes ferociously, there is little evidence of year-round territorial behavior with the roe deer. There are, however, indications that the doe attaches importance to property rights when seeking a suitable spot to drop her young in May or June.

This rearing zone is, of course, extremely important to the well-being of fauns. The young animals do not cling to their mothers, but spend their first weeks largely alone. The mother does little more than feed and clean them.

The rearing area is usually in a warm, dry, sunny position. It must, however, have sufficient cover because the faun's defense is not flight but freezing reflexively into motionlessness. Its spotted coat provides efficient camouflage.

Shortly before and after the birth of their young, does do vigorously defend their rearing zones against other does. They do not engage in head to head fights, but merely stand erect and beat at the ground with their front hooves. Probably the boundaries of their preserves have been marked out with urine.

Soon after bucks shed their velvet in the spring, they begin organizing hierarchical systems. Fights are common but primarily between specimens of equal strength and stature.

Roebucks fight face to face with forelegs spread apart, antlers interlocked while trying to establish a firm foothold. After opening rituals, they relinquish their secure positions to circle round with lowered heads and antlers still interlocked. The battle is brought to an end as soon as it becomes apparent which animal is stronger. The victor displays a proud bearing, with antlers held high. The loser assumes a meek mien, with lowered head; it subsequently takes flight.

In the springtime, fights between roebucks are far more frequent than in summer or during the rutting season (1). It is likely that the animals fight only to establish a clear hierarchy in the herd. In early summer, the

Roe do not form large herds like red deer. They prefer to live alone or in small groups or families. The roe deer is extremely territory-conscious. When, in summer, fodder is plentiful, each group establishes and fiercely defends its territory against other roe (1, 2). Despite this separation, members of different groups maintain contact. Communication is mainly by means of aromatic substances secreted by glands in the animals' skins. In the case of the roebuck, the glands are situated between the horns and on the hindlegs.

When the animal rubs against a tree or bush with its antlers, the secretion adheres to the plant and is detected by other deer.

4 The faun is washed by its mother while being nursed.

5 Two roebucks fighting for position in group hierarchy.

6 Shortly before mating, the buck examines the vulva of the doe in rut.

7 The actual mating is rapid, taking place under cover, often in high grass.

8 Even individualists join up with a family for the winter.

September until April

3

7

8

mature bucks retreat to separate domains, which rarely overlap (2). Should a meeting between animals with rival territorial claims nevertheless occur, fights are unlikely to take place because the weaker animal acknowledges its weakness and retreats with head lowered submissively. The stronger buck intimidates its rival but does not attack it.

However, both victor and vanquished seek out suitable bushes or small trees to serve as substitute enemies and to do combat with them. In the process, they can do serious damage to vegetation. The marking out of territory at the time is enhanced by the secretion of an odorous substance from a gland situated between the animals' horns.

As soon as fauns become independent of their mothers' care in July, the does' defense of the rearing zone ceases. Bucks relinquish exclusive rights to their domains after the rutting season. During the winter, when deer retreat to the woods and spend less time in open country, family group cohesion is more difficult to sustain (3). The family has by now increased in size to consist of the mother, six-month-old fauns, usually also female yearlings from the previous year, pregnant for the first time, and occasionally one or more bucks which have chosen to latch onto the group. When fodder is short, the local deer population temporarily congregates at the few accessible feeding places. Does

without fauns or fauns without mothers join up with other groupings for the winter.

In spring, the large groups which have wintered together split once more. Female yearlings start scouting for places to drop and rear their young. Male fauns leave their mothers and, together with other males of the same age, form loosely defined fighting groups (1). Female yearlings prefer the company of older bucks. Mother does retreat to their new breeding grounds to give birth to new fauns.

95

Rescue of the Alpine Ibex

Once decimated but now firmly established again, the ibex has an impressive, sturdy appearance. It is a dazzling climber for whom no rock face is too steep and no peak too high. Its hooves are broad and have sharp edges. Their inner surfaces act as suction pads to enable the animal to cling to the smallest surface of rock and uneven ground.

Millions of years ago, *Tossunnoria,* the ancestor of all sheep and goats known today, including the ibex, roamed the vast expanses of China. But paleontological dicoveries reveal that the ibex, together with the mammoth and the rhinoceros, had attained its present anatomical structure by the time of the last Ice Age, and thrived in many different regions. Today, in addition to the wild goats of North Africa, Europe and Asia, true ibexes are found in the Alps, the Caucasus, the Himalayas and Siberia. The *Capra ibex pyrenaica,* with its lyre-shaped horns, lives in Spain. The Nubian ibex inhabits the rocky desert land around the Red Sea. The *Capra ibex walie* is found in the barely accessible rugged mountains of Abyssinia.

The retreat of the glaciers, and the resulting climatic changes slowly forced the ibex from lowlands into higher, colder mountainous regions more suited to its needs. In summer, it lives among rocks and rubble at a height of up to eleven thousand feet above sea level. Sparse pasture on the stony slopes and strips of grass on rock provide sufficient nourishment. In winter, the ibex moves to lower regions although, unlike the chamois, it never goes below the treeline. Lichen provide its primary form of winter food.

The Alpine ibex boasts powerful, saber-shaped horns which curve backwards; they can measure up to three feet and weigh around thirty pounds. The age of the animal can be determined from the rings, superimposed on each other, on its horns. The ridges on the front of the horns are tell-tale signs of the various breeds. The gaze from the ibex's amber, slanting eyes has a cold, almost challenging aspect. In summer, the coat of the animal has a brownish-red shimmer which changes to yellow-gray in autumn, following the molt. These colors effectively camouflage the ibex among the rocks and stones of its habitat. Its scent glands secrete a penetrating odor, particularly during the mating season. The animal can easily be crossed with the domestic goat. It lives in herds and displays a highly developed sense of hierarchy; during the summer, the males maintain a running battle to establish their positions.

The ibex has always been much treasured game and its horns have always been much sought after as trophies. In Europe, emperors, kings and princes of the Church tried to prevent the animal's extinction. It became an endangered species in some regions, not because of any widespread passion for hunting and horn collecting, but because its horns contain a substance which was widely thought to be an infallible aphrodisiac. The bezoar stones found in the animal's stomach—small balls composed of hair, resin and small stones—and its droppings were transformed into various grandly named medicines for many types of maladies; they were sold to the gullible at exorbitant prices. An ibex's ossified heart muscle was even sold in bygone days for its own weight in gold!

Superstitious belief in the healing powers of these concoctions and of ibex organs was not without serious consequence, aside from the fact that they performed no miracles and effected no cures. The animal was hunted with great vigor and attempts had to be made to prevent it from vanishing forever from the face of the Earth. An archbishop of Salzburg once had an ibex poacher sewn into a deer's skin and savaged to death by hunting dogs! But, in spite of severe measures, the number of ibex declined drastically.

A small number of pure-bred ibexes was preserved in the mountains of Piedmont. King Victor Emmanuel II of Italy, for whom the ibex hunt was a jealously guarded personal privilege as well as a passion, in effect rescued the animals from complete extinction in Europe. Between 1861 and 1878, the game reserve "Gran Paradiso" was established under his protection—a biotope for ibexes covering almost fourteen thousand acres. In Austria and Switzerland, where the last ibex was legally hunted in the nineteenth century, attempts were also made to reintroduce the animal, but without success. To mark the opening of the Simplon tunnel between Switzerland and Italy in 1906, the Swiss asked the Italian king for a few ibexes. But this attempt also failed. A few years later, some nature-loving Swiss offered considerable sums for a few pure-bred specimens. In response, several Piedmontese *bracconieri,* or poachers, heavily laden with crates, secretly crossed the border from Italy into southern Switzerland over little-used paths. Not long afterward, the populace was invited to admire newly arrived ibexes in the local game reserve.

The young animals flourished and the first of the new ibexes were permitted to roam free in Switzerland in 1911. A young male named "Wucki," smuggled in from Italy with several females, became progenitor of the ibex colony of over four thousand animals which lives in Switzerland today.

The Chamois

Chamois choose their haunts according to weather, the time of day and the season. In summer, the animals rest at midday in shady, undisturbed areas and graze during mornings and afternoons on slopes rich with tasty vegetation. During snowy periods, they seek protection in wooded regions and climb to steep, snowless slopes to graze once the weather improves. In spring, they often descend into the valleys in search of sustenance.

The chamois occupies a special place among the cloven-hoofed game of Europe. Its closest relatives, the serow and the goral, live in Asia, and the Rocky Mountain goat is, of course, an inhabitant of North America. All of the so-called *Rupicaprini*—the family of the chamois—are, geneologically, comparatively old and have retained a primitive stage of development with regard to both horns and behavior.

The Rocky Mountain goat has dagger-like horns with which it is capable of inflicting serious wounds on rivals in battle. Unlike many more highly developed hoofed animals, it has no ritualized form of combat with definite guidelines for preventing fatal consequences. However, these animals seldom fight and, besides, have shaggy coats with remarkably thick skins.

The chamois also belong to that category of animals which do not fight according to an instinctive life-preserving ritual. Their thin, hooked horns are unsuitable for the kind of duels which are engaged in by the ibex and wild sheep, serving only to prove which combatant is stronger. The bucks engage in furious battles which usually end in mortal wounds being inflicted, rather than the withdrawal of the weaker animal. The gladiatorial skills of the chamois bucks are their only means of establishing an order of precedence.

The young can easily be recognized as inferior and accordingly ignored or expelled. But, in the case of an adult buck, the size of the horns does not necessarily testify accurately to fighting ability. But the possession of desired mating territory is regarded as a sign of precedence; the leader of the herd is recognized by its rivals through its territorial dominance and its position in the hierarchy is established without the constant need to do battle.

This system cannot, however, function when the chamois herds must move because of wintry conditions during the rutting season, in November or December. Battles are then frequent. However, the number of fights is limited by a natural instinct: the male chamois hardly ever attacks a rival when the latter is motionless. It usually waits until the rival attempts to flee. But should a chase ensue, the roles of attacker and defender can be reversed. During these encounters, the hooked horns of the chamois come into play. The pointed tips are used to grasp the fleeing opponent.

Even without serious injury, the expenditure of energy during these confrontations can have grave consequences.

The bucks take little nourishment during the rutting season and there is little time for the animals to recuperate from fierce combat and from serious wounds before the onset of deep winter. The results are recognizable from loss of game through natural causes: kids are the first to perish, because of their greater weakness and lower resistance; then come buck and, finally, the females. Comparatively more males die than females and the surviving bucks are usually younger than the surviving females. This means that the herds are made up of more mature females than males, which has a disruptive effect on the male–female relation in the group.

Like other hoofed animals, chamois react to over-density of population by becoming increasingly vulnerable to parasites and natural fatality. Aside from that, the basic living conditions of the herd are imperiled. In extreme cases, the vegetation on which the herd subsists may even suffer long-term damage, with a corresponding effect on the herd itself.

It would, of course, be for their own good if the chamois were able to prevent overpopulation. But their social organization does not permit controlled reproduction. The size of the herd and the number of

Top: Chamois are gregarious animals. The females with their kids and young animals prefer to join up with larger herds. The size and composition of the herds change constantly, so no fixed hierarchy can be established. Although adult females are always superior in strength to young animals, they decide amongst themselves which animal may, for example, be first to sample a salt-lick.

Bottom: The healthy buck enters the rutting season in prime condition, having grown plump and sleek during the summer.

herds are unlimited. Nor do the buck's rutting habits lead to birth control; each male is capable of impregnating several females. The rate of population increase can only be checked by the condition of the females and young animals. Weak females tend to be unable to conceive and weak kids are rarely able to survive the first winter. It is part of nature's ruthless culling process which helps promote survival of the healthiest of the herd.

Chamois populations in newly colonized areas are characterized by two-year-old mothers and a relatively high proportion of twin births, while herds which live in areas barely capable of supporting their needs usually produce no twins and few mothers younger than four years. Where the rate of population increase is nevertheless too great, parasites and hard winters are left the task of ensuring the maintenance of population balance. Hunters also assume part of the responsibility and can contribute meaningfully through selective chamois hunting.

Aside from that, a hard winter can drastically reduce the size of the herds, even without the intervention of hunters and beasts of prey. A succession of hard winters in regions which chamois inhabit can totally eliminate the threat to the animal of population explosion.

The Wild Boar

Wild boar are primitive and comparatively unspecialized even-toed ungulates. They are, however, sly and highly intelligent animals.

They can perceive extremely faint sounds and can sniff out the most meager scent from great distances. Their eyesight, however, is poor and if the wind is against them they might practically stumble across a concealed hunter before detecting his presence.

Wild boar do not leave the undergrowth to follow their accustomed trails in search of fodder and wallow puddles until dusk. They are omnivorous and feed on grubs, worms and insects which live on the forest floor, as well as roots and tubers found in the fields, and acorns, beechnuts and windfall fruit.

They are not averse to mice, grasshoppers, frogs, snakes, or incapacitated or dead game.

The male reaches maturity at the age of five years and joins the ranks of old boars by the time it is seven. In the cold damp areas it favors, a wild boar can reach the age of fifteen and weigh up to 450 pounds.

The tusks of the sow are relatively unimposing. The protruding upper and lower canines of the boar grow blunter with age and curve further and further backwards. Its tusks are coveted hunters' trophies.

The Mating Season

The boar in heat: Fierce battles between male boars usher in the mating season as they rush at each other with wild leaps, head cracking against head, each trying to overwhelm its rival.

The treatment subsequently accorded by the victor to its mate is not much gentler, during the November to January courting period. He drives her before him, or around in circles. He administers violent blows to her ribs and energetic bites to her neck and throat. Caressing thrusts, blows of his hooves and the aroma of his

repeated urinations are apparently intended to inflame the passions of his mate and clearly to indicate his intentions. Both animals utter squeaking noises during copulation. The pairing act is repeated several times. But it is a passing phase. As soon as the rutting season is over, the boar reverts to his solitary habits in the peace and quiet of his own territory.

The badger in heat: The badgers' rutting season begins in the summer. But these are dusk and nocturnal creatures and not many

humans can claim to have seen them copulate. The male badger chases the female around bushes and trees. During this pursuit, these normally quiet animals utter strange sounds—loud snorts and fox-like barks from the males, panting and contented grunts from the females. Like the roe, the female badger sometimes rolls over and over and turns in circles before the actual mating, at which time the male clasps the neck of the female for a comparatively long time, all the while nipping at her ears and neck. Like the marten, badgers lie down on their sides after mating. The significance of the badgers' weird mating cries is not yet completely understood.

The hare in heat: During mild, dry weather, the hare ruts as early as January and right through to late summer. The females usually produce three to four young a year, ensuring survival for this relentlessly hunted animal. Scraps of fur on the ground testify to violent fights between rival males. However, it is the female which does the actual courting. By lifting her black and white tail, she displays her anal gland which indicates her readiness to mate. The excited male pursues the beckoning but fleeing female, attempting to leap over her while urinating. The male is a furious lover and beats his bride violently with his forepaws during copulation. A distinctive cry of the female brings the mating to an end.

Though foxes mate between December and March, the wild cat's rutting season is in spring. It is accompanied by much meowing and spitting. In the case of the polecat, the procedure is somewhat different. In the period roughly between February and June, the male pursues the female with loud cries which can be heard from great distances. The chase ends only when he has caught her. He grasps her neck, thus overpowering her, and she allows herself to be carried around by him. Finally, the male clutches her with his forepaws and the two animals lie down to mate. Copulation is repeated several times.

European Predators

Below: Once the lynx could be found everywhere in Europe. Today, the northern European branch of the lynx family survives only in Scandinavia, Russia, Poland, Czechoslovakia, Hungary and Yugoslavia. On the Iberian peninsula, in Sardinia and the Middle East, a smaller and more strongly speckled lynx makes its home. Efforts are being made to reintroduce the lynx into some other parts of western Europe.

The bear, the wolf and the lynx were once the most important regulators of European cloven-hoofed game, focusing their attentions mainly on young and sick, and old and decrepit animals. All three of these predators have, however, become virtually extinct in parts of Europe densely populated by humans. It is a process which has been going on for almost two centuries. In western Europe wolves can be found in extremely limited numbers, particularly in the highlands of Spain and Italy, although they are more common in less heavily populated regions of eastern Europe.

Fortunately, many hunters today recognize the need for ecological balance. They assume responsibility for preserving reasonable populations of game in relation to prevailing vegetation, thus assuming the role once primarily played by the now declining numbers of animal predators.

Far-sighted authorities are trying to reintroduce the lynx into western Europe as a natural regulator of game. In northern and eastern European countries, much exemplary work has already been done to encourage propagation of the lynx. The same is true for the lynx's smaller cousin, the almost extinct European wild cat. Thanks to the common sense and goodwill of conservation-minded hunters, this species has increased in number to over a thousand in West Germany alone.

The most widespread European animal predator today is undoubtedly the fox, which is extremely adaptable and has a high birth rate. The fox is to be found in all European environments, from sea level to the treeline, although its favorite habitat is woodland and meadow with plenty of cover. This is also the home of its favorite rodent food.

As one of the primary carriers of rabies, the fox is an intensively hunted animal. Despite this, its numbers have barely decreased, unlike the badger which often lives in the same areas but which, because of its greater vulnerability to anti-rabies chemicals, is extinct in many places.

The badger is a marten-like predator. It is omnivorous, but is particularly partial to the eggs of ground-nesting birds. Another adaptable marten is the polecat which prefers to live in damp, marshy lowlands. It subsists on small animals, insects, snails and amphibians. It

Left: The beach marten is the most common European marten. Unlike the yellow-throated pine marten, it has a white throat and is often nicknamed accordingly. It frequents regions of human habitation and lives mainly on poultry, eggs and rodents.

Right: The red fox is the most common European predator. It ranges from the Mediterranean to the Polar Circle and from sea level to the treeline. The fox reproduces prolifically. It lives mainly on mice and sometimes on poultry and on deer fauns.

Bottom: The wolf, primary regulator of the moose and deer populations, is the most highly developed wild dog. Almost extinct in those regions of western Europe colonized by humans, it can, however, still be found in parts of Spain, Italy, the Balkans and eastern Europe. It is the ancestor of many breeds of domesticated dog.

stocks its "pantry" with frogs paralyzed by its bite.

Though the river otter has become extremely rare in industrial countries because of river pollution, the pine and beach marten, whose hides are currently less in demand, have increased in number. Both animals are nocturnal and live mainly on rodents, birds and berries. The ermine and the weasel, the smallest European relatives of the raccoon, are, on the other hand, entirely carnivorous and are particularly fond of mice.

The reintroduction of the lynx, which lives chiefly on wild game, rarely attacking domestic animals, has been beneficial to the ecological balance. But two other animals which have been introduced into Western Europe for the first time have proved to be less than welcome. The marten, which originated in North America, and the raccoon-dog or enuk, which comes from northeastern Asia, threaten the balance of European fauna because of their tendency to spread and dominate.

The Wolverine

In the forests and on the plains of North America, northern Europe, and northern Asia, everywhere where the wolverine, or glutton, has made its home, awesome tales are told of this mysterious predator. Few hunters can claim to have shot one, or even to have seen one. Natives of the regions it inhabits fear it because of its wildness and hate it because it plunders their traps, breaks into their remote wooden camp huts, and leaves a trail of vandalism wherever it roams.

The wolverine has hardly any natural enemies. Other predators even leave part of their prey for this impudent, secretive, alert and distrustful creature. It is constantly on the move, sniffing the air continuously for omens and warnings, even when it is not being pursued. Every four hours, it rolls up and goes to sleep.

The wolverine is similar to a small bear in appearance, but belongs, in fact, to the weasel family. It is short and thick-set and reaches a weight of up to sixty pounds. Hunters and trappers value its thick, frost-proof coat. It is an excellent climber and has webbed feet which enable it to move quickly and safely through the snow. It easily covers long stretches, patrolling the largish territory which it claims by marking out boundaries with a glandular secretion and which it defends uncompromisingly against all enemies and intruders.

The wolverine's diet, determined by the time of year, is extremely varied. During

The wolverine, feared, mysterious predator of the northern wilderness, is an excellent climber. In winter, when food is harder to find, it has no trouble hunting animals larger than itself because of its strength, ferocity and agility in snow-covered regions.

Below: a young wolverine opening an egg with its teeth, and not losing a drop of the contents.

the summer, it eats birds' eggs, lemmings, wasp grubs, berries and young game; carrion is perhaps its favorite food. In winter, it hunts and kills game of various kinds. It has an advantage over larger animals which cannot move as quickly through the snow. Thus the wolverine is able to hunt moose, lynx, fox, marten, snow hen, hare and squirrel. It pursues its victim until the latter collapses from exhaustion. It kills small game with a single bite and devours it on the spot. With larger game, it springs onto the back, holds on firmly with its claws and bites the animal's neck to kill it. It does not, however, consume the whole animal. It tears it into pieces, some of which it stores.

In spring, the female produces two to four young. The mother, which cares tenderly for its young, refuses to allow the father anywhere near them. The cubs are fully grown after three months but remain with the mother until they are almost three years old. Orphaned wolverines can develop into amusing and trustworthy companions in captivity— unlike their kin in the wild which, in America, are called "Indian devils."

Animal Camouflage

3

1

2

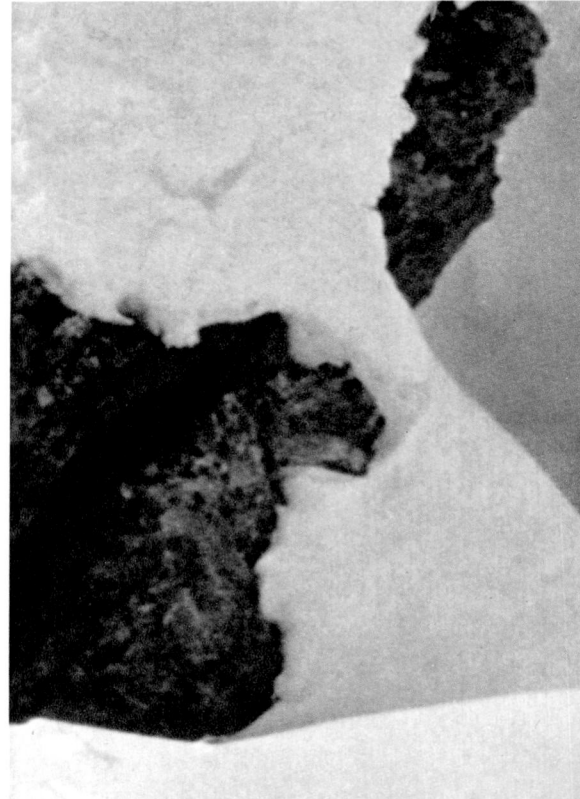

4

5

From the beginning, and until comparatively recent times, hunting served to maintain a balance among the living creatures of our planet. Natural defensive skills evolved by hunted animals served the same purpose. The methods of the hunter were countered by an impressive range of ploys brought into play by the victims of predators, human or otherwise. Warning off by shock effect, camouflage by freezing inconspicuously into place and simulation of death ("playing possum") are among the more common devices the hunter has come across and by which he has often been outwitted.

The vigilance and agility of the hunted animal often compensate for the hunter's advantages, which means that frequently his "catch" turns out to be only young, inexperienced, sick or senile animals. Everything else being even, healthy game stands a respectable chance of escaping the hunter. Its skills are nature's bounty. Its survival is the principle of natural selection at work.

But it is not only the hunted which benefits from innate skills of concealment and related talents. The tiger's camouflage, its ability to remain virtually imperceptible as it lies in wait before making its deadly leap, is truly remarkable. Even experienced tiger hunters have fallen victim to this giant cat, and some have taken many months to track down a dangerous man-eater which chooses to be elusive.

This camouflage skill has led many shikaris in India to believe that the tiger, the "great invisible one," casts a spell on the sambar deer by imitating its sound, lulling it into complacency and then moving in for the certain kill. It is a fact, however, that the growling of a hungry tiger in the jungle night is often answered by the metallic bark of the

sambar deer and that nocturnal dialogues of this kind can last for hours, with the sambar coming within a few yards of the tiger, giving the impression that both sounds are coming from a single animal.

Some time ago, a hunter in India reported a strange experience: at dusk, a tiger "announced itself" with a short, almost unearthly growl which was immediately answered by the warning cry of the sambar deer. Then hours went by with no further unusual sights or sounds. However, after midnight, there was a spine-chilling cry and a long growl, immediately answered again by the penetrating warning cry of the sambar. Then came a loud stamping of hoofs, which led the hunter cautiously to the scene of the clamor. There a tiger, standing over a dead buffalo, was about to begin its meal. But the sambar stood with apparent recklessness just a few yards from the tiger, distracting it from its freshly killed food. Suddenly, there was a great deal of activity and in a flash the dead buffalo had disappeared. The tiger had dragged it into the undergrowth, fleeing with its prey from the comparatively fragile sambar, as if the deer exercised a mysterious power.

It is now known that the sambar deer sometimes "pursues" the tiger for nights on end, remaining in regular communication with it. Many other animals are thus warned of the tiger's whereabouts. If a moral can be read into this phenomenon, it is that the hierarchical system among jungle animals, which ensures the victory of predators over their weaker prey, is never absolute. The defensive instincts of most hunted animals have been developed in such a way that they are capable of resisting or avoiding the attacks of predators to an extent sufficient to guarantee survival of their species.

The medieval hunter stalked his prey camouflaged by an accompanying ox (2). Prairie Indians camouflaged themselves with the skins and stuffed heads of elks to deceive live deer (1). Other hunters donned the skins and masks of wolves and, thus attired, crept up on bison herds (3) or they smeared themselves with oily substances to confuse their victims' senses of smell. Camouflage adapted to the environment includes the snow-white winter dress of the arctic fox (6),

and mountain hare (4), which retreated to mountainous regions in post-glacial times. Change in color of the mountain hare depends on the temperature. Arctic mountain hare remain white the whole year round, whereas those living in the milder climate of Ireland, for example, usually retain their reddish-brown coats, even in winter. Larger species of game are also adept in the art of camouflage. The fallow deer (5), which lives mainly in the dappled light and shade of lightly

wooded countryside, is skilled at evading the attention of hunters. Most fascinating of all is the camouflage of the tiger, the "invisible one," of the jungles of India (7).

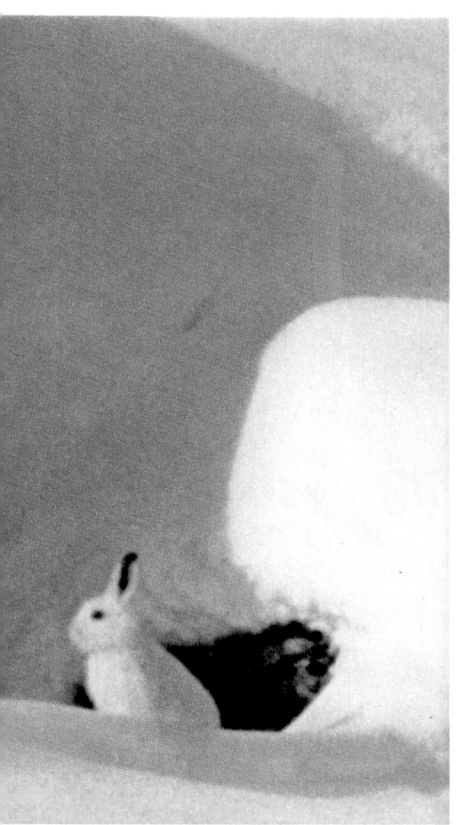

6

7

Animal Tracks

Wild animals and dogs can pick up a trail by using their sense of smell. Man, however, can only follow tracks when they are visible.

Tracks left by such cloven-hoofed game as red and roe deer, ibex, chamois and boar consist of clearly defined prints made in soft ground or snow. They vary considerably, depending on whether the animals were moving slowly or quickly; the hooves of cloven-footed game in flight are spread noticeably apart.

Animals which move on the soles of their feet, including the bear, fox, badger, marten, hare, rabbit, dog and cat, leave distinctive tracks. Those of the fox and badger emphasize their strong paw pads and claws. Those of the marten, polecat, weasel and hare show more of the whole paw. The marten hops with its fore and back-paws in pairs.

The tracks of many wildfowl are generally distinguishable by the structure (webbed or otherwise), size and shape of their feet.

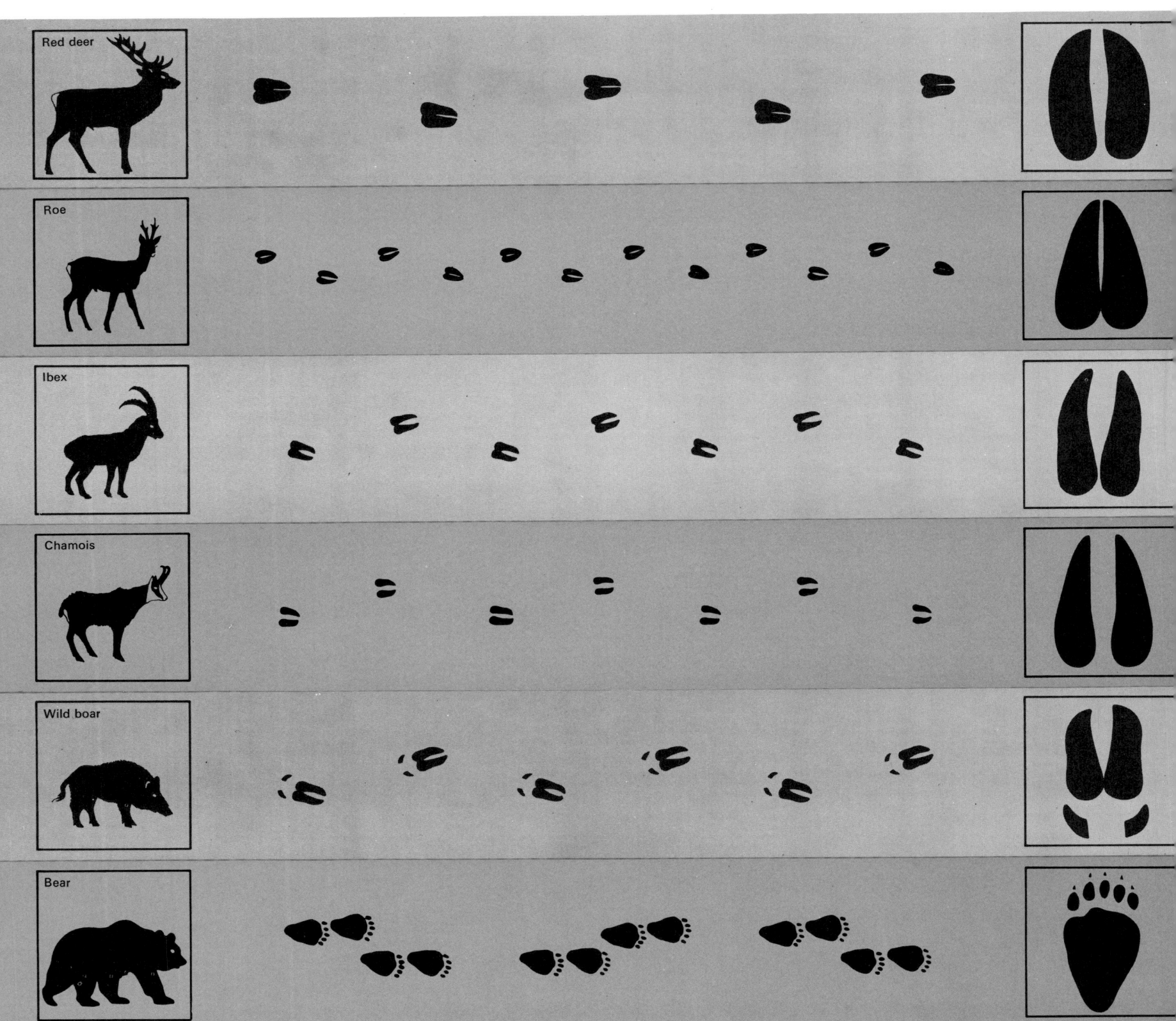

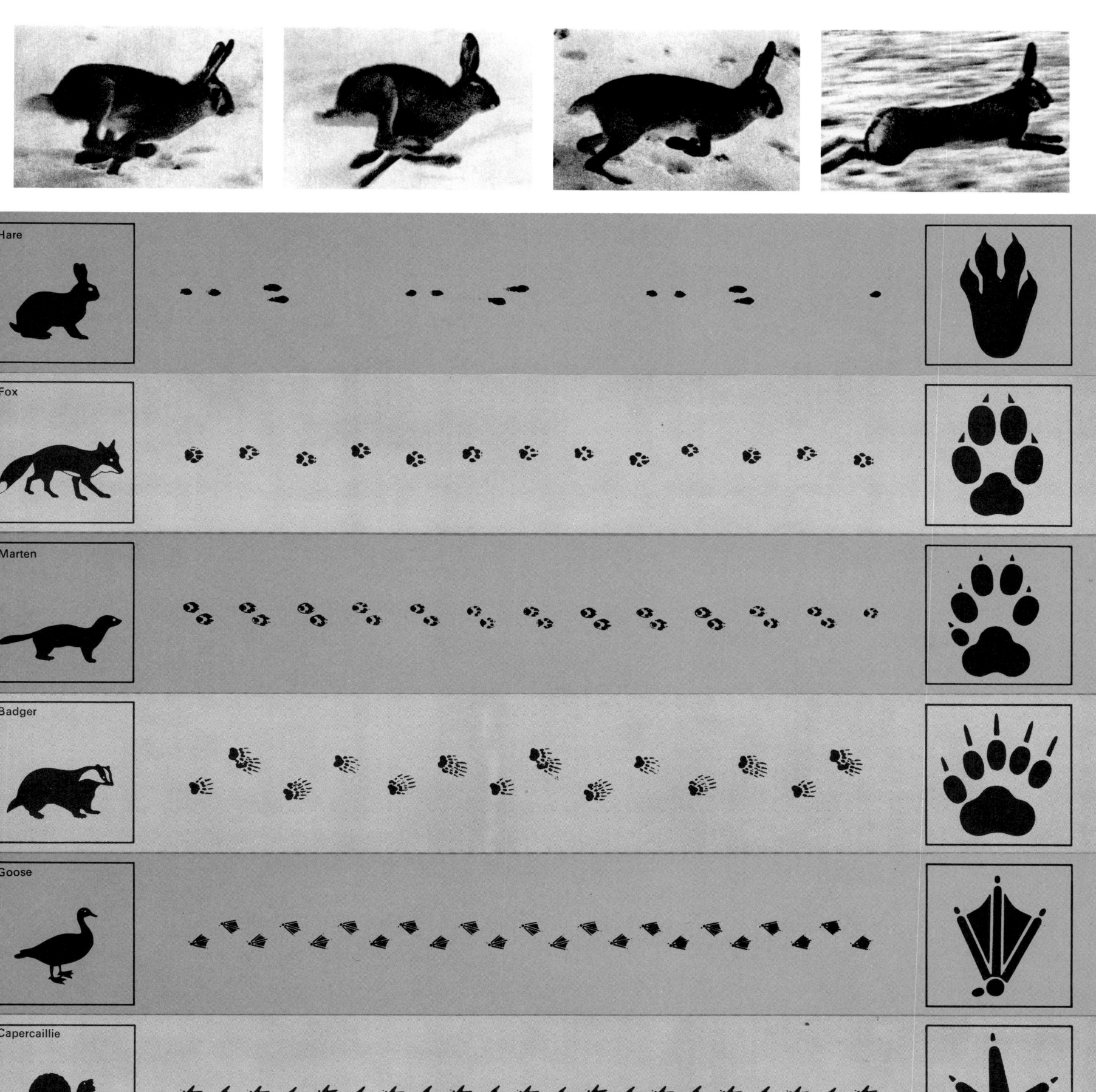

Hare

Fox

Marten

Badger

Goose

Capercaillie

Pictures in the Snow

Freshly fallen snow can provide hunters and other interested persons with remarkable revelations of secrets of nature. Game trails suddenly become glaringly clear, even to the most uninitiated observer of animal ways. The tracks point unmistakably to the hideaways of the fox and the badger and the marten. Countless hare tracks lead, surprisingly, to a single subterranean retreat. Clearly defined markings chart out the territory of an otherwise secretive buck. Predators on the prowl leave their "visiting cards." Fresh snow offers an opportunity to determine the kind and density of a game population. It provides a setting for nature's telltale winter hieroglyphics.

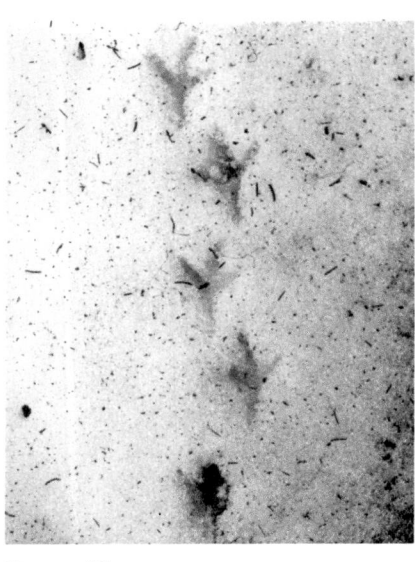

HAZEL HEN
Easily recognizable partridge-like tracks punctuate the snow.

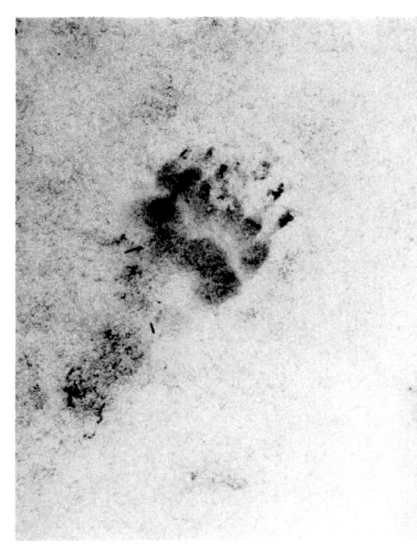

BADGER
A weighty print; the marks of the claws are clearly visible.

FOX
The more confident its movement, the straighter its tracks.

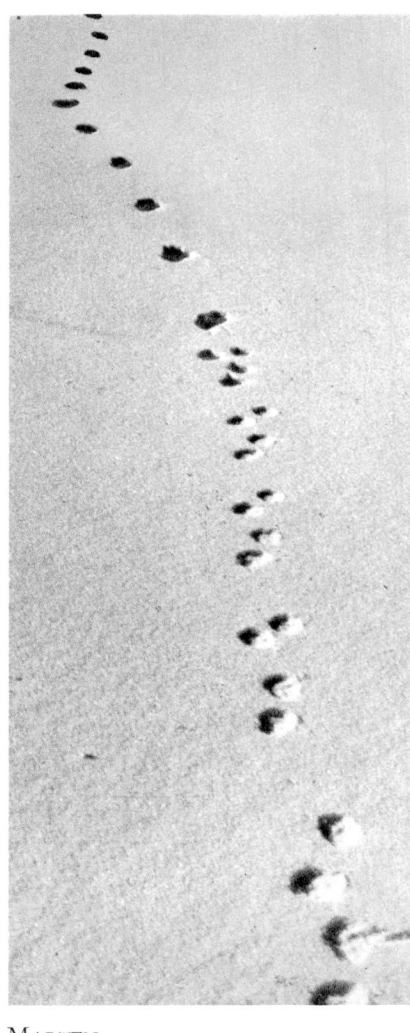

MARTEN
Positioning of prints changes as it traverses softer snow.

HEATHCOCK
Even, closely adjoining tracks across winter's white blanket.

HARE
Trail of an unruffled hare. When in flight, there is greater space between tracks.

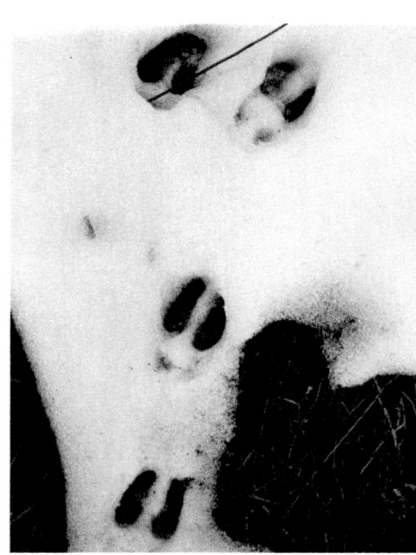

IBEX
The dew-claws of the ibex accentuate the animal's snow markings.

CHAMOIS
Almost rectangular, chamois tracks are unmistakable.

Right: Black grouse in fighting position.

Birds of Prey

Birds of prey are monarchs of the skies. Some species were once constant companions and pets of princes and falconers. Their existence was threatened when they came to be regarded as parasites and thieves. Today, more is known about their importance to ecology. It is known that they contribute greatly to the biological balance of their habitats. They kill young game, but concentrate primarily on sick and weak animals.

Birds of prey have the qualities of the perfect hunter. They have muscular bodies, extraordinary stamina, and exceptionally sharp senses of sight and hearing. Their weapons are short, curved beaks and the sharp claws of their talons. Contrary to general opinion, however, most of their attacks on prey end in failure.

In categorizing birds of prey according to beak, talons and type of prey, they may be

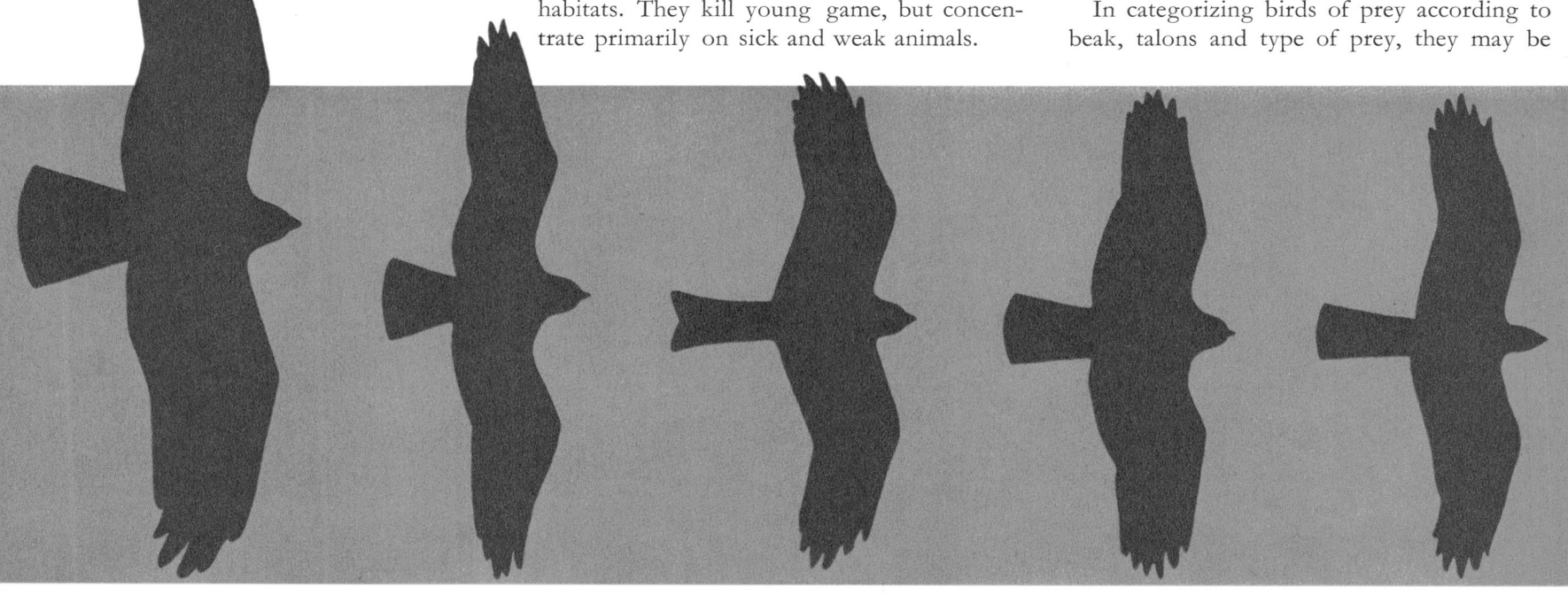

GOLDEN EAGLE
Aquila chrysaetos. Northern New and Old World. Non-migratory. Severely threatened. Prey: marmots, hares, etc. TL (total length) 30–35 inches.

OSPREY
Pandion heliaetus. Six sub-species, spread over almost the entire world. Swoops and dives for fish. TL 20–23 inches.

RED KITE
Milvus milvus. Mediterranean regions to Scandinavia. Migrates to Africa in winter. Prey: mainly carrion. TL 24 inches.

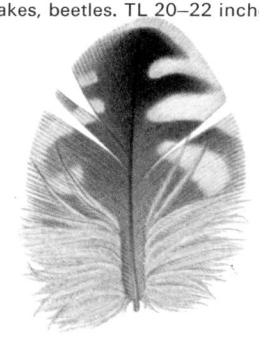
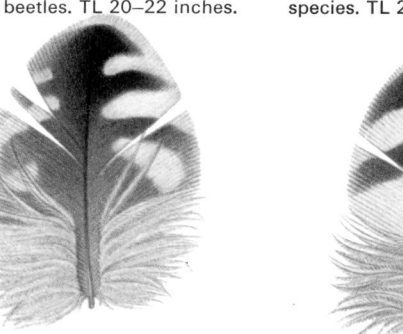

COMMON BUZZARD
Buteo buteo. Temperate zones of Eurasia. Non-migratory in central Europe. Prey: field mice, frogs, snakes, beetles. TL 20–22 inches.

HONEY BUZZARD
Pernis apivorus. Europe to the Caucasus. Winters in Africa. Prey: insects, especially wasp-like species. TL 20–23 inches.

divided into two primary groups. The eagle, goshawk, buzzard, harrier and Eurasian sparrow hawk, all of which have piercing, light-colored eyes, seize their prey with their dagger-like talons and, in effect, squeeze them to death. They move in quickly, seemingly out of nowhere, to make short work of their quarry. Buzzards and harriers usually lurk in trees or on fences to swoop down upon their victims from only slightly elevated positions.

All sixty species of the falcon, from the small European kestrel to the large gyrfalcon, belong to the second category of the birds of prey. With their long, tapered wings, they swoop swiftly down on their victims, seize them and dispatch them with mighty pecks to the head and neck. Capable of remarkable endurance in flight, these birds can reach seemingly effortless speeds of up to 200 miles an hour.

The role of birds of prey as natural regulators is undisputed today. They have been completely rehabilitated and, to a great extent, are protected by regulations. But this protection serves no purpose if their existence is undermined by the depletion of their natural food supply through the elimination of rodents and small game as a result of the increased and indiscriminate use of questionable insecticides.

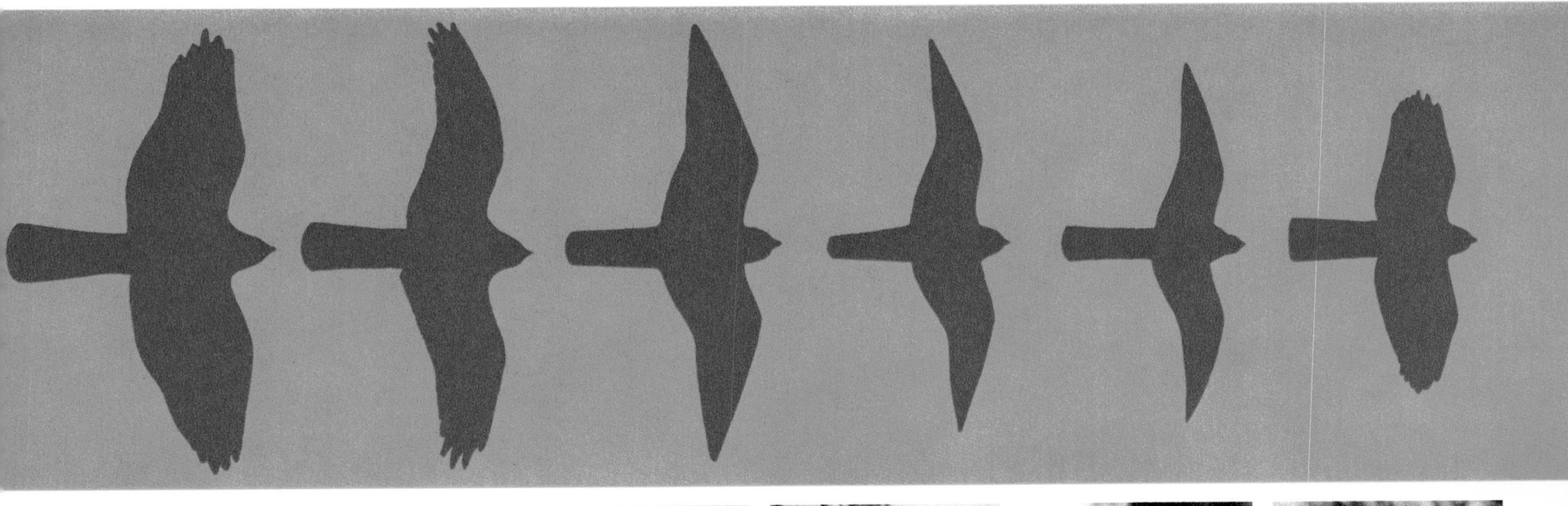

GOSHAWK
Accipiter gentilis gallinarum. Swift and powerful. Prey: mice to hares and cats. TL 19–24 inches.

MARSH HARRIER
Circus aeruginosus. Temperate zones in Eurasia, Australia. Prey: water- and song-birds. TL 19–22 inches.

PEREGRINE FALCON
Falco peregrinus. Also called the duck hawk. Particularly well known for its speed. Severely threatened. Prey: smaller birds. TL 15–19 inches.

HOBBY
Falco subbuteo. Small falcon of Eurasia's temperate zones. Prey: swallows, larks, insects. TL 12–14 inches.

OLD WORLD KESTREL
Falco tinnunculus. Hoverer. Common to Eurasia and Africa. Prey: mice, insects. TL 14 inches.

EURASIAN SPARROW HAWK
Accipiter nisus. Sometimes called the small goshawk. Temperate zones in Eurasia. Prey: birds, small mammals. TL 11–15 inches.

   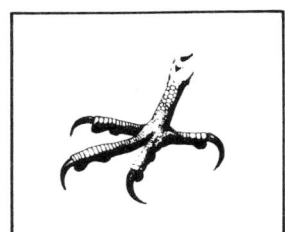   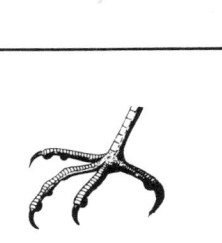

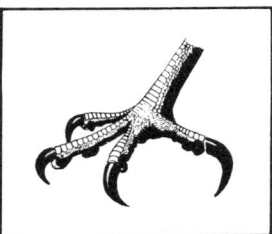 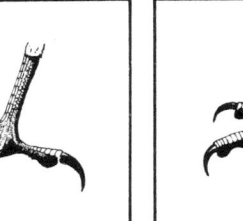

European Wild Fowl and Feathered Game

Almost all species of birds, including both migratory and non-migratory varieties, are threatened today, from the snipe to the gray partridge to the proud and sensitive wild goose.

The world and, particularly, man's relationship with its fauna and flora, have altered considerably in recent times. What we choose to call civilization now penetrates into previously untouched natural regions everywhere. Vast areas of marsh and swamp have been "improved." Fallow expanses of earth have been transformed into barren wasteland. Isolated coastal districts have been set back from their water boundaries and wading birds have been deprived of the special biotopes essential for their survival. All too few species, including the northern mallard, the wood pigeon and the pheasant, have been able to adapt to the altered environment and partake of the benefits of our civilization.

Winter cold, frozen lakes and rivers, and snow-covered pastureland compel northern wild fowl to seek sustenance in warmer zones. Wild geese and swans, ducks, grebes and coots migrate by the thousands to those coasts of Britain which are washed by the Gulf Stream, to the islands of the North Sea, to the open lakes of central Europe, or to the marshland of the Guadalquivir in Spain. The mild shores of the Mediterranean and the Black Sea are sought out by the common quail, the rail and other wild fowl. The stork, heron and crane migrate as far as Africa.

To rest from time to time during their long migratory flights, birds of passage seek out specific stopping-off places along their routes. Birds which are protected in northern countries are all too often decimated by irresponsible shooting, trapping and, above all, by oil-polluted waters during migration. No one can say how long nature-lovers will be able to delight in the poetry of sound and motion of wild geese in flight, and the music and beauty of other birds traveling to nesting and breeding grounds. The question is becoming increasingly acute. Much might be done to alleviate the situation if other countries copied the stringent North American regulations for protecting water fowl. But man's impact on the natural environment is having a deadly effect. Failure to take the necessary steps may soon have irreversible consequences.

BUSTARD *(Otis tarda)*

Once found all over Europe, now mainly in southern Europe where it is protected. Twenty-two species exist in Eurasia, Africa and Australia. Large, long-legged ratite, well camouflaged in exposed dry regions by its sand-colored, brownish-yellow feathers. The great bustard may weigh as much as forty-four pounds. A shy, cautious bird, it will flee from a threat 200 yards away. Its feather spread during mating display is impressive.

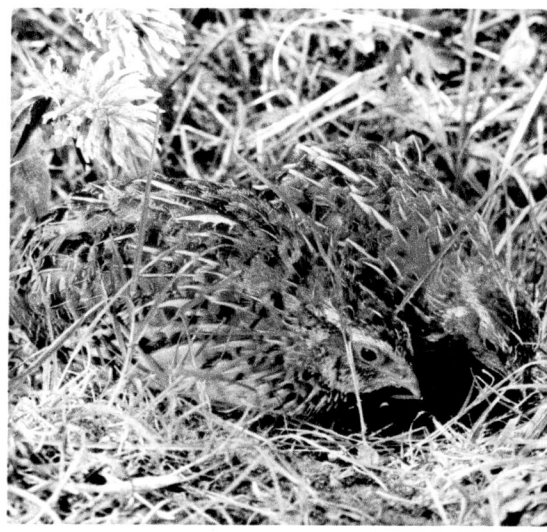

COMMON QUAIL *(Coturnix coturnix)*

Found all over Europe. A migratory bird which flies only at night and at low altitudes. Winters from northern Africa to the Equator. Earth-colored feathers bear ocher stripes along the back. The common quail is half the size of the grey partridge and lacks the latter's rust-colored tail. Favors cornfields; is severely threatened in agricultural regions. Monogamous. Calls "Peckwerweck-peckwerweck." Flocks of common quail are severely decimated during its migratory rests in Mediterranean regions.

COMMON SNIPE *(Capella gallinago)*

A migratory bird found in marshy areas all over Europe. Smaller than the woodcock, it has dark and light rust-yellow lengthwise stripes with dark tail feathers. Nests on the ground. Its mating flight at dusk is extremely swift and takes a zigzag course. Known as the "sky goat" because of its bleat-like sounds, produced by the swishing of its tail feathers. Cowers on the ground at the approach of danger.

WOODCOCK *(Scolopax rusticola)*

A migratory bird which usually winters in southern Europe and Africa. Spring is the woodcock's migratory season. A skilled flyer, it can maneuver between tree trunks. But its mating flight, during which it emits deep and high-pitched sounds alternately, is slow and similar to that of the owl. Its fine beak, which is permeated with nerves, is capable of extracting worms and caterpillars from the earth as if it were a pair of tweezers.

PHEASANT (*Phasianus colchicus*)

Most prolific in Asia, the pheasant was brought to Europe from what is now Soviet Georgia by the ancient Greeks. It was later crossed with the hardier Chinese–Mongolian pheasant. During this century, an almost black mutation, the "tenebrosus," has emerged. In its present form, the pheasant is particularly well adapted to lightly wooded territory. It is so adaptable that it has largely ousted the gray partridge from its habitat.

Below: GRAYLAG GOOSE (*Anser anser*)

The domestic goose is a descendant of the graylag goose which breeds in central Europe. It lives on the coasts of Scandinavia, northern England and Scotland and winters in Mediterranean regions. It has been reintroduced in northern and eastern Germany and is under protection in those areas. A cautious creature, it is careful to fly at great distance from any possible danger. Its feathers are gray-brown with silver-gray wings. Its ringed legs are pink. Its beak is orange. Its senses are very acute.

WOOD PIGEON (*Columba palumbus*)

One of the largest European pigeons, it lives in all types of woodlands. In autumn, it migrates southward in large numbers along the Atlantic coast. In mild winters, it remains in central Europe. The gray-blue-brown plumage is interspersed with white patches—one on each side of the neck and on the front edge of each wing. Monogamous. Incubation period comparatively long. Young birds are fed by glandular secretions.

NORTHERN MALLARD (*Anas platyrhynchos*)

Prolific in Europe, North America and many regions of Asia. Partially migratory. Winters in breeding areas. The northern mallard is the original form of the domestic duck. In summer, duck and drake both wear the same sort of brown feathers. After the molt, the drake develops its violet-green shimmering attire. The mallard is undemanding and adaptable. After mating, the birds often fly to distant breeding grounds.

The Grouse Family

1 GRAY PARTRIDGE *(Perdix perdix)*
Temperate zones in Eurasia.
Non-migratory. Favors barren
territory.

2 FEN PTARMIGAN *(Lagopus*
lagopus)
North America and northern Eurasia.
Favors moors and heathland.

3 RED-LEGGED PARTRIDGE
(Alectoris rufa)
Iberian peninsula. Small populations in
southern France and England. Prefers
dry, sunny areas.

4 HAZEL HEN *(Tetrastes bonasia)*
Europe and northern Asia. Lives in
pairs. Prefers mixed woodland.

Above right: PTARMIGAN *(Lagopus*
mutus)
Northern hemisphere. Lives above the
treeline. White in winter;
black-bordered tail.

Below right: BLACK GROUSE
(Lyrurus tetrix)
The Alps and northern Eurasia.
Prefers open territory and moorland.

1

3

2

4

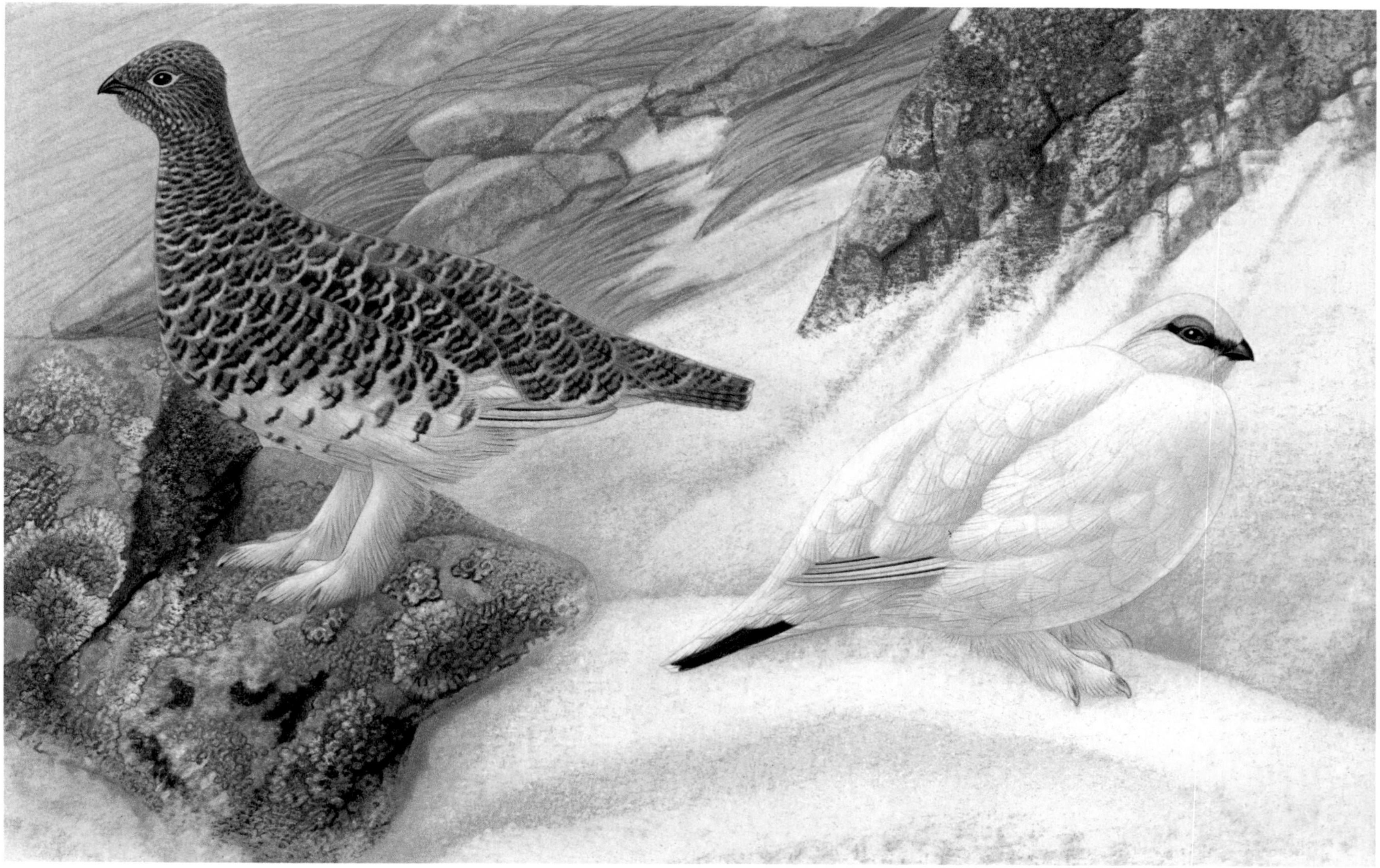

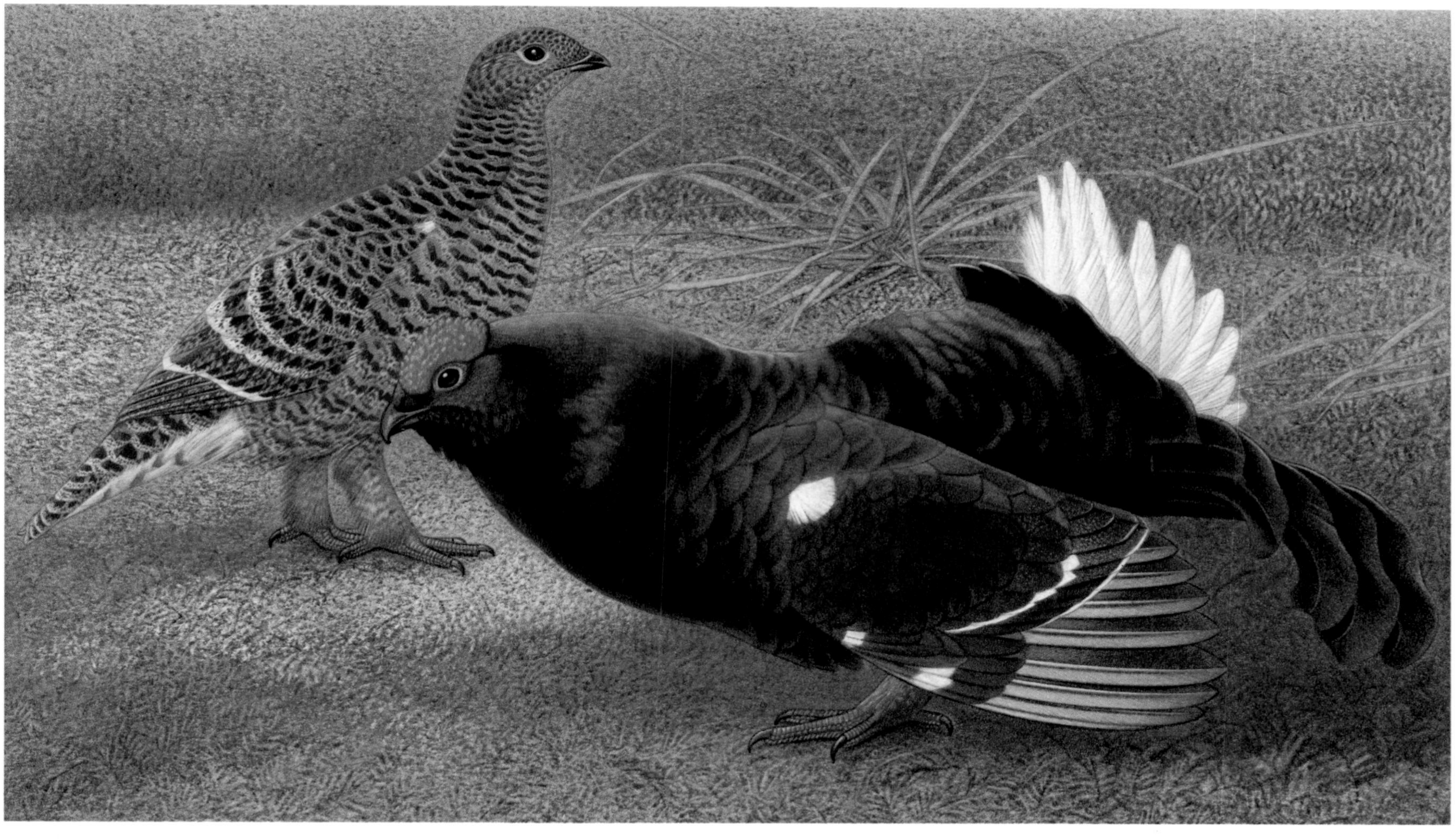

The Mating Dance of the Capercaillie

In the first rays of the morning sun, the capercaillie cock lowers himself to the ground where the seductive hen awaits him. Once more, the cock performs a brief, ecstatic mating display and, at the height of its excitement, mounts the crouching hen. Hunters should bear in mind that this is an endangered species.

Overleaf: Mating play of the heron.

Four stages of the mating song.

In March and April, when the snow melts, the mating season of the capercaillie begins. Its mating display is thought by many hunters to be at least as fascinating as that of the red deer or the chamois.

Year after year, the capercaillie cock seeks the same quiet territory. To be certain of observing its behavior, a hunter should seek out the mating locality on the eve of the event. Droppings under trees; tracks on scanty remains of snow; a soft, grating sound reveal the cock's presence. In windy weather, it is difficult, sometimes impossible, to hear the sound of the capercaillie.

The hunter should approach before dawn, silently and with great care, listening intently and constantly on the alert, until a timid scraping noise testifies to the near presence of the cock. Its "ko-lupp ko-lupp" becomes increasingly clear. As its ecstasy increases, the bird's cries become wilder and wilder, until the final notes end, trill-like, with a loud "tack" shattering the morning stillness like a popping cork. The excited cock is overcome by ecstatic trembling; its feathers rise and its wings spread wide.

After a brief pause, a hissing sound like a scythe being sharpened begins. The cock lowers, stretches and folds its tail feathers. Whether it is now overcome with passion or hindered by the closing of its eyes is not known, but for a few moments, the capercaillie can neither see nor hear and the hunter can take advantage of this strange moment to approach closer. Very likely, he will see the brownish-black outline of the cock silhouetted against the reddening sky. Its tail feathers are shimmering green, trembling with excitement. Its comb is a fiery scarlet. Its white shoulder patches gleam and its curved beak juts out unmistakably. This is the coveted capercaillie cock! With the approach of the sun's first rays, the bird begins to court the hen with its mating display.

When the time comes, the hen will construct a crude nest well adapted to the surroundings. She will sit on her brownspeckled eggs—there will be between five and ten of them—for around four weeks. In early autumn, the cock will no longer tolerate the presence of the young capercaillies and they are made to leave to seek territories of their own.

As with many other birds, polished peppercorn-sized stones are found in the stomach of the capercaillie. The birds swallow these stones to aid digestion of the resinous pine needles to which they are partial. In bygone times, the stones were believed by many to have miraculous powers.

The numbers of capercaillies have decreased sharply in recent years. It is, however, interesting to note that in the vast natural forests of the East, where the lynx, fox, badger, marten, eagle and goshawk are also still in residence, they have survived fairly well. The depletion of capercaillie populations elsewhere is not primarily the result of unrestricted hunting. Other factors are involved. These include unfavorable alterations to their habitats, especially the destruction of mixed woodlands where undergrowths had always been full of berries, seeds and red ants. Young capercaillie feed on these ants, as well as on beetles, caterpillars and flies, and where they have disappeared, the capercaillie population has correspondingly declined.

Only carefully planned conservation measures, and the availability of suitable breeding grounds, can save the capercaillie from total extinction.

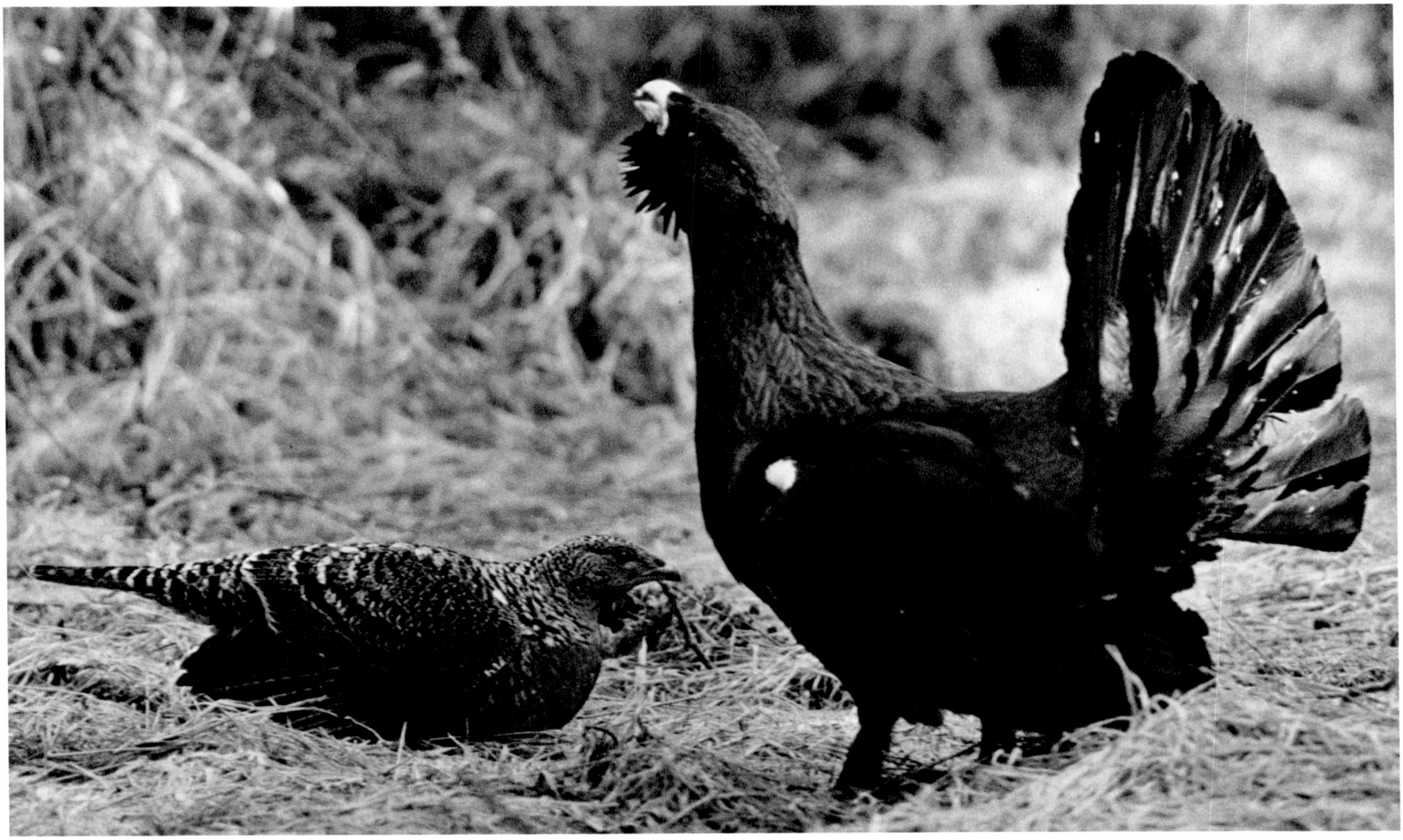

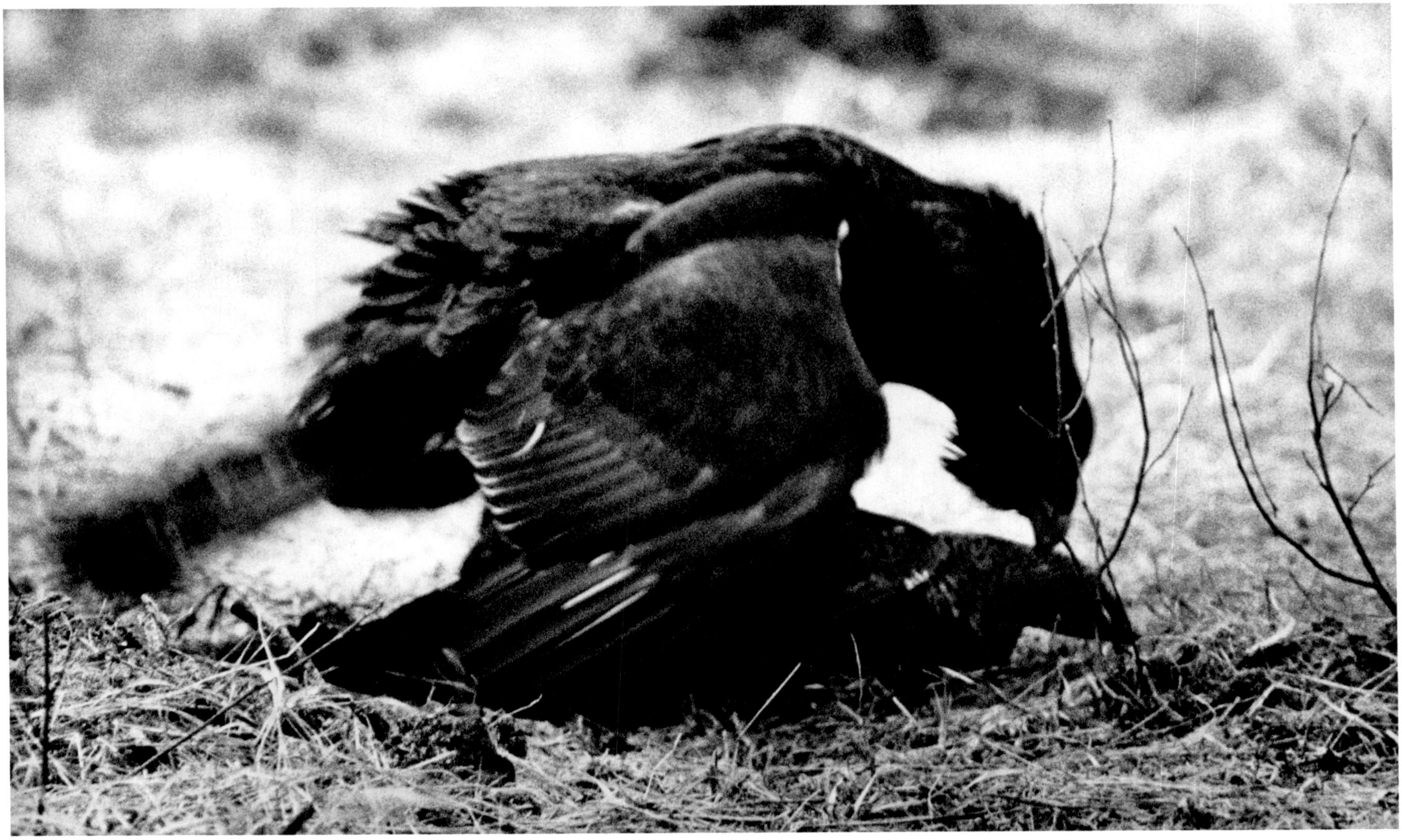

Fauna and Vegetation in Asia

The colors on this map indicate various vegetation belts, determined
by climate and geographic location, from northern tundra (pale blue)
to tropical rain forests (dark green). Corresponding bands of color
on the right provide a survey of the important large wild animals
indigenous to the various zones. Some of these species,
including the lion and the barasingha, are today confined to
narrow sections of their vegetation belts.

Deer of Asia

1   The barasingha—its Indian name means "twelve-pointer"—is severely threatened with extinction. This marsh deer, which bears fine antlers, lives in male or female herds or in mixed groups of young animals.

2   The sturdy nilgai antelope can be found in lightly wooded regions of India. It is also known as the "blue bull"

because of its blue-gray coat. Only the bulls bear small horns.

3   Sambar deer are particularly numerous near rivers, lagoons and lakes.

4   The chital, or axis deer, lives exclusively in savannahs and open woodland territory. Sambars and chitals are usually six-pointers.

Unlike antelopes and gazelles, which are not nearly as abundant and varied in Asia as they are in Africa, the deer family has developed in Asia into a remarkable variety of species. They range from the mouse deer and the muntjak in the tropics and sub-tropics to the mighty moose in northern regions. Many species are today threatened with extinction. These include Thorold's deer in Tibet, the thamin in Burma and Thailand, and the barasingha in central India. As far as is known, Pere David's deer has not lived in wild herds since records began to be kept; the approximately six hundred specimens known to survive are in captivity or preserves. Large-scale environmental changes, for which man is responsible, have had the most impact on highly specialized species. This applies particularly to the barasingha or marsh deer, an animal about the same size as the red deer which, by virtue of its body structure and behavior, is dependent on a marshy grass jungle environment.

Once upon a time, countless barasingha made their way in large herds through the wide Indian river valleys. However, when the vast expanses of marshy land were converted into fertile fields in the nineteenth century, the barasingha's existence was threatened. Although the survival of the northern sub-species seems to be secure in the Kaziranga Reservation in Assam, the central Indian barasingha was not able to survive in the Kanha National Park. In the early 1940s, the barasingha population was estimated at around three thousand; by 1965, the number had dwindled to a mere seventy. Their retreats have lacked the moist areas, with rushes, sedges and other marsh vegetation on which the animals feed.

The Indian sambar has proved far more adaptable. Its tracks can be found both in mountainous regions and in the rain forests. It prefers the jungle to open savannah and is able to move through dense undergrowth with remarkable skill and silence. These primarily nocturnal deer can still be found in the remote lagoons of Sri Lanka as they bathe in the cool, brackish water. Sometimes they even make their way in herds toward the rocky coast, to be refreshed by the foaming waves. In Sri Lanka, sambar deer gather in herds of sixty to eighty animals at dusk. At such gatherings, does with their fauns stand in the center surrounded by the stags. Although sambar deer are generally peaceable amongst themselves, fights sometimes break out between stags because only the dominant stag may mix with the females. Only he may control them and mate with them.

Like many other species of tropical deer, the sambar does not shed its velvet in any specific season; antler-bearing stags in rut are always in evidence. Does are also ready to mate and conceive at any time of the year. Often, however, only the fauns dropped during the rainy season are able to survive.

In India and Sri Lanka, man has created huge savannahs by clearing for cultivation. One effect has been the spread of the chital, or axis deer, one of the most beautiful of all deer, whose coat is pleasingly spotted all its life. The chital has adapted to the new living conditions over the past century with remarkable speed and has been found in cultivated areas in ever increasing numbers. Its large herds of up to six hundred animals can present so heavy a burden to pasture land in the dry season that vegetation is often completely destroyed and the soil eroded.

The chital has been successfully introduced into a number of countries, including New Zealand, Australia, Hawaii, Brazil and Argentina. Ironically, sometimes it has been introduced too successfully. In some areas, professional hunters have been employed to reduce its numbers.

1

Big Cats   **Bears**   **Dogs and Hyenas**   **Perissodactyls**

ndra
d Taiga

untain
getation

ciduous
 Mixed
rests

pical
n
rests

nsoon
ests
 Dry
pical
ests

annah
 ppes

sert

Lynx

Snow leopard

Leopard

Tiger

Leopard

Clouded leopard

Tiger

Lion

Cheetah

Caracal lynx

Polar bear

Brown bear

Giant panda

Asiatic black bear

Asiatic black bear

Malayan sun bear

Malayan sun bear

Indian bear

Wolf

Wolf

Wolf

Red dog

Red dog

Hyena

Jackal

Red dog   Jackal

Hyena

Great Indian rhinoce

Sumatran rhinoceros

Tapir

Javan rhinoceros

Przewalski's horse

Asiatic wild ass

Boars

Deer

Cattle and Wild Camels

Goat Antelopes, Sheep, True Antelopes

Moose

Reindeer

Isubra deer

Argali

Tahr

Wild boar

Musk deer

Tibetan antelope

Markhor

Blue sheep

Wild boar

Cashmere deer

Yak

Thorold's deer

Takin

Chevrotain

Goral

Wild boar

Pygmy hog

Hog deer

Barasingha

Water buffalo

Serow

os

Pygmy hog

Pygmy hog

Muntjak

Sambar

Gaur

Babirusa

Four-horned antelope

Indian gazelle

Axis deer

Banteng

Nilgai

Sambar

Oryx

Two-humped camel

Saiga antelope

Dromedary

Animals of Asia

From the ice-bound wilderness of northern Siberia to the steaming sub-equatorial rain forests of Indonesia, from the Urals, eastern Mediterranean and Arabia in the west to the Pacific Ocean and the islands of Japan in the east, Asia, the Earth's largest continent, lies spread out in inexhaustible variety, a world with a thousand different aspects. All types of climatic regions and environments are represented: arctic coasts, tundra, coniferous and mixed forests, steppes, deserts, jungles. So wide a spectrum of climatic conditions boasts an even broader range of animal life.

The wild boar, one of the most adaptable of species, is found in almost all Asiatic regions. Its wide propagation is a consequence of both its astonishing fertility and the fact that it can sustain itself on various kinds of nourishment. Such adaptability is by no means common to all large animals. In the southern part of the Asian continent, natural limits to the propagation of different kinds of species are fixed by environmental conditions. This is particularly true on the islands of southeast Asia. There, particular species, peculiar to their immediate areas, have evolved over the course of time. Although listed in zoological systems and described in detail, many aspects of their ways of life remain a mystery. But our ignorance of the Asian animal world is not confined to isolated and inaccessible species; it applies to greater or lesser extent even to more popular forms of Asian wild life, including the tiger, elephant, gaur and rhinoceros. To complicate existing mysteries, the same drama which has been played out in North America and western Europe since the nineteenth century is now being acted out in Asia as well: the last natural reserves of many kinds of game are rapidly being obliterated by man, through his indifference, irresponsibility or ignorance.

Let us, however, begin our survey of the continent in an area still untroubled by human overpopulation—the far north. Northern Asia, Europe and North America are regarded by zoological geographers as forming a single vast fauna habitat. The Bering Strait, which separates northeast

Asia from North America, did not submerge the landbridge joining the two continents until the Tertiary Period. As a result, many northern animals, including the fox, wolf, brown bear, polar bear, red deer, moose and reindeer can be found clear around the North Pole. Polar bear and various kinds of seal live on the Asiatic–Arctic coast, as do formidable walruses, amongst whom tusk-bearing bulls may measure as much as twelve feet in length and weigh over two thousand pounds.

Adjoining the regions of eternal ice is the tundra, where the ground thaws only slightly in the summer. Its vegetation is inhibited by extreme cold most of the year and the brevity of the summer; only a few animal species can survive such conditions. Among them are the reindeer, which feeds mainly on lichen, and the snow hare, arctic fox, fen ptarmigan and various kinds of wild geese.

The biggest forest in the world, the Siberian Taiga, is about one-third as large again as the entire United States. Its endless coniferous woods, interspersed with birch, aspen and alder trees, make a setting for the moose, reindeer, beaver, lynx, wolf, fox and several different species of fowl. Both tundra and taiga have relatively little rainfall; only on the eastern rim of the continent do the summer monsoons, with their rain-bearing winds, extend to the north and promote the growth of vegetation. Thus, Manchuria and parts of Korea and Japan have mixed forests with rich coverings of undergrowth. Swamped lowland plains and wide, marshy, grassy areas are also common in that part of the world. Those regions provide a habitat for the tiger, panther and Asiatic black bear. The deer family is also represented there by the isubra deer, sika, moose, roe and musk deer.

In central Asia, the tundra borders on a wide, dry belt of steppes and desert, extending from Iran to Mongolia. This region is inhabited by nomadic hoofed animals such as the Asiatic wild ass, the Mongolian wild horse (already very rare), numerous species of gazelle, the saiga antelope and the camel. Beasts of prey include the caracal lynx and the wolf. But

these vast Asiatic desert expanses are only a small part of the Earth's most extensive dry belt, which stretches from the Sahara in the west, across Arabia, Turkey, Iran, the lowlands border in the Caspian Sea and the Aral Sea, Afghanistan and the Gobi desert. This huge area is inhabited by few, but highly specialized, species of larger animals—various kinds of gazelle, the oryx antelope which now lives almost only in Arabia, the Asiatic wild ass, and the extremely rare cheetah.

The world's highest mountain range runs horizontally across the Asian continent from east to west, and forms the habitat of numerous kinds of wild sheep, wild goats, goat antelopes and snow leopards. In the south, the palearctic fauna area is clearly cut off from the Indo–Malayan region by the Himalayas. In these mountain woodlands and bamboo jungles an unparalleled variety of rare species can be found—the giant panda, small panda, clouded leopard, Asiatic black bear, tahr, serau, takin, goral, and many varieties of deer. To the south of this mountainous realm, between the Indus and the Ganges, lies the broad Indian dry belt which extends westwards and is home for the nilgai and the blackbuck. The alluvia of the Indus and the Ganges, now densely populated by man, are covered in the east by extensive grass jungles which were inhabited by lions and cheetahs over a thousand years ago. Today, the huge, damp grass forests of Assam provide the last refuge for the water buffalo and the great Indian rhinoceros. The tiger, elephant, gaur, axis deer, sambar, Indian bear and red dog are found all over the Indian peninsula.

Parts of India which are, geologically, relatively young and which are often characterized by rugged, craggy coasts and huge rain forests, are the home of an ancient animal world of spectacular variety. Wild cattle are represented by the gaur, banteng and kouprey. The great Indian rhinoceros is superseded by the Sumatra and Java rhinoceros—now almost extinct. The strangely marked black-and-white Malayan tapir is another distinctive inhabitant of this exotic part of the globe.

2

3

4

Rhinoceroses of the East

More than four and a half centuries ago the German artist Albrecht Dürer immortalized the Indian rhinoceros in drawing and woodcut. His remarkably lifelike portrayals were made all the more extraordinary by the fact that the artist had never even seen the huge animal, which happened then to be on show in Lisbon. Dürer worked entirely from drawings and descriptions from Portuguese sources.

He did, however, make one mistake. Misinterpreting what was probably an accidental flourish on one of the drawings from which he took his inspiration, he added a horn on the shoulder of his rhinoceros. This so-called "Dürer-horn" was inherited by other artists and did not disappear until two hundred years later when, in the middle of the eighteenth century, a rhinoceros was once again brought to Europe, to Holland this time. Ironically, later research indicated that horn-like protuberances can occur in unlikely places on the rhinoceros.

Depending on species, rhinoceroses boast one or two horns on the front of the nose. These horns are regularly sharpened on trees. They continue to grow during the animal's entire life and are seldom shed. They cannot be compared with the antlers of deer or the horns of cattle because they are not made of bone and are not enclosed by horny sheaths. Rhinoceros horns are composed of countless compressed hair-like structures. In many ways, the

What appears to humans to be the awkwardness of rhinoceroses in no way interferes with their mating rites. The animals remain motionless, then circle round each other. They inflict powerful blows upon each other, sniff each other, grunt and snort.

Below left: two Indian rhinoceroses.

The family of rhinocerotidae consists of five species. The Indian rhinoceros (1) and the Javan rhinoceros (2) bear a single horn and display their proverbial "armor." The smallest known species, the Sumatran rhinoceros (3) has thick hair and two horns. Two African species, the black rhinoceros (4) and the wide-mouthed rhinoceros (5) are also two-horned; their horns often grow to enormous size.

horns have been the undoing of the animal. It has been relentlessly pursued by man for centuries because of those protuberances which, in many places, are still regarded as made of a substance which can serve as an aphrodisiac. In Chinese pharmacies in Hong Kong, Singapore and Bangkok, rhino horn has literally been worth its weight in gold.

During the last century, it has been mainly the white hunter who, for commercial or sporting reasons, has systematically pursued the rhinoceros, though hunters in India cannot be said to have been sparing in their efforts either. In Cooch Behar, in West Bengal, over two hundred rhinos were shot by local hunters between 1871 and 1907. Irresponsible hunting by poachers has played an important role in the sharp decrease in the rhino population. Once abundant in the grass jungles of the Indus, Ganges and Brahmaputra, the rhinoceros now lives only in eight nature preserves in Nepal, Bangladesh and Assam and in small isolated groups in the wilderness. About four hundred of the seven hundred known surviving animals live in the Kaziranga National Park.

The Basel zoo in Switzerland has for many years been particularly committed to the task of preserving the Indian rhinoceros, as well as its closest relative, the Javan rhinoceros. This creature is somewhat smaller than the Indian variety. It has similar "armor," but it lacks the striking folds of skin which stand out like heavy, riveted joints on the Indian species. In the Udjung Reserve, the thirty last known Javan rhinoceroses are currently objects of intensive observation and study by zoologists. It is not certain whether further specimens of the rare animal exist in areas outside this West Javan protected region, though some may be roaming free elsewhere in Java as well as in Sumatra, Malaysia, Thailand, Burma and Assam.

The third and smallest of the Asian rhinoceroses, the Sumatran rhinoceros, has, unlike the other two, two horns. Its relatively small size and its thick dark-brown to black hair have earned it the name *badak kerbau,* "buffalo rhinoceros," among local hunters. Hardly any of the experts sent by international nature-protection organizations have ever caught a glimpse of this elusive creature, though it is still energetically hunted by the people of the regions it inhabits.

The last few of them live in the mountain forests of Borneo, Sumatra and India. Latest estimates on the size of the surviving population are based only on the discovery of distinctive tracks the animal leaves. The footprints of this three-toed animal, like those of other rhinoceroses, reveal a kind of cushion on the soles of its feet, formed by the fusing of its toes, which carries the main weight of its body. Like its relatives, the Sumatran rhinoceros regularly visits specific waterholes to wallow and cover itself with cooling mud.

All rhinos have extended, pointed upper lips which enable them to hold the leaves on which they feed. Their incisors, partially reduced in size, play only a small role in their feeding process. The African wide-mouthed rhinoceros has developed differently. It carries its head low. Its wide mouth and sharp upper lip are specialized for "plucking" grass.

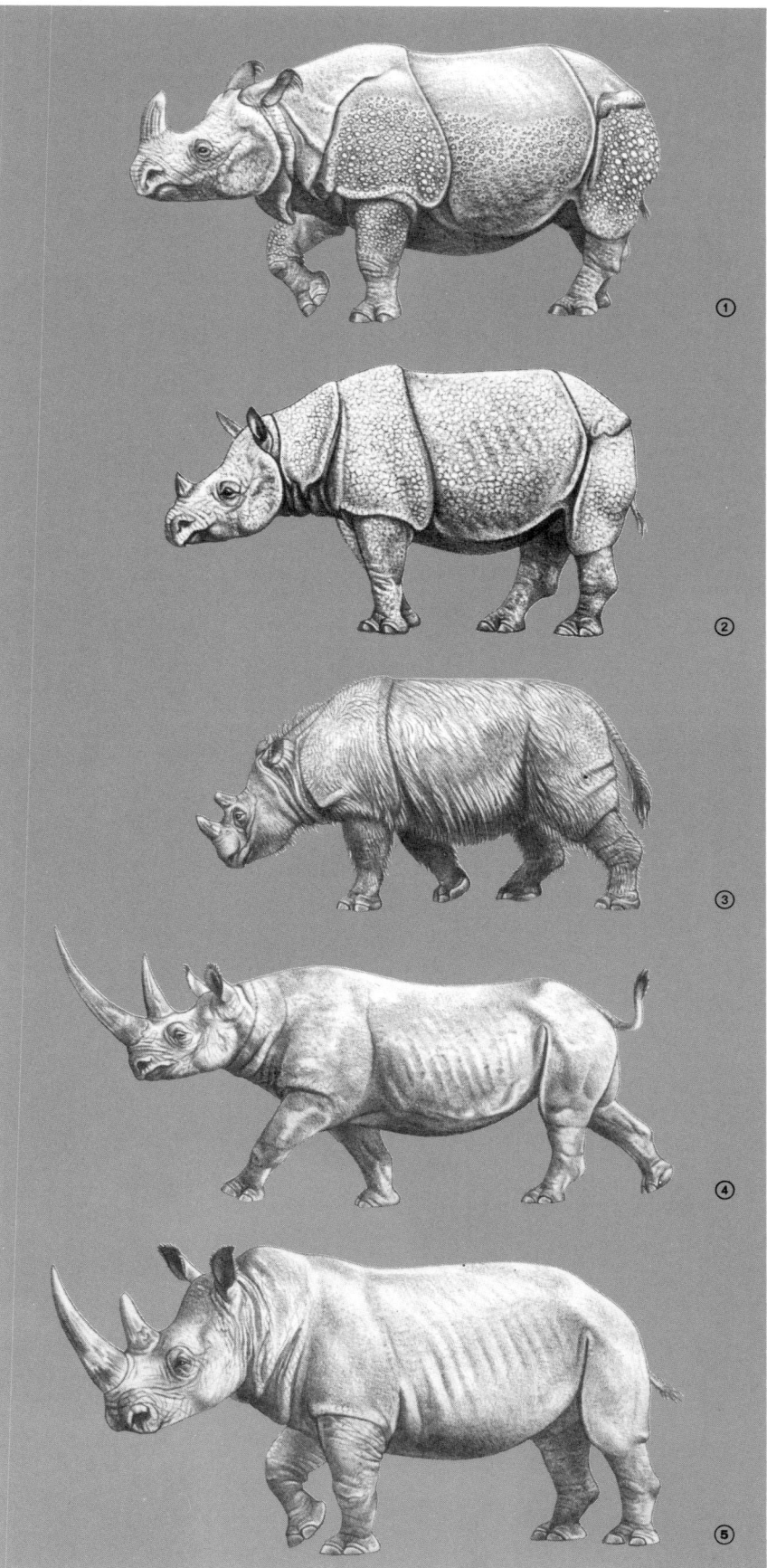

The Big Cats

One of the best-known nature writers and tiger hunters of India forecast not long ago that the tiger would be extinct before the end of the 1970s. His prognosis has not proved accurate—not yet anyway. But there is no doubt that the tiger is seriously threatened with extinction. There are only a few isolated specimens still roaming free through the great forests of India—excluding those in Gujarat, Punjab and Kashmir. Even in the so-called tiger reserves in the Corbett, Kanha and Kaziranga National Parks, the big striped cats have become so rare that they are seldom seen. In other Indian protected areas, encounters with tigers are hardly more frequent.

Over the last few years, the tiger's environment and its natural prey have been seriously affected by the spread of agriculture and cattle breeding. The tiger has often been compelled to seek sustenance by raiding domestic

1

Wild Sheep

The true wild sheep of the Ovis genus inhabit a wide area covering the highlands of Asia and North America. They constitute only a few species but as many as forty geographically separated sub-species.

1 The mouflon is the smallest but most distinctively marked wild sheep. The remnants of long resident mouflon populations still live in Corsica and Sardinia. The animal has recently been introduced into several European countries as an adaptable, huntable game species.

2 Urials comprise thirteen geographically isolated breeds of medium-sized wild sheep, spread out across the eastern Mediterranean, through Turkey, Afghanistan and Pakistan to northwest India.

3 The argali is the giant of the wild sheep. There are fifteen sub-specis in central Asia, from Karatau through Pamir, Tibet and Mongolia to southern Siberia.

4 The American snow sheep appears in three sub-species in Alaska, the Yukon, the Northwest Territories of Canada and northern British Columbia. The four breeds which live between Transbaikalia and Kamchatka are transitional forms between American and Asian species.

It is believed that wild sheep evolved from chamois-like animals at the beginning of the Ice Age. Fossils indicate that the evolution of this family of ruminants took place at a remarkably rapid pace.

The central Asian and European giant sheep of the *megalovis* genus, which were as large as buffalo, are known to have existed during the period when the climate gradually deteriorated. But the European wild sheep of the early and middle Ice Age were also much larger than the mouflons which were forced southwards and to North Africa by the steady expansion of the glaciers. True wild sheep became extinct some time later in North Africa and were superseded by the barbary sheep of the *ammotragus* genus which was related to the wild goat. In Europe, wild sheep have survived only in Corsica and Sardinia.

An undemanding mountain animal which favored cold climates, the wild sheep populated the entire habitable northern hemisphere during the Ice Age. In fact, it flourished at the time in an area larger than that ever before or after inhabited by any other species of ruminants. In Eurasia, however, wild sheep were obliged to share their environments with chamois, takin and wild goat. One consequence of this competition was the goat family, including the Tibeto-Himalayan blue sheep, taking possession of the steep, rugged mountain regions, while true wild sheep inhabited the foothills and high plateaus. This is also why, even today, all species related to the chamois and the ibex flee up into steep rocky regions when alarmed, while Asian wild sheep seek to escape into more level, undulating areas.

The evolution of the American mountain sheep, the American

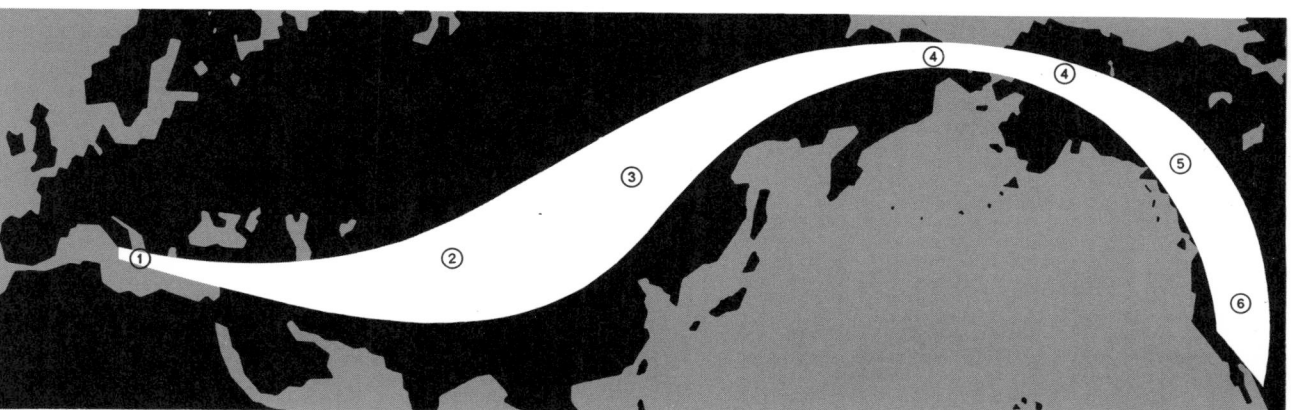

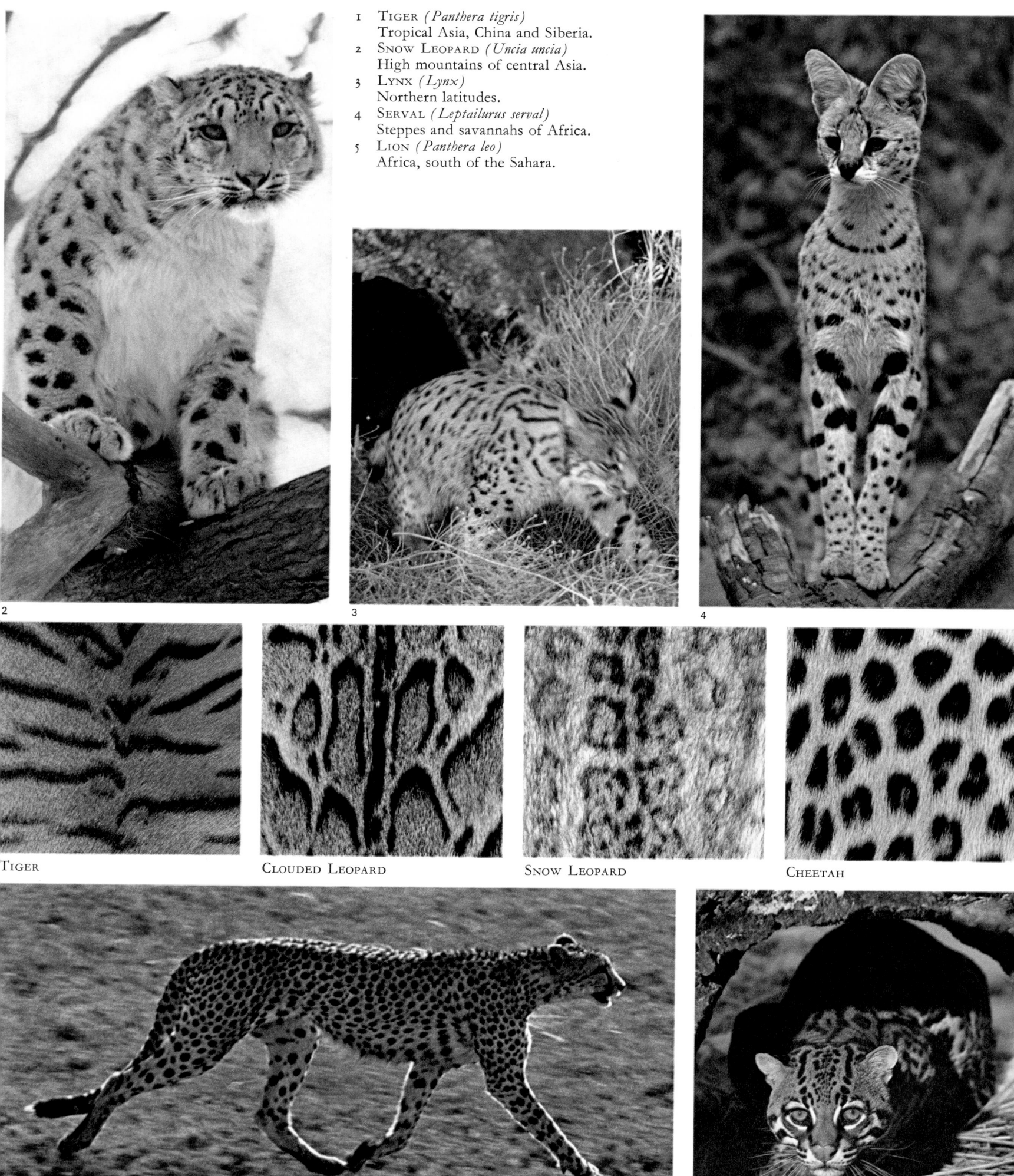

1 TIGER *(Panthera tigris)*
Tropical Asia, China and Siberia.
2 SNOW LEOPARD *(Uncia uncia)*
High mountains of central Asia.
3 LYNX *(Lynx)*
Northern latitudes.
4 SERVAL *(Leptailurus serval)*
Steppes and savannahs of Africa.
5 LION *(Panthera leo)*
Africa, south of the Sahara.

TIGER   CLOUDED LEOPARD   SNOW LEOPARD   CHEETAH

6 LEOPARD *(Panthera pardus)*
  Africa, South Asia.
7 CHEETAH *(Acinonyx jubatus)*
  Africa. Very occasionally in Asia.
8 OCELOT *(Leopardus pardalis)*
  South and Central America.
9 PUMA *(Puma concolor)*
  Western North America, Central and South
  America.
10 JAGUAR *(Panthera onca)*
  Central and South America.

5

6

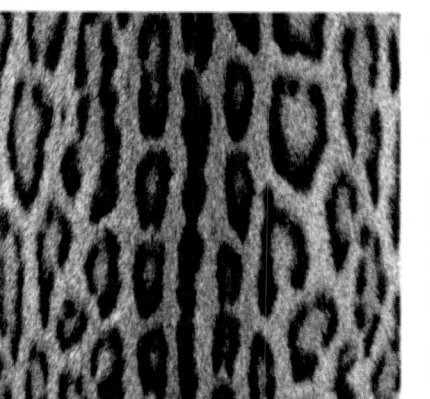

OCELOT

LEOPARD

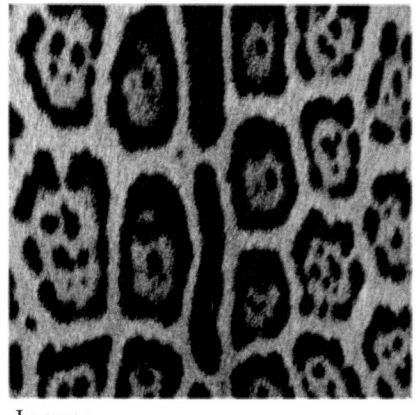

JAGUAR

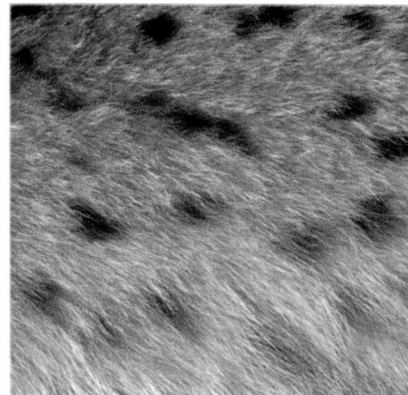

LYNX

9

10

animals, giving man an additional reason to hunt it. Until a few years ago, licenses to kill tigers were handed out to all and sundry and were ridiculously cheap to acquire. Before 1958, there was neither a limited hunting season nor any other legal limit on tiger shooting. Methods for hunting the animal were left entirely to the discretion of hunters. Usually, they lay in wait for them by one of the few water holes, or pursued the animals with cross-country vehicles, using their headlights at night. During the 1950s, tigers came under additional threat from shepherds and cowherds who put down chemicals to poison the animals. It is now believed, however, that only one out of every five tigers they eliminated in this way was a cattle thief.

The descriptions and tales told by hunters who "liberated" Indian villages from the threat of man-eating tigers were often repeated endlessly in distorted and exaggerated form. The result was often irresponsible and relentless hunting of the "man-eaters" by poachers and by foreign tourists who had been persuaded to take up the thrill of the chase by travel agencies both in India and in other parts of the world. Worse still, the tiger, while being hunted, was frequently surrounded by beaters or transported live to its bait, which had been tied up under the high shooting platform used by the visiting hunter. The tiger hunt was also inexpensive in India—at least it was far cheaper than an African lion hunt—and it had the additional attraction of possible financial gain. The tiger's skin still fetches a high price today—three times as much as it did in 1950. Although the Indian government has forbidden the export of tiger skins, they are still to be found in tourist stores and tax-free emporiums at airports. Only recently has the tiger been placed under complete government protection in India. Prime Minister Indira Gandhi herself ordered the protection of the remaining two thousand tigers, just as the maharajahs and British colonial rulers once secured the survival of the Indian lion. The tiger lives in the forests and reed thickets of large parts of Asia. Its habitat extends across much of Korea, China, Malaysia, Sumatra, Java, and India to Turkistan. In Siberia, it lives in the sub-arctic tundra.

The panther is a solitary hunter, like all felines except the lion. It mounts an attack on its quarry only when it is close enough for a reasonable chance of success. Both big cats, the tiger and the panther, are excellently camouflaged despite their conspicuous markings. The black stripes of the former and the dark rings on a light to reddish-yellow background of the latter make them almost invisible when they lie in tall grass or on the forest floor where bright stripes of light are interspersed with black shadows. This camouflage, as well as its powerful jaws and claws, makes the panther an extremely competent hunter. In Sri Lanka, it does not have to compete for its prey with tigers, which never reached the island, or with vultures or hyenas. Here wild boars are its worst enemy. After a panther has killed its quarry, wild boars often move in quickly and try to make off with its prey. The panther can manage to feed in peace only if it carries that prey— an axis deer, for example—up into the branches of a tree. Its favorite delicacies are heart, lungs and cartilage. It often does not consume the rest of the animal for a day or two. The carrion-eating wild boar is so persistent a competitor that the panther is obliged to kill almost twice as much as it actually needs for its own sustenance.

In the rain forests and mountainous regions of southeast Asia live two leopard-like cats, the clouded leopard and the snow leopard. Their mysterious ways of life in isolated areas have only recently been examined. The basic color of the clouded leopard is ash-gray to yellowish-gray, which appears on its shoulders, flanks and pelvis as a pattern in which dark, almost angular forms dominate. The clouded leopard, whose anatomical characteristics and behavior form a bridge between the small cats and the big cats, is a highly specialized tree climber. It is somewhat awkward on the ground because of its comparatively short legs. It hunts monkeys and other small mammals and birds in the branches of trees.

Like the clouded leopard, the snow leopard also is a link between big and small cats, as well as a distinctive species in its own right. It has long, light-colored hair with yellow tones over its thick undercoat. Dark brown patches mark its head and limbs and there are black rings on its body. Its quarry includes such animals of high mountainous regions as wild sheep, goats, deer and pheasants.

Two of the most widespread species of wild cat are the Bengal or leopard cat and the jungle cat. The jungle cat is long-legged and has a short tail. Its color varies between yellow-gray and red-brown, according to sub-species. Its ears, like those of the lynx, are tufted and it is, therefore, sometimes known as the "marsh lynx." It is seldom heavier than thirty pounds and lives primarily in marshy areas, lightly wooded territory and by lagoons. The "marsh lynx" feeds mainly on water birds, frogs, fish and crabs, which it skillfully removes from their shells by beating at them with its paws.

The leopard cat is about as big as a wild cat. Its color and markings are largely similar to those of the leopard. It is a voracious hunter and feeds on small mammals, birds and reptiles, and sometimes even on musk deer and muntjaks.

ow sheep, the bighorn and the
esert sheep took somewhat differ-
it lines. These species did not
oss the Bering isthmus to pene-
ate North America from Asia
itil the later Ice Age. With the
ception of the native Rocky
ountain goat, they met with no
ompetition for survival. The
merican mountain sheep devel-
ed into a robust, short-legged and
oad-breasted, goatlike animal,
apted to prevailing conditions.
ke the Eurasian ibex, the Cau-
sian thur, the wild goat, the blue
eep and species related to the
amois, the mountain sheep is a
illed climber in rocky terrain. It
also well adapted to wooded
untry. This is particularly true
bighorn sheep which live in the
ocky Mountains. As far as its
mands on space are concerned,
is far more adaptable than the
ologically and anatomically more

specialized Asian descendants of
its ancestors. They, however, have
a higher reproduction ratio, possibly as a result of environmental
pressure.

The wild sheep of Eurasia can
be divided into three clearly defined
evolutionary groups: the 65- to
90-pound mouflon in Europe;
the urial of the Near East which
can weigh twice as much; and
the huge argali wild sheep of
central Asia which can weigh up
to 450 pounds. Despite considerable differences in size, all three
groups possess the same basic
characteristics. They all belong to
the *Ovis ammon* family, whereas
the American wild sheep is divided
into a number of different species.
All wild sheep are adaptable to
varying climatic conditions, although they tend to avoid damp
climates and areas with heavy
winter snowfalls. They prefer dry-

ish regions and favor tough, dry
fodder.

Wild sheep live in sexually
segregated herds, strictly ordered
hierarchically, which meet only at
rutting time. The female herds,
which include the young, imma-
ture rams, are led by older,
experienced ewes. In the male herd,
the strongest rams are dominant.
Homosexual relations within the
herd are not uncommon, with
leading rams treating younger ones
as females.

All wild sheep are extremely
territory-conscious. Removal and
reintroduction of populations are
generally accompanied by great
difficulties. The animals live about
fifteen years, although wild sheep
kept in reserves sometimes live to
the age of twenty. Their natural
enemies are wolves, though lambs
may sometimes be seized by
eagles. Their senses are highly

developed, particularly their
eyesight. A wild sheep can spot a
potential enemy half a mile away.
Their extreme shyness and caution
makes them both a challenge and
an interesting quarry for the hunter.

Present-day domesticated sheep
are believed to be mostly descendants of wild mouflon and urial.
Sheep were first domesticated
around 5000 B. C. and evolved
subsequently in different ways,
according to natural environments
and use.

Horned Animals of Asia

In contrast to Africa, Asia boasts only a small population of antelopes and gazelles. Among them, however, are some species which have adapted to extreme environmental conditions. The Tibetan antelope, which lives at altitudes of up to 16,500 feet, can warm the air it breathes in a bladder-like "wind breaker." The muzzle of the saiga antelope has developed into a kind of trunk which filte[rs] dust from the air.

Most species of Asian antelopes and gazell[es] inhabit wide open territories which a[re] subject to sharp climatic change. The anima[ls] live mainly as nomads in big herds whic[h] often cover large distances in search of fodd[er] and water. Antelopes and gazelles are entire[ly]

Four-horned Antelope (*Tetracerus quadricornis*)
The four-horned antelope, or "chowsingha" as it is known in India, lives in family groups in the forests of the Indian subcontinent. It stands about two feet high. Its most striking characteristic is the four horns of the ram. The smaller forehorns are at most an inch and a half long; the rear horns generally measure from three to four inches long, but can reach a length of seven inches. The four-horned antelope usually lives near water. Its gestation period is eight weeks.

Blackbuck Antelope (*Antilope cervicapra*)
Bucks of this fine species of antelope can weigh up to eighty pounds and can stand up to thirty-two inches high. Their spiral horns can be as long as twenty-four inches. The fauns and hornless females are colored light brown on the back, neck, head and outside of the legs. The buck's coat darkens when it is about three years old and finally becomes black—whence the name "blackbuck." The animal once lived in huge herds on almost all open savannahs in India and West Pakistan. Today, however, its habitat is considerably more restricted.

Nilgai (*Boselaphus tragocamelus*)
The bull of this deer-sized antelope is dark blue-gray; the cow an earthy brown. The bull boasts a short, dark-colored mane and a tuft of dark hair on the underside of its neck. Its horns are modest single spike[s]. The nilgai lives in small groups in wooded areas of the Indian subcontinent. By virtue of its similarity to India's sacred cows, it is seldom hunted. Extremely territory-conscious, the nilgai always leaves its droppings in the same spot.

Saiga Antelope (*Saiga tatarica*)
During the past hundred years, the saiga antelope was almost exterminated. But, excellently adapted to the cold steppes of Asia, its populations have now increased again, notably on the Kalmuck steppe and in western Mongolia, although over one hundred thousand animals are still shot each year. The saiga is about thirty inches tall and weighs at most eighty pounds. Its comparatively large head has a clumsy appearance. Its inflatable nose is larger with bucks than with does. In summer, its coat is short and smooth; in winter, it is long, thick and woolly.

Mountain Gazelle (*Gazella gazella*)
Although sometimes also known as the "ravine deer," this animal is unquestionably a true gazelle, about the size of the roe. It lives in India and prefers dry forests, bushy savannahs and, above all, gorges offering plenty of cover. The upper half of its body is nut-brown; the underside and lower part of its flanks are white. The horns of the buck are slightly S-shaped when seen in profile; the horns of the doe are smaller or non-existent.

Tibetan Antelope (*Pantholops hodgsoni*)
Little is known about the habits of this animal. It stands about the size of a fallow deer. Its thick, woolly coat and its ability to warm the air it breathes into its lungs make it possible for it to exist in extremely cold climates. During the rutting season, which takes place in the coldest time of the year, the bucks fight duels with their two-foot-long, forward-curving horns for dominance over the female herd. For the duration of the rutting season, the buck lives main[ly] on the body fat it has accumulated in the autumn.

sent from the dense rain forests of Asia in which, however, live various species of deer, including the mouse deer, muntjak, sambar and ka. Open, dry, deciduous forests are inhabited by two rare species: the four-horned ntelope, slightly smaller than the roe and the nly animal to bear four horns; and the nilgai ntelope.

The ram of the wild sheep which roam the steppes or mountains of Asia is conspicuous for its huge, more or less snail-shaped, spirally twisted horns. Marco Polo probably discovered the most striking form in the thirteenth century—the pamir sheep, a light to dark gray animal about the size of a red deer, with truly impressive horns which can be as much

as seventy-five inches long, with base circumferences of sixteen inches.

The bezoar goat, markhor, thur and ibex are all wild goats which, according to geographic location, vary considerably in the shape and size of their horns.

SEROW (*Capricornis sumatraensis*)
The serow inhabits mountain forests all over southern Asia up to the Himalayas—with the exception of the Indian subcontinent. By virtue of its high degree of adaptability to humidity, it is also found in equatorial regions as far as Java. The buck reaches a shoulder height of forty-one inches and weighs up to 80 pounds. Its ears are long; its horns curve slightly backwards. Its coat is rough and one of the fourteen sub-species has a very thick coat, with a thick wool underlayer. Northernmost breeds sport white manes. The gestation period lasts seven to eight months.

GORAL (*Nemorhaedus goral*)
Although the goral often inhabits the same geographical regions as the serow, it favors lower dry valleys and steep eroded gorges between 1500 and 6000 feet high. Steep cliffs and naked rock faces are among its favorite landscapes. There are seven sub-species of the goral. They are found from Kashmir to Tibet and all over China as far as the Amur River. The goral weighs up to seventy pounds. Its horns, between eight and ten inches long, curve slightly backwards.

MARKHOR (*Capra falconeri*)
The markhor is one of the largest species of wild goat. The bucks grow to a height of three feet and may weigh over 200 pounds. Its giant horns, measured along the spirals, measure up to sixty-four inches. The horns of the doe are much shorter. The buck has a mane and hair hanging from its neck, breast and legs. The markhor is found from Turkestan to Afghanistan and in the western Himalayas. All breeds favor steep, isolated, rocky terrain.

TAKIN (*Budorcas taxicolor*)
It is possible that the "golden fleece" which Jason brought to Greece from Colchis came from a takin. The animal, which is still surrounded by an aura of mystery, is found in three sub-species between western China and the eastern Himalayas. This animal, with its primeval appearance, is about fifty-two inches high and weighs about 900 pounds. It lives in deep, densely wooded mountains at an altitude of 9000 to 13,500 feet. Old bulls lead solitary existences but cows and calves live in large nomadic herds.

TAHR (*Hemitragus jemlahicus*)
The tahr is related to the goat and appears in four sub-species. It lives in three separate regions in Asia: the Himalayas, the Nilgiri hills in southern India, and the Oman mountains in eastern Arabia. Both males and females bear horns. Those of the buck are considerably longer and stronger than those of the ewes. The horns are comparatively close together at the base and are characterized by a sharply wedged front surface. The tahr of the Himalayas has a conspicuous mane. The Arabian tahr has bearded cheeks and hair on its breast and legs.

BEZOAR GOAT (*Capra aegagrus*)
The bezoar goat is the original form of the present-day domestic goat. Formerly an inhabitant of the mountains of Asia Minor and the Greek islands, its numbers outside Iran have been sharply reduced. This wild goat, with its saber-shaped horns, was hunted primarily for its so-called bezoars, densely felted balls of hair which lodged undigested in its stomach. Superstition endowed these bezoars with miraculous healing powers. The bezoar goat climbs to a height of 12,000 feet on Mount Ararat.

Asian Wild Cattle

1 Light-brown banteng cows and their calves form medium-sized herds which are led by bulls.

2 The gaur, the largest species of wild cattle in Asi often lives in mountain forests which it leaves at evening to graze in glades. It feeds primarily on bambo leaves which it grasps with its long tongue.

3 Few people not native to its habitat can claim ever to have seen a wild kouprey. There are very few specimens in zoos. It is not certain whether this

1

2

3

The arni buffalo, one of the Asian buffalo species of *Bubalus,* is superbly adapted to its life in marshy terrain. Its broad hooves and protruding dew-claws ensure that its heavy body—it weighs up to 2000 pounds—does not sink. This characteristic led to its early domestication. It is one of mankind's oldest domestic animals, the water buffalo, bred and used to plow flooded rice fields as far back as prehistoric times in India and probably in Mesopotamia as well. In recent times, the domestic water buffalo has spread to warm countries all over the world, from Australia to the Mediterranean and America. At the same time, however, the old habitats of the original, undomesticated breeds, in Assam and Burma, have dwindled.

The closest relative of the six-foot arni is the four-foot anoa, which lives on the island of Celebes and in the Philippines. The smallest and most primeval of all existing wild cattle, the anoa is a secretive inhabitant of the jungle and is gradually becoming extinct. The gaur, however, still lives in sizable herds in many forested areas of India. Each of these is generally led by a black bull whose hump-like withers emphasize its powerful appearance. The banteng differs from the gaur in that it has no similar "hump." It is smaller and has a striking white spot on its posterior. The banteng is found from Burma and the Malayan peninsula to Borneo and Java.

The wild yak is one of the world's rarest animals, widely known by name though few people outside its habitat can claim ever to have seen one. This primitive aurochs-like wild ox, a resident of Tibet, has long, black, shaggy hair. The domesticated yak is smaller and differently colored and is widespread in central Asia, where it is used as a source of meat and milk and as a beast of burden.

Not until 1936 did zoologists stumble across the existence of the kouprey, another species of wild cattle, which lives in Cambodia. The horns of the kouprey are particularly unusual, curving backwards and outwards at the base, then upwards and forwards, and finally inwards at the tips. Even more remarkable is the wreath-like rosette formed by long horn fibers below the horn tips. Its bodily structure is also very different from that of its relatives—it is finely built, with a gray coat

...an-height wild ox is a species in its own right or ...cross between the gaur or banteng and the zebu.

The arni bull, which weighs about a ton and boasts ...rmidable horns, defends its territory against all ...truders. This predecessor of the domestic water ...ffalo was once present in great numbers all over ...dia; but comparatively few remain.

...nd a long tail with a tassel reaching almost ...o the ground. Both sexes have strongly ...eveloped dewlaps. It is not known for ...rtain whether the kouprey is a true species ...n its own right or merely a cross between the ...aur and domestic cattle. It is doubtful, ...owever, whether many researchers will soon ...ave the opportunity to observe this six-foot-...ll animal in its natural habitat because of ...nsettled political conditions in southeast ...sia.

4

Animals of North America

WOLVERINE
Gulo gulo

Large marten with an almost bear-like appearance. Found in arctic and subarctic regions all over the northern hemisphere. This "Indian devil" is a restless wanderer which claims dominance over exceptionally large territory which it fiercely defends against all rivals. Omnivorous, preferring carrion. Strong body and jaws; can kill large deer.

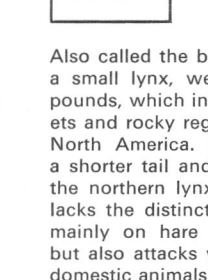

BOBCAT
Lynx rufus

Also called the bay lynx, the bobcat is a small lynx, weighing about twenty pounds, which inhabits swamps, thickets and rocky regions in many parts of North America. It has smaller paws, a shorter tail and a smaller body than the northern lynx, and almost entirely lacks the distinctive ear tufts. It feeds mainly on hare and cottontail rabbit but also attacks young deer and small domestic animals.

MULE DEER
Odocoileus hemionus

Confined to the North American West. Supersedes the white-tailed deer at high altitudes and in Pacific coastal areas. A sub-species, the black-tailed deer, can be found on the Pacific coast as far north as southern Alaska. The mule deer prefers dry, open territory and is therefore more severely threatened with extinction than the white-tailed deer. Its antlers are characterized by forking of the tines.

COLLARED PECCARY
Tayassu angulatus

Of the two species of peccary, only the collared peccary has penetrated from South America into the southwest of the USA. It lives in groups of up to thirty animals and, despite its small size (less than two feet high), it can be very dangerous. Will attack hunters even on horseback when threatened. Omnivorous, it feeds on roots, fruit, cacti and rattlesnakes. Marks its path with back-gland secretions.

WOLF
Canis lupus

Possibly an ancestor of the domestic dog. Found in all northern regions. Lives in herds with definite hierarchical orders. Chief regulator of caribou populations. Unlike smaller coyotes, the timber wolf has become extremely rare. Many color variations, from jet-black to snow-white (in arctic regions). Average dimensions: three feet high, four feet long, 100 pounds, but can be bigger.

AMERICAN RACCOON
Procyon lotor

A pointed face, hand-like forepaws and black rings on its bushy tail mark this creature, found from southern Canada to South America. Omnivorous, it often causes much damage to corn crops, melons, sweet potatoes and other farm produce, making it a ready target for farmers and hunters alike. But its high reproductive rate and nocturnal way of life appear to have assured its survival.

BEAVER
Castor fiber

A rodent which lives by fresh water. Weighs about thirty pounds (though prehistoric antecedents may have been much larger) and has a flat, ladle-like tail. Builds dams of mud and twigs. Occurs in several sub-species from Alaska to the Rio Grande. Almost extinct in the USA in latter part of nineteenth century but conservation measures in USA and Canada have since permitted numbers to increase.

COTTONTAIL RABBIT
Sylvilagus

Found all over the USA and southern Canada in various sub-species. Does not burrow; expert at surface concealment. Large ears, fluffy tail and short legs. Other American hare-like species include the white-tailed jack rabbit, the snowshoe hare, the piping hare and the pygmy rabbit.

GRAY FOX
Urocyon

Though similar in appearance to the fox, the gray fox is a separate species of wild dog. A nocturnal hunter, it flees up into trees when threatened and is thus also known as the "tree fox." It feeds on fruit, eggs and insects as well as on small mammals and poultry. Found from Venezuela to southern Canada. The red fox, the kit fox and the arctic fox are also native to North America.

TURKEY
Meleagris gallopavo

Once abundant in all wooded areas of eastern and southern USA, the turkey was later threatened with extinction because of over-hunting. Recently reintroduced in many regions and placed under protection. The wild turkey is the largest and heaviest of North America's fowl-like birds. Shy, it prefers areas with plenty of cover and sleeps on tree branches.

BISON
Bison bison

North America's most powerful hoofed animal, millions of which once lived on the prairies. Wanton killing by white settlers almost wiped out the breed by the turn of the twentieth century. Lives today in protected areas in the USA and Canada. About 20,000 buffalos have managed, thereby, to survive. Once the primary game of American Indians of the Great Plains. May be closely approached without danger.

MOOSE
Alces americana

This large deer is widespread through northern USA, including Alaska, and most of Canada. Favors marshy forest territory with plenty of cover. Will flee if approached too closely. Excellent swimmer. Due to its high reproduction rate, the moose still exists in large populations and is a notable source of food for peoples of the regions it inhabits. The Alaska moose can weigh up to a ton.

WHITE-TAILED OR VIRGINIA DEER
Odocoileus virginianus

The most common hoofed animal in North America. Found also in South America in the Andes and Amazon districts. Like the roe, to which it is related, the white-tailed deer is a territory-conscious follower of human habitation, capable, because of its high degree of adaptability, of surviving even near large towns so long as sufficient cover is available. Its acute senses make it difficult to hunt.

ELK OR WAPITI
Cervus canadensis

Species of large deer formerly abundant over all of North America. Closely related to European red deer. Shy fugitive from civilization. It has acute senses and a whistling rutting cry. Already extinct in eastern parts of the USA and Canada, it is found today almost exclusively in the Rocky Mountains. Has very powerful antlers; five or more points on each branch and an antler spread of up to five feet.

CARIBOU
Rangifer tarandus

Of the deer which inhabit the arctic and subarctic zones, this is the most abundant. Its origins can be traced back to the Ice Age. Both sexes grow antlers; the male's are larger than the female's. Curious by nature, the caribou may be approached closely. It migrates from treeless tundra to more southerly wooded areas in the autumn and returns to its summer haunts in the spring.

GRIZZLY BEAR
Ursus arctos horribilis

Ferocious North American bear; brownish, greyish or yellowish in color. Once widespread in western North America from the Arctic to central Mexico, but hunted almost to extinction. Now largely confined to national parks, with only huntable grizzlies in northern Canada and Alaska. Derives its name from its "grizzled" fur. Up to seven feet long and weighs up to 750 pounds. Preys on large mammals.

PUMA
Puma concolor

America's most abundant "big cat," the puma is found from Patagonia to the borders of subarctic forests. It has, however, become rare in the USA and Canada where it is mainly confined to the Rocky Mountains. The chief regulator of hoofed game, from the South American pudu to the mighty elk. In North America, it lives mainly on white-tailed deer.

PRONGHORN
Antilocapra americana

The oldest species of hoofed game in America; not seen anywhere else. The horny sheath of its horns, which is shed annually, is forked. North America's speediest hoofed animal, the pronghorn existed by the millions in the West before white men settled there. Threatened with extinction at the turn of this century, it now lives in huntable populations under strict protection.

BIGHORN SHEEP
Ovis canadensis

The most abundant representative of wild sheep in America; found in the high mountains of both North America and Eurasia. Threatened in its wild state, it exists only in isolated groups. Larger herds in national parks in the USA and Canada. A shy species of mountain game, it lives in herds segregated by sex, except during the rutting season in late autumn. The ram is much larger than the female.

ROCKY MOUNTAIN GOAT
Oreamnos americanus

The only example of a chamois-like species in the Americas. Found in the Rocky Mountains from Montana to southern Alaska. Large numbers in the national parks of Banff, Jasper and Montana. Extremely hardy game which usually remains at high altitudes the winter through. Relatively fearless, intelligent animal; capable of skillful maneuvering in steep, tricky terrain.

The Study of Wildlife in North America

Professor Aldo Leopold, who gave the very first lecture on wildlife biology in North America, at the University of Wisconsin, opened a new world with his comprehensive study, *Game Management*. The most striking innovation of this remarkable work was to explore the wide field embraced by the concept of game management as based on ecological principles, in contrast to purely empirical considerations related to game and hunting.

Many North American universities now offer courses of study in wildlife biology, ranging from individual lectures to specialist curricula leading to degrees in the subject. The influx of students interested in the field has been enormous, amounting to several thousand, far exceeding most expectations. This interest continues to be expressed, although the number of available jobs related to the subject is still very limited. The contrast inevitably raises questions about why students pursue the subject when their chances of moving on from their studies to a career in wildlife biology are so meager. A number of educators have suggested that the reason might be found in what the subject has to offer, other than job prospects. They point out that the wildlife biology study program deals more intimately and extensively with a general ecological education than most available alternatives. The problem-oriented manner of presentation, which enables students to relate their studies to human society and thus to extract added significance from them, is said to increase their interest in the subject. It has been noted that many students have been shifting from such traditional related studies as zoology and botany, seeking to study instead "real live animals," their behavior and social structure.

Aside from college study, comprehensive

research programs have been organized by government authorities in addition to their normal administrative duties. Almost all states in the USA, and the Canadian provinces, have active, efficient institutes of one kind or another in which wildlife biologists work with regular technical staffs.

Wildlife biology research has concentrated in recent years on huntable animals, species and populations threatened with extinction, and animals which cause economic damage. Game research also makes a considerable contribution to our knowledge of insecticides and their effect on the various ecological systems of the world. Many kinds of game are sensitive indicators of dangerous or potentially dangerous developments in the interaction between the countryside and the technological world. For example, wildlife biologists were well aware that DDT resulted in the infertility of the eggs of the brown pelican long before the menace inherent in indiscriminate use of the chemical was widely known.

For examination of the habits of migratory birds, the research capacities and the size of the countries participating in the program are factors. In Europe, water fowl from the Soviet Union or the Scandinavian countries traverse many central European countries on their migratory flights to Africa, flying over regions with widely diverse hunting laws. But similar birds from Canada only fly over the USA on their way to winter quarters in Mexico. It is thus not surprising that a migratory bird treaty between Canada, the USA and Mexico has been in effect for some time now, while such treaties have been more difficult to arrange where many countries are involved. The main migratory routes of North America have now been sufficiently investigated and steps have been taken to ensure constant adjustment of hunting laws to suit the stamina and strength of each migrating species.

North American regional characteristics extend from the arctic tundra to the subtropical climate of Florida, the deserts of Nevada and Mexico and the soaring peaks of its mountain spines. A wide variety of animals —from the musk oxen, seen below in their distinctive defensive posture, to the alligators of the Florida marshes—are influenced by the activities of man. Ecological research is required to save many of them from extinction. The technical standard of North American wildlife biology and game management is superb. Many procedures developed in the USA and Canada—including locating animals by radio waves (already tried with the use of satellites) and counting game from the air with film sensitive to heat—are now being adopted by other countries. Links between American and Canadian wildlife conservation organizations, and similar organizations in other countries ensure the dissemination of a rapidly growing body of knowledge in these fields. Meetings of experts from around the world take place periodically and new efforts are being made to forge even closer links between wildlife biologists.

Below: Musk oxen in defensive posture.

Following double page: Caribou on the move.

The Big Bears of North America

The Kodiak or Alaskan bear is the large dry-land predator in the world. Its massiv body is almost nine feet long and it can weig over 1700 pounds. The cubs are born durin a winter interval when the animal withdraw to a secure retreat. These new-born cubs ar astonishingly small compared to their im mense parents. At birth they weigh only on pound and are hardly larger than guine pigs. The Kodiak bear feeds chiefly on grass

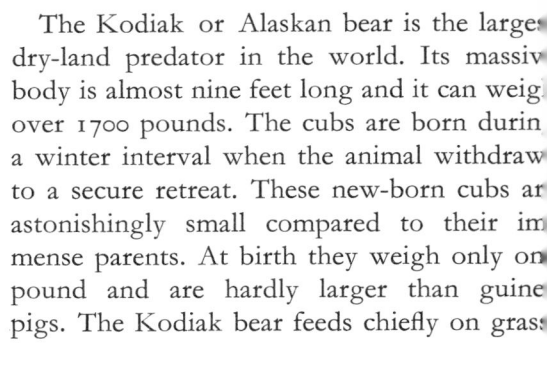

Right: The largest sub-species of brown bear is called the Kodiak after Kodiak Island.

A silver-tip grizzly, a relative of the true grizzly, has silver-colored ends to its long, dark hair.

The grizzly's coat varies in color from yellowish-gray to black and brown. Like all northern big bears, it spends the winter in caves in hibernation, during which its pulse and breathing remain normal. It can be awakened by serious climatic changes.

Unlike the grizzly, with its shaggy coat, the black bear has silky, shiny fur.

rries and roots. In the spring, when salmon ngregate in large numbers just offshore fore migrating upriver to spawning grounds, e Kodiak bear demonstrates its great skill as fisherman. Some even follow the salmon ong the coast and swoop them up out of allow waters. But fishing in rivers and aterfalls tends to be more productive. The ear wades into the water and simply seizes its ey with its paws.

The grizzly, another sub-species of the American brown bear, is rarely encountered by humans outside zoos because its breed has been unable to survive in regions anywhere near human habitation. However, enough is known of the animal for its reputation as a dangerous predator to be firmly established.

The black bear, or baribal, and its relatives the cinnamon and silver bears, have been rescued from extinction and live wild in many areas. The black bear is capable of adjusting to altered environments and survives without trouble in regions near human habitation. Visitors to American national parks are familiar with the antics of this friendly though sometimes dangerous animal.

The Wolf

There is probably nothing which more clearly dramatizes the desolation of the northern wilderness than the howl of the wolf. Even the mere sight of this graceful creature is, despite morbid legends, a thrilling experience. But comparatively few people can claim to have observed the wolf in the wild. It has been so systematically hunted that it has long been in danger of total extermination, and remains so when even airplanes and helicopters have been recruited to track wolves down and assist in their slaughter. There is, however, a glimmer of hope as recognition grows that this formidable wild dog plays an important role in maintaining the balance of nature.

To most people, raised on stories of how fierce and destructive the wolf is, the animal is still regarded as a bloodthirsty beast of no value whatsoever, a threat to any community it approaches, even capable of attacking its own kind. It is not unusual to describe someone who has been abandoned to disaster as having been "thrown to the wolves." But, in fact, few animals have such a well-ordered social system. Wolves live in marital pairs, in relationships which, it is believed, are maintained for life, and which are considerate and disciplined. They hunt singly or in packs of about thirty animals, led by the strongest and most experienced. They observe a strict hierarchy and the position of pack leaders is repeatedly confirmed through gestures of submission by the others. Facial expression and position of the tail are indicators of hierarchical attitude. Leaders carry their tails erect and their ears pricked. The others let their tails droop in normal position. A sign of deep submission, as is often the case with domesticated dogs, is the tail between the legs.

If a subordinate wolf presumes to challenge the leader, a fight is unavoidable. The animals rush at each other with bared teeth and hairs bristling. These confrontations rarely end, however, in fatality; as soon as the stronger wolf proves his supremacy, the weaker assumes an attitude of submission. It lies on its back and exposes the soft, vulnerable parts of its body. The victor is then usually content with a victory ceremony: it raises its tail, shows its teeth, circles round the defeated wolf and urinates on it. It is believed that an inner survival-of-the-species mechanism restrains the victor. Occasionally, however, this mechanism fails to function and, for all its groveling, the defeated wolf is killed.

Apart from communicating through body posture, the wolf is able to use its voice in a variety of ways. Neighboring packs communicate by "singing." While hunting, however, the pack remains silent. Constantly alert, it is capable of going immediately on the attack if it stumbles across prey, even at close quarters. But usually, its victims are approached cautiously, stalked, and pursued when they attempt to flee.

Far left: The wolf out hunting often covers up to forty miles a day.

Left: A wolf pack on Isle Royale in Lake Superior trying to corner a moose. This powerful animal can be dangerous to wolves and is, therefore, only actually attacked when in flight. If it shows no signs of weakness or defeat, the pack will not attack and will soon withdraw.

Generally, healthy adult animals are in no danger from wolves. Usually only young or senile, wounded or sick animals are attacked. Wolves seem to have an acute feeling for the slightest sign of weakness displayed by their potential victims. They quickly give up pursuit of a healthy animal. But a weakened creature will be relentlessly run to ground.

The wolf is thus a regulator of animals which share its terrain. When wolf populations in Alaska sharply decreased because of over-hunting in the 1950s, caribou herds expanded. But the proportion of sick and malformed caribou also increased. It was the wolf which had kept the health of their normal prey up to a high standard. They also ensured against over-population in their habitats and thus helped keep a balance between animal life and vegetation. In North America, campaigns to lay poison traps for wolves have been abandoned and there is a growing tendency to regard the wolf as a valuable animal whose extinction should be energetically avoided. This belief has been reinforced by recognition that random hunting can inflict damage to the wolf pack, whose strict hierarchical structure can easily be upset and in which each individual animal has a specific position and function. Rigorous hunting of wolves can only be justified in areas contaminated by rabies because rabid wolves are a serious danger to man and to many domesticated animals.

American Deer

The elk (or wapiti) appears in six sub-species in North America. The most southern variety is a very small animal, found only in the Sacramento and San Joaquin valleys of California, under strict protection. The northernmost elk, on the other hand, can weigh up to 1000 pounds. Its crownless antlers have ten to twelve prongs and can weigh as much as fifty-five pounds. These large deer were called elks by the first white settlers because their size was reminiscent of the European elk. The old Indian name, wapiti, is, however, increasingly used by zoologists. The animal once claimed the largest domain of all American deer, but its numbers sharply declined after the arrival of settlers.

The domain of the Virginian or white-tailed deer extends over the southern half of North America and the northern part of South America. It is the most widespread deer in the Americas today. The most distinctive feature of this medium-sized deer is its long tail, which it carries erect when in flight. It is very much tied to its territory, rarely leaving it unless compelled to. It lives in small groups which may join together into larger gatherings in severe winters. The animal is skillful at utilizing all kinds of protective cover. There are more white-tailed deer in America today than before the arrival of white men.

The mule deer is closely related to the smaller white-tail and lives mostly in higher altitudes and in arid desert territory. Unlike the white-tailed deer, which is often absolutely dependent on protective cover, the long-eared mule deer prefers more open country. A strong stag can weigh up to 450 pounds. The main axis of its usually ten-pointed antlers is marked by fork-shaped branching. Double forking can result in multi-pointed antlers with up to fifty points.

The black-tailed deer, related to the mule deer, is a sort of in-between breed though, because of its geographical isolation, it may soon be judged to be a species in its own right. It makes its home in rainy temperate regions of the Pacific coast, from California to Alaska. Its distinguishing characteristic is its long tail, colored black on top.

In some areas, where its natural enemies have been severely decimated or even exterminated, the mule deer has increased so greatly in numbers that its populations have reached dangerously large proportions. In the early 1920s, for example, about 100,000 mule deer lived in the protected zone of the Grand Canyon alone—one deer to every seven acres. In the hard winters of 1924 and 1925, three of every five of them died of starvation.

Left: The elk—a splendid twelve-pointer.

Above right: A white-tailed deer.

Below right: A mule deer in velvet.

Status Struggles of the Bighorn Sheep

Bighorns fight for position in their hierarchical order.
Top: an older ram is challenged by one of the herd.
The challenger rises on its hindlegs before clashing with its rival.
Bottom: A mature eight- to nine-year-old ram (right) approaches an older ram for a trial of strength.

animals, which tend to be more individualistic within the bounds of herd existence.

In late autumn the rams gather together in rutting areas. The ewes, which are not yet in season, are courted there, but fights do not take place. Even during the mating period serious fights between rams for the favors of ewes do not occur. But battles for position and respect are not uncommon. When ewes come into season, the ram with the most formidable horns ousts all rivals with threatening gestures. It is backed up by troops of younger rams which, however, do not get a chance to mate. They are obliged to work off their sexual energies on each other. Should the leading ram show signs of exhaustion, the young ram with the biggest horns takes over his role. the older leader returns, the younger animal withdraws without protest. Thus, it is usually only the rams with the most impressive horns which mate with the ewes.

The wild sheep which inhabit mountainous regions clear across the northern hemisphere have barely changed at all since the Ice Age. But only recently has there been some understanding of mating behavior and the struggles for hierarchical position among the bighorn sheep which live in the Rocky Mountains, and which are seriously threatened with extinction.

The bighorn lives in herds segregated by sex and age group almost the entire year. Development of the body and horns of the female ceases when the animal reaches full maturity, but the ram continues to develop for a further six to eight years. This accounts for its greater size—it is almost twice as big as the female—and its enormous horns, which can weigh up to forty pounds.

Mature and competitive, three- to four-year-old rams separate from the female herd and join up with others of the same sex. The strongest assume dominant masculine roles while the others act somewhat like females in rut. It is not unusual for the leading ram to court and attempt to mate with weaker male animals.

Unlike the deer family, whose herds are led by younger stags with undeveloped antlers (except during the mating season), the ram with the largest horns dominates the bighorn herd. The size of the horns determines the position of the ram in the hierarchy and the

submission it receives from other members of the herd. Rams with horns of approximately the same size and strength rarely fight for status. As a rule, all rams unquestioningly obey the leading animal. The degree of respect each offers increases in inverse proportion to its place in the hierarchical system. Young rams are much less independent and confident —in a certain sense, more feminine—than older

Arizona bighorn ram. This smaller, more delicate breed of American bighorn belongs to the desert sheep which live north of the Colorado River. It is also found in small groups in the provinces of Chihuahua and Sonora in northern Mexico.

The Pronghorn and the Rocky Mountain Goat

For a long time, zoologists were unable to decide whether the pronghorn was related to the antelope (it bears similar horns) or to the deer (which also periodically sheds the horny sheath of its horns).

The Rocky Mountain goat is related to the chamois. This snow-white mountain animal has changed little since primeval times in either appearance or behavior. The buck is often merciless in the use of its short horns when fighting a rival.

Deer and horn-bearing animals such as cattle, antelope and chamois are distinguished from each other partly through differences in their horns and antlers: deer bear multi-pointed antlers of bony matter which are cast off in cycles and replaced; the others bear a pair of single-pointed horns which continue to grow over the course of the animal's entire life, which are encased by a horny sheath, and which are not shed.

On the North American prairies, however, between the Missouri and the Rocky Mountains, there lives a species of cloven-hoofed animal about the size of a roe or fallow deer, the pronghorn, which belongs to neither the antler-bearing nor the horn-bearing group. Its forebears lived in America as long as 200,000,000 years ago, considerably earlier than such other even-toed ungulates as the moose, elk and bison. Pronghorn bucks, and occasionally the does as well, bear horns which, as is the case with true horn-bearers, consist of bony matter encased in horny sheaths. But this sheath is forked rather than single-pointed. In addition, it is cast off annually. A new horny substance forms under the old sheath before it is shed. It is covered with a velvet-like protective layer which hardens after about four months.

There has been much debate about whether the pronghorn and its ancestors should be regarded as deer or horned ungulates. They have finally been classified as a distinct family of hoofed animals. Pronghorns used to live by the millions on the American prairies but they later shared the fate of the bison when settlers conquered and tamed the continent, hunting them down in the process.

The animal is known, among other things, for its reaction to threatening smells. If it picks up any unusual or menacing scent— for example, that of a wolf or a coyote—it spreads the long, stiff hair on its posterior in the shape of a fan. This warning signal is recognized by other animals at great distances. Its effectiveness as an alarm is enhanced by the strong odor secreted by the animal's glands when the hairs are raised. This smell can be recognized even by man at a distance of several hundred yards. During the rutting season, bucks maintain small harems of three or four does. Does usually give birth to twins which, like roe fawns, spend most of their time alone during their first few weeks of life; the mother does no more than suckle and clean them.

The pronghorn is the swiftest animal on the North American continent. It has an astonishingly large heart which permits it to cover over a mile at a speed of fifty miles an hour.

Like the pronghorn, the Rocky Mountain goat is a primeval hoofed ungulate. Its four subspecies all live in the northern Rocky Mountains. These snow-white animals are not true goats, despite their name, but are related to the chamois. Their long coats are raised at the withers and croup by manes and their woolly undercoats are noticeably finer than cashmere wool. The cast-off wool was once gathered by Indians who spun and wove it into cloth.

The Rocky Mountain goat confines itself to its habitat, above the treeline, the whole year through. When descending a mountain, it is capable of astounding leaps. When ascending, however, its movements are so slow and cautious that even a man can keep up with it.

The bucks and does live in separate herds which join together during rutting season, when battles between bucks for the favors of certain does are not uncommon. During these fights, rivals position themselves side by side, but facing in different directions. They stand as tall as possible on stiff legs, with the hairs on their backs standing on end. Should this display fail to impress their opponents, they begin to circle slowly round each other, finally striking at each other with their horns. These fights often result in serious wounds and, more often than not, end in fatalities. In contrast, the bucks court the does with considerable restraint and the does are not reluctant to ward off undesired attentions with powerful butts to the ribs of their suitors.

North American Birds

1 FRANKLIN'S GROUSE—*Canachites franklini*
Small populations in Montana, Idaho, southern Oregon, Alberta, British Columbia and southern Alaska. Their curiosity often costs these birds their lives.

2 RING-NECKED PHEASANT—*Phasianus toquatus*
Introduced from China at the end of the last century. Adapted excellently to its new environment. The cock is multi-colored; the hen, earth-brown. Swift flight; little stamina.

3 ROCK PTARMIGAN—*Lagopus mutus*
Lives above the treeline in arctic regions around the world. Slightly larger than the partridge. Lives in pairs in summer; in coveys in winter.

4 CHUKAR—*Alectoris graeca chucar*
Mating call of the male—"chuk-ar, chuk-ar." Introduced from Asia. Olive-brown-green feathers; hazel-striped underside. When disturbed, runs uphill or flies downhill.

5 EASTERN BOB WHITE—*Colinus virginianus*
Its name derives from its soft call: "bob-bob-white." Common from southern Florida to Louisiana. Swift in flight. Lives in coveys during the winter.

Mountains and deserts, plains and forests, polar reaches and subtropical regions—North America's range of habitats can accomodate a wide variety of feathered creatures with a wide variety of behavioral characteristics: females of the spruce grouse—which inhabits the forests of Canada and northern USA—call upon the males of the species in mating time; turkeys lay up to sixteen eggs in a single clutch; the turkey vulture, clumsy on the ground, is graceful in flight.

The male sage grouse engages in elaborate displays, posturing and strutting at courting time, seeking to attract the female with its bold masculinity. The female must, however, not respond too energetically or it might be attacked by the highly nervous male.

Gambel's quail, of the American southwest, generally live in groups of about forty, but they split into pairs and establish exclusive territories for breeding.

No more than a hundred years ago, three types of prairie chicken lived in various parts of North America. But the last pair of the eastern sub-species *(Tympanuchus cupido cupido)* died in Martha's Vineyard in 1932 and the threatened *T. cupido attwateri* was only rescued by the creation of the Natural Landmark Reserve.

In Indiana alone, in 1850, over 20,000 heath chickens—the largest grouse and threatened with extinction—were brought onto the market. To replace them, several species were successfully introduced, including the ring-necked pheasant from Asia in South Dakota (present population almost 50,000,000), the chukar (80,000 shot in 1966) in California and Idaho, and the gray partridge or hun from Hungary.

1

3

4

2

5

WHITE-TAILED PTARMIGAN—
Lagopus leucurus
Alaska to New Mexico. Tail pure
white in winter; speckled brown in
summer. Lives chiefly on willow. Flees on
foot when frightened.

NORTHERN SHARP-TAILED
GROUSE—*Pediocetes phasianellus*
Lives in Alaska and from Hudson Bay
to New Mexico. The cock coos like
a pigeon during mating.

8 BLUE GROUSE OR DUSKY
GROUSE—*Dendragapus obscurus*
Loud, penetrating, rumbling sound during
energetic mating display. Behavior
similar to the Eurasian capercaillie.

9 SAGE GROUSE—*Centrocercus*
urophasianus
Lives on American west coast. Large
specimens weigh up to eight pounds.
Pheasant-like tail. Favors mugwort
plains.

10 HUDSONIAN SPRUCE GROUSE—
Canachites canadensis
Primarily resident in pine forests of
Canada and North America. Known as
the "fool hen" because of its lack of
caution.

11 GRAY PARTRIDGE—*Perdix*
perdix
Called "the hun." Introduced from Hun-
gary. Slightly larger than the bob white.
Easily recognizable by its reddish tail.

12 HEATH HEN—*Tympanuchus*
cupido pinnatus
Abundant in the Mississippi regions.
Remains of populations in Canada.

Overleaf: Canada geese ascending.

8

9

10

11

12

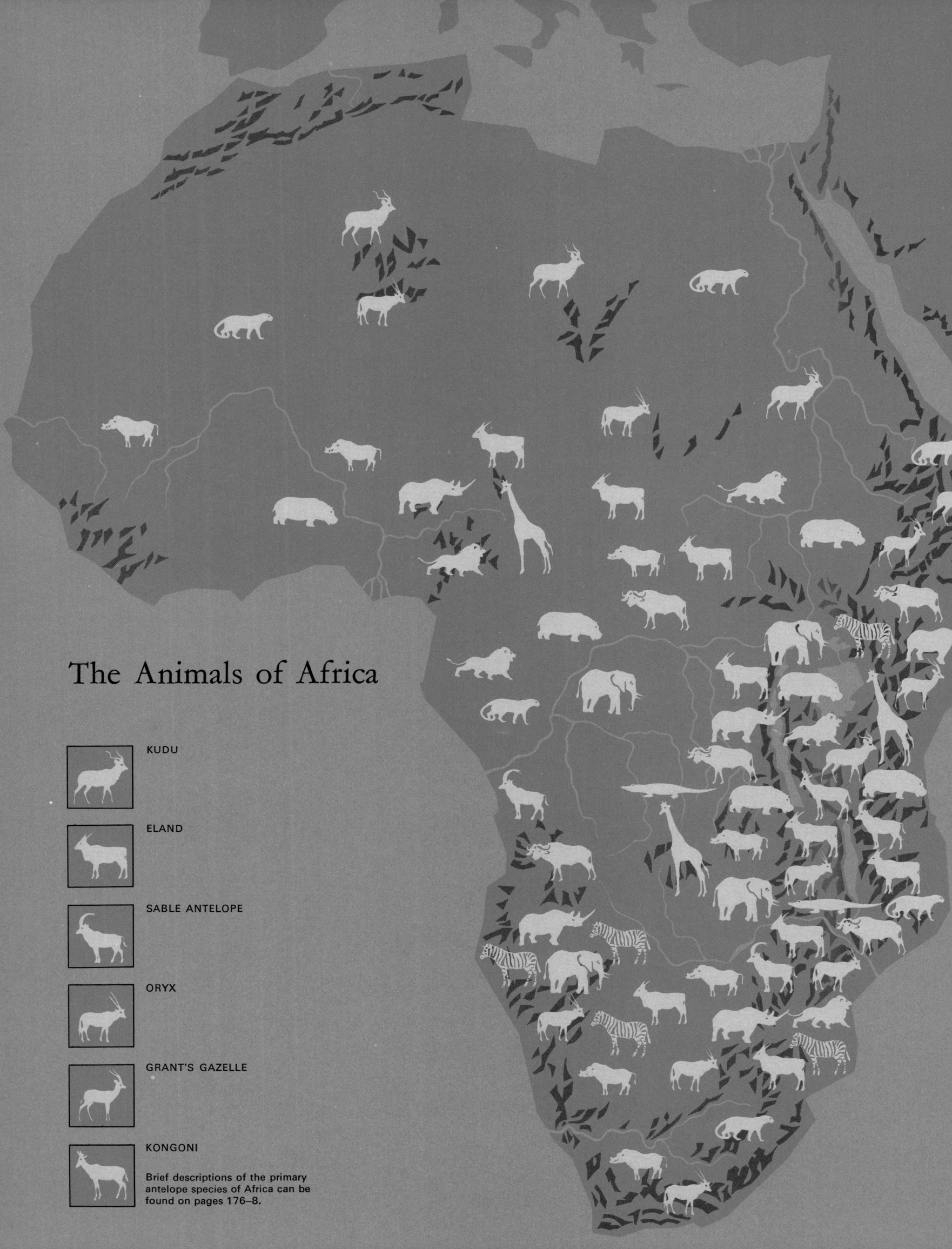

The Animals of Africa

KUDU

ELAND

SABLE ANTELOPE

ORYX

GRANT'S GAZELLE

KONGONI

Brief descriptions of the primary
antelope species of Africa can be
found on pages 176–8.

CHEETAH
Acinonyx jubatus

The cheetah, a long-legged big cat, is the fastest mammal on earth. It can attain speeds of more than sixty m.p.h., but only for brief spurts, so that it must calculate its attack on its prey. It hunts mostly gazelles and antelopes, which it seizes at full gallop. Avoids dense woods. The cheetah is the most common big cat in Africa; found even in South African farming districts. Almost extinct in India.

SERVAL
Leptailurus serval

Medium-sized, long-legged, spotted cat of the open savannahs and lightly wooded bush. Avoids dense jungles. Found from south of the Sahara to South Africa, but nowhere in great numbers. Nocturnal hunter. Prey consists mainly of rodents, fancolins and small antelopes. Despite its long legs, the serval is an excellent climber. Can be tamed like the domestic cat if captured young.

RATEL OR HONEY BADGER
Mellivora capensis

Found in tropical Africa and parts of India. Extremely aggressive. Has a symbiotic relationship with the honey-guide bird which leads it to bees' hives, where the ratel feeds on honey and grubs. Thick coat to protect it against stings. Has short legs and strong claws for climbing. Distantly related to the skunk; has anal scent gland.

BUSH PIG
Potamochoerus porcus

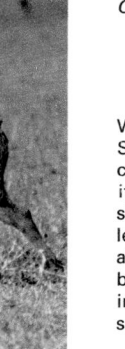

The nocturnal bush pig is found in most parts of sub-Saharan Africa. Similar to European wild boar in behavior. Lives in large herds. Where its primary enemy, the leopard, is not evident in any substantial numbers, the bush pig causes considerable damage to peanut plantations and other crops.

AARDVARK
Orycteropus afer

Of the two species of aardvark, one is found in central Africa, the other in the southern part of the continent. About six feet long, it has a long snout and a tongue about sixteen inches long. It claws open rock-hard termite mounds to suck out the insects, its primary food. The extensive, many-branched burrows it digs are much used as shelters by other animals as well.

SPOTTED HYENA
Crocuta crocuta

Found in all sub-Saharan regions which are rich in game. Contrary to commonly held opinion, it does not live exclusively on carrion, but hunts in packs by night, and often during the day as well. Its prey includes young and weak animals, notably antelope, gazelle and zebra. An important regulator of game populations. It is also known to have attacked children.

CARACAL LYNX
Caracal caracal

The caracal lynx, distributed all over the bush savannahs of Africa and southwest Asia, is a sleek animal with tufted ears. It hunts alone at night, its prey consisting of rodents, small antelope, guinea fowl and fancolins which it approaches stealthily and catches with a sudden leap. It can even bring down birds on the wing with its powerful high leaps.

AFRICAN HUNTING DOG
Lycaon pictus

African wild dogs are primitive but highly specialized animals. They hunt in large packs. They have acute senses and powerful jaws. Unlike that of the wolf and jackal, their social organization appears to be minimal. They often cause great damage to cattle and game populations. Found in East and southwest Africa as far as Chad.

BLACK-BACKED JACKAL
Canis mesomelas

Wolf-like wild dog found in sub-Saharan Africa. Together with the common jackal and the striped jackal, it occupies a position in African legend similar to that of the fox in western legend. Feeds mainly on carrion, but also kills young animals, rodents and birds and is not averse to fruit and insects. Lives and hunts in pairs or small packs.

AFRICAN CIVET
Viverra civetta

This relative of the cat family, though not a true cat, is found in most of sub-Saharan Africa. It secretes an oily strong-smelling substance from an anal gland when excited or in danger. This secretion was once used to make perfumes. In its wild state, the African civet is a nocturnal. It lives on small mammals, reptiles, amphibians and insects. In areas of human habitation, it is also notorious as a thief of poultry and eggs.

166

LION
Panthera leo

Once in great abundance all over Africa, today concentrated in regions with plenty of game, especially East Africa. Absent from jungle territory. The lion lives and hunts in groups, or prides. Its prey is generally antelopes, zebras and other herbivorous animals. The lioness does most of the hunting. Barbary and Cape Lions are now extinct. Once also inhabited parts of southern Europe.

LEOPARD
Panthera pardus

Extremely adaptable big cat. Hunts mainly at dusk and at night. Preys mostly on baboons, wild boar, gazelles and antelopes; also raids domestic cattle. It carries remains of victims up into trees to guard from parasitic jackals, hyenas and vultures. Black leopards are often called panthers.

ELEPHANT
Loxodonta africana

The African elephant, the largest extant dry-land animal, is monarch of its environment. Formerly resident all over Africa, it is now extinct north of the Sahara. Still abundant in many parts of East, West and southern Africa. In national parks, where it flourishes in great numbers, the elephant tends to disturb the ecological balance and has to be culled.

AFRICAN BUFFALO
Syncerus caffer

The largest of the African buffalo live in the savannahs of East Africa in herds of up to one hundred animals. Smaller red buffalo, which bear thick hairy coats, are more common in West African forests. Their numbers have increased following recent cattle plagues and culling is necessary in farming regions. Old bulls are often unpredictable in behavior.

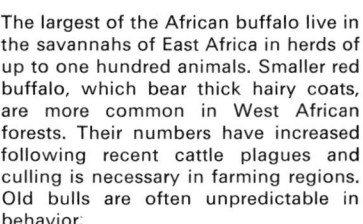

HIPPOPOTAMUS
Hippopotamus amphibius

Once found in many parts of Africa, the hippopotamus survives today only in areas uninhabited by humans and in national parks of tropical Africa. Related to the pig, it has its eyes close to the top of its head so that it can see when almost completely submerged. Spends much of its time in rivers or lakes. Feeds on water plants and, nocturnally, on shore vegetation. Few natural enemies other than humans.

BLACK RHINOCEROS
Diceros bicornis

Unlike the wide-mouthed rhinoceros, which has barely been saved from extinction, the black rhinoceros exists in substantial numbers, particularly in East Africa. Poor eyesight, but acute senses of smell and hearing. Irritable and easily aroused to attack. More feared than most animals by local inhabitants.

NILOTIC CROCODILE
Crocodylus niloticus

The nilotic crocodile is one of the largest of the armored lizards. Once abundant in rivers and lakes all over Africa, it is now found almost exclusively in southern and central regions of the continent. Lives mainly on fish and animal carrion, but sometimes attacks large mammals at watering places and is not averse to attacking man. The crocodile suns itself on the banks of river or lake, often with its mouth open.

GRÉVY'S ZEBRA
Equus grevyii

Grévy's zebra is found in the region between northern Kenya and Ethiopia. It is the largest equine animal living outside captivity. It differs from the more common steppe zebra and mountain zebra in its narrow stripes and large, fan-like ears. Like the mountain zebra, it lives in small groups led by a stallion. The southernmost sub-species, the quagga, died out a century ago.

WART HOG
Phacochoerus aethiopicus

The most common of the African species of wild boar. Found south of the Sahara in all regions except rain forests. Speedy runner. Very gregarious, except for old boars which prefer to live alone. Diurnal; mainly vegetarian. At night, often preempts lair of the aardvark. Name derived from warts on its cheeks between its eyes and its large, inward-curving tusks. Main enemy is the lion.

GIRAFFE
Giraffa camelopardis

The giraffes—together with the okapi, the last vestiges of a primeval family of even-toed ungulates—were once at home all over Africa. They are still abundant on the acacia savannahs and have no natural enemies, except the lion. Under strict protection. Females bear a single calf, which can be up to six feet tall at birth.

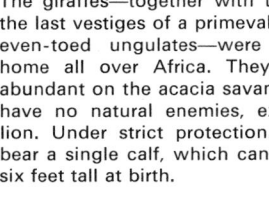

Africa's Animal Kingdom

This image of zebras and gnus on an East African plain studded with acacia trees is a symbol of much of the African continent. It shows one of the large animal communities which are common in many parts of tropical Africa's sprawling terrain. They are veritable paradises for observing and hunting wild game.

With regard to fauna, the area north of the Sahara belongs to the Eurasian zone—the Paleoarctic. Not only true wild sheep, but also fallow deer were once found in this region; and the Barbary deer, now extremely rare and found in the Algeria–Tunisia border country, are true red deer. Kin of the wild goat, including the African Barbary sheep, have advanced as far as the southern rim of the Sahara, and the ibex lives in scattered groups in the high mountains of Ethiopia.

The West African jungles, between the Niger and the Congo, have become a refuge for many species of primitive small animals, including the pygmy hippopotamus and the okapi (the "pygmy giraffe"). Even the forest elephant and the red buffalo which live in the rain forests of West Africa are smaller than their relatives which inhabit the open plains. Exceptions to this rule are the gorilla, which can weigh as much as 500 pounds, and the chimpanzee. In East Africa, especially in the elevated regions of Kenya, Tanzania, Uganda and Ruanda-Urundi, as well as south of the jungles of Angola, Mozambique, Malawi, Zambia and Rhodesia, the evolution and development of the African animal world is truly astonishing. The same wonder world exists in Botswana, Swaziland, Lesotho and South Africa. The world-famous parks of Tsavo and Amboseli, as well as the Ngorongoro crater and the Se-

rengeti plains, are also extraordinary settings for Africa's remarkable animal world. Here live the greatest ivory-bearers to be found anywhere, as well as the largest rhinoceroses. Huge herds of hippopotamuses still wallow in vast lakes and unspoiled rivers. Also abundant are the wart hog, with its imposing tusks, and the bush pig; less so, the giant forest pig. The wild horse family is represented by three species of zebra: Grévy's zebra in the northeast, the steppe zebra in the center, and the mountain zebra in the far south and southwest of the continent. The gazelle and larger antelope have evolved into such a great variety of sub-species that it is impossible to mention them all in a brief summary. The African buffalo is in evidence in herds of over one hundred animals. Fortunately, the biological and ecological balance has been preserved in important areas; Africa is still comparatively sparsely populated. The chief regulators, apart from man, are wild dogs and hyenas and, above all, lions, leopards and cheetahs.

Legends and tales of old Africa tell of the peaceful mingling of various species of game. Closer examination has revealed that such coexistence, where it occurs, depends on common behavior patterns.

The African Buffalo

For the big-game hunter, and for those who prefer to go on safari armed only with cameras, the dangerous "big five" are the most coveted African game: the elephant, rhinoceros, lion, leopard and African buffalo. The elephant and rhinoceros are both unpredictable and of uncertain temperament. The lion and leopard will occasionally attack human beings. The African buffalo is rarely aggressive—so long as it is not goaded or irritated by man or animals. But as soon as a buffalo is wounded or otherwise threatened, the peaceably grazing animal is transformed. Many a hunter in Africa, unaware of the reactions of this animal when hurt or enraged, has paid with his life for his inexperience or carelessness.

The habitat of the African buffalo extends practically all over Africa south of the Sahara, from sea level up to altitudes of 9,000 feet. The African buffalo is one of the most adaptable of all African mammals. Its environment is restricted only by its need for water to drink and in which to bathe.

The African buffalo embraces a variety of sub-species, including the red buffalo and the Sudanese buffalo. The largest of them live on the plains of the southernmost and coolest part of Africa, as well as in the eastern high plateaus. They are examples of the general rule that animals which live in warm climates are smaller than others of their species which inhabit colder zones. The red buffalo has adapted to the conditions of the West African rain forests and the Congo basin. It is smaller than the black, thinly coated plains variety and is red-brown in color. The edges of its funnel-shaped ears have long orange fringes. The red buffalo of the forest often lives alone or in pairs, though sometimes in groups of around twenty animals. The plains buffalo, on the other hand, is a gregarious herd animal; average populations of about sixty animals join together in the dry season to form huge herds of several thousand animals.

Evading Predators

Hoofed animals of the African plains are the main prey of the lion, leopard, cheetah, hyena and wild dog. With few defenses except for their speed, they frequently interrupt their feeding to take soundings and make certain no predators are nearby. Surprisingly, however, they allow their enemies to come remarkably close before taking flight, the specifi[c] distance varying according t[o] type of predator and situation[.] The speedy Thomson's gazelle o[f] the Serengeti often allows th[e] slower hyena to come as close a[s] thirty yards before making of[f.] When lions approach, they retrea[t] somewhat sooner and the swif[t] cheetah is allowed no closer tha[n]

to 400 yards. The African nting dog can put a gazelle to ght at a distance of over a half le.

These animals can not only ntify their enemies from afar, ey are also able to decipher their entions by observing their behavior. Little attention is paid by em to a lion lying placidly in the grass. But if, some hours later, that animal rises threateningly, the game takes to flight in a twinkling.

Larger species of hoofed game, such as buffalo, eland, zebra and giraffe, often protect themselves by lashing out with their hooves or horns and it is not unusual for them thus to kill their attackers. But flight remains their safest defense.

It offers each of a large number of fleeing animals the best chance of survival because predators find it difficult to concentrate their attack on individual animals when confronted with a rapidly dispersing group. As a rule, fugitive animals do not permit themselves to be driven in a specific direction by predators.

Impala flee from their enemies with huge leaps, scattering to make the predator's task more difficult.

The Uses of the Horns

The original, primitive hoofed animals we small, short-horned inhabitants of the woo and forests. More recent species, which a considerably larger and which live mainly open country, boast a wide variety of, son times almost oversized, horns.

The difference in the ratio between t sexes in different species is particula: interesting. In the case of primitive spec: which still inhabit wooded regions, t

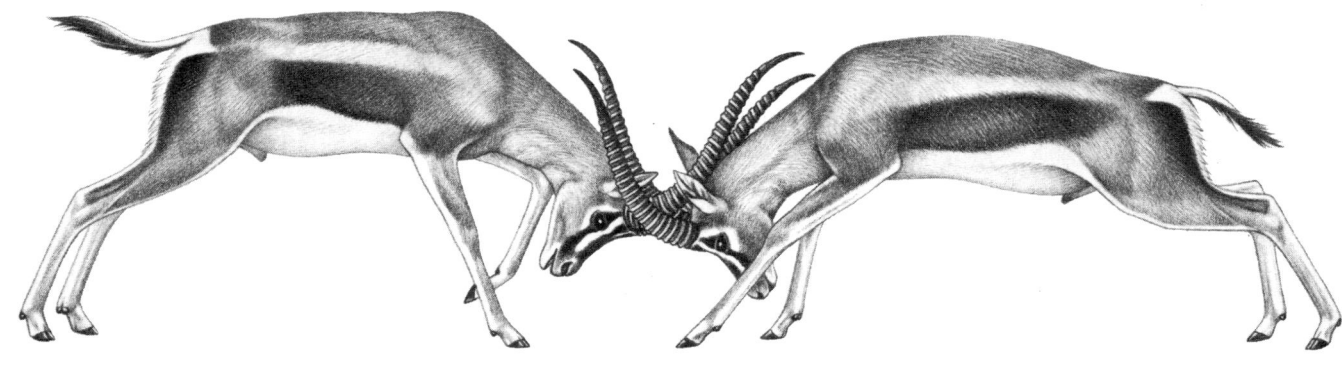

Thomson's gazelles use their horns against rivals of the same species to defend their territories. They mount repeated attacks involving the violent clash of horns. They often also interlock their horns and clash forehead to forehead.

Horned ungulates are "distance animals" which tolerate others of their species only at certain distances. If the lines are overstepped, flight or attack follows, depending on the relative hierarchical positions of the animals involved. However, direct contact is, of course, necessary for mating. Males court females with long

preliminary rituals and seek to draw near by use of various calming gestures. The most important of these is licking.

Before the actual mating, the male pursues the femal which takes to more or less ritualized flight. This pursuit can cover long or short distances, along straigh lines, arcs, circles or spirals. With some species, after catching up, the male lays its neck on the female's bac During mating, the male of the sheep and goat clasp

The mating foreplay, including mock fighting, is common to many species: the oryx bull, for example, courts the female by kicking at her back legs with his forelegs. The female thereupon assumes a humble, deferential posture, with her head lowered. A similar ritual is observed by the waterbuck and the gerenuk.

Biting and kicking, as practiced by the nilgai antelope represent much older forms of fighting than comparatively sophisticated battle with horns. Originally, animals mounted their attacks on all accessible parts of rivals' bodies.

umber of male and female animals tends to be oughly equal. With the horned ungulates of he open plains, females distinctly outumber the males. This could lead to the onclusion that the highly evolved, usually xtremely strong horns are effective weapons hich cause mortal injuries during battles beween male rivals. In reality, however, this is ot the case. The intricate horns of many lains dwellers—whether they are the long "daggers" of the oryx, the "screws" of the kudu, or the curved horns of the gnu—are primarily used to impress opponents and to determine victor and vanquished in conflicts which stop short of fatalities. The outcome of such strictly ritualized battles is generally the acceptance by the loser of its subordinate position, whether in the herd hierarchy or with regard to possession of a disputed territory or a female herd. The vanquished leaves the field of battle after the fight and often also separates itself from the herd. In such cases, it becomes easier prey for predators. That is why the balance of the sexes among the plains dwellers tilts in favor of females.

The females of many species of horned ungulates bear only poorly developed horns, or none at all. When they fight, they do so by means of kicking, biting and butting.

trictly ritualized combat between vals of the same species is a sign of gh development. Sable antelopes ght horn to horn and assume kneeling sitions in battle.

e female's flanks with its forelegs. Gazelle bucks, on he other hand, stand on their hind legs and may even erform the mating act on the run.

The "neck fight" is part of the mating play of the greater kudu. The bull slides its neck over the neck of the female, and then onto her croup. The horns play no part in either pre-mating mock blows or the "neck fight." Many species do not use their horns at all in the mating foreplay. Ritualized behavior

convinces the female of the male's momentary supremacy.

he horns of some species of hoofed game have eveloped into such specialized shapes that they can ly be used as weapons against animals of the same ecies. The hooked horns of the gnu, for example, have d to forms of fighting exclusive only to gnus.

The thrust and blow are the most primitive forms of fighting; present-day species of horned ungulates rarely practice them. Most of them, like the sheep, ram their rivals. Others, like the oryx and sable antelope, fight with their horns, while kudus wrestle forehead to fore-

head. Their spiral horns serve only to lock the rivals together. Some highly developed species often break off battle to sniff at each other, nose to nose.

Antelopes and Gazelles

KONGONI
(Alcelaphus buselaphus cokii)

Habitat: Kenya, Tanzania, the Masai plains, and Tanzania east of Lake Victoria. Often in large herds. Height at withers: fifty-two to fifty-six inches. Color: a variety of sandy tones; back and underside lighter. Both sexes bear horns. A swift runner with much stamina, it favors the open plains. Also known as Coke's hartebeest.

BRINDLED GNU
(Connochaetes taurinus albojubatus)

Habitat: still abundant in East Africa as far as the Tana River. Height at withers: about sixty-three inches. Wanders in large herds in search of pasture land during the dry season. Light gray to black-and-white striped. Dark face with light tuft on its forehead. Straggly hanging mane on throat and chest. Both sexes bear horns.

GREATER KUDU
(Strepsiceros strepsiceros)

Habitat: south of the Nile over most of East Africa and as far as Mozambique, Angola and Southwest Africa. Height at withers: around five feet. Possibly the most beautiful and impressive of all antelopes. Its spiral horns are coveted by hunters. Favors lightly wooded savannahs or rocky hill country interspersed with thorn bushes. Strong bulls; can weigh up to six hundred pounds. By virtue of its pale gray-brown coat, marked with six to eight whitish stripes, it is excellently camouflaged among the acacia bushes, the leaves of which are its favorite food. Bulls court hornless females through strictly ritualized mating ceremonies. The maneless lesser kudu, similar in most ways to the greater kudu, is found only in isolated regions of East Africa.

KIRK'S DIK-DIK
(Rhynchotragus kirki)

Habitat: East Africa. Height at withers: about one foot. Dik-diks normally live in pairs or in groups of three with a young animal, in strictly confined territories where they remain for many years. Large eyes. Strongly developed hind-quarters. Only the bucks bear short, pointed horns. Humans can approach closely before they take flight. Prefers dry, bush country.

ORIBI
(Ourebia ourebia)

Habitat: sub-Saharan Africa. Height at withers: up to two feet. Only the bucks bear horns. Coat: fox-red to dun on upper parts; underside whitish. White marking round eyes and on muzzle. Raised hind-quarters. Favors the open savannah, with water not far off. May be approached closely. Lives alone or in families.

BOKOR REEDBUCK
(Redunca redunca)

Habitat: East Africa—greater reedbuck, central and southern Africa. Height at withers: about three feet. Coat: reddish-brown to yellowish-gray; lighter on the flanks; belly whitish. The reedbuck forms a link between bush and savannah antelopes. It prefers areas with tall grass or reeds and remains closely tied to its territory. Makes a strange whistling sound when in danger.

WATERBUCK
(Kobus ellipsiprymnus)

Habitat: from Sudan over all of East Africa to Transvaal. Various different species. Height at withers: four to four and a half feet. Only the bucks bear horns. Shaggy coat, gray to red-gray, with collar-like mane and light-colored stripes. Lives near water, reeds and marshes. Faithful to its territory, which tends to be extensive. Often flees into water when endangered.

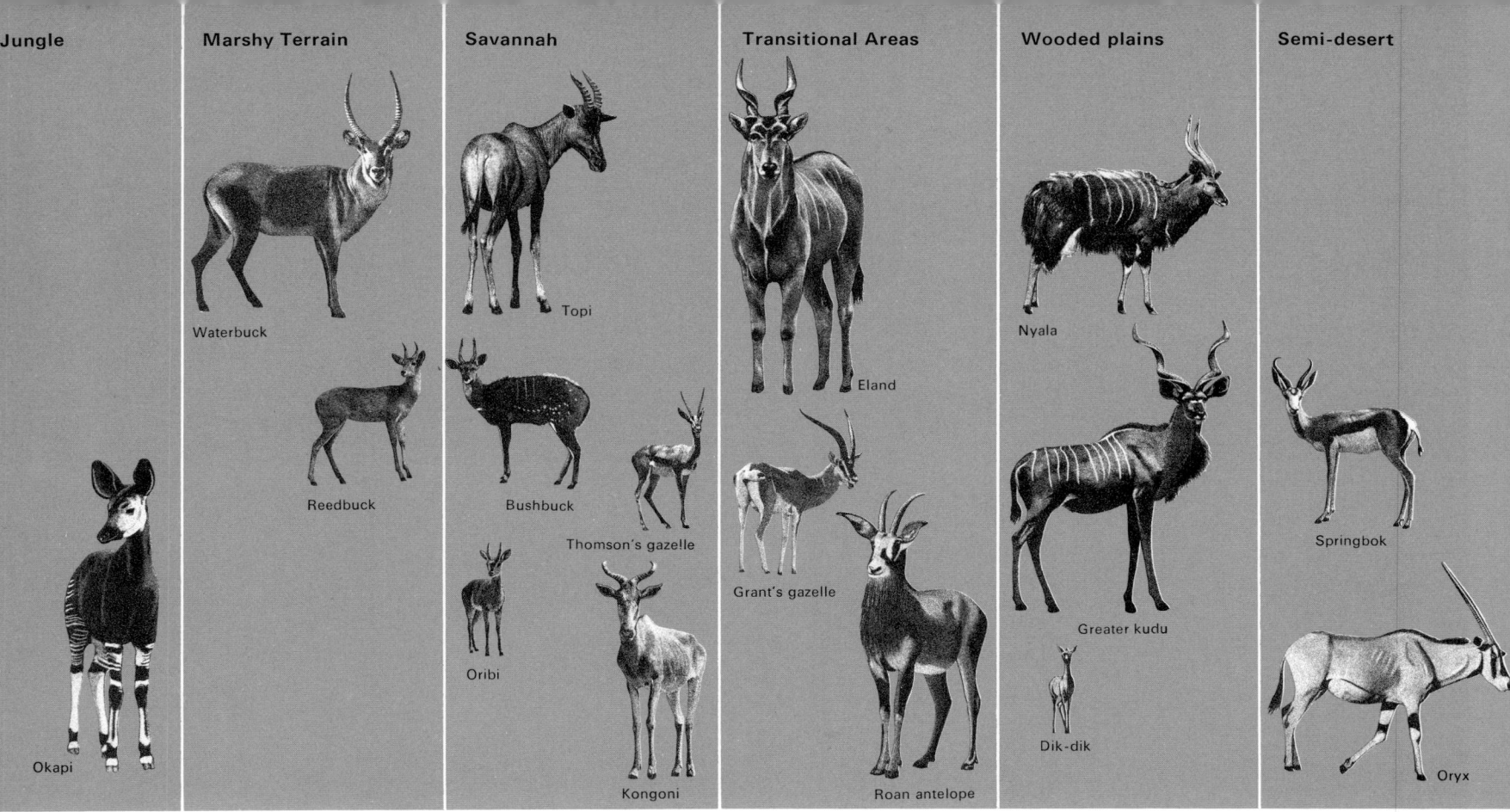

| Jungle | Marshy Terrain | Savannah | Transitional Areas | Wooded plains | Semi-desert |

Waterbuck

Topi

Eland

Nyala

Reedbuck

Bushbuck

Thomson's gazelle

Grant's gazelle

Greater kudu

Springbok

Oribi

Kongoni

Roan antelope

Dik-dik

Okapi

Oryx

More than one-third of the 190 known species of hoofed game are African antelopes. At least seventy species in all, they form the main group of African ruminants which also include the African buffalo, the Barbary sheep, the giraffe, Nubian and Ethiopian ibex, the atlas deer and the chevrotain. Only nine species of antelope are known outside Africa.

The African antelope and gazelle occur in a wide variety of sizes and characteristics. The smallest, the dik-dik, weighs little more than a hare. The largest, the eland, for example, and the giant sable antelope, can weigh as much as a domestic ox.

The variety of horns they display is also remarkable. Sometimes they are grown by both sexes; sometimes only by the male. Some species of antelope use their horns as weapons for fighting their rivals. Other employ them against enemies of other species. The greater kudu, the nyala and the bongo all bear long, spiral-shaped horns. The impala and other gazelles have elegant, lyrated horns. The oryx sports long, straight horns. Those of the gnu are similar to those of the buffalo.

Antelopes have adapted to all types of African environment, from the grasslands, where tens of thousands live as nomads, to the forests, where several species live quietly and secludedly. Some species have penetrated into the mountains of Africa—the klipspringer can climb steep rock faces. Others live in swamps and marshes, including, for example, the sitatunga whose slender, pointed hooves have flexible toes which it can spread wide to keep from sinking in soft ground.

Habitats have, of course, had considerable influence on the development and habits of antelopes. Species which live in regions with dense undergrowth have short, back-curving horns to permit them to move easily through thick vegetation, rather than the larger, more imposing horns of other species which do not have the same need. Their compact bodies, with raised hind-quarters, are set on short forelegs and longer hindlegs which propel the animals through the bush. In contrast, species which live on the plains are strong runners which can cover long stretches without great effort and which, in many cases, live with a minimum of water. They can reach extremely high speeds in flight, but forest dwellers, which have limited heart and lung capacity, react to danger by taking cover and remaining motionless.

Virtually constant conditions prevail in the tropical rain forests. The various species are distributed uniformly and are not usually distinguishable by regional characteristics. Territorial organization and behavior, in which the different species live alone or in families in specific regions which they defend against intruders of the same species, are most highly developed in wooded areas. Visibility is limited in dense vegetation and sense of smell, rather than vision, is the primary instrument of recognition for forest dwellers. Small inhabitants of the forests possess glands near their eyes to produce a secretion with which they mark out their territories.

Most of the medium-sized and large antelopes, and primarily the gazelles, live in wide, open country, such as savannahs and deserts subject to extreme ecological fluctuation. These creatures usually live in large communities and are nomadic. Their environment makes visual communication easy and their eyesight is, therefore, considerably better developed than their sense of smell. Their horns are often oddly and extravagantly shaped, and they often bear striking markings on their skins. These frequently make it possible to distinguish male from female easily, as well as old from young, and play an important role in the social behavior of these highly developed hoofed ungulates.

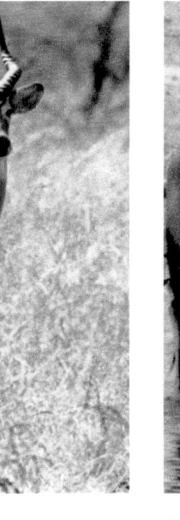

BUFFON'S KOB
(Adenota kob thomasi)

Habitat: eastern Zaire, Uganda to Sudan. Height at withers: three feet. Its territories tend to be isolated and confined to small areas. Coat: red-brown with white markings round the eyes, on the chin and throat. The kob is possibly the most elegant of the marsh antelopes and is related to the waterbuck. Prefers open bush and savannah territory. Only the buck bears horns.

ORYX
(Oryx gazella)

Habitat: from Ethiopia and Sudan, across Uganda and Kenya to south of the Tana River. Height at withers: about four feet. Both sexes bear horns. Those of the cow are longer and thinner. Coat: cream-colored on upper parts; broad, dark stripes on the belly. Favors savannahs and semi-desert regions. The oryx can live without water for months. Combative by nature.

ELAND
(Taurotragus oryx)

Habitat: from Sudan over all of East Africa; the giant eland only in West and East Sudan. Height at withers: up to six feet; small bump on the withers. Bulls can weigh up to a ton. Both sexes bear horns. Bull's coat is light gray-brown; that of the cow is reddish. Light, vertical stripes on the stomach not uncommon. Despite its massive size, the eland is a remarkably high jumper.

Favors savannahs, feeding on leaves of trees. Climbs to a height of 12,000 feet in the East African mountains. Shy; will flee from even distant humans. Attempts now being made in Africa to domesticate these antelopes.

GERENUK OR GIRAFFE GAZELLE
(Litocranius walleri)

Habitat: southern Ethiopia and Somalia to Kenya and Tanzania. Height at withers: thirty-five to forty-three inches. Only the bucks bear horns. Coat chestnut-brown; underparts whitish. Light markings round the eyes and on the muzzle. Prefers dry bush forest territory. Highly specialized feeder; often stands on hindlegs to reach acacia leaves.

BUSHBUCK
(Tragelaphus scriptus)

Habitat: sub-Saharan Africa except for rain forests and deserts. Height at withers: thirty-two to thirty-five inches. Only the bucks bear horns. Coat brown to dark brown—some sub-species have whitish stripes. Fringes on neck; white marks on throat and chest. Raised hindquarters. Stays close to its territory. Requires water nearby; a good swimmer. Prefers solitary existence.

NYALA
(Tragelaphus angasi)

Habitat: plains nyala from southeast Africa to South Africa; mountain nyala only in the Arussi Province of Ethiopia. Height at withers: thirty-two to forty-five inches. Only the bulls bear horns. Coat gray-brown, dark, shaggy mane on back, throat and belly. Whitish horizontal markings; more distinct on the cow which is also redder in color. Nyalas live in small groups.

OKAPI
(Okapi johnstoni)

Habitat: Congo basin. Height at withers: fifty-nine to sixty-seven inches. Only the bulls bear small, skin-covered horns on their foreheads. This rare, strictly protected animal was first discovered by Sir Harry Johnston at the beginning of the century. Coat shiny, chocolate brown with broad white horizontal bands on the forelegs and hindlegs. Secretive; lives singly or in pairs.

TOPI
(Damaliscus korigum eureus)

Habitat: northern Uganda, Kenya to central Tanzania, westwards to Lakes Edward and Kivu and northwards to the Juba River. Height at withers: about four feet. The topi roams grasslands for pasture with nearby waterholes, but has been known to stand on elevated ground, such as termite mounds, for hours on end. Both sexes bear horns. Distinctive alarm and mating calls.

SABLE ANTELOPE
(Hippotragus niger)

Habitat: wooded savannahs in Mozambique, Rhodesia, southern Tanzania, eastern Kenya. Height at withers: about five feet. Both sexes bear horns. Bulls have black and white markings on the face, black, erect manes and shiny, brown-black coats. Females are reddish-brown. Very aggressive. Strictly protected populations of the giant sable antelope still exist in Angola.

ROAN ANTELOPE
(Hippotragus equinus)

Habitat: plains and thornbush savannahs south of the Sahara to Oranje, East Africa westwards to east Cameroon and Nigeria. Height at withers: sixty to sixty-four inches. Both sexes bear horns. Together with the eland and kudu, the roan is one of the most striking of all the antelopes. Typical features are a thick neck mane with dense fringes, unusually large,

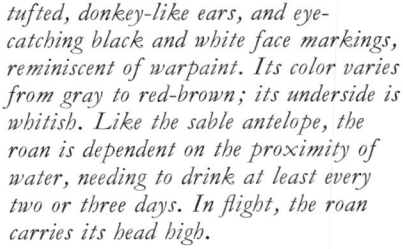

tufted, donkey-like ears, and eye-catching black and white face markings, reminiscent of warpaint. Its color varies from gray to red-brown; its underside is whitish. Like the sable antelope, the roan is dependent on the proximity of water, needing to drink at least every two or three days. In flight, the roan carries its head high.

IMPALA
(Aepyceros melampus)

Habitat: East Africa as far as Transvaal; westwards as far as Lake Edward. Height at withers: thirty-two to forty inches. Only the buck bears horns. Smooth coat, gleaming rust-red on upper parts; underside whitish. Black tuft of hair on back legs and, therefore, also known as the "black-heeled antelope." Feeds on leaves and grass. Extremely committed to its territory.

SPRINGBOK
(Antidorcas marsupialis)

Habitat: south Angola and Transvaal to Cape Province. Height at withers: thirty-two to thirty-six inches. Both sexes bear horns. Coat cinnamon-brown to sandy yellow; flanks and underside whitish. In the middle of the back, the skin is doubly folded. Long white mane stands on end when animal feels threatened or is otherwise excited. Powerful jumper.

GRANT'S GAZELLE
(Gazella granti)

Habitat: East Africa. Height at withers: thirty-two to thirty-six inches. Horns of the buck considerably more formidable than those of the female. Coat light sand-colored. White tail with black tip; slight flank stripes. Unlike Thomson's gazelle, it has a monochrome appearance. Many mating and fighting rituals. Older bucks defend a territory of their own.

THOMSON'S GAZELLE
(Gazella thomsoni)

Habitat: East Africa, west of Mount Kenya to Tanzania. Height at withers: twenty-four to twenty-eight inches. Both sexes bear horns. Coat sand-colored, dark stripes on the flanks, belly whitish. Light stripes from ears to muzzle. Distinctive kind of leap. Huge herds often congregate to search for new pastures.

The Cheetah

These big cats, of the kind which once served as tame hunting companions for Asian and European potentates, and are here pictured cavorting playfully together, are dreaded thieving predators in their wild state. Taller than the leopard, the cheetah is an extremely swift daytime hunter.

It stealthily approaches its victim until it comes close, and then gives chase at speeds which can reach more than sixty miles an hour. The gazelle has no chance of surviving if the cheetah succeeds in overtaking it and striking it down with its forepaws. But if the gazelle manages to survive the first 500 yards of its flight it might very well escape completely unharmed, because the cheetah soon tires and must give up the chase.

The Great Predators

Left: The reproductive activities of lions are not strictly restricted to any single season. In East and South Africa, however, mating usually takes place between March and June, while in West Africa it is usually in November and December. The male lions are polygamous—at least the strongest of them are. They live singly or in groups with lionesses which will eventually drive them away.

Right: Lionesses drop their cubs in hiding. But as soon as they are able to stand, the proud mother presents them to other members of the group. Young lions are tolerated as participants in the kill, but their fathers often treat them roughly.

On Africa's vast savannahs, the natural balance between predator and prey has largely been maintained. Significant scientific research has recently examined this process in depth, particularly the behavior and ecological roles of the great predators—the lion, leopard, hyena and African hunting dog. These investigations revealed, among other things, that the lion, so long known as "king of the beasts," is often obliged to break off its hunt because its victims, so long thought to be helpless and hopeless, regularly detect its approach soon enough to make good their escape. As a consequence, the lion is frequently the uninvited dinner guest of the hyena and hunting dog, whose hunting methods are generally more successful than its own.

Predators and their prey, having lived more or less side by side for millennia, have influenced each other's development. The speed of hoofed game compelled their predators to develop exceptionally powerful muscles for leaping, strong claws and powerful teeth, as well as a refined sense of cunning. Propagation of game was intimately related to the success or failure of predators. Only the fastest and most alert animals survived; the others were killed, along with old and weak specimens of sturdier breeds.

People for whom hunting has been a sport and recreation, as well as a search for trophies and sometimes commercial gain, have tended to speak of "bloodthirsty beasts" and greatly to have overestimated the hunting skill of the mighty predators. A researcher working in Serengeti Park observed that a pack of African hunt-ing dogs killed 281 specimens of hoofed game in a year. His studies also brought to light other interesting details: the larger the pack, the fewer the quarry killed per head. A pack of twenty-one animals killed about four pounds of meat a day per dog; a pack of six animals could boast of exactly twice that amount. A lion, however, kills an annual average of nineteen animals, weighing about 240 pounds each—corresponding to a monthly consumption of about 380 pounds. Lions do not eat every day, although the males in particular do not consume only their own kill but also as much as a tenth of the kill of other, smaller predators in their territories. Once they settle down to eat, however, a lion can devour up to sixty-five pounds of meat at a sitting. When their appetites are satisfied, they retreat and leave what is left to hyenas, jackals and vultures.

As a rule lions, like hyenas and African hunting dogs, hunt in groups, in which each individual animal plays a specific role. Before the hunt begins, the pride of lions divides up. Two or three of them, usually lionesses, lie hidden in the grass a distance from a grazing herd of game. The others approach the prey from the far side and drive them toward the concealed lionesses. The lion is a quick killer. Usually it springs on its prey from the side or front, seizes it with its powerful claws and tears it apart. Some of the fallen animals die of broken necks; others from savage bites on their throats.

The African hunting dog hunts by sight. It has far greater stamina than the lion and can reach speeds of thirty-five miles an hour. Its quarry, which includes the reedbuck, impala, Grant's and Thomson's gazelles and zebra, is seized from behind or by the flanks and is rapidly devoured by the pack. Twenty-five of twenty-eight hunts observed in the Ngorongoro Crater were successful.

It is not only when hunting that herds and packs of predators form communities, but also in other fields, for example, the rearing of the young. The lion lives in groups consisting of generally two or three males and five to ten females with their offspring. Though the adult lionesses stay together all through their lives, the lions are permitted to remain in the group only as long as they can fend off other male competitors. As soon as a leading lion is overcome by a new candidate, it is forced to leave the community.

Crocodiles and Rhinoceroses

Left: During the day, the crocodile dozes on sandy banks in the hot sun with its mouth wide open. When moving on land, its short legs brace its massive body just above the ground.

Right: The black rhino's upper lip is elongated, somewhat like a finger. It is often raised when the animal sniffs the air.

Overleaf: Gertie, the female rhinoceros from the Amboseli Park with its strange, 54-inch-long front horn—probably the world's most photographed black rhino.

The crocodile, one of Africa's most fearsome predators, has a hide on which humans have placed great value. Therein lies the threat to its existence. But the extinction of the crocodile is not yet imminent and it remains a very active example of the large predators which seldom specialize in their feeding habits, preferring to adjust their diets according to what is available.

The crocodile is extremely fertile. The female lays about twenty eggs at a time, each the size of a tennis ball. Some dig pits for them on river banks; others construct nests of vegetation in which the eggs are hatched not only by the warmth of the sun but also by the heat generated by the gradually decaying nest lining. The mother crocodile regulates this incubator by adjusting the amount of cover-

their numbers have been kept small by lions and by man, the hunter. This may have contributed to the fact that the rhinoceros has a very low reproduction rate: its gestation period is about sixteen months and it only gives birth every four years or so. Young rhinoceroses are suckled for two whole years and remain with their mothers for about three and a half years. They do not reach sexual

totally undisturbed by huma predators.

"Territorial awareness" is on of the mechanisms for propagatio and survival of animal species. Th black rhino is particularly terri torially aware. It is not onl extremely cautious and aggressiv when dealing with potential ene mies of different species, but als with regard to other rhinocerose which it drives from its domain The rhino habitat is divided int feeding areas, drinking places an sloughs—which these herbivo rous creatures regularly visit—a well as numerous specific place where they deposit their dropping The animal tramples on these drop pings to obtain a substance wit which it marks off the boundarie of its territory.

According to one African legend however, this particular habit ha a different origin. When animal were created, the rhinoceros i said to have received a needle fror its creator to sew the loose ski of its body tighter together. Bu while engaged in this task th original rhinoceros lost the needle The animal was obliged to con tinue with the sewing, using horn—no easy task. However, th idea dawned on it that it migh have swallowed the needle b accident. It began searching fo the missing needle in its dropping with its horn and back feet . . . an is still searching.

Generally, crocodiles subsist on fish and tortoises, which they are skilled at catching. They often remain motionless below the surface of the water for hours on end and then snap up their prey in fractions of a second, spurting forward with mighty lashes of their powerful tails.

Crocodiles seem able to sense the presence of carrion at relatively great distances; they often leave their favorite haunts on the banks of rivers and make their way inland to feed on dead buffalo and other dead animals. They also stealthily approach drinking animals from below the water's surface and drag them into the water.

ing matter, according to the temperature. In addition, she defends her brood against such nest thieves as mongooses and monitors. After the young crocodiles are hatched, they are kept together in a kind of kindergarten, with the mother protecting them from enemies, including, in addition to large birds, cannibalistic crocodile fathers! It is estimated that only two to five of every one hundred crocodiles actually manage to reach maturity.

The aggressive rhinoceros and the elephant are large tropical animals which occupy exalted positions in the hierarchy of the animal kingdom. Historically,

maturity until the age of seven. The two African species of rhino, the black rhino (which feeds on foliage) and the wide-mouthed rhino (which lives on grass) are found today in a number of reserves, where they are under strict protection. Under such conditions, black rhinos in particular reproduce at an astonishing rate because local (and visiting) hunters, once its most dangerous natural enemies, are prevented from killing them in reserves. It should be remembered, however, that these parks, regardless of size, are merely small parts of an almost boundless ecological system in which wild animals once could live

The Death of a Giant

Though the heaviest of dry-land mammals, the elephant is highly sensitive and exceptionally intelligent. Its strictly hierarchical social system is characterized by personal relationships which last many years and by the constant readiness of each individual elephant to help other members of the herd. It sometimes seems that these giants of the plains, constantly driven into ever-smaller habitats by encroaching civilization, are aware of what is becoming their increasingly ominous and totally unnecessary fate.

Even after most commercial ivory hunters, who killed enormous numbers of elephants during the nineteenth century, were finally compelled to give up their cruel pursuits, the imminent extinction of the African elephant seemed unavoidable. Some colonial administrators, who had themselves not done badly out of the ivory trade, expressed doubt whether there was any point in sparing the last few of these huge animals. Why, they asked, was it necessary to preserve the remaining specimens of this primitive species which was, after all, notorious for damaging plantations which had been cultivated in the bush with so much effort? In addition to laying waste vast areas of vegetation, they claimed, the elephants also threatened the local inhabitants.

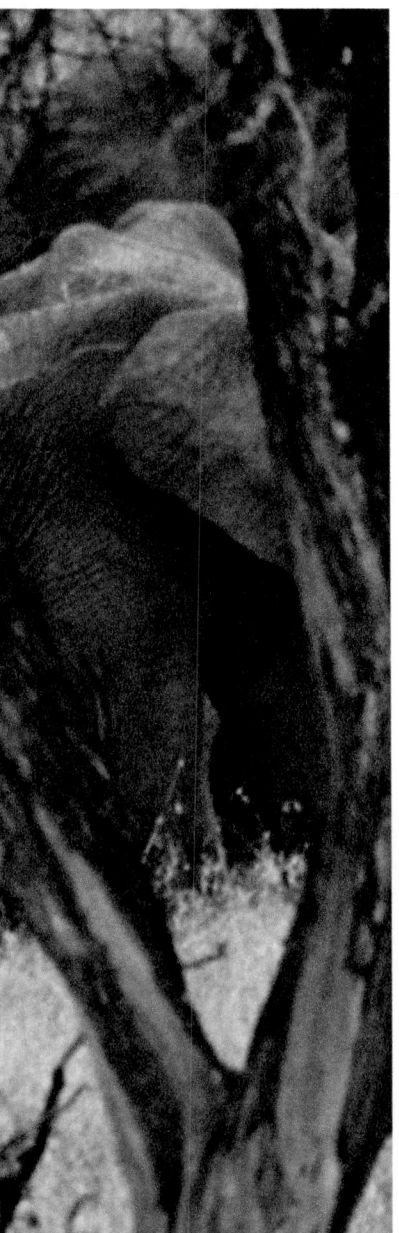

However, common sense fortunately prevailed. Responsible authorities, hunters and nature conservationists founded national parks in which our wildlife heritage could be preserved. Elephants congregated in the protected areas and sizeable herds developed in such places as the Tsavo Park in Kenya, Serengeti in Tanzania, the Kruger Park in South Africa, the Amboseli Park in the Masai region and the Etoscha enclave in South-West Africa. Today large herds of elephants can be found even in wilderness areas. However, in the national parks, they have increased to a point where they pose a threat to the ecological balance because they have forced certain rare species of antelope to seek habitats elsewhere and they have destroyed vast patches of vegeta-

tion—each of these huge animals devours over one hundred pounds of vegetable matter each day. The consequence has often been starvation, and game wardens have been required to cull a certain number of elephants in the reserves.

The death of an elephant, whether from hunger, sickness, old age or any other reason, is a tragic event for the entire herd. The only pictorial account of such an occurence yet produced provides a poignant image: the old, emaciated female elephant, aware that death is near, has separated herself from the herd. Her huge ears, still flapping rhythmically, are barely able to assume their normal, semi-erect position. Her flanks are sunken; the line of her back is no longer straight and

firm. Slowly, the mighty colossus collapses. The entire herd approaches to form a silent phalanx of protective bodies around the dying animal, as if seeking to screen her from the gaze of waiting vultures. Just as elephants, trumpeting loudly, bravely stay by their lead bull hit by a deadly bullet, the herd now tries to help the dying animal to its feet.

Only after a long vigil does the herd reluctantly withdraw, leaving the corpse to the waiting vultures and hyenas. It will not be long before only a few bleached bones remain as final witness to the life and death of this once hulking creature.

Man's Hunting Companions

No one knows exactly when man began hunting animals with other animals. But reference is made in ancient documents to four-legged hunting companions. The Greek writer Arrian (A.D. 95–180) reported in great detail on the hunting practices of the Danube Celts. Their favorite pastime appears to have been hare coursing with horses and speedy grayhounds (*vertragi*). "Not for itself, but for the lord, the fiery vertragus hunts, and brings the hare undamaged in its jaws."

Probably the most significant event in the history of hunting was the introduction of the use of the dog for sporting purposes—this domestic predator had thus entered the service of man! Some time later, these terrestrial companions were joined by others which flew, birds of prey trained to hunt for man. When that happened is also lost in the mists of time, as is the moment when the great horsemen of the steppes of Asia first used their equestrian skills in pursuit of game. The Hunt, into which horseback hunting developed as it moved westward into Europe, became a ritualized event, with impeccably trained hounds, prescribed attire and upper-class social status.

Hunting Dogs—Their Characteristics

The following table describes the five different types of hunting dog—their appearance, characteristics and use. The standard features regarding head, hair, color and size are noted in the captions. HW stands for height at withers; D for dog; B for bitch.

Hounds: Among the most typical representatives of the hound category is the Jura-basset, or bruno, a direct descendant of the

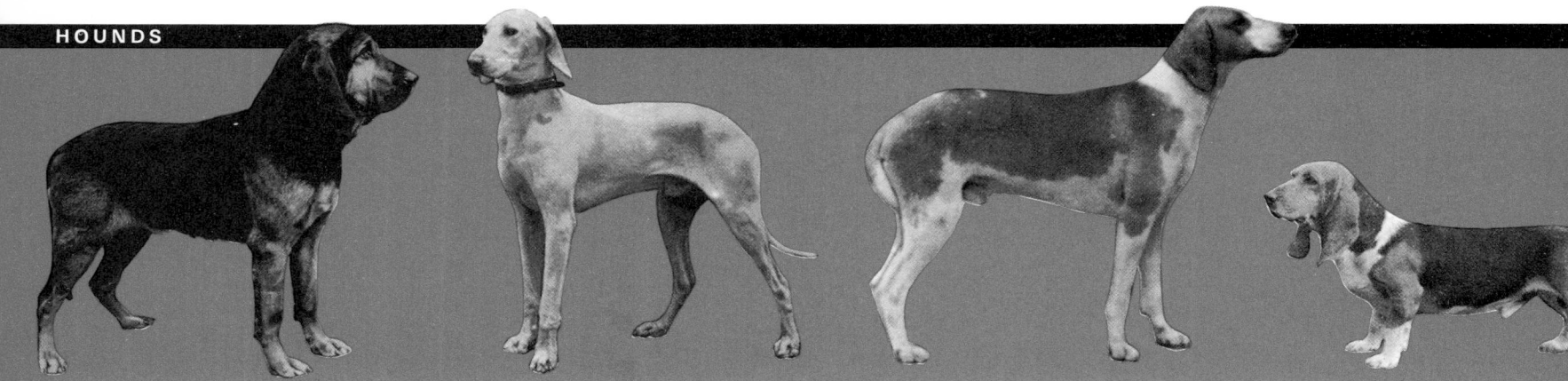

HOUNDS

CHIEN DE SAINT-HUBERT
HW: about 26 inches. Large, somewhat narrow head. Upper back legs strongly developed. Eyes black to brown. Low-set, long, delicate ears with silky hair. Long tail. Coat smooth and dense. Colors: black and red, red and tan, dun.

CHIEN DE BILLY
HW: D 24–26 inches, B 23–25 inches. Medium-length head, finely cut. Narrow forehead, lightly arched. Distinct stop. Dark eyes. Medium-length ears. Long, powerful tail. Hard, smooth coat. Color: pure white, light brown, white with orange spots.

POITEVIN NORMAND
HW: D 25–28 inches, B 23–26 inches. Generally of similar appearance to the Billy, but slightly more heavily built. Dark eyes. Lively expression. Square, well-developed muzzle. Abundant, smooth-haired coat. Colors: three-hued—red, black, white spots.

ARTÉSIEN-NORMAND BASSET
HW: 10–14 inches. Head lean, powerful, slender. Distinct stop. Large, dark eyes. Long, sharply tapering tail. Smooth, flat coat. Colors: bi-colored—white and red; tri-colored—yellow on head, white and black.

SPANIELS

BERNESE BASSET
HW: 12–15 inches. Medium-sized head, moderate stop. Long ears and tail. Dark eyes. Short, stiff coat. Colors: like those of the Swiss hound. Long-bodied.

JURA BASSET
HW: at least 16 inches. Powerful, heavy head, distinct stop. Long, folded ears. Flat, smooth coat. Colors: yellow or red-brown, black with red-yellow points, sometimes white patch on breast.

HAMILTON STOVARE
HW: D 23, B 21 inches. Long, clean-cut head, ill-defined stop. Dark brown eyes. Top hair thick, strong, flat; short, dense, soft undercoat. Colors: black, brown with white markings.

GERMAN SPANIEL
HW: 18–21 inches. Head clean-cut, ill-defined stop. Brown eyes, long ears with curly feathering. Coat strong, wavy, shiny, curly at the neck and legs. Colors: brown, blue or red roan, tri-colored.

ENGLISH SPRINGER SPANIEL
HW: about 20 inches. Head medium-length, moderately broad, stop distinct. Hazel eyes. Coat smooth. Colors: all recognized spaniel colors, preferably brown and white or black and white.

WEIMARANER
HW: D up to 28, B up to 25 inches. Medium-length head, ill-defined stop. Amber eyes. Broad, medium-length, pointed ears. Coat—smooth-haired: fine, coarse; wire-haired: thick, wiry, rough; long-haired: up to two inches long, feathering on legs. Color: gray.

GERMAN WIRE-HAIRED POINTER
HW: D up to 26, B not under 23 inches. Moderately long head. Powerful jaws, sufficiently long. Brown eyes. Medium-length, broad ears. Coat dense, wiry, with soft woolly undercoat. Colors: brown or mixed with white or gray-brown.

GERMAN GRIFFON
HW: D up to 24, B up to 22 inches. Large, long head, sloping stop. Very hairy, with eyebrows, moustache and beard. Eyes brown to yellow. Medium-length ears. Coat rough, bushy. Colors: brown or steel-gray, usually with brown patches.

POODLE POINTER
HW: D up to 26, B up to 24 inches. Head moderately long, broad, covered with hair, heavy eyebrows and beard. Pointer's stop. Jaws broad and long. Eyes yellow to yellow-brown. Coat medium-length, dense, rough, wiry. Colors: brown or russet.

Hunting Dogs—Their History

The hound is considered the original ancestor of all the various breeds of hunting dog. Ivory carvings with hunting themes bear witness to its existence in ancient Egypt, around 4400 B.C. Hunting dogs probably came to Europe as merchandise at first, brought from the Middle East by the Phoenicians. Unmistakable images of hounds, with their slender bodies and long ears, are conjured up in the early documents of the Celts, Gauls and Romans.

Earlier still, however, around 10,000 to 5,000 B.C., a hunting dog is believed to have accompanied hunters as they pursued game, using spears and throwing sticks as weapons. It was a watchdog as well as a hunting dog and was particularly useful as a bloodhound. It was a bold and tenacious fighter when its master encountered strong wild game.

As the forerunners of present-day hunting dogs evolved through breeding, two primary functions became distinct: locating game and attacking the quarry. Different breeds developed which specialized in different skills. During the Middle Ages, a clear line was drawn between "attacking" and "tracking" dogs. The hunter on foot, with his attackers and trackers, was joined by the mounted hunter in the later Middle Ages when the style of hunting known as the chase evolved. Fast dogs were developed to keep up with swift horses. Particularly in England and France, where a form of the classic chase is still practiced, the original Egyptian hound gradually developed into a standard which was always deployed in packs. Certain characteristics were a passion for hunting, an ability to pick up a scent, aggressiveness, and baying. It also offered breeders excellent material for creating new breeds.

For a long time, the form of hunting was determined by the availability of packs. It was a situation which did not really change until the political and social revolutions in Europe in the nineteenth century. With the collapse of the feudal system, court hunting with the use of large packs of dogs disappeared. After hunting possibilities had been considerably extended by the introduction and perfection of hunting firearms, the pastime took a far more varied form and dogs were given more specialized tasks. The genuine chase hound became less important and was replaced by spaniel- and pointer-like dogs trained and adapted to new hunting methods. Attempts at selective breeding, dating from antiquity and intensified during the Middle Ages, show that man was unceasingly involved in efforts to improve and enhance the hunting abilities of canines. Above all, the desire to develop specialized skills, such as relentlessly following a scent and, in the case of the lead dog, leaving a clear track of its own, going aggressively into the attack, diligently flushing out where bird dogs were involved, ardent baying in the case of hounds, led to experiments in breeding. As early as the fourteenth century, the breeder's interest concentrated on a specific type of dog which was mentioned in the Salic law of ancient Germanic tribes as the *segusius magister canis*. It was the lead dog which did all the scenting in the hunt, with the pack of hounds following in full cry. In medieval poetry, exact descriptions of this type of dog can be found, with special mention of the unusual length of its jaw and ears and of its arched, vertically carried tail. While the lead dog was employed in the chase in France as a *limier,* to carry out the preliminary task of picking up the scent of game, in Germany it was later assigned the more difficult task of determining the trail of a specific deer. Later still, it was trained as a bloodhound. In the nineteenth century, central-European dog breeders tried to produce a blend of the three best breeds of lead dog, the Sollinger, Harzer and Hanoverian. This led to the development of a new breed of lead blood hound, later known simply as bloodhound.

Almost at the same time, loudly baying breeds caught the interest of breeders because of their reliability when tracking game. The oldest type is the hound, the original ancestor of all types of brach. The original large form gradually became smaller to adapt to ever-decreasing animal territories.

The development of long-haired bird dogs, both large and small, was also determined by the needs of the hunter. Their task was to mark hare and wildfowl or to flush them from the cover of fields and hedges. The spaniel is the original type of these bird dogs and its tasks were much more varied than those of the hound. It proved to be just as reliable in flushing for the falconer as in setting for the wildfowler. Later it was also used to drop to shot and developed into a real working dog for field, wood and water hunting. The retriever was produced by crossing the water spaniel with the Newfoundland dog. With the introduction of firearms, setting became less important and was largely replaced by pointing. For this, larger dogs which could be seen in high grass were usually used. The pointer evolved from the large family of hounds by crossbreeding with sheepdogs.

The qualities of a good pointer are calm searching, careful flushing, confident and reliable retrieving and indefatigable pointing. The oldest known form of pointer is the Spanish perdiguero, which was imported into England on the strength of its famous nose and its skill in wildfowling. It was crossed with the foxhound and grayhound, the result being the present-day pointer.

In contrast to the English breed, which is a direct descendant of a primitive breed, the German pointer is a true product of cross-breeding traceable back to the seventeenth century. It was originally a rather slow dog. Its breeders, therefore, tried to introduce English pointer blood into the breed to make it faster and racier. The result was that the German pointer became more elegant and eager and what had been a "field sniffer" became "a searcher with a raised nose."

The ground dog is often used for hunting small predators, for example foxes and badgers. Most suitable are the dachshund, fox terrier and hunting terrier. The fox terrier, for example, can be trained for use not only below ground but also for pointing, flushing and tracking by scent.

Thanks to its inherited qualities, the present-day hunting dog is able to provide the hunter with valuable service, so long as it is trained early enough by a skilled trainer. The best work is undoubtedly done by dogs which possess all the advantages of inherited characteristics, skilled training and knowledgeable direction.

was crossed first with the French form of the breed and then with the foxhound. The pointer is large, powerful, elegant, and has a deep chest and round, low-set ears. The tail is carried horizontally.

Retrievers: English hunters have bred dogs for virtually every type of hunting. Retrievers are used to fetch game after it has been brought down. They must have an acute sense of smell and derive pleasure from the act of retrieving. Probably the most popular of the breed is the golden retriever, a medium-sized, long-haired dog with short ears and a long tail. The Labrador retriever is thick-set, black or golden, and with a smooth-haired coat and an otter-like tail.

Ground dogs: The most popular ground dog is undoubtedly the dachshund which comes in various forms—long-, smooth- or wire-haired, black, brown or tan-brindled. The wire-haired dachshund owes its development to a cross between the English wire-haired terrier and the German miniature schnauzer. All three types of dachshund are used as blood hounds and flushers. The dwarf dachshund is best used for flushing out polecats, martens and wild rabbits, which it can pursue into their narrow burrows.

HOUND
Distinctive head, ging lips. Muzzle brown eyes. Full, lors: dark to light ith black.

BEAGLE
HW: 16 inches; dwarf beagle under 10 inches. Head powerful. Clearly defined stop. Eyes dark brown. Long ears. Coat: smooth- or wire-haired varieties. Colors: white, black, brown.

BLOODHOUND
HW: D 25–28 inches, B 25–27 inches. Head narrow, up to 12 inches long. Lips overhanging squarely in front. Eyes dark brown to yellow. Thick dewlap. Coat short and hard, silky on head and ears. Colors: black and white, reddish, pale red.

FOXHOUND
HW: about 23 inches. Head powerful, elegant. Ears docked almost an inch at the ends, rounded. Coat short, thick, hard, shiny. Stern set high. Colors: black, brown, white, badger pied, yellow.

SWISS HOUND
HW: at least 16 inches. Long, narrow head, pronounced stop. Very long ears. Smooth-haired: thick; wire-haired: hard, wiry. Colors: white background, yellow-red or dark red patches.

...
s. Head long, clean-cut. Good eyes. Medium-sized ears, with e sides. Tail and legs feathered. gth, flat, fringe on belly. d, gold shimmer.

ÉPAGNEUL BRETON
HW: D up to 20, B up to 19 inches. Medium-length head. Pronounced stop. Dark amber eyes. Ears shortish, rounded, with wavy hair. Stumpy tail. Fine coat, flat or lightly waved. Colors: white and brown or orange, gray.

SPINONE
HW: D up to 28, B up to 25 inches. Head long. Sloping stop. Eyes dark yellow to ocher. Ears triangular, without fold. Coat hard, dense, flat, not curly. Tail docked. Colors: pure white, white with orange or brown markings and spots.

GERMAN SMOOTH-HAIRED POINTER
HW: 24–28 inches. Head clean-cut, distinctive. Slightly overhanging lips. Nose always brown. Medium-length ears, rounded. Coat short, dense, coarse. Colors: brown, with or without markings, white with brown patches or spots, black.

GROUND DOGS

LABRADOR RETRIEVER
HW: D up to 25, B up to 23 inches. Head broad, ill-defined stop. Long, powerful jaws. Eyes brown and black or yellow. Medium-sized ears. Broad muzzle, open nostrils. Otter-like tail. Coat short, very dense, hard. Color: black or golden.

DACHSHUND
HW: Usually about 10 inches. Long head, protruding cheek bones, no stop. Eyes black to dark brown. Medium-length ears. Tail long, not too tapering. Coat and colors: many variations. Picture above: wire-haired dachshund.

FOX TERRIER
HW: D up to 15, B up to 14 inches. Wedge-shaped head, ill-defined stop. Powerful jaw, rather long. Black nose, dark eyes. Small, V-shaped ears. Coat: smooth- or wire-haired varieties. Colors: white with black markings or patches.

GERMAN HUNTING TERRIER
HW: up to 16 inches. Rather heavy hea ill-defined stop. V-shaped ears. Dark ey docked tail. Rough coat. Colors: bla with red or yellow markings, brown, r yellow-red with black specks.

Celtic brach and closely related to the chien de Saint-Hubert: powerful, long-bodied, a heavy domed head, very long, large ears and a medium-length tail. It is particularly useful for wooded regions since its loud baying can be heard from a great distance. Agile, versatile and equipped with an acute sense of smell, it hunts with certainty and fervor.

Spaniels: While the hound often pursues game over long distances for hours on end, the spaniel works close to the hunter, flushing out birds and ground game alike and giving chase, but not far. English breeds of spaniels have particularly good reputations. The original spaniel, the springer, has a heavy, narrow head with long, silky ears; a docked, feathered tail; and a long smooth or wavy coat. The cocker spaniel was previously used exclusively for hunting woodcock. The Irish water spaniel is as intelligent as the poodle, has senses as acute as the setter, and is a dedicated hunter, as are all spaniels. It is medium-sized and bears a topknot. Its coat is curly and its tail is short and tapering—a "rat tail."

Pointers and Setters: English pointers and setters are the result of careful breeding which has done much to perfect both form and character. The pointer is a first-class dog, descended from the Spanish perdiguero which

[GR]IFFON VENDÉEN BASSET
[H]V: 15–16 inches or 13–15 inches. [He]ad lean, powerful, slender. Muzzle [sh]orter and squarer than that of artesien-[no]rmand. Medium-length ears covered [wit]h long hair. Coat wiry, not too long. [Co]lors: as artesien-normand.

GERMAN BRACH
HW: under 16 inches. Long head. Undefined stop. Clear, light-colored eyes. Thickly coated belly; hind legs feathered. Colors: red to yellow with black saddle. Breast and muzzle white; white collar and tail tip.

WESTPHALIAN BADGER BRACH
HW: 12–14 inches. Long, narrow head. Undefined stop. Eyes dark. Ears broad and medium-length, stumpy and rounded. Tail carried horizontally. Coat dense and rough. Colors: red to yellow; black saddle or patches and white points.

BAVARIAN ALPS BLOODHOUND
HW: D up to 20 inches, B up to 18 inches. Broad skull, flat-domed. Dark brown eyes. Straight hanging, medium-length ears. Dense coat, flat, moderately rough. Colors: deep red, copper, red-brown, pale yellow, red-gray.

HANOVERIAN BL[OODHOUND]
HW: about 24 inc[hes.] powerful jaws, ov[er] large and broad. [Ears] smooth, shiny coa[t.] red, streaked or fla[me.]

POINTERS AND SETTERS

[EN]GLISH COCKER SPANIEL
[H]V: about 16 inches. Heavy head, [pro]nounced stop. Square jaw. [Br]own eyes. Long ears covered with [lon]g, straight hair. Coat straight, [sil]ky, with feathering. Colors: many [va]rieties.

POINTER
HW: about 26 inches. Long head, pronounced stop. Dark eyes. Thin, silky ears, rounded. Ratio length to height: 9:8. Coat thin, dense, hard, shiny, flat. Colors: white with patches and spots of black, brown, orange and yellow.

ENGLISH SETTER
HW: 23–25 inches. Long, clean-cut head, good stop. Dark brown eyes. Moderately long ears with fold. Tail and legs heavily feathered. Slightly wavy coat, long and silky. Colors: white with black, yellow or liver markings. Tri-colored. Spots preferred.

GORDON SETTER
HW: D up to 26 inches, B up to 24 inches. Head deeper than broad, wrinkles on the forehead, good stop. Dark brown eyes. Moderately long ears, covered with long hair. Well-feathered tail and legs. Soft coat. Colors: jet black with shiny red markings.

IRISH SETTE[R]
HW: 25–27 i[nches.] stop. Dark br[own.] fold, fringed [ears.] Coat mediu[m.] Colors: brow[n.]

RETRIEVERS

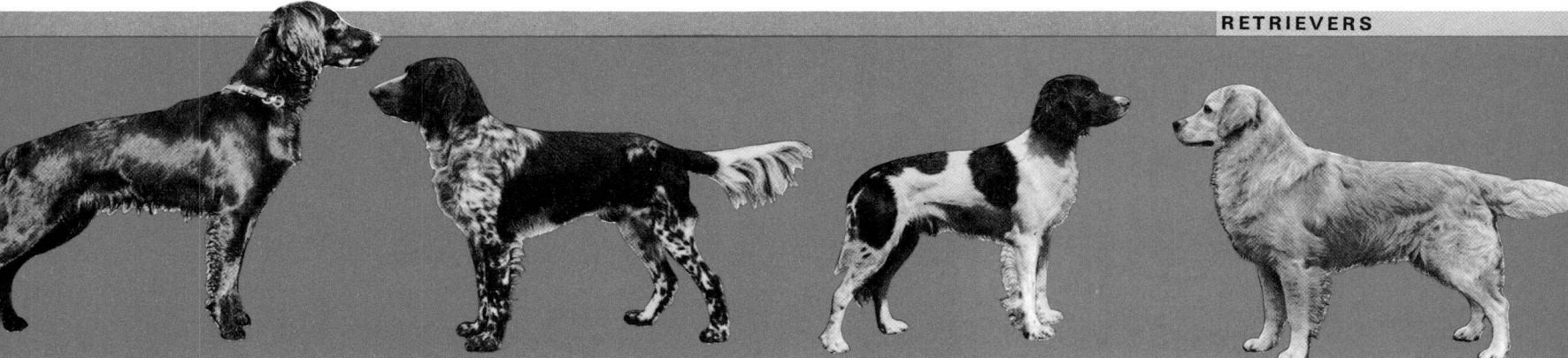

[GE]RMAN LONG-HAIRED POINTER
[H]V: 25–28 inches. Head long, clean-cut. [Sto]p steeply sloping. Broad jaw. Dark eyes. [Ea]rs not very long, with a lot of hair. No dewlap. [Sli]ghtly wavy coat, feathering on legs. Colors: [bro]wn and white, with specks or patches.

LARGE MUNSTERLANDER
HW: about 23 inches. Long head, clean-cut jaw. Black, flat nose. Dark eyes. Broad, rounded ears, fringed. Feathered tail and legs. Coat smooth, slightly wavy. Colors: white with black head, large black patches and small specks on body.

SMALL MUNSTERLANDER
HW: D up to 22, B up to 20 inches. Head long, clean-cut, jaw long. Brown nose. Dark eyes. Ears slightly pointed, fringed. Coat smooth, flat. Colors: white, brown and white with yellow or reddish patches.

GOLDEN RETRIEVER
HW: D up to 25, B up to 22 inches. Head set gracefully on muscular neck. Pronounced stop. Powerful jaw, dark eyes. Black nose. Medium-sized ears. Long, straight tail. Coat thick, slightly wavy. Color: rich gold.

Hunting in the Field

long distances, even when badly wounded. For that reason, the hunter will keep his eye firmly fixed on the wounded pheasant and search for it, with the help of his dog, at the point where it seemed to fall to ground and disappear. Proper pheasant hunting required reliable retrievers and skilled searchers for wounded game. All breeds of dogs descended from the ancient species of bird dogs are particularly well suited for hunting in the field.

The pointer is the noblest specimen of bird dog and the most skilled in the field. Its perfectly suited body structure, its excellent character and its masterly command of the tasks allotted to it combine to make this dog incomparable. It was these characteristics which led to an attempt in Europe to cross it with the somewhat slower, smooth-haired German setter. The hope was that the result would be a dog with an even finer nose as well as a brisker temperament. The success of the experiment was soon evident: the one-time "field sniffer" was transformed into a finer, more spirited German smooth-haired pointer with an exceptionally fine nose.

Hunters often speak a language which, to non-hunters, may sound like an obscure form of Latin. Non-hunters may, for example, find it difficult to understand why hunters talk of "work" when, after all, it is the pleasure of hunting which draws the hunter into the fields and woods. The fact that real work is performed both by the hunter and his dog will, however, become clear in the following chapters, which describe aspects of hunting with dogs.

Hunting with a pointer in a well-stocked partridge field, with the early morning mists rising around him and his gun under his arm, is as thrilling an experience as the dedicated hunter could ask for. With its nose raised, positioned one to two hundred yards from the hunter, the pointer ranges over wide tracts of open country in search of winged game. All cover, regardless of how thick, is carefully examined. The dog repeatedly zigzags to the left and the right over the field, making certain no inch of ground is left unexplored.

An ideal bird dog has an excellent nose. It has a brisk, confident, far-ranging way of

quartering game. It has a highly developed and reliable capacity, not only for pointing, but also for remaining still for comparatively long periods without attempting to approach the quarry too closely. A field dog must be absolutely obedient. It must not be subject to extraneous diversion from, for example, hares or rabbits that might suddenly cross its path. It must be thoroughly unperturbed by the sound of gunfire. Its task includes reliable tracking of feathered game and retrieving to hand without the slightest damage to the bird.

The skill of the hunter is demonstrated by his method of shooting. The good hunter will not waste his ammunition. He will under no circumstances merely shoot at random at a chain of rising partridges and hope that at least one of his cartridges will hit a target. He will take aim at individual birds to the right and to the left. If two birds fall, one on each side, the hunter can claim to have scored a doublet.

When hunting pheasant, the skilled hunter will refrain from long-distance shots. He knows that this bird is hardy and able to fly

Hunting in the Woods

Retrieving, searching for game and following a blood trail are among the most important tasks of the dog in the woods. It must be able to kill small forest predators and chase and bring to bay wounded game. Size permitting, it should also be able to work in animal burrows.

Hunting in the woods demands much more independence and initiative from the dog than does hunting in open fields. In the fields, the "high nose" makes the running; in the woods, it is the "low nose" which dominates. A track-sniffing dog generally comes equipped with the right qualities for work in the woods. Among them is the ability to vary its baying according to whether it is hunting at random or following a specific trail. The better a dog can pick up a trail, the better is it likely to be able to follow that trail and retrieve to hand. It is possible to train a dog to follow a single trail without deviating from it—a quality essential in a dog of the woods. Its baying when it finds a track, its tenacity in holding to the trail, its passion for tracking— all these are basic attributes of a dog suitable for training in the most varied forest tasks.

Most important, of course, is the relationship between the dog and its master. Few circumstances better illustrate a dog's true grasp of its function than when it operates under the rifle in undergrowth. Instantaneous, disciplined response is essential, with the dog pointing as soon as it scents the game. The German pointer, the hunting terrier and the spaniel are particularly well suited for this kind of work.

Searching a wider area requires greater initiative from the dog because its explorations often take it into places where the view of its master is obstructed by dense thickets, high grass and other cover. The dog's task in this sort of territory is not only to flush out the game but also to chase it, baying loudly, toward its master or the line of hunters. Pointing is not required in these circumstances and the dog must be capable of working completely on its own in dense woods. For this assignment, it requires a fine sense of smell, a loud bark, a passion for pursuing, and stamina. The dachshund, spaniel, fox terrier, hunting terrier and small basset are among the dogs well suited for this kind of work. These breeds all have the necessary ability to bay loudly while following the trail and are not upset if the luck of the hunt shifts them from chasing one animal briefly to going after another when the first trail runs dry.

The dog of the woods must be able to spurt into action after the shot has been fired, following blood trails when necessary, to prevent wounded game from being lost or dead game from remaining unfound. The desirable qualities for reliable dog work after the shot has been fired are much the same as those applicable beforehand: adherence to the trail, passion for tracking and enthusiasm for retrieving. A good dog of the woods, which has been well trained, will never disappoint its master, regardless of the kind of game it is sent to flush out or track down.

Following the Blood Trail

Below: Locating the stag wounded by the hunter's bullet precedes the successful end to the day's hunting. The dog follows the trail on a long leash, at least six yards in front of the hunter.

Right: Off the leash, the dog finds the dead or severely wounded deer and begins its loud baying, which continu until the hunter arrives.

If there is such a thing as a crowning point to the hunter's day in the woods with his dog, it is undoubtedly the skill displayed and energy expended following a blood trail. There are various ways this is done.

The hunter can keep his dog on the leash and follow it to the fallen game. He can turn his dog loose to find the dead game and bay long and loud until the hunter reaches the spot. Or, turned loose to find the dead game, the dog can return to its master and indicate, by jumping, barking and running back and forth between hunter and game, that it is to be followed to the quarry. If the game shows any signs of life, the dog will dispatch it quickly before summoning its master.

A refined technique sometimes used in tracking down dead or wounded game involves the dog in more sophisticated action. It clasps a piece of wood or leather hanging from its collar between its teeth and returns to its master, thereby indicating that its search has been successful and that it should be followed to the spot.

Each of the different methods for following a blood trail has its advocates and detractors. It is impossible to say that one is better than the others. It is, however, perfectly clear that following the blood trail with the dog on a long leash is the most reliable, if not the most convenient, way to find a fugitive, wounded animal. Work with the leash forms the basis of all bloodtrailing. It is the method by which the dog learns to stick to the trail. In contrast to turning the dog loose, this type of work is carried out under the immediate control and with the immediate collaboration of the hunter, permitting him to retain uninterrupted influence over the dog. Many hunters testify to the satisfying feeling of following leashed dogs, catching sight here and there of traces of blood on the ground or on low branches, or tracks, to establish undeniably that they are on the right trail.

Following the blood trail with a dog on the leash requires complete understanding between hunter and dog. The leash must be welcomed by the dog, increase its determination to find game and offer the promise of reward. The skilled hunter never forge this last inducement. The old custom rewarding the dog with the warm innards the dead animal is seldom practiced thes days because it is feared that dogs subse quently bloodtrailing off the leash might b tempted to tear open a dead animal on its ow to seek its reward.

It is, incidentally, unwise to punish or pu the dog around roughly if it loses the trail. Th leash represents a link between the hunter an the dog more significant than merely length of leather. On no account should it b allowed to arouse the slightest feeling displeasure in the dog. If it does, successfu leash work is impossible.

Searching for wounded game is a predator instinct of ancient origin and almost all breed of dog are, therefore, suitable for this kind task. There are, however, definite specialists the job, notably the Hanoverian bloodhoun and the Bavarian mountain bloodhound.

The closer to the ground the dog is, th more reliable is its work in following th blood trail—a rule which applies to all breed This is because the low-slung dog has muc less difficulty in keeping its nose to the groun than a long-legged one. It is, therefore, n surprising that the dachshund is an exceller breed for following the blood trail.

Other breeds used for this work include th small Munsterlander, the spaniel, the huntin terrier and the fox terrier. With carefu training and skilled direction, the Germa pointer may also be used, despite the disac vantage of its larger size. It is unsurpasse for bloodtrailing off the leash.

In Reeds and Rushes

The hunter has followed his dog into the water to have a better field of fire when the ducks rise. He sends the dog into the reeds to scatter the birds.

A major attraction for the hunter in this form of hunting is the reliable performance of a water dog which excels in both seeking out and retrieving the hunter's quarry.

When hunting duck, the hunter sends his dog into the reeds or rushes to flush out the birds. The hunter himself remains on the bank, positioning himself according to where his dog is in the reeds. If he stays too far behind his canine companion, or stays fixed to one spot, the firing distance could become too great and, more than likely, he will miss the ducks when they rise and scatter. As soon as a shot has been fired, the dog leaps forward at its master's command. If a duck is wounded and unable to fly and tries to take cover in the reeds, the dog swims after it, barking loudly, until it can seize it. With the bird held firmly but gently in its jaws, it swims to shore and delivers the prey to its master.

The dog leaps elegantly into the water to retrieve the duck shot by its master.

Hunting tradition holds that ducks may be shot only when rising or in flight; never on the water. A wounded duck may trail one or both of its legs in the water and may no longer be able to swim. Birds with wounded wings may try to escape from pursuing dogs by diving and remaining under water. There may be a long wait before the duck comes up for air again.

The hunter often conceals himself, especially at twilight, in places where he knows ducks will land and congregate. A hunter familiar with his territory knows where ducks alight to seek food and a place to spend the night. To ensure that he does not wait in vain, he will sometimes scatter food—corn or acorns, for example—on the ground. To avoid discouraging birds from landing there, however, the hunter who can tell the difference is advised not to shoot ducks which feed there regularly. Only when flights of migratory birds begin arriving in great numbers and frequency at a given location can the hunter feel complacent about testing his skills there.

The dog swims, baying, after the duck until it can seize the bird. If the duck is wounded, the dog will have no difficulty catching up.

In the early morning hours, stalking can also be successful, so long as the hunter, under cover of a raised bank, can approach the ducks on the water closely enough.

Even temperament, a hunting instinct and pleasure in its work are the three most important characteristics of a successful water dog. In summer and autumn, the dog may be delighted to splash around in the water. But that is not always true for frigid winter waters.

Its pursuit successful, the dog swims back to land through the rushes, the dead duck in its jaws.

The dog climbs out of the water, still firmly holding its prey.

Right: A German smooth-haired pointer at work. A wounded duck tries to flee; a second duck flies away. It will not be shot because the dog is in the line of fire.

Only dogs which are hardened to all sorts of weather conditions can work in water when the thermometer plummets. Wire-haired species are more suited to such chores than smooth-haired ones. The thicker the woolly undercoat of a wire-haired dog, the less sensitive it will be to cold and damp. Whether the dog is wire-haired or smooth, the wise hunter will make sure to rub the dog down and cover it after hunting.

Ideal hunting companions for work in or near water include the German pointer (especially the wire-haired variety), poodle pointer, griffon, spaniel, hunting terrier, fox terrier, and retriever. Of retrievers, the Chesapeake Bay retriever is a particularly fine water dog.

Dogs the World Over

Dyre hound (Norwegian moos
hound). A medium-sized, thick
coated dog with raised ears and
curled tail. HW: 18–20 inche
Powerful, compact hindquarters
deep, broad chest. Coat: hard
thick, flat. Color: gray with blac
tips to top hairs.

Swedish Grayhound (3). A mec

1 Basenji   2 Canaan dog   3 Swedish Grayhound   4 Jamtland dog

Primitive Dogs

Shensi Dogs. Examining the large number of primitive dogs of undefined breed in the African and Asian tropics makes it possible to reconstruct the gradual domestication of the dog over the ages.

The dogs in question here, from a semi-cultivated tropical zone (cultural epoch of the Middle Stone Age, around 9000–8000 B.C.), are still in the beginning stages of domestication today. They are probably killed and eaten by man in times of need. The German cynologist Werth gave them the name "shensi dogs" (*Canis familiaris shensi*) in 1944. From the wide variety of shensi dogs the:

Basenji (1) has emerged from anonymity and has been declared a breed in its own right. It serves many of the inhabitants of Central Africa as a hunting dog and as a regulator of small predators. It has been bred in England since 1895 and in America since 1937. The English Basenji Club has published the following standard description: the basenji is a medium-sized, long-legged, thick-coated dog with a conical skull, prick ears and a curly tail. HW: D 17 inches, B 16 inches. Wrinkles

on the forehead are characteristic. Short, shiny, silky coat. Supple skin. Colors: chestnut-brown, pure black, black with light points. White breast, paws and tail tip. The basenji is probably the only dog in the world which never barks.

The other seventeen or so kinds of shensi dogs are not genuine breeds but can be described as variations of the species.

Wild dogs. The Australian dingo occupies a special place in the wild dog category, standing somewhere between the shensi and pariah dogs (see below). It was already domesticated in the Stone Age and emigrated with man to Australia where it became wild. Its usefulness as a killer of small predators and wild rabbits is offset by the damage it inflicts to herds of sheep. The dingo is medium-sized, long-bodied, short-legged, with a thick coat and raised ears. HW: about 22 inches. Colors: red to pale yellow.

Pariah dogs. These dogs are classified under the collective description "ownerless street dogs of the Orient." They are native to Iran, India, Japan, Australia, Asia Minor, Egypt and North Africa. Whether the pariah dog is a wild

descendant of earlier domestic breeds or of a dingo-like original species is not known.

The Kennel Club of Israel recently published an official standard description of the *Canaan dog* (2), according to which the animal is a medium-sized, collie-like, short-haired dog with short, relatively broad raised ears set low, dark eyes, deep chest and bushy tail. Coat: medium-length, thick—males with manes undesirable. HW: 20–26 inches. Colors: sandy to red-brown; black and white.

Dogs of the North

All northern dogs have a characteristic in common: their genuine passion for hunting. This is a product of predilections which have been inherited from their wolf forebears and which have been maintained while, with the Pomeranian dog for example, the hunting instinct has been sacrificed to develop watchdog skills. Northern hunters have virtually created canine specialists for each type of game and all hunting procedures.

Moose Hounds

From the large number of local breeds, the Scandinavians tend to favor three especially:

ium-sized, powerful, thick coated dog with prick ears and curled tail. HW: 19–21 inches Powerful, compact, short hind quarters and broad, deep chest Coat comparatively long, straight haired, stiff, with black-tipped hairs. Color: gray.

Jamtland Dog (Great Swedish moose hound) (4). HW: 21–2 inches. Similar in appearance to the Swedish grayhound. All three moose hound breeds are fast robust and have good powers o endurance and initiative. They are intelligent and energetic and are passionate hunters of moose and other game; in America, they readily pursue lynx, mountain lio and raccoon.

Bear Hounds

Karelian Bear Hound (5). A med ium-sized, sturdy dog with thick coat, raised and pointed ears and a curled tail. HW: 19–2 inches. Long, powerful hindquar ters; straight back; muscular slightly sloping croup. Large deep, oval chest. Straight, stif coat. Color: black, with clearly defined white points. Courageous daring, dedicated hunter of bear lynx and moose, with specia skill for finding bears' winte quarters. Its senses, particularly its sense of smell, are exceptionally sharp. It is distinguished by its headstrong delight in fights and scuffles.

Tahltan Bear Dog (Bear hound of the Canadian Tahltan Indians). This dog exists only in a northern environment; its breeding is,

to search for birds' eggs on steep rock faces. It is a small, long, wire-haired dog with prick ears and a curled tail. HW: 9–10 inches. Coat: dense, rough top-coat; soft, woolly undercoat. Colors: black, gray, brown; sometimes white points.

Laika (8). The laika is probably

9

5 Karelian bear hound 6 Finnish Pomeranian 7 Lunde Hound 8 Laika

therefore, restricted to a limited area. It is a small, fox-like, long-haired dog with vertically pricked, bat-like ears and an extremely thick, straight, vertically carried tail. HW: 12–16 inches. Coat: dense and long. Color: blue-gray with white markings and black head, or pure black.

The Tahltan Indians carry their dogs in animal-skin sacks as close as possible to the bear, then prod them on. Without attacking, the dog encircles the bear, barking loudly, until the hunter is able to take aim and shoot. Apart from bears, these dogs hunt lynx and porcupine. Its bark is much like that of the fox; its howl resembles that of the coyote.

Bird Dogs

Finnish Pomeranian (6). A medium-sized, fox-red, densely coated dog with fine, prick ears and a curled tail which it carries sideways on its back. HW: 15–19 inches. Coat: short and flat, longer on the body, stiffer on the neck. The Finnish Pomeranian is used as a many-sided hunting dog in Finland and specializes in capercaillies and grouse.

Lunde Hound (Norwegian Bird Dog) (7). Bred for many centuries

the most interesting northern dog. It occupies a position somewhere between the Pomeranian and the mastiff and bears a remarkable resemblance to the wolf. This Russian dog is primarily a hunting dog particularly noted for hunting feathered game. When it has a bird at bay in a tree, it barks ceaselessly until the hunter arrives at the scene. If the bird flies away, the dog follows silently until the bird again settles on the branch of a tree.

Common characteristics of all laika are: medium size, powerful appearance, wedge-shaped head with slanting eyes, triangular prick ears, tail carried rolled over its back. They are lively, energetic and, because of their coarse, dense coats, weather-proof. They are alert and dedicated hunters. As well as for feathered game, the laika is used for hunting sable, marten, ermine and polecat.

The following breeds of laika are recognized in Russia: the Finnish-Russian laika, the Russian-European laika, the West and East Siberian laika, and the north Russian Samojeden laika which is chiefly used for hunting reindeer in the Archangel region.

African Lion Dog (9 and 10). Called the "pronkrug" by the

10

local population. This dog, the most popular breed in South Africa for use as a hunting and watchdog as well as a household pet, is rare outside South Africa and Rhodesia. The South African kennel club describes the pronkrug as follows: medium-sized, powerful, muscular. HW: D 25–27 inches, B somewhat less. Broad, deep chest. Coat: smooth, hard, light-brown in color, sometimes with small white markings on the chest and paws. Its name comes from the word *pronk*, meaning a dark stripe of hair, which begins

between the hips, runs across the back, curves over the shoulder blades and ends in a crown. This *pronk* runs against the grain of the hairs, from rear to head. The tail is long and round and carried limp except when the dog is working, when it is borne horizontally. This dog is a remarkable jumper, capable of overtaking and challenging lions.

Dogs in Action

1

3 A setter determinedly pursuing a hare which has been wounded by the hunter. The hunting dog is essential for finding and retrieving wounded game and thus saving it from a slow, more painful death. Although the setter has a longer pedigree than the pointer and is a direct descendant of the "sitting dog," which is absolutely reliable for pointing purposes, the pointer is more popular among hunters. Nevertheless, the setter has many faithful advocates because of its skill in retrieving and questing as well as pointing.

2 and 4 The German pointer is considered today a jack of all trades. The smooth-haired and wire-haired varieties are the only kinds of pointers which can be considered truly all-round hunters. Their reputation in America and Africa is steadily increasing.

In the picture below, the hunter has shot a duck which has fallen into dense reeds at the water's edge. The dog, turned loose from its leash, has been commanded to search and retrieve. The photograph on the right shows the German wire-haired pointer emerging from the water with the duck in its jaws.

There are those who contend that, despite all his skill and experience, a hunter without a good hunting dog is like a ladder without rungs. Undoubtedly, a dog can "see" further across camouflaged countryside than the sharpest human eye. Other skills it brings to the fields, the woods and the water make it an invaluable hunting companion.

The dogs pictured on these two pages, and the tasks they are shown performing, symbolize hunting dogs and their abilities the world over, whether they descend from noble canine lines or are the chance products of incidental pairing. The photographs illustrate situations with which each dog was confronted while performing its function—often alone and often required to make its own decisions in the absence of a guiding hand or command from its master.

1 A smooth-haired German pointer has located and challenged a fox, blocking its path to its burrow. The dog now barks loudly until the hunter arrives at the scene. If the fox tries to turn tail and get away, the dog will give chase and go for the kill.

2

3

Fox Hunting

"It's a glorious day." Glorious or not, those words are on everyone's lips, because it is the occasion rather than the weather that matters. Greetings are exchanged; horses are appraised and praised. One is among friends: experienced huntsmen in red coats, novices in tweed and bowlers. Horses are impatient to be off. The hounds are excited and panting. The spectators gaze curiously. The master of the hunt, upon whose leadership, knowledge of the countryside and experience the success of the day's activities depends, discusses final details with the whipper-in, who keeps the hounds from straying. In fact, the weather is glorious. Yesterday it rained but today the sun is shining; the best possible conditions for the hounds. A blast of the horn—and they're off. At the head, the whipper-in turns the hounds loose. Then the master and the rest of the hunt, the best in front, first in groups, later in single file, the thunder of hooves in the wind, a gallop over fields and meadows, over hedges, through wall gaps, over moorland and streams, on and on. Dirt and water are thrown up by powerful hooves. It is part of the hunt. At last, the leading hound sounds off, cautiously at first, then the whole pack opens up with a music all its own. The whipper-in cries: "Forrad, forrad away!" They spurt forward even faster, following warm tracks over open country. Suddenly the hunt comes to a halt. The huntsmen have come to a road. The hounds have lost the scent. They search for it, their muzzles to the ground. A farmer points toward a bog. Off they go in a new direction—a flash of red among the rushes. The master sounds his horn: "Tally ho!"—fox in sight! The hearts of horses and riders beat faster. There is an excited baying of hounds. Riders jostle to be in at the kill. "Over there! Over there!" The whipper-in waves his cap and reins in his horse.

Then the fox displays its cunning. It flees from the bog to sandy hills nearby and disappears into its underground retreat. "He's gone to ground," someone cries.

The horn sounds: "Hunt over." This time the fox has won and even small terriers brought along will not be able to drive it from its intricate burrow. Nevertheless, it was a "glorious" day for all concerned—including, this time, the fox.

Origins of Falconry

The sharp eye of the falcon, the audacious beak of the goshawk and the wild nature of the eagle have excited the admiration of mankind for longer than recorded history. Though birds of prey have been man's hunting companions since ancient times, they have never been domesticated. They have always remained creatures of nature, symbols of freedom and dignity.

The Egyptians worshiped the falcon as a god and considered it a messenger of light. But the origins of falconry lie not in Egypt, nor in the gloom of thick, primeval European forests, but in the wide open expanses of the East—in distant Asia. In regions where hordes of horsemen thundered over endless steppes, it was the privilege of now long-forgotten chieftains to hunt with eagles and falcons. Long before the light of civilization dawned in the West, falconry and the cult of the eagle were established as far as the shores of the Yellow Sea.

In old feudal Korea, all birds of prey were protected by the threat of severe punishment for those who did them injury. Records of magnificent hunts with eagles and falcons exist for China in the Han period (around 200 B.C. to A.D. 200) when Buddhism is believed to have reached Central Asia from India and when hunting with chariots partially superseded hunting on horseback.

In the fourth century, the art of hunting with falcons and white-headed sea eagles developed from Korea to the Japanese islands. No less a personage than Tenno Mintoku, a predecessor of the Japanese emperor, wrote a work of eighty-one volumes about falconry.

Around 1400, the Venetian explorer Marco Polo provided the western world with its first report —contested by his contemporaries —of hunting with birds in far-off Cathay. This discoverer of new worlds had become a trusted friend and adviser of Kublai Khan, the Mongol emperor of China.

It is, therefore, reasonable to assume that his detailed descriptions of the emperor's ways were not totally far-fetched. He describes how Kublai Khan went hunting accompanied by thousands of falconers, fowlers and hunting flunkeys, hundreds of falcons, goshawks and tame cheetahs: "The emperor sits on a wooden sedan borne by elephants, gilded on the inside and covered with tiger-skins on the outside . . . He has his chosen goshawks with him. As soon as pheasants, cranes and other game are sighted, the sedan door opens and the emperor

sets his birds free. Seated on a ma[ ] he now watches the play an[ ] fights of the birds with obviou[ ] delight . . ."

Mongol dominance in China wa[ ] followed by the emergence o[ ] the Ming Dynasty and then by th[ ] Manchus. Great cultures and dy[ ] nasties rose and fell. But the fin[ ] art of hunting with eagles wa[ ] maintained and is still pursued i[ ] Central Asia, at the foot of th[ ] Tien Shan mountains and on th[ ] steppes of Kazakhstan. The peopl[ ] of Kirghiz still practice the art o[ ] falconry according to their ancien[ ] traditions, riding on horsebac[ ]

its sense of direction), it sits for days on end on a swaying rope without food. In classic prisoner-disorientation procedure, the rope is kept in constant motion so that the eagle will forget its identity and all other frames of reference it may have acquired. Only when, weakened by hunger, it can barely keep its balance, even with its wings spread, is the blinding hood removed from its head.

The falconer then shows the bird a piece of meat for the first time since its capture. He gives it a small piece, compelling it to move toward him to receive it. Then another piece. Then he mounts his horse and the eagle, to get more food, flutters to grasp another morsel of food from him. The game continues until the bird, tamed, rides with its claws firmly grasping the gloved wrist of its master.

All this sets the stage for actual hunting training for the bird. When it soars up to attack and kill its prey, the bird is rewarded with bits of meat which the hunter keeps in his boots. The eagle, confident of this reward, invariably returns to the saddle and allows its master to replace the hood over its eyes. "It has," according to an old description, "forgotten freedom, forgotten the mountains, yes, forgotten even itself."

pursuit of wolves, small deer and gazelles with their *berkut*—golden eagles. Foxes too are more often hunted with birds of prey than with rifles.

Like all falconers, the Kirghiz prefer to hunt primarily with fully fledged mature birds which need no special training to swoop down on their prey. To acquire eagles for hunting, the Kirghiz erect large, tent-shaped nets in which the hearts of newly killed wild sheep are laid as bait. The bird-catchers, concealed in nearby natural caves or among rocks, often have to wait days before they can spring their traps. Golden eagles are not only rare, they cover enormous distances in their unceasing search for hares, marmots, squirrels, foxes, pheasants and Caspian snow-cocks.

When the eagle, soaring high in the sky from valley to valley, spots the bait on the ground it appears to stop in mid-air. It then swoops with folded wings only to become entangled in the nets laid out to take it prisoner. The eagle caught, the job of taming and training the bird begins. Tied by its legs and blinded by a leather hood (and thus robbed of

Hunting with Trained Birds

Falconry is the ancient art of hunting with trained birds. Among the birds which have been falconers' companions in the annals of hunting, acting on command to seize their prey while in flight, are the falcon, goshawk and eagle. The training of these winged creatures is a protracted, often tedious affair which is completed only when the hunting bird forgets its original free state and comes to recognize and accept the falconer as its master. After that, practice sessions involve a decoy made of feathers tied to a piece of meat which is thrown into the air. The falcon, if that is the bird being trained, attacks the decoy as if it were real feathered

1

2

3

game. But this is only the beginning. The falconer now rides out into hunting territory, his newly trained falcon on his wrist. Should a partridge or a pheasant take to the air, the falconer hurls his falcon in its direction. Feathers fly, the game falls dead to the ground, followed by the falcon which covers it with its wings before feeding. The well-trained falcon will always return to its master's wrist—a phenomenon almost inconceivable to the uninitiated, who find it hard to understand that the bird does so of its own free will. The falconer may have had the bird for years and they may have become true companions.

To train a falcon, it is necessary to take it from its nest when it first begins to fly. The training must begin as soon as possible. Experienced falconers, however, sometimes catch and train fully grown birds which are used to living free and wild.

There are differences between the hunting

4

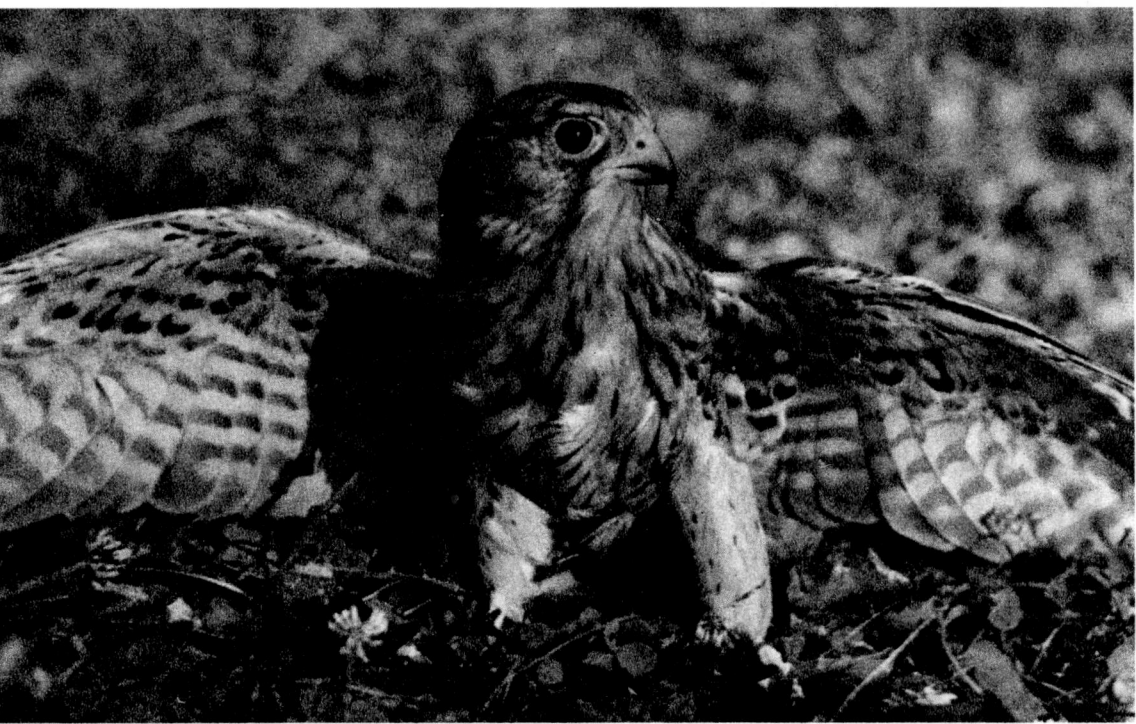

1 Young goshawk which still has its vertical markings.

2 Hooded hunting birds on a perch.

3 A bell on the bird's leg.

4 The bird is "thrown" by its master. The falconer often carries the bird on his left wrist.

5 The goshawk pursues its quarry, a hare this time, flying low over the ground. The hare attempts to escape with leaps and zigzags. But the goshawk wins out. After a short pause for breath, it will begin feeding on its victim. The falconer allows the bird a certain portion of the quarry as a reward for a job well done.

6 The peregrine falcon squats on its quarry, covering it with its wings before starting to feed.

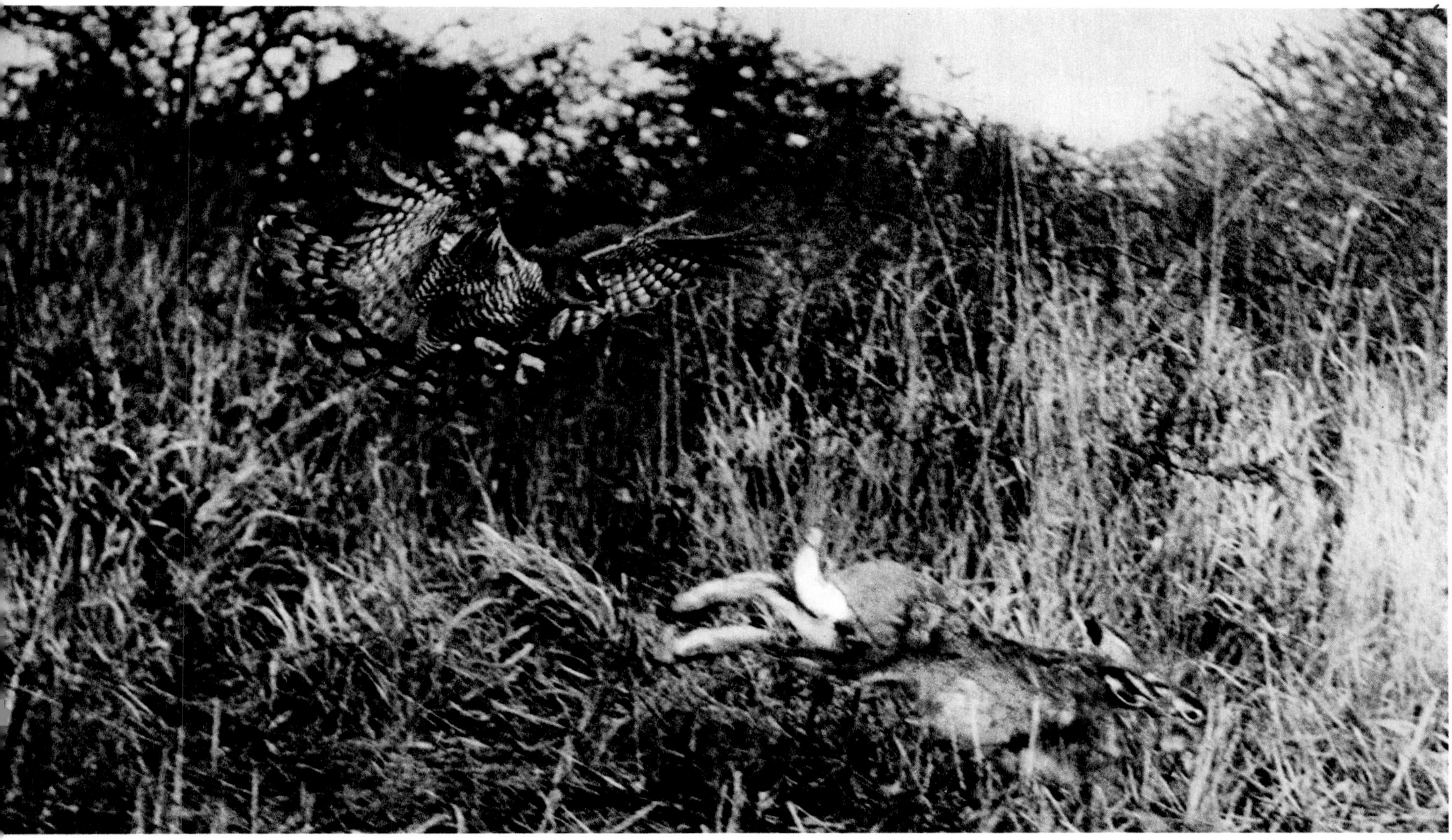

ethods of the goshawk and the falcon. The lcon hunts in high flight; the goshawk in ow flight. When the falconer turns his falcon oose, the bird tries to gain height as quickly s it can. At a certain altitude, it circles round ie falconer in wide arcs. When feathered ame rises, it swoops rapidly down, seizes the ame in its long claws and kills it with pecks) the neck and throat. Its swoop is often so ist that it cannot keep hold of its prey and has to go back for it.

In the case of the goshawk and sparrow awk, the birds fly over low ground, circling ushes and other obstacles, and kill their prey n the ground—mice, squirrels, jays and ıbbits.

Both types of hunting bird share one haracteristic, however. They both feed on ie ground at the spot where the game has ıllen, and falconers attach small bells to the ·gs of their birds, to locate them and their rey.

6

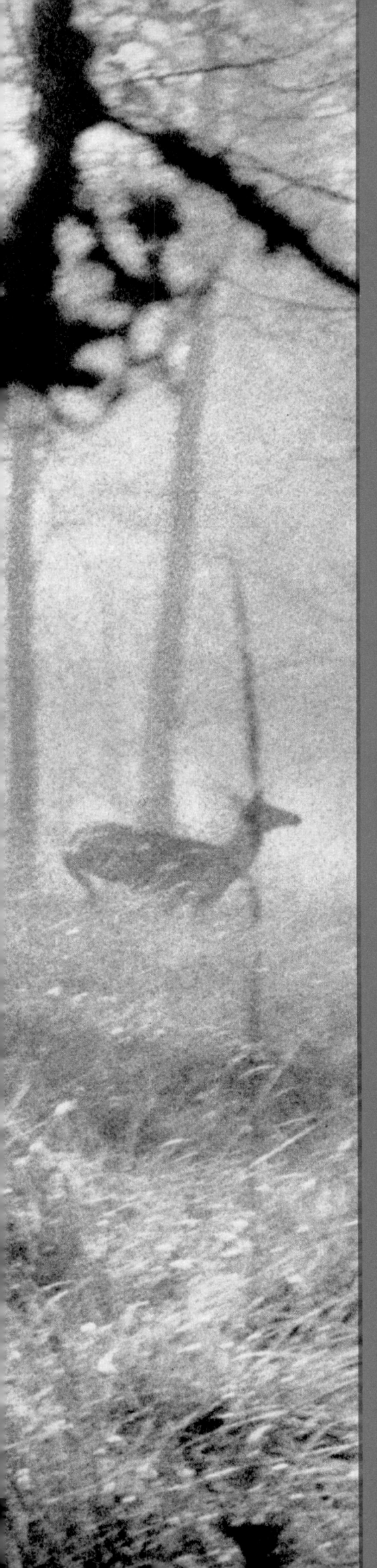

Hunting Magic

Hunting I reckon very good
To brace the nerves and stir the blood.

So said poet Matthew Green, seizing upon just one aspect of the magic of hunting. But whatever thrills it provides, hunting has always been primarily a means to a specific end—a source of food to perpetuate the human species. But it was always something else as well. Man the killer, who killed to live, was in turn influenced by his victim. In time, the victim became an adversary who could only be understood by means of a system of cultish rituals. That same victim was the instrument of trials of courage, skill and determination, by which qualities man could be classified. Primitive peoples believed the awesome wildness of animals could be assumed by hunters who vanquished them. Hunters today also feel linked in almost magical fashion to the animals they hunt. They too sense a primitive unity. The element of competition— the challenge of the often shadowy adversary—remains part of the hunting ritual. There is often a powerful tension which can only be resolved by the death of the hunted animal. The harder the hunt, the greater the endurance and sacrifice required, the more complete the satisfaction. Most recently, however, the hunter has had to assume a new responsibility. The satisfying moment of conquest has had to be subordinated to a sense of responsibility for the balance of nature, threatened by the vulnerability of many species to extinction or depletion. The most crucial task for today's hunter is the fulfillment of his role as preserver of the ecological and biological balance. He must be a conservationist in the most comprehensive sense. Hunting traditions can survive only if they are adapted to changed conditions. Mankind's technological superiority, which has jeopardized the natural balance, must now be employed to set it right once more.

Concealment

Although skill in stalking may be considered by many the hunter's greatest talent—it certainly was before the invention of firearms— patience is without doubt his most rewarding quality. Patience is the primary skill when hunting from concealment, from a pre-prepared hide. And since patience is a quality anyone can develop, and patient vigilance carries this virtue just a step further, hunting from hides has become increasingly popular in some parts of the world —notably central Europe.

Today's hunter is often a man with a trade or profession which permits him to indulge his hunting passion only when work permits. He is, therefore, frequently pressed for time. He is also limited by conservation laws and practices with regard to the species, age and sex of the animal he hunts. The hunter, as a consequence, seeks a method for meeting time and hunting restrictions most easily. Many consider hunting from concealed hides the most reliable way.

This does not mean that stalking is an inferior approach. Hunting from the hide is simply different. It offers hunting experience of a special kind. When a hide stand has been erected and the hunter's rifle and binoculars are set in place, his personal existence dissolves into the awesome silence of his surroundings. It is a curiou transformation. Some minutes be fore, the determined hunter wa rushing to take up his position now he is suddenly careful not t intrude upon the silence, not t reveal his presence, not to displa any identity of his own. Hig above the surface breeze, out danger of having his scent picke up by wild game, the hunter ma be part of a spiritual communio transcending the hunt. His strivin

r identification with the tree
.mouflaging his observation post
iks him with the green world
ound him, a world in which
cavy footsteps and other human
bises are remote.

The hunter waits unmoving,
erged into his surroundings,
rreful not to anticipate the mo-
ient when his purpose in being
iere will be fulfilled. Suddenly an
iimal form emerges from a thick-
:, or from the mist, and with it a
ew dimension of the hunter's
ristence. A decision must be
iade. The weapon in the hunter's
and becomes more a part of him
ian the tree which had, an
istant before, meant so much,
iut which is now just camouflage.
rom the hide, he makes the
ecision for the animal in his
ght—life or death.

There are no rigid formulas for
deciding on the position and
design of the hide. Local conditions, the animals' approach and
the hunter's intentions vary according to time and place. Generally, the hide should be erected
in a commanding position but
accessible to the hunter by a route
as distant as possible from the
path usually followed by game.
It should be built to make it
possible for the hunter to remain
still and vigilant for hours on end.
It should be sufficiently solid and
comfortable—a covered hide is
essential for cold winter nights.

A structure which uses as little
material as possible, which har-
monizes with the surroundings,
and which fulfils the above-stated
objectives is ideal. As for choice of
materials, oak and conifer woods
are admirably solid and durable.

The Stag in Rut

Left: To imitate the roaring of a stag in rut, the hunter may use a triton horn, an ox horn and various other devices, including even the glass cylinder of an oil lamp.

Right: A roaring stag—a symbol of majesty.

The climax of the deer hunting season is the so-called ten sacred days—the brief period at the end of September and the beginning of October, before the mists and night frosts set in: the rutting season. At other times, the stag tends to be a timid creature whose remarkably acute senses serve its extreme caution and discretion. Come the rutting season, however, the animal exhibits a full measure of self-assertion and aggression, with only the strongest assuming responsibility for propagation of the species.

at first from far away in a mist-shrouded hollow, then nearer and louder. Again the challenge, more certain and determined; and again a reply. And soon these exchanges are superseded by the sound of clashing antlers; wood-dull in the case of weaker animals, almost metallic when mighty stags clash.

The hinds, the reason for and goal of these angry confrontations, stand seemingly unconcerned on the borders of the clearing where the contest takes place, patiently awaiting the result of the duel.

neuvered animal. Bleeding from a gaping wound, the once-proud adversary, beaten in its struggle for dominance over the hind, might stagger away to die in some secluded spot.

However, a third party might be present to benefit from the uncontrollable urges of the stag in rut. An experienced hunter can use a shell horn, or even the glass cylinder of an oil lamp, to imitate the cry of a stag so well that he himself might be sought out and approached by an animal believing it had been challenged. The deceived creature would thus stand unprotected before the armed hunter, angrily roaring its vain challenge into the morning air, its breath vapor rising skyward. The hunter must quickly decide whether to shoot or spare the animal, according to the laws of conservation and his own predilections.

The stag in rut is an easy target. But to bring it down properly requires a high caliber rifle and a well-aimed shot. The stag's strength and powers of endurance appear greater during the rutting season. It often seems to ignore wounds which are not fatal or severely incapacitating. Stags have been known to romp off, sometimes only to seek the safety of nearby thickets, even after two or three wounds have been inflicted by hunters.

The antlers of the stag are sometimes called the "crown of the hunt." But this trophy is a mere souvenir, the memory of a dramatic moment, perhaps only a decoration for a hunter's den. The weight, size and number of tines of the antlers are of secondary significance. It is the moment of an encounter which is meaningful.

Struggles for status and for possession of hinds are fierce and merciless at this time of year. At first only grumpy and sullen, the sounds of the stag develop in an increasingly confident crescendo, with stag calls warning the hinds of encounters to come. The sounds themselves seem to goad the stags on to further belligerence. Tentative calls become firm challenges, and they are answered—

The lowered antlers crash together. Stags' hooves dig deep into the ground. Each animal tries to force back its opponent and put it to flight. For brief intervals, the locked antlers disengage, possibly a strategic withdrawal for a canny stag, which might follow through with a lightning thrust to the unprotected flank of its rival. If the ploy is successful, it can result in a painful end for the outma-

Deer at their winter feeding places appear to have their senses dulled, and their morale shattered, as they go about eating their fodder despite the presence of curious human onlookers. It is, however, a mistaken impression which anyone who has observed the animal in the wild can testify. No matter how powerful his rifle, a hunter stalking deer is doomed to failure if he lacks patience, tenacity, shrewdness and skill. In short, he must display the qualities for which good hunters have been known since the beginning of human existence.

Stalking

Without doubt, stalking is the most demanding form of hunting. It requires enormous effort, experience, stamina and skill. In stalking, the odds on hunter and hunted are more even than in other forms of hunting. A foot inadvertently placed on a dry branch and the animal world is alerted at least a hundred yards in every direction. The warning cry of a passing jay and the hunter is betrayed. And the most meticulous attention paid to the rules of stalking are totally in vain if a treacherous ground wind carries the scent of the hunter well ahead of him and sends the game scrambling off before he has even had a chance to see it.

Generally, cloven-hoofed game is the prey of stalkers. Both furred and feathered game may also occasionally be hunted in this fashion, but this would not be regarded as stalking in the usual sense of the word.

As for the tools of the trade, a good pair of binoculars can be of great assistance, but in wooded areas there is no substitute for observation by the naked eye. Every bush, every hollow, every clump of trees must be scrutinized if the stalk is to have any prospect of success. The hunter must, in short, spy out the game; not the other way round. A thorough knowledge of the characteristics of the intended victim is essential, as is familiarity with local weather conditions, the animals' usual routes, congregating places and bathing, mating, drinking and feeding habits. Nor must prevailing or likely wind conditions ever be overlooked.

High up in mountainous regions, preliminary observation through a good telescope, capable of enlarging forty times, can be particularly useful. Cover in elevated areas is much less dense than in forests of the lowlands. But scanning a wide area with a telescope with a narrow field of vision requires a lot of experience. As a general rule, the stalker should aim at a higher location when morning sunshine is likely to draw his prey upwards, and at shady lower slopes when the cooler evening begins to draw in.

Hunting Chamois

The greater the difficulties, and the more arduous the hunt, the greater the pleasure and fulfillment at its success. Such sentiments are easy enough to express, but they are confirmed by chamois hunters, who pursue their quarry despite the toil and trouble that such pursuit entails. The chamois has clear advantages over its two-legged adversaries. Man is an awkward, clumsy creature compared to the sure-footed, speedy chamois. And when the hunter finally climbs to a spot where it seems that his reward is simply waiting to be gathered in, a warning cry from an animal, seemingly on sentry duty, will send a whole tempting herd scampering away out of reach.

It is not enough for a chamois hunter to be able to climb and shoot. Everything takes on new dimensions at mountain heights. Even his rifle, accurate at two hundred yards in the valley below, can no longer be relied upon for the same precision—thinner air permits the bullet freer passage.

At an altitude of 6000 feet, on the slope of a high peak, this means an aim that would be accurate in the lowlands could completely miss its target. A shot upward or downward similarly requires corrected aiming. These essential ballistic considerations are compounded by the necessity to remain absolutely motionless—however tired or breathless the hunter might be—while keeping the hunted animal in view, calculating its likely fall and waiting until the chamois assumes a position from which it can best be picked off. All this requires a robust constitution and strong nerves.

The would-be chamois hunter would do well to study the animal carefully, systematically and unhurriedly during the summer. Judging the game is no simple matter for beginners. Although the horns of the buck are more distinctly hooked than those of the doe, there are also "buck-horned" does and "doe-horned" bucks. Judgment based on the animal's anatomy as a whole tends

eft: A good pair of binoculars is as nportant as a rifle on a chamois hunt.

Right: Real duels between chamois are are. But there can be furious mock attles between rival bucks during the utting season.

Below: A herd of chamois, startled by unters, flees out of range.

o be more reliable. The thick-set rame and short, thicker neck of he buck, and the apparent break n the line of its back, clearly istinguish it from the doe.

Skill in tracking chamois is less nportant than it is in hunting ther cloven-hoofed game. It is arely possible to follow a trail ver long distances in the mounains. Occasionally, however, old ucks leave unmistakable tracks in he winter snow.

The chamois' predilection for omparatively moderate tempertures helps the hunter choose the est stalking territory. After grazng on slopes warmed by the norning sun, the herd moves into he shade with the increasing varmth of the day.

Apart from poachers and avanches, the most dangerous enemy f the chamois is mange, the skin isease caused by parasitic mites, which they catch from sheep and which can be dealt with only hrough ruthless culling of inected animals.

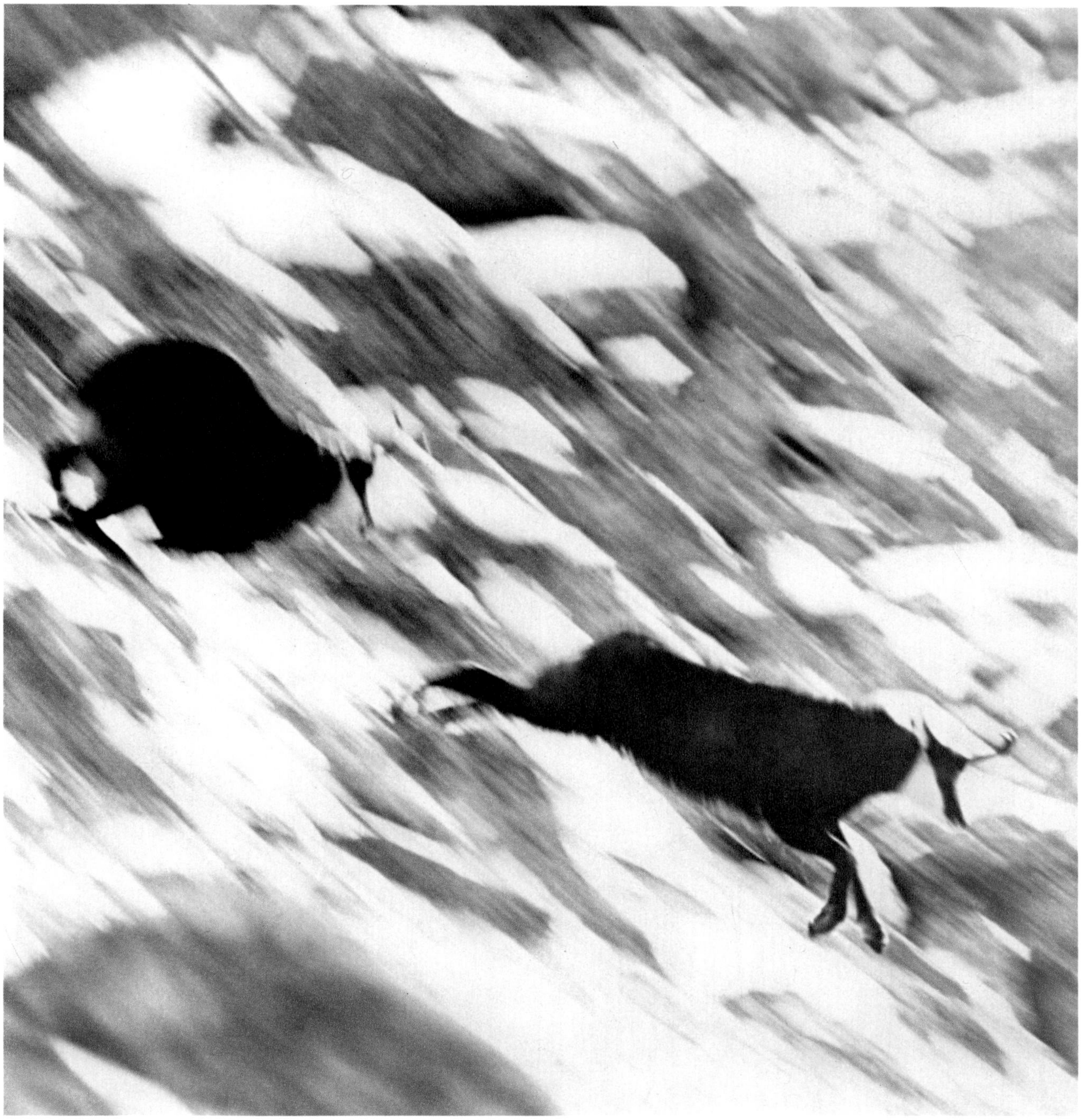

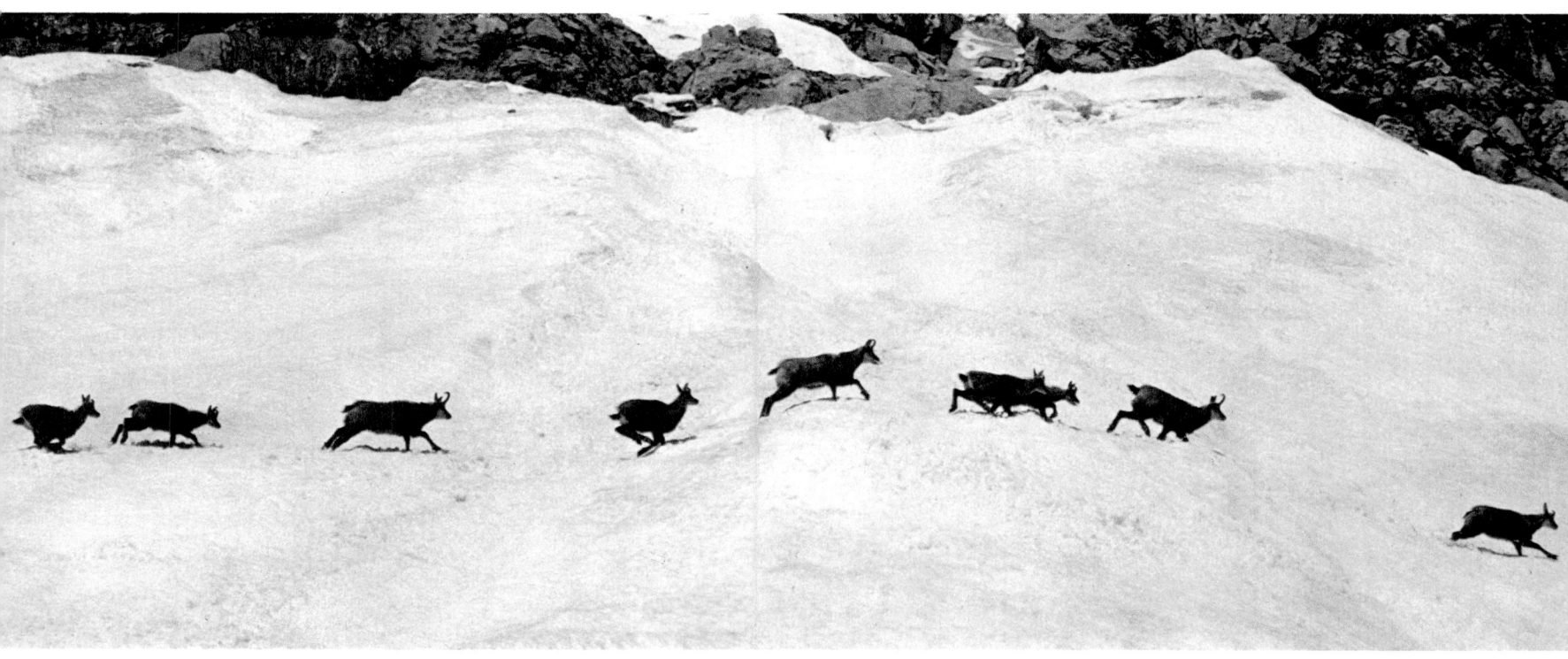

Boar Hunting

There are several different ways in which wild boar are commonly hunted. Where there are a number of hunters, and where beaters are available, a kind of stampede hunting is devised to permit as many of the hunters as possible to get a chance to line the animal up in their sights. Wild boar are suspicious, tough and aggressive, and often unpredictable.

Early in the morning, long before an actual boar hunt begins, the presence of the quarry must be confirmed. One of the hunters dispatched to scour the territory, keeping safe distance from where boar are believed to be to prevent the animals from becoming alarmed and scattering prematurely. When he comes across fresh boar tracks, he cautiously follows them until they disappear into thicket. If they do not lead out again, the presence of boar is confirmed.

The other hunters are then summoned and silently take up positions within sight of the thicket. They gingerly remove twigs and branches which might block their view, and begin a motionless, silent vigil. Not long afterward, the first calls of the beaters, muted by the snow, rise in the distance. This is followed by the cry of a hound, then of other hounds, until the air resounds with the baying of the whole pack, moving in on the prey.

From time to time, the howling of a wounded hound is heard, the anguished yelp of a boar's victim. The hunters, still motionless, wait breathlessly. At last, a swift, black shadow against the trees, a boar breaks from the thicket, plowing up the white-blanketed ground with its flailing trotters. A shot rings out—a little too hastily, too impatiently. A second shot meets its target. The boar shudders convulsively and tumbles over.

Foresters and farmers see the boar differently. The forester values the wild boar highly. It is his most reliable ally in his struggle to control parasites which damage the trees of the forest. Farmers, however, are less enthusiastic about these animals, because the boar is indiscriminate in its ravaging, laying waste to crops as well as exterminating vermin.

Hunting Wolves

n parts of Europe, traditional ways of olf hunting die hard. The wolves, hose locations are determined by their acks in the snow, are often still iclosed in circles of rags joined by rope, nd are thus exposed to the hunters' fles.

In all northern wilderness regions, the wolf was once the primary instrument for the maintenance of biological balance. But they caused extensive damage to domestic cattle in many places and have been almost exterminated in several countries.

The hunter respects wolves more than he does other predators. There are several reasons for this. The wolf possesses highly developed instincts which make it an intelligent adversary, a shrewd opponent, a tricky target. Its cunning is legendary. Even experienced hunters confess that it is extremely difficult to outwit the wolf.

Clear evidence for this frustration is manifested in the shewel hunt still common in northern Europe. To the despair of the hunters, the wolves manage repeatedly to escape from an enclosure ringed with rags linked together by rope, if, in fact, they permit themselves to be so surrounded in the first place. Even compared to other canny game, like the wild boar and the bear, the wolf is a master of shrewdness. The inhabitants of the Carpathian Mountains in Romania, who hunt all three species of game, testify readily to this. Their experience is that boar and bear are comparatively easy for hunters to bag, while the wolf, more often than not, makes good its escape.

A member of a zoological expedition, who spent four years in the mountains of Tibet, found wolves there as successful in evading death at the hands of hunters as those in other parts of the world. He concealed himself for several days in the local white wilderness but was unable to attract a single wolf—and there were many in the area—to bait which he had laid out. Toward the end of his stay, however, the tables turned in his favor:

"I had been sitting for several hours in a deep hollow while wolves circled the bait, keeping a safe distance. Only one old, gray-faced animal began to approach rifle range. Holding my breath, I assumed firing position. But the wolf then sat down, just out of range, and for what seemed like an eternity sniffed the air with head raised and mouth half-opened, turning its head in a circular motion. It had not yet spotted me, and the wind was in my favor, but the animal's inbuilt caution was aroused, and it seemed ready to wait for the cover of dusk.

"I despaired; I had never before seen so clear a demonstration of distrust and suspicion. It was made even more evident when, though the bait was still there, the wolf rose, turned and disappeared into the distance. During the same long day, I spotted three other wolves, none of which came close enough for me to risk taking a shot. The reason for this remarkably unrelenting caution became evident when my Tibetan guide approached on horseback to help me back to camp.

"The following day, I went again to my place of concealment. This time, however, I had the guide stay clear until I was in place and then circle the bait on horseback at a distance of a half-mile. The object was to make the wolves feel confident with a potential enemy safely in view. It worked. This time, I did not have long to wait. Half an hour after the guide began his slow peregrination, his silhouette clear against the horizon, the first wolf approached the bait, tentatively at first, then at a slow trot, and finally at full gallop, with a second wolf at its heels. The animals snatched at pieces of the meat on the ground. Marvelling, I whistled reflexively through my teeth. The wolves froze in their tracks. I took aim and fired. The front wolf leapt into the air, somersaulted, crumpled and lay still, while its companion bolted toward distant safety."

The Mighty Bear

When the bear approaches the bait, the hunter, positioned in a well-camouflaged location nearby, takes aim. But a bear is hard to kill with a single sh and is, generally, highly unpredictable. Despite poor vision, it has acute senses of smell and hearing.

Since time immemorial, the bear has been considered a symbol of strength, more powerful than any other predator in the northern hemisphere.

In ancient Europe, the bear was the coveted prey of royal princes. The mighty animal was captured and put in enclosures so that hunting bears was made less difficult and less dangerous for them. However, even after the invention of firearms, some hunters preferred to match strength and cunning with bears and went after them with spear and dagger. Such exploits are, however, increasingly rare.

For one thing, bears are no longer as common as they once were. Only rarely, in harsh winters, do they approach districts inhabited by humans. While many hundreds can be found in American and Canadian national parks, and in nature preserves in some other countries, only a comparative few still survive outside these protected areas. As a regulator of cloven-hoofed game in western Europe, the bear has long since lost its preeminence. Alpine valleys, the Abruzzi Mountains of Italy, the Pyrenees and parts of Scandinavia provide the last retreats in western Europe for this severely threatened species. In eastern Europe, the bear is more effectively protected by exemplary conservation measures. Yugoslav examples of these survivors wander regularly over the border into Austria where bear-protection regulations have been less stringent. In the Balkan countries, permission is granted for the shooting of very few bears each year, and that permission is usually parcelled out by eminently responsible hunting societies. And those bears marked off as expendable are generally those which have developed reputations for savaging sheep, goats, cattle and other domestic animals and for causing serious damage to forest vegetation. In the

spring particularly, when there is generally shortage of fodder, bears tend to damag young and maturing fir trees by gouging hug portions of bark from the trunks in order t lick up the trees' sap. These damaged tre rarely recover.

Although the hunter after bear usual positions himself not far from the bait he ha laid out, he must often contend with bad lig conditions and the possibility that the fir shot will only wound his target. Hunte are, therefore, advised to use high-calib rifles.

Bears shot directly behind the should blades succumb quickly. In cases where direct hit is impossible to predict, it is ina visable to aim for the heart; the bear's e ceptionally compact muscular system ca foil what seems like an extremely accura shot so that the result is only a wound rath than a fatality.

This was the experience of an Italian hunt who wounded a powerful brown bear dusk in a Yugoslav hunting area. Althoug the animal was seriously wounded, it was ab to flee and proved impossible to find agai before darkness made further searching i possible. The following day the hunte determined to claim his kill, set out with bloodhound to find the bear. But again th search had to be abandoned; the dog wa unable to pick up any trace of the wounde animal. But the hunter refused to quit. On th next day he hired the services of a renowne dog trainer and his equally famous dach hund. This remarkable dog was immediate able to pick up the bear's trail—already tw days old—and by midday was able to loca the first place of refuge the wounded anim had dug for itself and then abandoned. Late the dog detected a fresh scent in a water-fille trench used for transporting logs. The bea it seems, had cooled itself in the trench. The more than nine miles away from the sp where the bear had been shot, the dachshun pulled its master, head-over-heels, into a gorg covered by a thicket of wild raspberries. Th trainer broke both his hands in the fall, but h extraordinary dog had finally found th wounded bear which the hunter, coming u quickly behind, dispatched with a sing bullet.

The Drive

Left: In late fall, the drive is often preferred to stalking or hunting from concealed vantage points. For the drive, there are no massive formations of hunters and beaters. The drive is as silent as possible and requires considerable experience and skill.

Below: Around a crackling fire, during the midday pause.

Right: Before the drive begins, the hunt master instructs the others on which animals are not to be targets and on the general course of the day's activities

For a whole week, a northwesterly gale had blown across the woods. The deer had vanished as if they had never existed. When the wind veered to the northeast, it was bitingly sharp, whipping the snow into hip-high drifts on the fringes of the woods.

In the morning, when the sun rose burning red over the white ridges, a small group of veteran hunters gathered in the silence of the woods: six guns, three beaters and two rough-haired dachshunds which, with their whiskers sheathed in white, struggled their way through the snow on their short legs.

The usual few words of greeting were quickly passed and the master of the hunt proceeded to give his instructions to the hunters and their aides. "All leading animals will be spared. All other deer, and particularly weak fauns, female yearlings and inferior stags with up to eight brow tines, are fair game." He continued in muted tones—sound carries easily on such clear, frosty mornings. To the beaters he said: "Take care not to alarm the deer prematurely. Approach their thickets only against the wind. Avoid all unnecessary noise. Rely completely on the dogs!"

The beaters nodded wordlessly. The breath of the cluster of men rose in white clouds in front of their faces. Not to alarm the deer, it had been decided to forego the customary preliminary horncall. Time for beginning the drive was fixed and, with the exception of two men who were to secure the return trail, the hunters made their way into the forest.

At a lichen-covered tree-trunk, one of the hunters stopped, gazed about and loaded his rifle. He checked the direction of the wind and gently shook the branches of nearby young beech trees. Snow silently fell from those branches, freeing his field of fire. In front of the hunter, a stream gurgled under a cover of ice. On its far side was a thicket punctuated with treeless patches. The winter morning was deathly still. The only sounds were the

hattering of a congregation of long-tailed tits
and the tapping of a distant woodpecker.

Half an hour passed. The drive was to have
begun already but the hunter heard nothing
to indicate it had. Then, suddenly, the warning
cry of a blackbird and the shrill laugh of a jay
rang out. A streak of red flashed across a
nearby slope—a jittery fox was the first to
flee. Then came the excited barking of the
dogs. A few seconds later, a deer dashed
through the trees to be followed by another,
half-hidden by pines, a darker shape in the
shadows, but its crown flashing; fourteen-
branched antlers. It sniffed the air, its ears
raised. It glanced backward, laid its antlers
flat on its back, then disappeared amidst the
trees. In five years, it would be a lead stag, a
master of the herd.

But the hunter had no chance to dwell upon
the future. The whole herd of deer suddenly
stormed into view. He stood stock-still,
making his decision. The first deer, an old
leader, was to be spared. So was the family of
hind, stag, yearling and faun which followed
it. But stragglers brought up the rear, including a two- or three-year-old stag whose
antlers were barely twelve inches long and
which bore weak tines instead of well-
formed forks. This was to be the hunter's
target.

He took aim, and waited. The stag had
momentarily paused. As it was about to
resume its flight, it was checked by the
hunter's bullet. It fell, enveloped in a miniature
avalanche of snow, and it rolled head over
heels toward a ditch. A second bullet cut down
the weakest faun in the herd.

There were no woundings that day. All
animals hit were killed. There was no need to
go searching for injured game.

Still Hunting

This is a form of group hunting in which a comparatively large number of hunters, pooling their efforts, can go out into the fields together in pursuit of hare, water birds and wildfowl. Aside from the sport involved, still hunting helps reduce the stocks of small furry and feathered game to agriculturally supportable proportions. This is an objective which could never be fulfilled through hunting individual animals, as is the case in deer or bear hunting, for example.

There are many kinds of still hunting. Without going into detail on all of them, it is nevertheless useful to distinguish between its practice in open country, in woods and forests, and in the mountains.

Hunters, beaters and dogs set out to scour one territory after another according to set methods suited to each territory. The rules of this particular pursuit hold that hunters are permitted to shoot only certain stipulated types of game. Strict adherence to the rules is governed by the observance of horn signals and exact timing. The countries where still hunting developed are mostly in central and western Europe—Austria, Hungary, Czechoslovakia, Germany, France and Switzerland. Rules there held that certain animals, including fox, hare and rabbit, could only be

shot while fleeing, and fowl, including pheasant and partridge, only when in flight.

Apart from the fact that individual hunters would never be able to make any serious contribution to the long-term control of stocks of small game, this form of hunting has an additional function. It serves the purpose of educating young sportsmen in the laws and traditions of hunting. It is also an extremely revealing test of character. Only while hunting in the company of others, particularly in a still hunt situation, is the true character of each individual hunter revealed to those hunting with him. Only then can his attention to detail and general behavior when suddenly confronted by fleeing game be properly judged.

It may happen, for example, that a hunter will shoot a hare so close to the feet of a man standing near it that the ricocheting bullet will bounce off his boots. Or two hunters may feel compelled to argue about ownership of a pheasant at which both had aimed. One of the company may go off with his dog in search of a hare wounded by another hunter. Another, mindful of the hunt master's instruction that no shots are to be fired after the hunt is declared over, may allow his first fox of the day to escape unmolested although it passes

temptingly near his line of fire. Different hunters will respond differently. Their behavior on the still hunt is likely to reveal what sort of stuff they're made of.

An old hunting proverb contends that "wet hunters and dry fishermen are not worth very much." This maxim, based on the accumulated experience of centuries, is particularly valid in still hunting. It is true not only because hunting in dripping foliage and wet pine thickets is not much fun, but also because the game—and primarily the hare, the main target in this kind of hunt—shies clear of wet undergrowth, preferring open country racing for cover when threatened. Still hunting is best not begun until the early November frosts have stripped the leaves from the trees, thinning out obstructions to vision, and a steady, cold, but not yet strong wind is blowing.

Stalking, hunting from concealment and still hunting—the three main methods are equally valid and all three have been practiced by various animals—the fox, puma and wolf as well as human hunters of the past and present. Each method has its advantages according to habitat, hunter's intention and the kind of game.

Left: Hare and rabbit often turn cartwheels when struck by bullets in the chest or forepaws.

Left and right below: Late fall is the best time of year for still hunting. Attention is paid to positioning hunters and beaters as evenly as possible and to a steady approach in an unbroken line. In open country, the animal most commonly hunted is the hare. In marshy, reedy regions, it is wildfowl.

Right: When shooting at pheasant in flight, the shot should be aimed slightly ahead of the target.

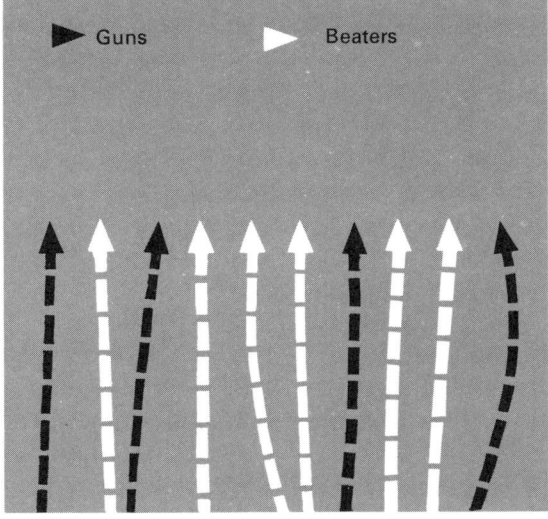

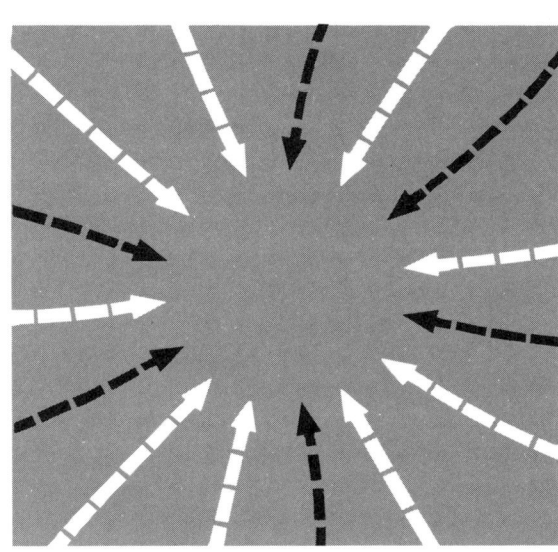

According to the number of guns in this particular drive, the territory is surrounded on three sides and approached from the fourth by a line of beaters interspersed with a few good guns (see diagram). If there are few hunters, then only the downwind side is blocked, and the beaters work on three sides. All the guns must be able to maintain visual contact with each other. Start and finish are announced by signals, and no gun may leave his position until the signal to do so is given.

Guns and beaters, spaced out at regular intervals, take up their places in a line downwind of the game. Under the leadership of hunters who know the ground, the flanks keep in advance. It is essential that everyone is in sight of everyone else, and that the chain of guns and beaters is kept as straight as possible. This kind of drive is especially suitable for hunting hares, rabbits and pheasants in open or lightly wooded country, and is considered a particularly sporting method as the game has a good chance of escape.

This is a worthwhile method only if there is a large number of guns and beaters. A selected territory is encircled, with the leader signaling to the men to position themselves until the circle is closed by an evenly spaced line of guns and beaters. Beating begins toward the center, but when the circle becomes so small as to be dangerous, then the signal is made for the guns to fire outward from the circle.

Hare and Rabbit Hunting

The hare, chief character of many a fairy tale and cartoon, portrayed as a lovable, roguish, basically harmless creature, is the "small fry" of the hunting grounds. It is among the most prolific of all smaller species of wild game. Because of its abundance, many consider hare hunting an inferior sport. But anyone who has taken the trouble to study the hare as a wild creature in its own right cannot fail to respect this alert animal, not least because of the meticulous efficiency with which it organizes its life. This characteristic is particularly evident in its high degree of adaptability.

Despite its comparatively high reproduction rate of an average of twelve leverets per pair per year, the hare is becoming less and less common in the modern landscape. Apart from its natural enemies, both large and small, the hare is a victim of the vastly increased use of insecticides in agriculture and the growing number of automobiles on the roads.

Tens of thousands of hares are run over each year. If it is estimated that cats, foxes, weasels, farm machinery and poachers leave the mother hare with an average of four of its original twelve leverets, of which another two fall prey to hunters, then we can say that, at most, only two leverets per pair per year survive.

Attention is drawn here to the sharp increase in the mortality rate of the hare to encourage an interest in the protection and preservation of this interesting species of game, and to instil in hunters a sense of responsibility toward it. It is possible, given reasonably favorable conditions, to make good, within a few years, stocks of deer which have been decimated. But for hares, such rehabilitation is only possible if all protection and conservation

measures are scrupulously observed. It also requires long-term careful distribution of fodder and rigorous control of hare hunting with traps and rifles. By way of reward, hare hunting offers the hunter satisfying experiences which make strong demands on his skill.

The hunter's satisfaction is derived from what he feels before actually shooting and not on the weight of the limp game he carries from the field. Few things are more exhilarating for him than the sound of the horn on a cold winter's morning. He listens attentively to the sounds of the beaters, interpreting each noise, judging every shot, whether far or near. Motionlessly he waits, hoping a hare will come within sight

while trying to break through the chain of hunters. "The hare!" one of the beaters calls and a small creature streaks across the ground, to turn a somersault in a flash of fire and powder. Nods of congratulation from the others acknowledge the hunter's skill.

That is part of the pleasure—the ungrudging sharing of success. There is also the sight of well-trained dogs performing as they should, and, before all that, the pleasure of anticipation at morning twilight. A wide range of pleasures are brought into play while hunting hare in the field.

The mountain hare, a cousin of the field hare, can make its home in virtually all arctic or subarctic regions of the northern hemi-

European brown hare. The length of its legs compared with those of the rabbit (picture 3) is particularly striking. Its ears are also much longer.

A quick eye, a sense of distance and velocity, and thorough control of the firearm are essential for hunting hare in open country.

3 Wild rabbits live gregariously in burrows which often have extensive systems of tunnels.

4 Alpine hare. Thick fur on its feet enable it to scamper quickly over snow. Though smaller than the field hare, it leaves larger tracks.

5 Ferret on a long leash. If released, it might devour part of the rabbit it pursues and then roll over and go to sleep.

Young hares are born unprotected and usually barely camouflaged. They weigh around four and a half ounces at birth and are obliged to fend for themselves against various predators as well as bad weather conditions, insecticide-contaminated plants and automobiles. It requires strong nerves to remain motionlessly camouflaged until the last moment, and the way the hare confuses the dogs with its erratic escape route when it breaks from cover reveals a

superior intelligence. The hare's only defense weapons are its long, tireless hind legs.

4

...phere. This animal is also a favored target of hunters, though in some elevated regions—in the Alps and the Carpathian Mountains of Europe for example—it is generally stumbled across by accident. Smaller than the field hare, it has shorter, black-tipped ears. Its coat is white in winter and grayish-brown in summer.

The wild rabbit is considerably different from the hare in shape, habits and reproduction rate—each female produces an average of thirty young rabbits a year!—and it is hunted all through the year. It is also hunted in a completely different way. At the first sign of danger, the rabbit disappears below ground. Hunters use ferrets to follow the animals into their subterranean burrows and to drive them toward waiting guns. Wild rabbits are extremely alert and swift in flight. The drive and still hunting are the most common form of rabbit hunting.

Unpredictable in direction and velocity, rabbits put hunters with shotguns to difficult tests. But they offer a tempting challenge to experienced sportsmen. The rabbit, with its phenomenal reproduction rate, presents a serious threat to agriculture. With both its skin and flesh in demand, it seems a natural target. This alone should be enough for responsible hunters to place limits on their catches.

5

The Red Fox

Hunting has always been one of the ways by which men have tried to prove themselves. Hunting has always been a challenge and a hunter's prey has always been his adversary, matching its skills against his. The wild animal's sharper senses, more reliable instincts and greater agility had to be compensated for. The hunter made up for his inferior physical attributes by devising weapons and optical tools to give him the advantage.

But even with the instruments of modern technology, the hunter has to be just that bit more crafty than his prey—and this is particularly true in the case of the fox, one of the craftiest of all animals. Cunning, suspicious, cautious, audacious and insolent, the fox also possesses a measure of stamina and tenacity which has made it more than a match for many a hunter.

Killing a fox is no cut-and-dried undertaking. If wounded in one of its limbs, it will continue to run on three legs as if they were four. It will often bite the hunter who presumes to consider it dead. It will appear cornered and exhausted, only to dash away as if only beginning the chase.

However, a fox can become careless, and when it does it is the time for the hunter to prove his mettle. He must then display his knowledge of the paths and trails the fox is likely to use. Cover is extremely important to the animal and the hunter must know how to lure it out into the open, by imitating the sounds of a mouse or a hare or by laying bait.

The hunter must expect to endure hours of brittle silence while he waits for the right moment. A fox hears everything within a radius of hundreds of yards. A cough, a sneeze, a cleared

The nickname "reynard," from the French "renard," was first given to the fox in the eleventh century. It means the unbeatable cunning one." The fact that the fox has survived to the present day is primarily due to its cautious inclinations and high reproduction rate.

Right: The hunter examines the thick winter coat of the fox he has shot.

Below: The fox has been killed by a dachshund in its labyrinthine underground burrow.

throat, a loose button dropping on a rifle barrel—any of these can give the game away. Nor may he allow himself to be startled by the noise of others. He is not alone. An owl might soar out of the night, a ghost in motion, swooping down on a helpless mouse—its hunting a success already.

The shadows of the night grow longer and then disappear as the morning begins to take shape. On the rim of the woods, on the far side of the brook, there is a sudden, brief movement. A fox at last, but still well out of range. To lure it on, the hunter invokes his skill at mimicry. From his lips rises the cry of a hare in trouble. The fox halts in its tracks, its ears pricked. Another cry breaks the silence, an imitation of the truncated sound of a hare suffocating in the snow. The fox is hooked. It approaches, at a trot at first, then faster, toward the source of the hare's anguished noises. As it comes close, it slows and stops, a forepaw raised as it peers into the darkness for its prey—and, at that instant, becomes the prey itself. The crack of a rifle shot rings out and it falls, dead before its face hits the snow. And the silence is once more complete.

A less dramatic way to hunt the fox is to break into its underground burrows with specially trained dogs (fox terriers, other hunting terriers or dachshunds). The fox is sought out, trapped and killed or, as is often the case, driven out into the open. Hunters, their rifles at the ready, keep watch at possible exits.

The red fox has an indelible reputation as a thief. But apart from stealing chickens, it does not usually intrude on domestic animals. In fact, in many places it is considered a useful aid in maintaining a biological balance, preying as it does on weak fauns and hares. Its main food is, however, the field mouse, and forty-eight mice were once found in the stomach of a dead fox. One fox, which was killed for the strange tassle-like protrusions from its muzzle, was found to be carrying thirteen mice in its teeth, their tails hanging from its mouth like a bizarre moustache.

The fox's diligence as a destroyer of mice makes it popular with foresters and farmers, who tend to overlook the occasional stolen chicken or pheasant.

Hunters wanting to know the ways of the fox should take the trouble to watch young foxes at play in the spring. Aside from the knowledge and understanding that can be thus acquired, it probably will lead them away from any temptation to indulge in senseless slaughter when it comes to this cunning creature.

Hunting Traditions

Hunting traditions are as old as hunting itself. Some developed spontaneously to meet the needs of the time, the tools and the circumstances. Others sprang from the mystical and cultural elements associated with hunting in different places and in different times.

Many of the more down-to-earth hunting traditions date no further back than the middle ages. These include ritualized methods for interpreting tracks, procedures for dressing dead game and laying out the bag, and many other ways and quirks. All served important functions when they were first used and most are still valid today, sometimes even when they are not fully understood by those who perform them. But traditions in themselves, devoid of immediate significance, can turn into empty, often farcical, formalities.

Horn signals, for example, are not merely relics of feudal times. They are useful messages from the master of the hunt and can contribute meaningfully to the safety of the hunters, beaters and dogs. They are even more useful in these days of high-powered firearms than they were at the time of the bow and arrow and the wheel-lock rifle.

The use of hunting jargon may, at times, merely be an affectation, serving no serious purpose whatever. But it is the mark of an experienced and responsible hunter and can save time and energy at crucial moments in the field or forest. Anyone familiar with hunting procedures, and the recurring need for clear, quick communication between hunters, understands the importance of the specialized hunting language.

Hunting traditions, of various kinds, exist all over the world—from Africa to Canada, from Europe to the Arctic, from Japan

to the Indian subcontinent. They have always existed during man's tenure on Earth and they will exist as long as there are hunters. But anyone who believes that knowledge of hunting customs alone makes good hunters is making a mistake. Content is more important than mere form. Those who practice the pursuit of hunting without real interest in or sympathy for wildlife do damage to the reputation of hunting and should be advised not to bother with the sport in the first place.

The hunt is over. The bag is laid out for counting and evaluation. An exchange of congratulations between hunters is in order. The diagrams below indicate the order of placement as practiced in parts of central Europe though, even there, it was not rigidly observed. According to likely precedence when alive, the game is set down—red deer before fallow deer, fox before hare, male before female. The quantity of game killed is announced by horn signal. Fires are lit and the horn has announced the hunt's end. It is, for some, a strangely melancholy moment.

Grouse and Snipe Shooting

Left: Dedicated sportsmen turn out in great numbers when the grouse-shooting season begins in the Scottish highlands. For this kind of hunting, the more skillful the hunter, the more birds he will bring down.

Right: The woodcock, on the other hand, is always hunted singly. In spring, a restricted quantity of birds permitted to be shot. They are always males.

Grouse shooting: This particular pursuit has an added dimension. August 12—"the glorious twelfth"—opening day of the Scottish grouse season, is still considered *the* event of the social side of the shooting season.

The extreme speed and the low flight of this short-winged wildfowl is a formidable challenge. Each year, when the early fall starts to tint the Scottish highlands, competition begins between hunters positioned in well-camouflaged butts all over the region. When the drive begins, the novice may have little idea of where to aim and when to shoot. The fowl materialize in thick formations, to the right, to the left, barely skimming over the heads of the hunters, and darting through the air as swift as arrows.

Originally, the Scottish ptarmigan lived only in Scotland, northern England, Ireland and Wales. It was later introduced into Belgium, where it failed to spread to any great degree. The favorite habitat of this dark brown species of grouse—the only fen ptarmigan not to have white feathers in winter—is the peat moors where numerous and varied berry bushes grow.

Snipe shooting: This form of hunting is particularly popular in Europe where it has more romanticized overtones—one hunter against one bird. The experience is deemed more important than the size of the bag. When the sun settles toward the horizon on

a mild evening in early spring, and dus begins to fall, the "long-faced bird" starts h silent mating flight over the hen, sitting c the ground in the woods. The hunter ma hear the call of a distant thrush, but it's tl snipe he's after, and suddenly its "pssie pssiep" call rings through the air, followe by a deep, rhythmic "quorr, quorr"—and fleeting shadow. The hunter raises his ri and waits, spots a flash against the evenir sky and fires. His dog then runs out retrieve the first snipe of the season.

Despite the temptation to open the seaso this way, shooting snipe in their matir flights remains a questionable practice, pa ticularly in view of the declining population the bird. However, research has indicate

that the bigger part of the problem li elsewhere. The deep decline in the numb of snipe—a delicacy among winged game is due to a much greater extent to uncontrolle shooting in the winter habitats of the bird, southern Europe and North Africa.

Water Fowl

Dawn is the best time for hunting wild geese. Dull, hazy weather, with a ground mist—those are the ideal conditions. The hunter sits in a ground depression with a free field of fire in all directions. He picks a location which experience has taught him to be frequented by geese seeking pasturage. The advance guard of the birds arrives first, followed by dozens of geese in close formation, their wings making whistling sounds in flight. The wild goose is extremely swift when winging through the air. Experienced hunters aim for the head and neck; the strong body feathers can deflect even well-aimed shots.

The special character of each water-covered region of the world and the distinctive experience of local hunters both contribute to the specialized form water-fowl hunting can take from place to place. A few basic principles are, however, valid just about everywhere.

Water birds are among the more fidgety and alert forms of game. Hunting them requires a considerable degree of skill, patience and aptitude on the part of the hunter.

A knowledge of the biology and behavior of the birds is essential for the successful water-fowl hunter. For example, if a hunter knows that the wild goose passes the day on land and the night on water, he will not drift in a boat through reeds during daylight hours, seeking in vain for a glimpse of a goose. He might, however, look for the northern mallard, which spends its days among the weeds on the banks of lakes.

Even the most functional boat and the most reliable hunting companion cannot make up for the absence of a well-trained, water-loving dog. The duck is swift as it wings through the air. Bringing it down with a single shot requires considerable skill. Wounded, it will dive and make for the shore. Even when it falls like a stone into the water, its exact location is extremely difficult to judge from a boat. Without dogs, only a small fraction of the number of birds shot would be recovered. Most would be left to the tender mercies of foxes, crabs and rats.

Capercaillie Hunting in Finland

Left: This small, lively and highly intelligent Suomenpystykorvat, the spitz, with its pointed ears and curly tail, is specially trained for capercaillie hunting. Like all dogs with such specialized training, its sense of smell is extremely acute. The Finnish spitz probably came to Finland with the country's first prehistoric settlers and probably evolved from primitive wild dogs.

Below: Startled by the dog, a capercaillie has taken t the branches of a tree. The spitz utters its haukku *sound, the bark which lets the hunter know that the bird is at bay. The hunter silently makes his way through the undergrowth. It is often difficult to spot the bird in the branches, even from nearby.*

Hunting habits are influenced from place to place by considerations of fairness, discretion and delicacy. In most places, hunters refrain from shooting game when it is mating—this applies equally to red deer in rut and wildfowl during their mating displays. Some hunters are particularly proud of the trophies they bring back from the field or the forest. Others consider the game they bag to be of no greater significance than it was to the original human hunters: pot luck, something for the day's menu at home. For some hunters, the number of animals they bring down is the most important element in their day's work. To others, the skill they were called upon to demonstrate is of prime significance, even if their kill is of modest proportions.

In Finland, hunting has for centuries been a profession as well as a sport. With its huge spruce and pine forests, its 50,000 lakes, its endless moors, swamps and tundras, Finland provides an ideal environment for wildfowl. The Finnish Game Research Institute has published almost incredible statistics for the country's game stocks: 300,000 snow hens; 600,000 hazel hens; 700,000 capercaillies; over a million black grouse!

Nevertheless, Finnish hunters are sharply limited in the quantity of winged game they can bring down. Only about 12,000 capercaillies are shot each year, with the year's bag

Left: The capercaillie is so mesmerized by the dog under the tree that it is heedless of other danger. The dog continues barking until the hunter has fired his shot.

Below: The capercaillie falls lifeless to the ground. Young cocks are considered gourmet food; older ones are tough and their flesh tastes of resin.
The dog is given a wing as a reward for its work, a tradition dating back to the middle ages. The hunter quickly removes the entrails, which would otherwise soon go bad and taint the rest of the bird.

or the individual hunter seldom more than three or four birds.

And the hunter must work for his reward. He sets out usually at dawn with his rifle, map, compass and dog, as often as not a red spitz. It might take him hours to reach the hunting grounds he has chosen. But moors and forests are full of ripe berries in fall; the capercaillies on the ground are less alert, less ready for flight, less likely to be frightened off by dogs.

The spitz roams free over a large area, always maintaining contact with its master. Ignoring even warm tracks of the hare or the scent of hazel hen, its sole interest is to pinpoint a capercaillie and to sound off when it does. When its cry, its *haukku*, rings out, the hunter moves gingerly toward the spot. By tradition, the capercaillie should not be shot once in flight. The hunter must aim for it while it is still perched on a tree branch, and the spitz completes its task by retrieving the bird after it has fallen to earth.

In areas where capercaillies and black grouse are prolific, the two species are inclined to interbreed. The most usual cross is between a black grouse cock and a capercaillie hen. The cock of the hybrids produced are known for their pugnacious temperament and often disturb the mating of other feathered game.

Duck Shooting in North America

Wildfowling in North America is a national sport. Strict controls and supervision of habitats by game wardens and protection commissions ensure that legal stipulations are for the most part obeyed.
Shooting is mostly during the fall and winter months, mainly in low-lying coastal areas. Duck and goose decoys are set out to attract the birds and fifes which mimic their calls are also used.

At the beginning of this century, stocks of water birds in North America were so depleted that experts were seriously concerned that many species would become extinct. This situation had been brought about by the drainage of moors and marshes, as well as by unrestricted bird hunting.

By 1930, it had become clear that random and irresponsible hunting had to be curtailed and that measures had to be invoked to promote perpetuation of the bird populations. Artificial ponds and lakes were created. Arid stretches of land were irrigated. Shooting was prohibited in the spring. The use of live decoys was prohibited and other restrictions

were initiated to end the uncontrolled slaughter of birds.

It had also become clear that such steps would, by themselves, not be enough. There had to be trained game biologists and precise research to determine what efforts were producing the desired results and what other steps it was advisable to take. The overall effort was so comprehensive and successful that the management of water birds in the United States and Canada has become the model for such programs in other countries. The proceeds from the sale of duck stamps, which hunters buy for a few dollars each to stick on their shooting licenses, go toward improving conservation 'measures in regions which lie astride the four great migratory routes traversed by North America's water

North American ecologists keep close watch on wild-fowl populations which breed in the north and migrate southward in the winter. Authorities in Canada and the United States set limits on the number of birds hunters may bag.

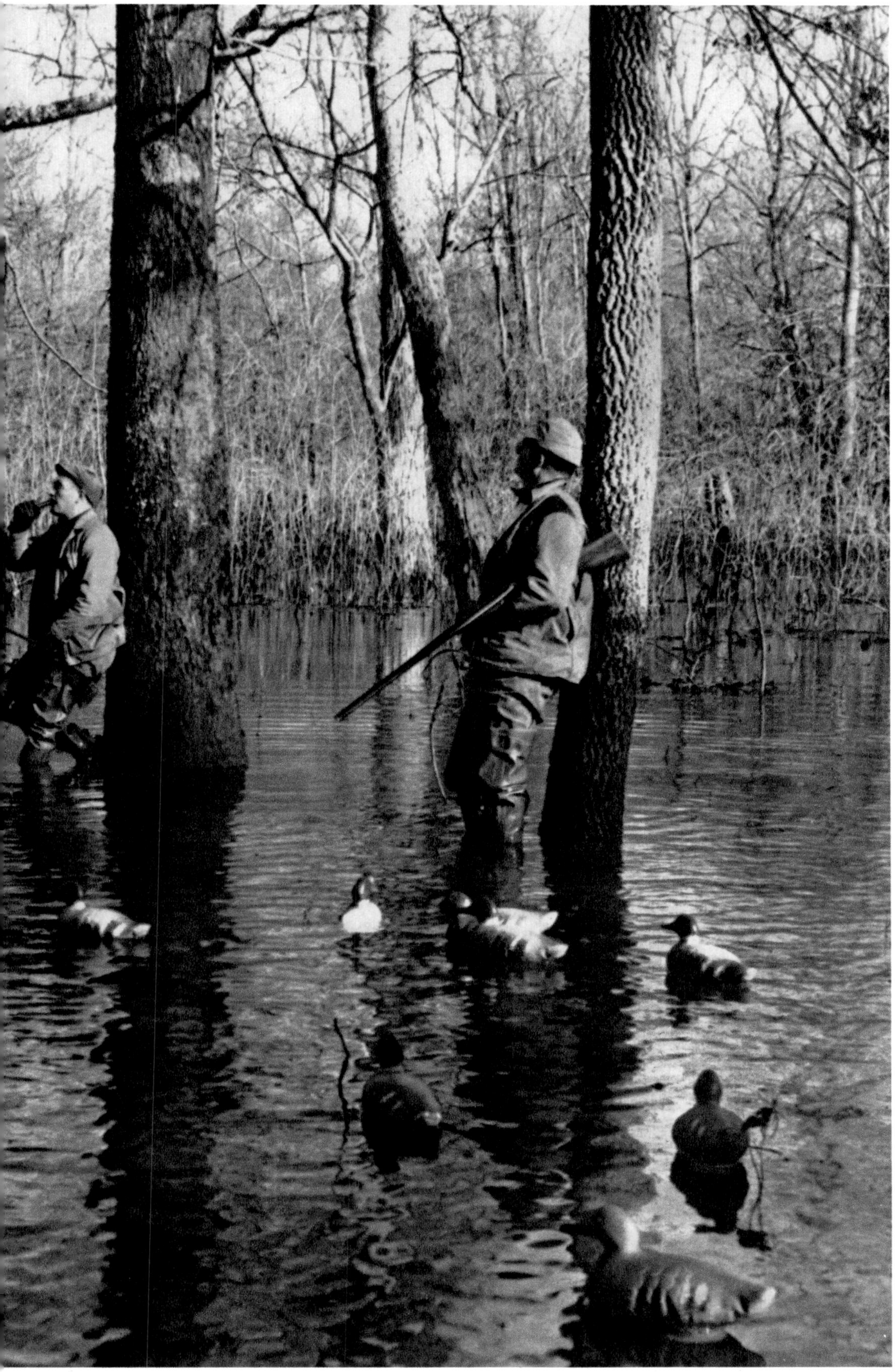

birds. These funnel-shaped *flyways* extend from breeding grounds in the north to wintering places in the south.

After only ten years of concentrated conservation measures, the first results became evident. The populations of wild geese and ducks had increased fourfold! Today, North America's prairie lakes and low-lying coastal regions are populated or visited by hundreds of thousands of water birds and, of course, by thousands of hunters as well. Only a few thousand snow geese used to spend their winters in California's Sacramento Valley; today, over two million birds winter on the region's artificial lakes.

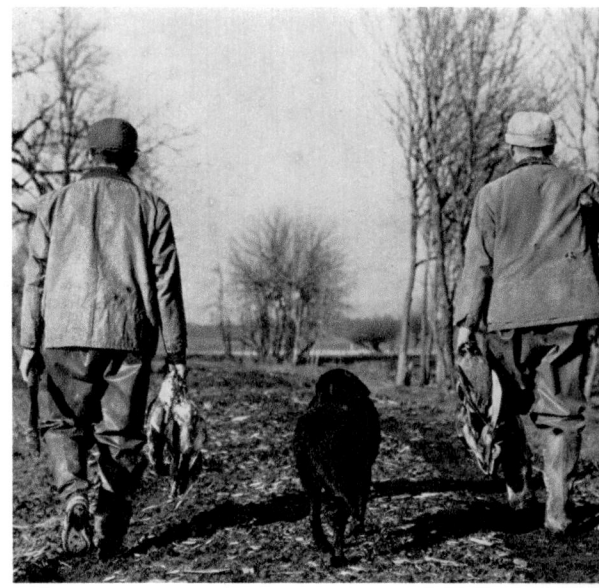

With a few exceptions, including the blue-winged teal, black-headed duck, bufflehead, red-headed duck and Carolina wood duck, the same species of wild fowl are found in North America and Europe; the gadwall, widgeon, northern shoveler, blue-billed pintail, common goldeneye, greater scaup, black scoter, and much-hunted northern mallard.

Probably the most coveted of all is the canvasback, not only because it is delicious, but also because its great speed in flight requires considerable shooting skill on the part of the hunter. Typical American geese include the blue goose, snow goose, emperor goose and various kinds of Canada goose. The brent goose, barnacle goose and white-fronted goose are found both in America and Eurasia.

Hunters of the Frozen North

breed of hunters will be able to resist the pressures of less agreeable ways.

In addition to seal and walrus, polar bear have been among the most valued prey of the Eskimo hunter. It is believed that the polar bear population of the far north has been halved during this century alone. It is known that during the 1969–1970 hunting year, about 1300 polar bears fell victim to hunters. The following year about 900 are

the other in the Hudson Bay region—th[e] authorities try to enforce a quota system. A[ll] bear-skins, including those acquired by Esk[i]mos, have to be indelibly marked. Wheth[er] the decline in the polar bear population can b[e] effectively checked by this and similar metho[ds] is questionable.

Eskimos are believed to have come originally from northeast Asia. Less than 5,000 years ago, the ancestors of present-day Eskimos probably made their way across the Bering Strait to Alaska and, subsequently, along Canada's arctic coast to Greenland.

The Eskimo's entire way of life is determined by his adaptation to a harsh environment, by his efforts to survive and thrive in a polar climate. Eskimos are a tenacious hunting people. They live almost exclusively on meat and fish. They have invented weapons, means of transport, dwellings and clothing specifically suited to their ways of life and environment. These include the harpoon, sledge, kayak, igloo and parka. Despite their austere living conditions, Eskimos are among the most peaceful people on Earth, capable of engaging in individual conflicts but not in wars. Dedicated to a common aim of survival, they share their kills and catches. A different kind of civilization is, however, rapidly approaching the North Pole. It is impossible to predict whether this self-sufficient, amiable

believed to have been killed. Of that 900, one-third were shot by hunters visiting Alaska.

But statistics are at best estimates and at worst completely inaccurate. The unwritten law is that Eskimos in Alaska still have the right to kill up to three polar bears per head per year. While some may go through winter after winter without seeing a single polar bear, there are more than 20,000 Eskimos in Alaska alone.

Since 1973, using airplanes for hunting has been prohibited. Nevertheless, the "kill statistics," such as they are, continue to rise. This is true partly because many Eskimos have taken to driving motor sledges over the frozen wastes, and some of them are not reluctant to use these vehicles in pursuit of bear. Visitors also find it easier, and safer, to go hunting across snow-blanketed regions with motorized transport and, as a sad consequence, the number of polar bears shot illegally has been climbing steadily.

In Canada, where two separate populations of polar bear exist—one on the Arctic coasts,

Left: An Eskimo hunter stalking seal with a shooting sledge. Camouflage screen and rifle have replaced the bow and arrow. Without an enormous abundance of seals, the Eskimo hunting culture would have developed along completely different lines.

Below: Dogs have been valued companions in the Eskimo adaptation to life in the polar environment. Though domesticated, Eskimo dogs retain closer links to their wolf antecedents than do their canine cousins elsewhere, and still howl like wolves, rather than bark.

Right: Restless wanderers of the white snow-deserts of the far north, polar bears are today threatened with extinction. Motorized sledges and other technological advances have put them at serious disadvantage when facing the well-equipped hunter. Many countries have introduced regulations to protect them.

Caribou

Although comparatively easy to hunt, the caribou is still the most abundant species of large deer to be found in North America. Sizes of herds vary, however, and in the United States they are now comparatively few in number, living under strict protection, mostly in Maine and the state of Washington.

In Canada and Alaska, they are found in greater numbers. There are three breeds: the barren-ground caribou, which makes its home between Hudson Bay and Alaska; the larger and darker forest caribou, which lives further south; and the mountain caribou, which can weigh up to 700 pounds and which is found in the Rocky Mountains, particularly in the Cassiar range of British Columbia. The more southern breeds have become rare because of indiscriminate slaughter, leaving the barren-ground caribou as the prime target.

Like the moose, the caribou's senses are notably less acute than those of more southern species of deer, such as the elk, mule deer and white-tailed deer. Hunting the

animal, therefore, requires less skill, especially since licensed guides, with whom most visiting hunters set out, survey suitable hunting territory before the visitors even arrive at base camps.

The caribou territory is studied from an elevated position with the help of a good pair of binoculars. The caribou prefers the cold climate and is usually found in small glacial valleys and in snow-fields above the treeline. The guides often try to block off animal escape routes at fords or mountain passes; the success of the hunt is frequently the result of the guide's ingenuity. The caribou is relatively bold and does not flee great distances so, aside from the pleasures of the unspoiled landscape, caribou hunting has little to offer the experienced hunter who happens to be seeking a challenge as well as a conquest. Nevertheless, hunting restrictions are severe for visitors, with only Eskimos and local Indians permitted to hunt the animal the year round.

These animals, and the reindeer of Eurasia, are the only deer in

which the females as well as the males bear antlers—probably to help them survive in the harsh, snowy winters. Although the antlers of the female are considerably weaker than those of the males, they too have broad, branched "snow shovel" antler-tips.

During the brief arctic summer, the upper layers of earth thaw in the caribou's biotope. But the water cannot drain away and the areas become transformed into vast marshes, interspersed with countless lakes. The broad, spreading caribou hooves keep the animal from sinking into the bog-like earth. A characteristic of the animal on the move is the snapping sound of its fetlocks.

The harsh environment forces barren-ground caribous to wander great distances. In the fall, when snowstorms start to gather, and sparse vegetation disappears beneath a white shroud of snow (which will stay there for half the year), long processions of caribou wend their way hundreds of miles southward. The following spring, the animals return—first the pregnant cows which drop their young

on the way in carefully chosen sheltered spots; then, some days later, larger bulls which, after the rutting period during the days of the midnight sun, grow new antlers.

The first white pioneers in caribou country, the daring hardy French *coureurs de bois* of the Canadian wilderness, encountered countless caribou. The jostling animals were said to have pressed together so closely in the narrow valleys that for weeks on end the entire countryside, as far as the horizons, seemed to be covered by a single moving mass. With the exception of the bison herds to the south and large agglomerations of animals in Africa, it would seem that those surging crowds of caribou outmatched in numbers every other concentrated gathering of animals anywhere.

But these huge herds are a thing of the past. At the turn of this century, whalers from many parts of the world induced Eskimos to kill hundreds of thousands of caribou for their vitamin-enriched meat, superb for avoiding

Left: Small airplanes are often used to help in hunting caribou over the vast open spaces and trackless countryside of the far north of America. Hunters and their guides often land on lonely lakes and set up camp on the shore.

Below: The white-maned barren-ground caribou spends all year wandering from one place to another. Mature bulls, with their widely spreading antlers, can often be seen in small herds. After being killed the animals are brought by boat back to camp to be skinned immediately.

he threat of scurvy on whaling essels. Today, the ecological balance of the north is severely threatened by encroaching human civilization, and particularly by he discovery of precious oil beneath the perpetually frozen rctic surface.

The intrusion of civilization has lready reduced stocks of caribou o less than a tenth of what their number was not very long ago. In the 1940s, about one million caribou were counted; today they can be counted only in tens of thousands. Depletion of caribou stocks ushered in a tragic time for Eskimos and many northern Indians. Many tribes which lived exclusively by hunting barrenground caribou have suffered extreme poverty as a result.

The White Ram

Left: Its constant readiness for flight and its acute senses make the North American wild sheep a difficult animal to hunt. Camouflaged in white, hunter and guide approach a ram.

Right: High up on a treeless and stony slope, its rear protected by steep rock faces, this old ram is in a thoroughly protected position, out of reach of the hunter. Aerial photo.

The snow-white Dall's sheep lives wild in the northern reaches of North America. Bordering its habitat is that of the dark-colored Stone's sheep. True bighorns, the heaviest and sturdiest specimens of the breed, can still occasionally be found in the Rocky Mountains, from Canada to Mexico, though not nearly in as great a number as once roamed these heights. A smaller desert sheep also lives in the Rockies and parts of northern Mexico.

All these species of wild sheep have been hunted assiduously, with little concern about the danger that they might be totally exterminated. They all also suffer from comparatively meager reproduction rates, and from a reluctance to wander and adapt to new terrains. The result is that ecologists are now seriously concerned about depletion of wild sheep stocks. Only a few isolated populations of the various species are still in existence. Some, particularly those which clung to remote mountainous regions, are already extinct.

Much damaging poaching has been perpetrated by hunters who fly to mountain lakes, pick off their prey, load them onto their planes and take off before any ranger or warden can intervene. An incident like the following would be hard to duplicate today:

"The guide had spent weeks seeking out a huntable ram on Alaska's Kenai Peninsula. One evening, after a temporary camp had been made near a stream, the sun unexpectedly broke through a crack in black banks of clouds which had hung over the region for several days. A beam of light seemed to pick out a small white dot in the distant gray mountains. Focusing our binoculars, we were able to identify the dot as the ram we had set out to bring back. We watched it move in almost ghostly fashion along the craggy face of a glacier. It seemed to promise much for our efforts the following day.

"Early in the morning, we located the ram again, clearly silhouetted against the glacier in the early summer sunshine. Since last we had looked, it had climbed several hundred feet. It now stood motionless on a rocky cliff, like a proud monarch surveying its kingdom. The only thing to do was to follow the established rule: climb higher than the ram and approach it from above.

"On so tranquil and sunny a morning, the climb was extremely satisfying. The slopes, covered with birch and small willow, were alive with color. We climbed for four whole hours, establishing and maintaining an upward momentum. When we reached the first ridge, we gazed down through the binoculars into a crevasse in the fissured glacier. And there was a breathtaking sight: more than

fifty sheep were grazing peacefully on the mountainside—not one of them suitable for hunting.

"After a short rest, we resumed our climb. Now the wind was blowing steeply upward, permitting us to traverse the area without having our scent disturb the herd before descending to the spot where we believed we would find the ram. Great care now had to be taken; a false step or a momentary slip would send tell-tale stones and rubble cascading down into the valley.

"In the middle of an almost impenetrable labyrinth of rock, the guide suddenly stopped and stooped. In the distance, still well out of range, stood the figure of the white ram, posed majestically on a rock. Its head, crowned with ivory-colored horns, was raised—a snow-white silhouette. 'Too far,' the guide whispered, and so we moved cautiously after him down the steep slope.

"'Okay to try now,' he whispered after we had descended a fair distance. I signaled that I would take the shot. I positioned myself for slow, long-distance aiming. The shot resounded across the mountains. But it had missed. The ram leapt agilely to a nearby rock before the echo of the shot had faded. Speed was now necessary on my part as well. Caution had become a luxury. Racing to a nearby rock which commanded a clearer view of the region below, I focused once more on the elusive ram, took aim and fired. This time the bullet went home. I had accomplished in haste what I had failed to achieve with all the time in the world."

Moose

"For days on end, my guide and I had little to show for our exertions. The game seemed to have moved further north. Then one morning, as we were about to give up in despair, we spotted a huge moose on the other side of a deep, rain-soaked gorge. Its head thrown majestically back, the animal sniffed the air and moved off at a calm, unhurried pace. It was an impressive sight.

"'If we can't cover the distance between that animal and us in a half-hour,' the guide said, 'he'll be gone.'

"The two of us plunged into the damp, green wilderness and pressed on to reach the other side of the gorge and move on from there. Suddenly the guide stopped and pointed. There was the moose, on its way toward a valley up ahead, a region veiled by rain mist and half-hidden by foliage. The animal

had stopped. Its ears were raised; its snout-like muzzle sniffed about. It clearly sensed danger . . . and it was so near that I could count the tines on its mighty crown.

"The search was over. The target was in range. However, my pulse was hammering away, my heart was thumping, and the rifle sights were clouded by the vapor of my breath. But the moose was not about to wait me. I pulled himself together, aimed and squeezed the trigger. The shot rang out but nothing else happened. The moose still stood upright. Hastily reloading, I dashed forward, to be stopped by my guide, who called out to me: 'That's a dead moose you've got there.' And suddenly the mighty animal collapsed."

The attractions of the moose hunt are many and various. There is the challenge of tracking this proud, giant creature. There is

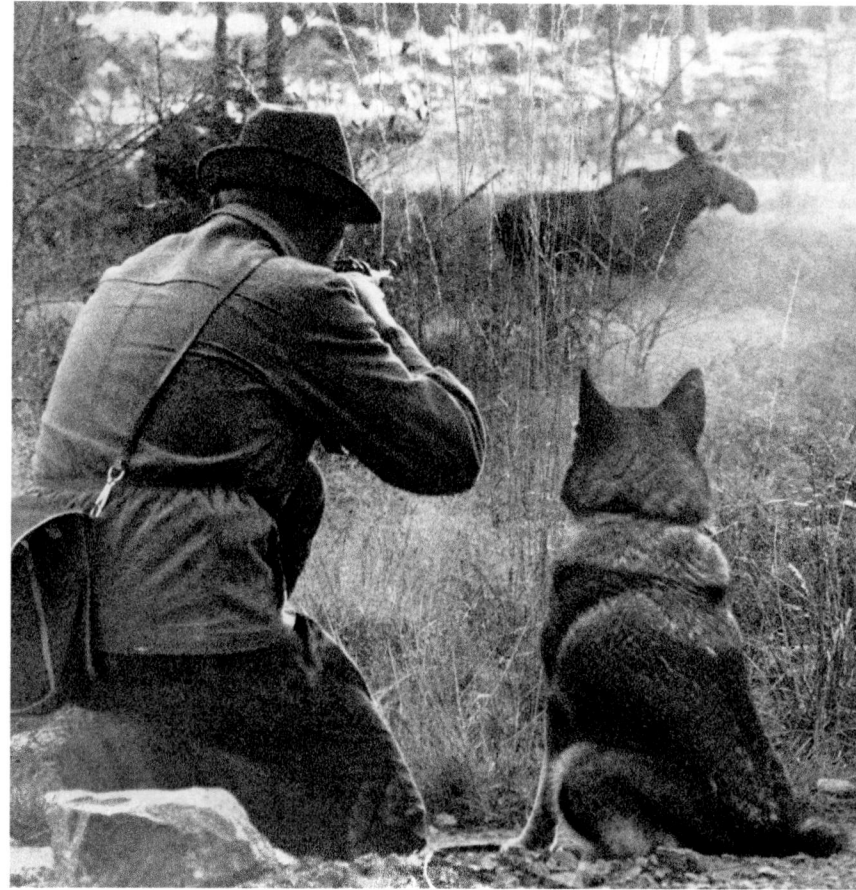

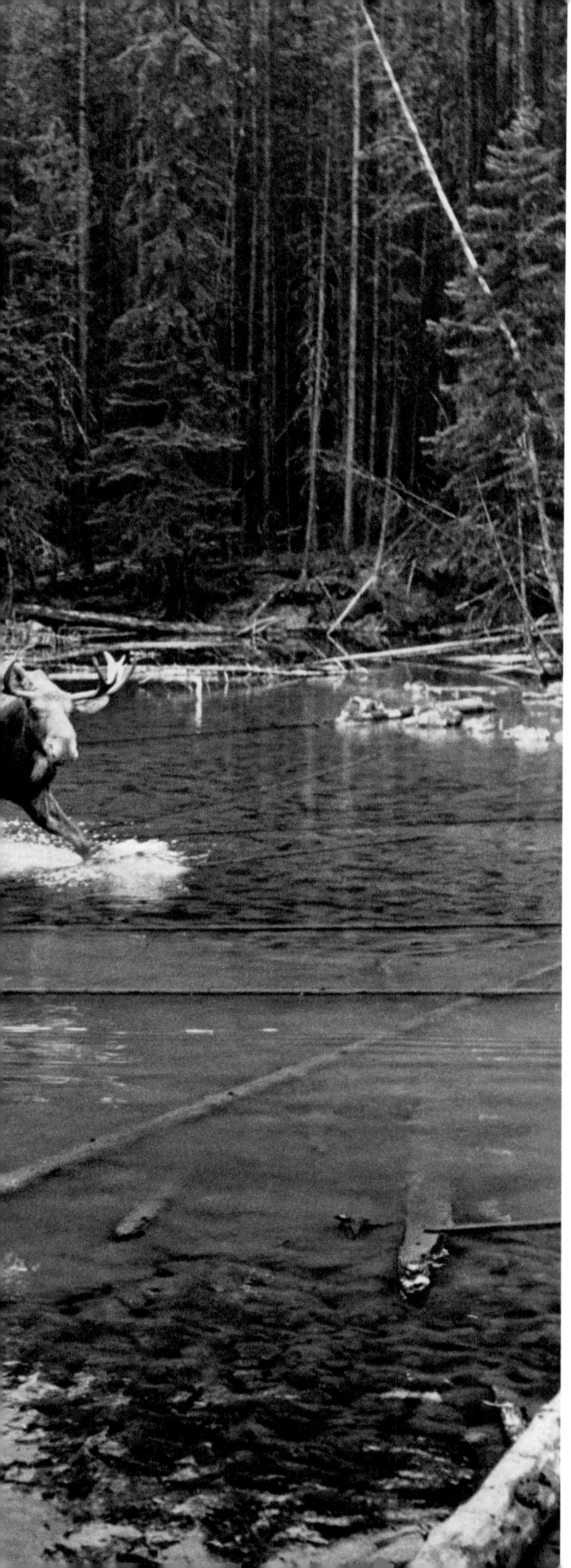

The moose is hunted by stalking or driving, or by following its tracks with highly specialized moose hounds. In Sweden, the animal is hunted with free-running hounds; in Norway, the hounds are held on long leash.

the lure of its powerful antlers. There is the experience of nature with which the moose hunt is inextricably linked.

This, the world's mightiest deer, lives in northern regions of North America and Eurasia. Once upon a time, moose were also widespread in the American heartland and in central Europe. But climatic changes and, later, the pressure of civilization drove them up into northern wildernesses.

The moose is a water-loving animal which prefers to frequent the banks of remote lakes and marshes. Despite its extraordinary antlers it is astonishingly nimble, and moose hunting requires great skill on the part of the hunter. These animals are restless wanderers, particularly during the rutting season, and can cover hundreds of miles, undeterred by lakes, rivers and even inlets of the sea because they are accomplished swimmers. The cry of the moose, echoing through the forest during rutting season, gives the hunter his lead; it is possible to lure it on by imitating the call of the female.

The most popular moose hunting regions today are in Canada and the Scandinavian countries, and especially in Alaska where the largest moose—weighing up to 1,800 pounds—can be found. In North America alone, about 90,000 moose are shot each year, but hunting restrictions are strict.

Those who have gone moose hunting will know what hunters mean when they speak of the "magic hour"—the time at dawn or dusk when these majestic creatures suddenly, unexpectedly, appear out of man-high, mist-shrouded willows, wandering monarchs of the animal kingdom.

The Last of the Bison

Energetic protective measures at the beginning of the twentieth century saved the bison from extinction in the United States and Canada. Today, a limited number of animals, mainly old bulls, are hunted annually for culling purposes.

White pioneers in America encountered the bison, the most powerful mammal in the American midwest, for the first time in 1691. They called it, incorrectly, "buffalo" and the name stuck, expanded to "Red Indian buffalo" in many of the popular adventure stories which the Wild West was later to spawn. But the American bison is a distinctive creature; with the European bison, it is an enduring representative of Ice Age wild cattle. There is, in fact, some controversy as to whether the two breeds are genuinely distinct species or merely sub-species, because it is known that they are capable of unrestricted interbreeding. At the beginning of the eighteenth century, the number of bison occupying the land between the Canadian north and northern Mexico was estimated at between sixty million and seventy million—probably the greatest concentration of hoofed animals ever.

In the fall, these primitive cattle would wander 200 to 400 miles southward toward gentler climate over well-trodden game trails. The following spring, they would return to their northern pastures. Sometimes it would take days for the enormous herds to pass a given spot along the trail.

The material and spiritual cultures of many prairie Indian tribes were based on the bison. It was also the primary source of food for the Indians who had learned to hunt them before they acquired horses—brought to the Americas by the Spanish *conquistadores*—and became excellent horsemen. They stalked them with bow and arrow or stampeded them over steep cliffs. The latter was a cruel and wasteful way to hunt, but there were so many bison and comparatively so few Indians that it resulted in no serious depletion in bison stocks.

The greatest animal tragedy in the history of mankind followed the advance of the white settler into bison country. The first of them regarded the bison as no more than a welcome source of meat; they shot some and drove others away into areas they considered unsuitable for breeding their own cattle. The real catastrophe had its roots in the construction of the first transcontinental railway. Untold numbers of bison were slaughtered to feed the men who cleared the land and laid the rails. When Indians organized fierce raids to try to halt the settler advance across Indian territory, men were sent out to exterminate great numbers of bison, simply to deprive the Indians of their main source of food and thus undermine their ability to fight. Wagonloads of bison skins were sent eastward; the meat was left to rot in the field, except for the tongues which were considered delicacies by Boston gentry.

The climax of this cruel slaughter was the organization by railway companies of pleasure hunting trips in which distinguished guests, including once a grand duke of Russia, took part. The participants

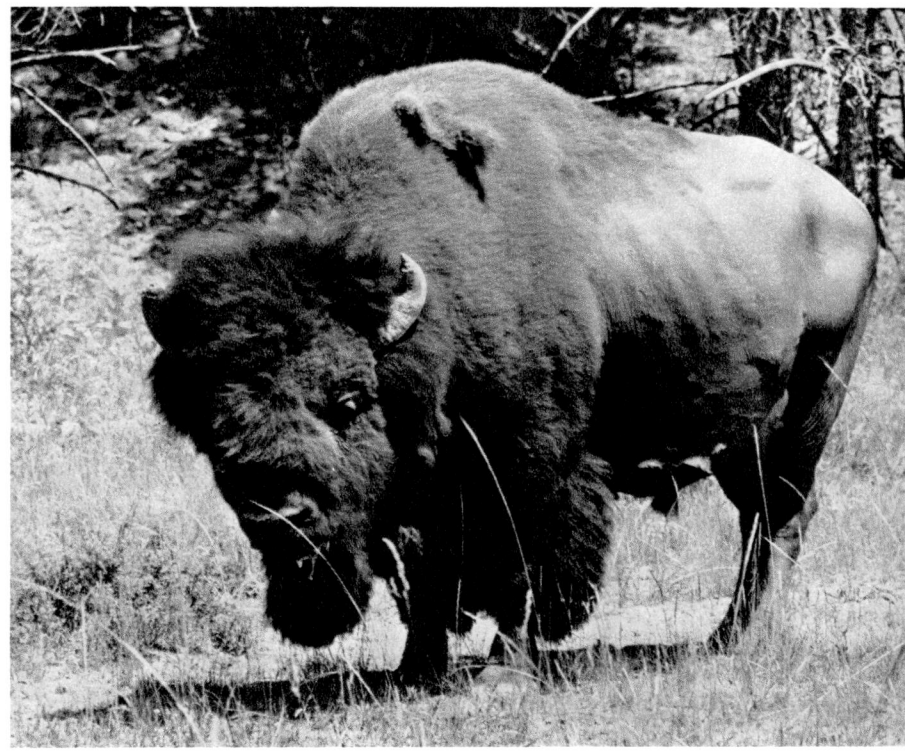

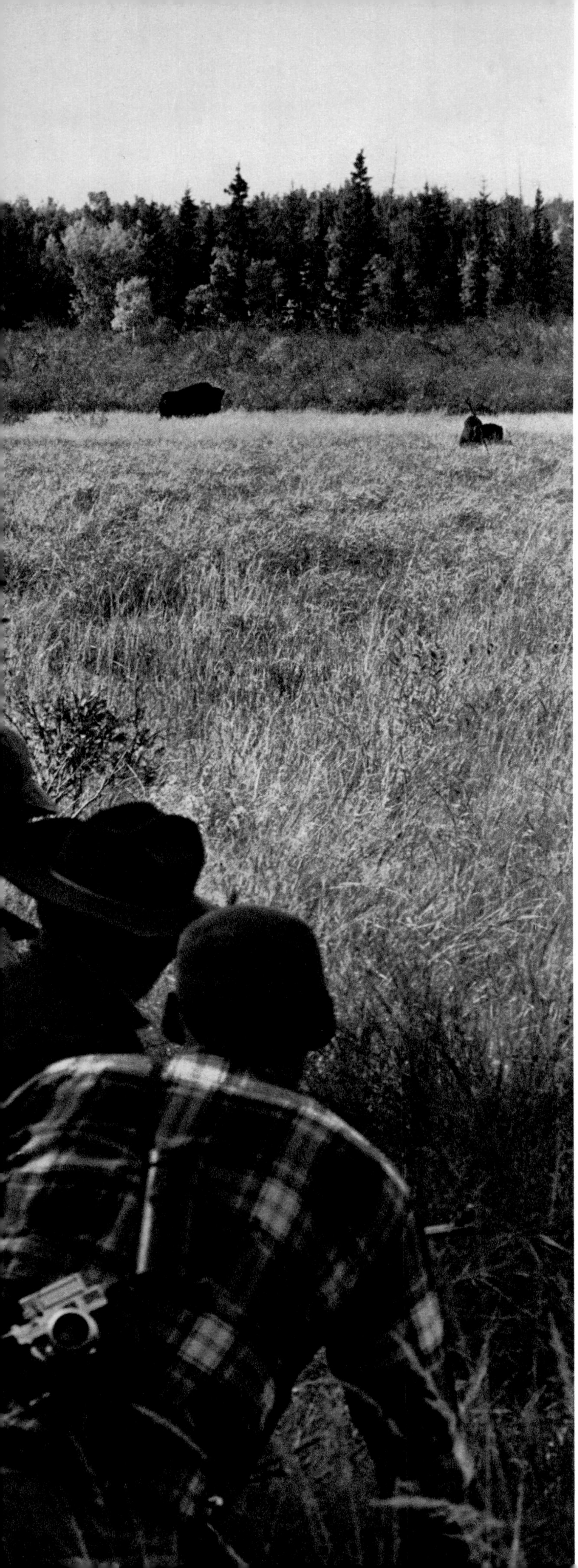

The "buffalo," as it is mistakenly called, is not a native of America. The bison first wandered over the landbridge that existed between northern Asia and Alaska during the Ice Age, and subsequently became extinct on the Asian side from which it had come. Hunting bison requires no great skill. The animal is placid and unaggressive. Its sense of smell is very acute, but it is not given to long-distance flight.

could shoot as many bison as they liked from the windows of trains. The air on both sides of the tracks was soon fouled by the stench of rotting flesh. Perhaps the best known bison exterminator was Colonel William F. Cody, better known as Buffalo Bill. At the end of his career, Cody, a national hero who also ran a circus, boasted that he had cut down no less than 4,280 bison in eighteen months while serving as meat dealer and butcher to the Kansas-Pacific Railway.

This dark chapter in the history of American hunting was, however, almost closed by this time. The national conscience gradually awakened. The *United States Game Report* recorded the existence of around one dozen bison in the 1890s (clearly an underestimate, but indicating the dimensions of the slaughter). This was partly responsible for the founding, in 1905, of the American Bison Society and for the efforts of President Theodore Roosevelt to save the last of the bison. Roosevelt, who was in office from 1901 to 1909, was a dedicated and responsible hunter. He became the greatest advocate of conservation America had until then known.

In 1907, the American government created a bison enclosure in the Oklahoma Wichita reserve, to which fifteen bison from the New York zoo were dispatched. Other reserves were set up in other places, including Montana, Nebraska and the Dakotas. The Canadian government too took steps to save the bison from extinction and was also successful in rescuing the somewhat larger sub-species of wood bison, which was introduced into the huge Wood Bison Park between Great Slave Lake and Lake Athabaska in 1915. Prairie bison in the various North American reserves today number around 20,000 animals.

Elk and White-Tailed Deer

The elk is one of twenty-three sub-species of large red deer. Like so many of North America's animals, it reached the "New World" by wandering over a landlink from northeastern Asia during the closing stages of the Ice Age. When the white man conquered and settled in North America the elk was abundant throughout temperate regions of the continent. But these large deer require plenty of space and they were gradually driven back by encroaching civilization. Elk are now few and far between in the eastern part of the United States.

Elk herds which withdrew to the mountains of the west are more abundant today than they were at the turn of the century. Their extinction was prevented by

protective regulations established by the American Wildlife Service. The elk has also been reintroduced into Canadian national parks from herds in Yellowstone Park further south. The density of the isolated and widely scattered populations of the Rocky Mountain elk is largely determined by the availability of pastureland in lower regions during the winter because, after the rutting season, when the first snows fall in the mountains, the elks move from summer ranges along well-beaten game trails to the lower valleys and foothills. In the national reserve at Jackson Hole, Wyoming, thousands of acres of land have been set aside to perpetuate the elk population. It is hoped by this means to sustain the local stock of about 20,000 elk—the densest elk population in the whole of North America.

Due to the inaccessibility of many of the mountains of the American west, an elk hunt usually assumes the character of an expedition. Good horses and bino-

culars are as important as long range rifles. The mating call of the elk is a whistle which is low pitched at first and then rises to high tremolo—a sound which can please a hunter as much as the belling of other red deer. An "elkpipe" is often used by elk hunters to lure the animal within shooting range.

The best hunting regions in the United States are those of the state forests of Montana, Wyoming, Idaho and Colorado. In good years, about 60,000 elk are shot there—half the annual quota for all of the United States and Canada.

Unlike the specialized hunting of such North American large deer as the elk and caribou, hunting the smaller white-tailed deer, mule deer and black-tailed deer has become almost a kind of popular sport. Millions of hunters set out in autumn during the few days in which hunting these animals is permitted. There is no doubt that the white-tailed deer is the most common species of

cloven-hoofed game in North America—possibly partly because it is not easy prey to hunt. During the rutting season, mature stags keep diligently to their small individual territories. They mark these out with glandular secretions on tree-trunks and urine-soaked patches of earth which they check each day and through which hinds are attracted. These animals are experts in the art of creating invisible scent barriers. Their mating battles often end in the death of one of the adversaries. This fight-to-the-finish behavior is much more evident in the case of white-tailed deer than the mule deer of the American west.

The white-tailed deer gets its name from the white underside of its tail. Around the turn of the century, their numbers were sharply reduced because of random hunting. But stocks of the animal are now estimated at several million, more than ever before in recorded memory. In the states of New York and Pennsylvania alone, the number of animals killed each year is over a quarter of a million.

The Track of the Puma

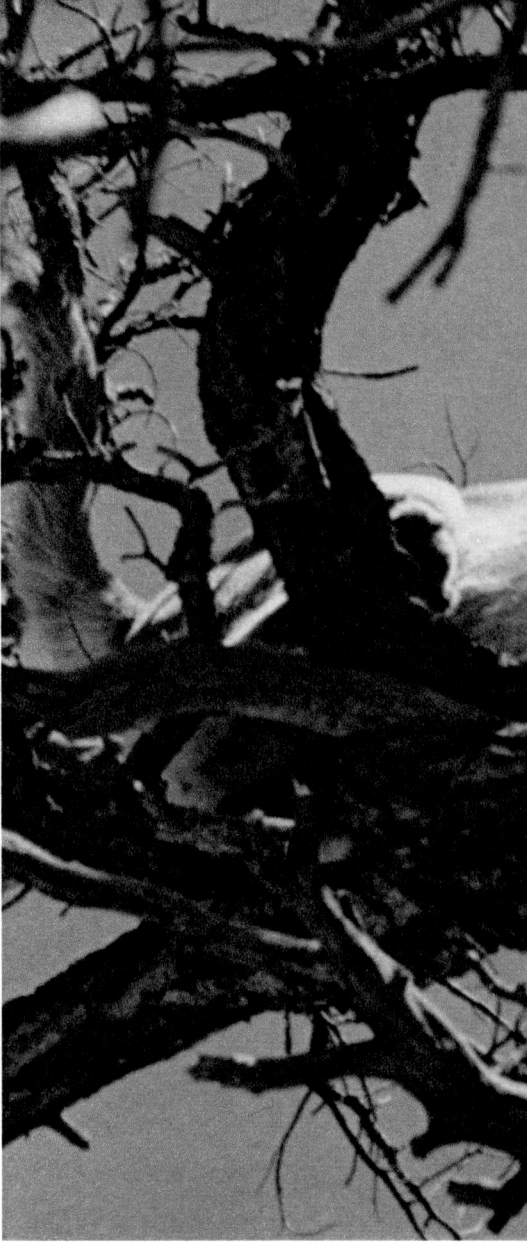

immeasurable damage is done to cattle b these "mountain lions," even today. It is fact that lone pumas do sometimes break int sheep stalls and kill as many as thirty sheep i a single night. No wonder that the pionee out west hunted puma with a vengeance an with all the means at their disposal.

The hunter hardly ever sees a puma face t face. It is a secretive, withdrawn, nocturn animal. Only in the rutting season do its wi cries echo through the night—cries onc described by a local farmer as sounding lik "a woman being murdered." At other time however, it is possible to live through almos the entire year without hearing, much le seeing, the slightest indication of the animal presence.

The puma makes its home today in th mountains and mountain forests of norther Canada, along virtually the entire Rock Mountain spine, in the dry cactus lowlands Central America and in many parts of Sout America. It once lived also in the east an middle west of the United States. It can b found from sea level (on the Caribbean coas to a height of about 18,000 feet (in the Ande

The wilder, more spacious and less developed a region, the greater the significance hunting has for its inhabitants. That has always been true for hunters in the wildernesses of the world and also in America in the days of the pioneers. However, unrestricted hunting combined with the development of ever more effective firearms sharply reduced the vast numbers of wild animals that once roamed North American expanses. Within just a few generations, the seemingly inexhaustible reserves of game in Canada and the United States have been cut back dramatically. That is why hunting the "cougar" or "mountain lion," as the puma is called in the mountains of the American west, has become a symbol of what once was unrestricted hunting in the wilderness.

The pioneering spirit lives on in the heart of the American hunter. Many retain a Western romanticism and a dedication to "free" hunting in which the prey is merely the object of the hunt and nothing else. It is a feeling which has no linkage whatsoever with ecological concerns, conservation movements or a feeling of responsibility of the hunter for the game. The most famous of all hunting clubs, the Boone and Crockett of New York, holds that the pursuit of hunting should perpetuate reliability, energy, resolution, self-confidence and self-reliance—qualities without which no people on Earth can develop a sense of fulfillment. There is no mention of game protection. The professional "lion killers" of the Rocky Mountains are imbued with these characteristics, when they set out with half-wild hounds in pursuit of puma, often returning to camp, exhausted, hungry and thirsty several weeks later.

According to farmers in puma country,

Setting out on a puma hunt. Fresh tracks have been scented; the chase can begin and will continue until the change in tone of the hounds' baying indicates that the puma has fled up into the branches of a tree. The hunters follow the hounds on horseback. The horses are left about a hundred yards off as the hunters approach cautiously to shoot the trapped animal.

swift pronghorn and the sturdy elk. Although an excellent hunter, the puma is not unremittingly aggressive. Proverbially, it "kills all animals which flee, and flees from all animals which attack." This not uncommon response to circumstances is perhaps due to the fact that the puma has few natural enemies and is confounded when one appears. It can become astonishingly tame if acquired young. Like all cats, it is naturally clean. Indeed certain anatomical and behavioral characteristics make it clearly recognizable as a relative of the small cat. In captivity, it never uses its teeth or claws against its keeper. Its friendly disposition as a pet is probably excelled only by that of a pet cheetah. Anyone familiar with what can be the lovable nature of the puma will find it hard to understand why hunters in general are reluctant to fix restrictions on the pursuit of the animal. It is this reluctance which has so sharply reduced the number of pumas in many parts of North America, and has, incidentally, also been partly responsible for the uncontrolled white-tailed deer "population explosion." Even in national parks, pumas have become increasingly rare because of intensive hunting in adjoining cattle breeding regions. The director of one such park admitted that it was necessary to cull the local elk population because there were not enough pumas to do the job according to nature's rules. He also admitted that, though he had grown up in the Rocky Mountains, he himself had never encountered a "mountain lion."

nd thus can occupy by far the largest and ost varied biotope of all cat species.

Unlike the jaguar, which tends to remain omparatively stationary and which is regard-d as the cunning recluse among the big cats, e puma is a highly adaptable individualist hich claims a large territory ranging from vo to twelve acres for males and from one to ve acres for females. In winter, the puma llows its prey into lower regions. Every bit s elegant and supple as the leopard, it plays a milar role in the Rocky Mountains as the now leopard does in the mountains of ntral Asia.

A Rocky Mountain puma can be as big as lioness. It is capable of taking on and killing powerful bighorn ram and the plucky Rocky ountain goat. On the other hand, smaller arieties of puma which inhabit the tropical in forests of South America feed mainly on namou, curassows, guans and chachalacas, as ell as monkeys, pacas and agoutis. First and remost, however, the puma is a major enemy f all species of cloven-hoofed game in both orth and South America, from the tiny udu and the larger white-tailed deer to the

Hunting Jaguar along the Orinoco

The jaguar, America's most powerful big cat, generally devotes its predatory attentions to its favorite game and long-established traditional prey, animals like the tapir and the capybara. But there are frequent exceptions. For example, for several months in succession, a jaguar accustomed to making off with domestic cattle terrorized a village on the Arauca, a tributary of the Orinoco River in Carabobo, Venezuela. After weeks of fruitless pursuit, the hunters and their hounds came face to face with the animal at last. But it was only a split-second encounter. The big cat disappeared like a flash into a jungle swamp. *"El tigre* is a sorcerer," one of the hunters moaned.

"There was no question of deep sleep that night. With feverish expectations, we all dozed, our senses half alert to the sounds of the jungle. Before dawn, a little way up the river, dozens of pairs of green eyes gleamed from the darkened sandbanks. The cayman alligators, secure under the cover of darkness, let us come within a few yards before abandoning the narrow strip of land between the jungle and the river and disappearing into the water. They drifted motionlessly just below the surface before rising onto the river banks again further downstream.

"Dawn rose as we clambered over fallen trees and up steep slopes to be swallowed once more by the darkness of the jungle. We slashed our way through the undergrowth with machetes, following the dogs. Suddenly one of the hounds became strangely excited. Sniffing the air, it ran around in circles and came back whining as if to transmit its excitement to us. At the next branch of the river, it led us to barely distinguishable fresh droppings. And a little further on, we came upon a tree on which the elusive jaguar had sharpened its claws the night before. The bark bore long scratches up to nine feet off the ground, and sap was still oozing from the trunk. Past the tree, undergrowth and bushes were flattened over an area of several yards square—as if someone had made camp there.

"Suddenly the excitable hound began trembling with impatience. In fact, the scent of the jaguar was now unmistakable. To mark out its territory, its *vivienda, el tigre* had liberally distributed its urine. Our leader whistled softly through his teeth—a signal that the jaguar was hiding nearby. The other dogs were, of course, also excited by now and two more *revolcaderos* where the jaguar had lain were quickly found. One of the dogs, its hair standing on end, found a six-foot-long cayman, its back bitten through and its flank torn open. The jaguar had heaved its prey up a nine-foot bank and had left it lying there.

"The climax of the chase lasted only a few dramatic minutes. In the brooding heat, amidst the confusion of jungle vegetation, with the smell of the big cat growing ever more penetrating, the baying of the hounds rose like the sounds of a cacophonous, angry choir. In savage reply, the jaguar grunted and growled in its nearby hiding place. We moved carefully forward, our rifles poised. In the jaguar's refuge all hell broke loose: roaring, spitting, hissing, the jaguar tried to defend itself against the attacking hounds, which scattered as it lashed out. One of us edged still closer to catch a glimpse of the unseen phantom at which the fury of the hounds was directed. A snarl! A leap! And two fleeing hounds almost knocked him to the jungle floor. But before he could move again, the jaguar was on the ground before him, hissing ferociously. The hunter took quick aim and fired. His bullet struck home . . . but the big cat leapt away into the undergrowth. 'Quickly,' the lead hunter cried, 'or he'll kill all the dogs.' The hounds had resumed their pursuit only to be stopped and thrown back by the fleeing jaguar. But its flight was now only a final effort. The bullet had done its damage and, as we caught sight of it again, it collapsed. The leader advanced with a spear and plunged it deep into the animal's breast."

The South American Jungles

1 and 2   Hunters make their way in long processions from their temporary camps through broad savannahs and forests. The fate of these tribes and of their cultures is largely dependent on the rate at which modern civilization penetrates their hunting regions. Indians living in the border areas between civilization and jungle already use firearms.

South America is a completely new world for hunters from other parts of the globe. Game animals with which they may be familiar from their exploits elsewhere are extremely rare, or altogether non-existent. There is, however, the red deer imported from Europe. Though not an indigenous in-habitant, it has—unlike smaller native species of deer which bear only minimal antlers—developed truly spectacular antlers in the southern Andes region of the continent.

South America's distinctive animal kingdom is a product of its long insular seclusion, dating back to early geological times. Through-out the Tertiary Period, there was no free movement of fauna be-

1

3 *After exhaustive stalking, which often lasts for days, a South American hunter has succeeded in killing a deer.*

4 *The whole community rushes to examine the catch. Young and old help to dress the game.*

5 *After an improvised camp has been set up, the fire kindled and the hammocks hung, the festive meal begins.*

4

ween South America and other parts of the world. The continent thus retained its singular animal world which, as is proved by fossils found there, included elephant-sized sloths and massive armadillos. Smaller descendants of these creatures survive today, as do anteaters, primitive rodents and monkeys—none of which offer much in the way of sport to the hunter.

The huntable game of South America includes various species of deer—such as the pudu, mazama, huemul, marsh deer, pampas deer and white-tailed deer—as well as the jaguar, puma and tapir. South America also offers a wide variety of winged game, including tinamou and chachalacas the size of capercaillies, geese and ducks. With its estimated 2,700 different winged species, South America has by far the most diverse and interesting bird life in the world.

The responsible hunter, for whom the preservation of the animal world is of deep concern, is often at a loss when confronted with prevailing hunting standards in some parts of South America. Such concepts as conservation and codified hunting procedures are often the product of totally different cultures. The continent that was once taken by *conquistadores*, soldiers and adventurers has not yet readily lent itself to the demands of restraint felt by hunters in many other parts of the world. This is particularly true for those South Americans who fight an unceasing struggle for existence and sustenance and for whom huntable game remains a significant part of the daily diet. It is easy to understand that close seasons and other restrictions will be ignored by men anxious to feed their families and themselves. Animal furs and hides often provide cheap clothing. It is a climate in which great interest in preservation and game management is often difficult to arouse.

But there also exist in South America huge areas remote from civilization in which archaic hunting cultures have been preserved and in which there is such an

5

abundance of game that questions of animal extinction do not arise. In the wildernesses of the upper Orinoco and the Amazon, and in the wide savannahs east of the Andes, ancient tribes of hunting peoples have survived. These remnants of primitive populations are, like the bushmen of the Kalahari Desert and the pygmies of Zaire, among the oldest hunting cultures still existing.

These tribes were not originally native to the region. Their immigration into South America probably took place in several phases. The first to arrive, possibly about 40,000 years ago, may have been pre-Mongolian hunters of Asian origin, to whom the Ainus of northern Japan and the few remaining Veddas of Sri Lanka are related.

A second phase of immigration from Asia is believed to have taken place around 20,000 years ago. These neo-Americans were descendants of peoples of northeast Asian origin who crossed the temporary landbridge from Asia to Alaska and who gradually made their way southward. Some of them fanned off en route to become the antecedents of North America's Indian tribes. Others continued southward across the Central American isthmus. The discovery of bone and stone tools indicate that they may have pursued herds of mammoth and bison southward, finally reaching South America where giant sloths and armadillos—which became extinct only about 8,000 years ago—became their favorite prey.

Their outsized bows and arrows made it possible for these Stone Age hunters to take on the giant mammals. These weapons are totally inconsistent with the demands of hunting the small species of game now most common in the jungles of South America. Indians there now hunt with poisoned arrows of more modest proportions and with blowpipes. Their prey includes fish, cayman alligators, tortoises, snakes, fowl, rheas, parrots, such rodents as the agouti, paca and capybara, tapirs, peccaries, monkeys and various species of deer.

The native jungle hunters of South America have a deep magical-mystical relationship with the animals they hunt. They kill only as many as they need to live. Among the Weikas on the upper Orinoco, the soul of each individual hunter is supposed to live in the form of a huge eagle, the fate of which is closely attuned to the fate of the hunter—almost to the point of being identical. Thus, for these people, the killing and eating of all large birds of prey is regarded as sacrilege. Anyone who kills one by accident is in breach of strict taboo laws and must atone for his crime before being reinstated in the community.

Although numbers and comparative evaluations have littl[e] place in these Indian culture[s] these primitive hunters can tell th[e] exact time of day from the positio[n] of the sun. Like all primitiv[e] tribes, their sense of direction an[d] orientation is also extremely highl[y] developed. They believe they go t[o]

eaven when they die and that eaven consists of a magnificent ngle teeming with game. The oon is their most highly revered eavenly body, its phases playing important role in their religious fe.

Indian jungle hunters return heavily laden with the game, killed with primitive weapons which are reminiscent of Stone Age implements. Huge poisoned arrows (left) and nine-foot blowpipes (above right) are used for killing peccaries and monkeys. The curare arrow poison has such a narcotic effect on monkeys that, unable to climb, they fall to the ground.

he South American porcupine is a dent which is seldom hunted.

he banded armadillo is regarded as a licacy.

uth America's smallest deer, the pudu, es primarily in the undergrowth.

nteaters live on the savannah and in dry rests.

he tapir is one of the largest uth American animals.

265

The Vanishing Tiger

From the Caucasus to the Yellow Sea, from Java to Siberia, the tiger hunt was once considered the most noble sport of all. In India, it was the favored pastime of maharajahs. A prince's status could be determined by how many tigers he owned and the size of the jungle to which he laid proprietary claim. In elaborately organized drives, the world's largest and mightiest ca[t] were hunted down and killed b[y] hunters perched safely on special[ly] trained hunting elephants. Or the[y] were concealed in elevated hide[s] to pick off the tiger when [it] approached strategically place[d] bait.

Tigers require astonishing[ly] large quantities of meat. The[y]

favorite prey is large animals, including deer, antelope, cattle and wild boars. But they are not likely to shun smaller prey if it is available. In places where the game population is scanty, tigers are sometimes compelled to prey on domestic cattle. In fact, their main source of sustenance in India today is domestic buffalo and cattle—a fact which gives the animal a reputation of national menace.

Man-eating tigers are an even greater threat in India than lions are in Africa. But tigers become man-eaters usually when they are too old or too sick to try to overwhelm other animals and are able to take by surprise humans who are less able to defend themselves and escape.

This giant cat, of which there are eight sub-species, is severely threatened today. Only the Siberian tiger, the largest cat on Earth, has increased in number in recent times, because of strict Soviet conservation measures. In India, once the classic home of the "king" or Bengal tiger, tiger hunting is now prohibited as well. While it is believed there were about 100,000 tigers at the turn of the century, today's figure is closer to 2,000. Now, on what seems like the eve of its extinction, serious efforts are being made to save the tiger.

Panther Hunt

Before the population explosion sharply reduced the numbers of all kinds of game in the Indian sub-continent, many Indian villages, regardless of size or isolation, had their own "local" panther. These great mysterious cats were at home everywhere and nowhere, living on the fringes of the jungle in gorges washed bare by monsoon rains, or on jutting rocks blanketed by thorny bushes, which provided the cover panthers gravitate toward. At the time, if stories handed down can be trusted, the relationship between the simple Indian peasant and the panther was friendly and peaceable. The peasants were happy to sacrifice a few goats to the panther deities, and they were pleased when an excess number of pariah dogs which strayed into their villages were eliminated by the spotted predators.

Man-eating panthers were, however, feared even more by the villagers than man-eating tigers. This may have been because those

The panther hunt is always highly dangerous. Before the hunt begins, the hide—known as the "machan"—is erected. Helpers armed with bows and arrows are situated in trees flanking the drive in order to prevent the panther from escaping.

attacked by panthers often escaped with their lives, to live on as cripples, while tigers almost always kill their victims. But so strong was the mystical link between villagers and panthers that peasants often preferred to abandon their ancestral homes and find other places to live rather than to help kill the offending panther. Even a professional hunter who came to free a village from the threat of a man-eating panther received no help from the villagers, who believed that the spirit of the dead animal would torment all who had been instrumental in its death.

Superstition went even further than that. It was believed that no panther was truly dead until it had been skinned. This belief was adopted by hunters who, considering the panther hard to kill, went out after it with rifles more powerful than were really necessary. They would hunt the animal either with drives or from elevated hides beneath which bait (usually goats) were tethered. Although a tiger is easily stampeded, panther driving has always been an uncertain undertaking, extremely dangerous for both beaters and hunters. Many a panther drive has failed because, instead of panicking, the panther hid in a tree to pounce on the unsuspecting hunter. There are many recorded cases in which panthers leapt upon, and seriously mauled, beaters—often several of them within seconds.

It is widely believed that the panther is the most dangerous of all beasts of prey in India. Buckshot fired from a shotgun is recommended for bringing it down, with the understanding that the hunter can at no time relax his vigilance when a panther might be nearby.

Traps in the Jungles and Forests

In the dense tropical forests of Asia, as everywhere else, it is far from easy for local hunters to approach large animals close enough to take aim for a sure kill. Those using bows and arrows and blowpipes, rather than high-powered rifles, are at a particular disadvantage because with such weapons distance is an even more significant factor. Primitive weapons are more suitable for hunting more clearly visible game, such as wildfowl and monkeys, closer to the leafy roof of the forest. For elephants, rhinos, deer and other large game, many indigenous hunters rely on traps which they themselves build.

The "trappers" of the forests of southern Asia hunt more or less selectively. They use particular types of traps for each species; the traps are designed and constructed with the specific animals in mind.

The Pannikiyas, elephant hunters of Sri Lanka, seek out an appropriate spot for the trap on the animal's game trail—often near a thick tree-trunk. Thick rope is attached to the tree and laid out round a circular, camouflaged two-foot-deep pit in the ground. Digging the pit demands expert knowledge and skill because the circumference should conform to that of the elephant's foot. The closing and releasing mechanism of the trap is remarkably effective, though simple. The rope with the noose is attached to another, thinner rope which is weighted with a heavy sack of stones, hung several feet up in the branches of the tree. The releasing apparatus, carved out of hardwood, holds the weight still until an elephant, stepping into the pit triggers the mechanism.

The Pawangs of northern Sumatra use dozens of different home-made traps in their hunting pursuits. As well as the "box trap" and the noose, they have developed a devastating rhino spear which can drop from about thirty feet up, right through the bodies of these massive animals.

Like other game hunting tribes which have developed their skills over thousands of years of hunting for sustenance, the Pawangs adhere strictly to codes of restricted hunting. They kill only what they need for food. None of the species they have preyed upon has ever become extinct.

Substantial changes in hunting practices have taken place on the second largest of the Sunda Islands of the Malay Archipelago. Encroaching civilization has eaten away at its rain forests. The last of the rhinos, elephants and tigers native to the island survive in steadily decreasing numbers in steadily declining jungle areas. Although the hunters are of the same people as before, their weapons have changed, and the demand for rhino tusks, ivory and young orang-utans has steadily increased.

The Pawangs, once armed only with long knives which they used in constructing their ingenious animal traps, were organized into groups of well-paid poachers, armed with rifles. Villagers buil[t] hides and platforms for thes[e] hunters, who proceeded to ki[ll] almost the last of the large animal[s] of the local rain forests.

When one of the last jungl[e] regions of Sumatra, the Leuse[r] Reserve, was taken over by na[-] tional conservation organization[s] in 1971, the Pawangs were allotte[d] a new and important task—t[o] become game protectors. Thi[s] "promotion" achieved thre[e] things: the Pawangs received [a] secure income; foreign poacher[s] with their sophisticated weapon[s] were unable to obtain the service[s] of qualified guides; and the natur[e] conservation project had the mos[t] knowledgeable experts on the rai[n] forests and local game at thei[r] disposal.

Above: "Prankat harimau" — *Sumatran tiger trap, made of bamboo. The bait, usually a young goat, is tethered behind the trap. Tigers and clouded leopards which fall into the trap trigger the release mechanism, making the heavy gate fall.*

Right: Orang-utans are sometimes captured by means of traps. A sprung bamboo platform forces the animals to climb through a sack when descending a tree. They are then unable to break free.

Fixing bait to a macaque trap. When it is seized by a monkey—which usually approaches from behind—the suspended plank falls, trapping the "thief" in a noose between two horizontal bars.

An elephant trapper has dug a pit in a suitable spot and has laid a strong rope noose. The rope is fastened to a thick tree trunk. Hanging from branches high above is a sack filled with stones, connected to the noose by a thin rope. The sack is held in position by the second rope until the release mechanism is activated.

Camouflaging an elephant trap requires great knowledge and skill. First, the opening is covered with thin, dry twigs. The thin rope which is connected to the release mechanism is clearly visible.

Finally, the trapper places large leaves over the noose and pit, and covers everything with earth.

Above: The release mechanism of the rino trap is so well hidden that even experienced hunters sometimes fail to spot it.

Above: Bird trap. Small ponds in which ground-living birds bathe are covered with fine bamboo trestles. The birds enter these "cages" through funnel-shaped entrances but are then unable to find their way out again.

Right: Small birds as well as large animals can be caught with noose traps. In this model, the noose is drawn tight as soon as the mechanism is touched and the stretched bamboo shaft springs up.

271

Hunting Living Fossils

By Dr. Ernst Schäfer, former chief curator of the State Museum of Lower Saxony and Professor of Biology and Ecology at the Central University of Venezuela in Caracas.

Asia, the largest of the continents, is widely regarded as the original region of evolutionary development and spread of many of the large mammals. It has thus always played an important role in the study of the animal world. In the secluded retreats of its remote mountain regions, a number of primitive and primeval species still survive—species which are justifiably known as "living fossils." These are among the rarest and least-known animals in the world.

Before they could be placed under protection—as they mostly are today—it was necessary to carry out a considerable amount of research into their habits and ways of life, and to acquire some specimens for scientific examination. This was the reason and justification for hunting expeditions some of us took into these far-off districts.

Exploration of the remotest regions of Asia was not completed until the 1930s, and even today some parts of the continent remain a mystery. The researchers found themselves proving over and over again that ontogeny, the development of the individual specimen, is a brief recapitulation of the history of the entire species. Like this writer, they were all primarily "hunters and collectors" for the world's finest museums, in which the results of their endeavors were to be preserved for the pleasure and edification of the general public. They were also responsible game biologists and protectors of nature whose most important task was the preservation of the Earth's animals. It is in this light that the following accounts of our trail-blazing hunting adventures in the mountains of Asia should be understood. Where the 13,500-foot-high mountain plateaus of central Asia are bordered by the towering range of the Himalayas, where four of Asia's greatest rivers, the Yangtze, Mekong, Salween and Irrawaddy, rise within only a few hundred miles of each other to follow the courses carved out over millions of years through wild, craggy mountain territory—this was the region of our exploration and research.

The Panda

It all began with one of the "living fossils," the bamboo bear, black, white-headed, the giant panda which has since become so famous—the rarest and most valuable animal in the world.

The panda now lives only in the almost impenetrable bamboo jungles of the Hsifan

Below left: The rarest and most valuable large animal in the world, the bamboo bear, or giant panda, has been adopted as the emblem of the World Wildlife Fund. Only four specimens are known to have been shot by wildlife biologists and researchers. Now under the strict protection of the Chinese government, it is a unique predator with a highly specialized vegetarian diet. It spread from China to Burma during the Pleistocene epoch. Today, however, it lives only in a small area in the mountainous region between China and eastern Tibet.

mountains on the borders of Tibet and China. This animal was the beginning of my career as zoologist and hunter. My encounter with it was a determining factor in my life as a researcher. The first giant panda was shot by Theodore and Kermit Roosevelt, the sons of the American president Theodore Roosevelt, on April 13, 1928. Four years later, Dean Sage and William H. Sheldon killed another panda, and in 1935 Captain H. C. Brocklehurst shot the last of the four pandas known to have been killed by white research hunters. I myself shot the second of these animals in 1931 while a member of the Brooke Dolan/Hugo Weigold Expedition. The memory of that moment is as fresh today as on the day it took place.

Spring 1931. We had penetrated into the mountain labyrinth in which the half-wild Wassu hunting tribe lived. Accompanied by Wang, a local guide, I had been fighting my way through dripping bamboo jungles for several weeks at altitudes ranging from 6,000 to 12,000 feet, but there was no sign of a panda. One day, however, I came upon a large clump of sour-smelling vegetable matter consisting of ground bamboo fibers. I had never seen anything like it, but my instinct told me that it could only be the droppings of the giant panda. I crept through tunnel-like trails in the silent wilderness for many more days until, suddenly, I found teeth-marks and whole "fortresses" of piled-up bamboo sticks obviously "built" by this rare animal. It seemed that I had reached the home of the panda. But where was it hiding? The search continued. And then one day I heard its growly voice. I tried to penetrate the bamboo thicket to "capture" it. But the panda made no further sound. Then I caught sight of strange scratch-marks on a huge tree-trunk which towered high above the green wilderness. There was no doubt that they were claw-marks and I even found white, wiry hair jammed between the bark and the wood, high above the ground. Now I knew: the panda could climb trees! Probably to dry its coat in the warmth of the sun after the nightly cloudbursts.

May 13, 1931. Morning broke over the mountains. Hunters tend to be superstitious people: the Roosevelt brothers had killed their bear on the thirteenth. There was no holding us back. Wang and I clambered from

Right: The takin is also one of the rarest and least known animals in the world. It is found in three geographically separate species in isolated regions of the eastern Himalayas and western China at altitudes of between 6,000 and 15,000 feet. This animal can also be regarded as a living fossil, a relic from a period long past. With its broad nose, the 900-pound animal looks like something from prehistoric times. The takin is extremely belligerent and only a few specimens are known to have been shot.

slope to slope, from peak to peak, to gain a view over the misty gorge. Suddenly I saw a movement in the foliage on the opposite slope. Was I mistaken? Once more a tremor shook the foliage and then the silhouette of an animal appeared. "*Beshiung-chin*," I whispered. "White bear." Wang stood as if turned to stone. Then he whispered hoarsely, "*Bu sche de!*" "It's nothing!" But something moved once again on the far side of the gorge, and then the black and white head of the panda appeared over the leafy roof of the forest. I judged the distance to be about 900 feet. But it was impossible to approach more closely in that wretched setting. Feeling my way, I groped for a support for my rifle and waited until the body of the panda was clearly in my sight—and then, with the mountains echoing to the sound of the shot, the panda fell.

The Takin

After hunting the giant panda, I concentrated on the search for the "golden ox of the Chinese," the takin, which was equivalent in the annals of our expedition to tracking down the Golden Fleece.

The takin is a belligerent creature, feared even by the natives of the region it inhabits. Even its bearing is imposing; its coloring—radiant gold on a black background—enhances its strange and mysterious appearance. The historical development of this primeval animal remains a mystery. Next to nothing is

known about its habits and way of life. Its head is similar to that of a musk ox, with its protruding eye sockets and its muzzle reminiscent of the chamois. Its body structure bears a resemblance to the buffalo. Its legs are short in relation to its huge body. It has thick muscles and spreading hooves which enable it to make its way through the jungle like a steam-roller and climb the steepest slopes with ease. The takin leads the restless life of a wanderer between deep valleys and high mountainous regions. I even encountered a bull on the borders of the eternal snows. But there is no doubt that the animal feels most at home in the impenetrable jungle.

The hunt for my strongest bull began harmlessly enough: Wang and I found its tracks in undergrowth thick with rhododendrons—it had broken trees as wide as arms into matchwood! Suddenly Wang pointed upward and I caught sight of the takin high up on a steep slope. I fired, though believing it impossible to hit my target. I sent Wang to where we had seen the animal, but he quickly returned and asked me to accompany him because he had no gun and the takin might have been wounded. I again ordered him to go on ahead, but he declined. So I shouldered my rifle and climbed the steep slope with him. After a quarter of an hour's hard climbing, Wang bent down, picked something up off the ground and disappeared like a bloodhound on all fours into the dense undergrowth, while I cocked my weapon and looked for a firm support for it. Several minutes passed in silence; then an angry snorting sounded, a

cracking and splintering, and with eyes almost leaping from his head, Wang stumbled out of the thicket, followed by the takin with its horns lowered. Wang threw himself to the ground. The bull stood with its head raised, ready to attack, almost vertically above me—a huge, wild animal determined to kill its enemy! Slowly, I raised my rifle, wanting to savor the sight of this rare beast as long as possible. My shot rang out only when it lowered its head to complete its attack.

Thorold's Deer

Some years ago, on my most exciting and successful expedition, our goal was the solution of the riddle of the Tibetan Thorold's deer. It was then an animal which no one could describe in detail and of whose habits no one knew anything.

For two years, I had been searching for this animal in the remote, unexplored regions of East Tibet, which was inhabited by the wild, aggressive Khampas. Several surprise attacks and several exchanges of gunfire had taken place but finally, after traversing countless passes, between 14,000 and 18,500 feet up, we arrived at Batang. Our horses were as thin as skeletons. My native companions had given up all hope; their strength had dwindled and the whole undertaking seemed hopeless.

But one day, it happened. As we toiled over yet another seemingly endless pass, two black heads with long, powerful, snow-white and shining antlers suddenly appeared from

the confusion of granite rubble that marked the landscape. By then, however, I was so exhausted that I could not get my rifle ready before the animals disappeared. So near and yet so far . . . And it was November 13, 1934. Another thirteenth! I did what I could, but my horse stumbled and fell into a fissure in the rock. It lost so much blood that it seemed unlikely that it would reach our distant camp. I was at the point of giving up and putting the horse out of its misery, but I didn't. Half dead from exhaustion and with senses dulled, I staggered after my Tibetan guide, still leading my poor horse. Suddenly, the Tibetan touched my arm. "Sir!" he whispered, "the deer!" And there they were, a whole herd of them,

looking down at us from a great height, elk-like, dark, truly primeval-looking creatures. And towering above the antlerless heads of the females were the shining antlers of a fine stag! Gathering what little strength I had left, I crept for cover and began to climb. One of the most adventurous stalks of my life had begun. After only a few hundred yards, my head began to spin and my heart thumped as I approached the level at which the deer had been. I slid and stumbled over slippery stones to the final ridge—and there, in the snow, were unmistakable tracks. Pausing to draw breath, I gazed about. Some 200 feet away was a mass of huge brown animals! Only the light-colored antlers and

the black face of the leading deer stood ou from the mass of female animals. Eye to eye I stood confronted by the legendary deer, bu only for an instant. The entire herd suddenl swept into motion, thundering wildly dow the slope toward protective rocks. Hidden b the females, the stag raced away with enormou leaps. Instinctively, I raised my gun and, a the animal came again into sight, I fired. I a fraction of a second, the deer had appeare above the herd, had been struck by the bulle had made a long, stiff leap, and fallen dead.

The Blue Sheep

After this success, we made our way heavily laden, down perilous slopes to th Yangtzekiang valley where I discovered a extremely rare variety of the otherwis common blue sheep—the pygmy blue sheep This time my destination was the towerin heights of Kanchenjunga. The ascent, wit twenty-five male and twenty-five female bear ers, presented no problems and we were abl to negotiate about 3,000 feet in altitude eac day. Finally the valley broadened out and th huge twenty-five-mile-long Zemu glacier ap peared like a dragon from the semicircula mountain spine. As we pitched our tents i the shelter of moraine, it began to snow. A biting wind howled around us and th thunder of an avalanche reached us from th far end of the valley. In this first night, ou tents were covered by several feet of snow an for two whole days it continued to fall in suc huge quantities that our tiny cluster of huma beings was soon buried under a thick whit blanket. This situation was made even mor serious by the fact that our supplies had ru out. As was my wont, I had reckoned o killing several plump blue sheep for sustenanc and, in retrospect, I marvel at my recklessnes

Right: The rare argali belongs to the group of central Asian giant sheep. The ram weighs up to 230 pounds and its horns weigh as much as 55 pounds. Unlike the Himalayan blue sheep, the Tibetan argali favors slightly undulating, almost vegetation-free territory at altitudes of 13,500 to 18,000 feet. It is thus regarded as one of the most difficult to hunt species of game of the Asian mountain plateau.

in embarking on this adventure in the middle of the winter, thereby risking the lives of fifty men and women.

The next morning, however, the mountains glistened in fantastic light. Our Bhutia headman rushed into the tent crying "Nawa, Nawa!" "Blue sheep, blue sheep!" An awesome silence descended on the entire camp. Then a few blankets were quickly tossed over the crest of the snow and, barely 300 yards off, on the opposite slope, we saw a huge herd of blue sheep moving slowly toward the valley. What followed cannot be described as good sportsmanship. But what choice did we have? It was genuinely a matter of life or death as far as we were concerned and, one after another, five powerful rams fell to their death in the snow. We let the others continue on their way. Toward midday, as clouds began to roll up to the icy peak of "the world's most beautiful mountain," the Siniolchu, I discovered a herd of sheep high above us. The lead ram, with its deep black breast and widespread horns, towered over the herd and gazed down at me as if from a throne. I had to have him! During the climb up the high snow drifts, I was overcome by a spell of dizziness and had to fight for my breath, but I quickly recovered and once again I experienced an unforgettable moment: I took aim, squeezed the trigger, and the ram fell.

The Argali

We had been making our way northeastward through a deserted no-man's-land toward the source of the Yangtzekiang. We steadily gained altitude, from 14,100 feet to 15,900 feet, until we reached trackless mountainous terrain where pyramid-shaped peaks, seemingly devoid of vegetation, towered into the sky like huge sugar loaves. As far as the eye could see, there was nothing but naked mountains, dull red hills and ocher-colored earth. I had been drawn to this wilderness as if by a magical force. But the further we penetrated this empty landscape, the greater grew the terror of my bearers and their conviction that we would not return alive. Trying to set an example, I made a point of leading the procession. And where I had least

expected it I came across the tracks of the giant sheep, famous for its timidity—an animal missing from my collection. I chose the place to set up camp and waited for my half-starved company of bearers, whose number of pack animals had been reduced by half, to catch up.

At dawn the next day, Wang and I set out to try our luck. The higher we climbed, the more unfriendly the mountains became— the mountains which the argali, this mightiest of horn-bearers of the Asian heights, seemed to prefer to all other available territories. Hour after hour, we climbed from ridge to ridge some distance below the summit of the mountain. Finally I spotted a footprint which was unmistakably the track of the wedge-shaped, narrow hoof of a giant ram. Now extreme caution became the order of the day and, as we gazed over the next ridge, I threw myself to the ground. There, before my eyes, a fantastic picture in the bleak landscape, were no less than nine argalis, their heads held proudly aloft. Although still out of shooting range, they had become aware of our presence and broke into their peculiar, lolloping gallop, much influenced by the considerable weight of their mighty horns. They soon disappeared into the next valley so we followed the clearly visible tracks over the hard ground for more than two miles, drawn on by the image of those nine rams. Whenever I thought one of them might be within shooting distance, these shrewd creatures fled toward

the valley, into the protection of plains surrounded by hills rather than, as I hoped, up toward the more exposed mountain summit. We finally ended up waiting about 1,000 yards from the animals, until the sun was low over the horizon. Then under cover of falling darkness, I decided to make a last attempt and approached cautiously to a distance of some 400 feet from the argalis, my rifle at the ready. When it was almost too dark to risk a shot, a hail storm suddenly blotted out the sky and rattled down upon the stony ground. Stung by hail stones, deafened by the echoing thunder and drenched to the skin, I raced madly after the fleeing rams. Throwing myself to the ground and releasing the lid of my telescopic sight, I took rapid aim and fired. The sound of the shots, the thunder, the flash of the powder and the lightning blended into a weird symphony. Then I dashed forward and knelt over three dead rams. What magnificent creatures they were, and what huge "ammonite horns" they bore— horns which I could encircle with the fingers of both my hands!

Wild Yak

In the same remote region, considered uninhabitable even by Tibetan nomadic tribes, I shot my first wild yak in 1935. This singular animal, the bull of which reminded me of an over-sized aurochs and weighs over a ton, is

without doubt not only the largest but also the least known of existing wild cattle.

For months, we made our way through lofty solitude, finding only bleached skulls of yaks, which looked like objects from another world. Each week, we lost several pack-animals; half-starved, they perished in the sticky slime of the Naka bogs or had to be mercifully dispatched with a bullet. And the men mutinied. If things had gone on like that, there would have been little hope for the expedition. One evening, however, my binoculars picked out five tiny black specks in the distance. I quickly plunged a spear into the ground on which to steady the glasses. My dream, in which I had almost ceased to believe over the previous weeks, was coming true. Ahead of us, a few miles off, clearly recognizable in the thin mountain air, was a herd of wild, fierce-looking yaks. I watched them until nightfall and made my plans for the following day.

A few hours after midnight, the camp came to life. The leader of the caravan was instructed to follow our tracks in the fresh snow at dawn. Wang and Gesong, my two scouts, rode out with me into the darkness. As day broke, we dismounted from our horses into the fresh snow. I went on ahead and soon discovered the yaks a mile or so away. I returned and told Gesong to remain in hiding with the horses while Wang and I stalked the

animals. As the sun rose steeply over the wide horizon, I recognized the clear outlines of the huge, curved horns. Not knowing how acute the yak's senses were, and with the terrain as flat as a plate, it was essential to weigh each move with the utmost caution. We crept closer, camouflaged with bearskin hats, from time to time lying still in the snow until it melted and we found ourselves in icy puddles. Then storm clouds arose and for the first time in my life I hoped fervently for a Tibetan snow-storm. Indeed it came, covering us with a white cloak of invisibility—and we set out once more against the wind and the snow. As the driving white screen began to thin out, we had almost come within shooting range. The massive, thickly maned bodies of the yaks jostled each other as they grazed. I chose the strongest of them, the lead bull which, thick-necked and broad, a primordial image of strength, lashed the air with its long, bushy tail. I had to get closer. I wanted to approach this king of Tibetan game alone—and exact my reward for all the trouble and sweat of the past twelve months.

I crept closer, my bearskin hat pulled down over my face, thrusting my rifle before me from knoll to knoll. I could have shot the bull at this distance, but I wanted to make absolutely sure of my target. Suddenly it reared its head, snorted and pawed the ground. After what seemed like an eternity, it calmed down

and began to graze again. I slid down into small pond on the moor and, stooping lo so that I remained under cover, I wade through the water. I was now only eight yards away. Letting my soaking sheepskin fa to the ground, I slipped off my jacket as we and, intending to throw it at the bull if attacked, held it in front of me as I advance foot by foot. The lashing tail of the bu whipped the air like a battle standard. Did think I was a bear? Suddenly it made fou or five wild leaps and, standing still once mor sniffed the air with its head held high. Did want to drive away the "bear?" Seemir uncertain, it approached cautiously, slowl with its head lowered. Then it again stoc still, snorted once more and stamped th ground. I remained motionless, my rifl poised, coldly reckoning my wisest course action. If I shot it in the head, the remain would be useless for a museum; if I shot anywhere else, it might not succumb imm diately and I would be fully occupied wi him while the others got away. The situatic was urgent, but I was obliged to wait for better opportunity. I pulled my bearskin h down over my face. Each second seemed last an eternity. Suddenly the bull turne toward me and, in that instant, I shot it clea between the shoulder blades. Dust and ha flew in all directions, but the huge beast ga no sign of being wounded. It fled in wi leaps—just as I had feared. I leapt up, too aim and fired at the next largest bull. I race after the fleeing bulls which had by no reached nearby rolling terrain. I raced u the nearest hill—and stopped dead in m tracks: five bulls had turned to face me! The was no time to think and before I could rai my rifle, a wall of massive bodies storme toward me.

I threw myself to the ground and fire again and again. It was life or death an when I was down to my last bullet I jumpe up and ran. Behind me the ground thundere I reloaded my rifle while in motion. An then—a dull thud, a snort and a groar Reflexively, I turned and saw the lead bull, th one I had shot first, sink to its knees an collapse. At the same instant, the other fou bulls gave up their chase. I stopped an approached the dead animal, seeing a wild ya for the first time from close quarters.

Discovery of the Abominable Snowman

The strange effect the bear has on man's imagination became clear to me when I went to Tibet in 1934 to try to discover the secret of the yeti—the so-called abominable snowman. My experience with this "monster" began with an audience I had with the governor of the eastern Tibet province of Sikong. He had given us permission to penetrate the land of lawless nomads of the region, and also asked me to bring him a pair of hairy "migus" for his private zoo.

The *London Illustrated News* and *Paris Match* had published photos of the "tracks" of the yeti; the Maharajah of Sikkim had told me that the hairy creature had violated women in remote settlements in his country. But the British mountaineer Frank Smythe asked me not to publish anything about my discoveries because the English Mount Everest expedition needed the fairy tale of the abominable snowman to finance its costly undertaking. So a blanket of silence was lowered over the second Brooke-Dolan expedition while the sensation-loving press seized upon the abominable snowman as its number-one story. Even professional zoologists came eventually to believe in the existence of the yeti and gave it the scientific name *Dino-pithecus nivalis*. What had been overlooked, however, was the fact that the magical-religious ties between men and bears virtually rule the cultural lives of the natives of the high altitude regions of Asia.

The "yeti," "migu" or "dremu" plays an important role in the mystical fabric of belief of those people. They believe in them as strongly as medieval Europeans believed in devil with horns and hooves.

In spite of this, the conqueror of Mount Everest, Sir Edmund Hillary, organized a "scientific" yeti expedition in 1960–61, which proved as fruitless as its predecessors. But it did prove that yeti scalps preserved in Tibetan and Nepalese monasteries were forgeries.

There remained only the possibility that the yeti had something to do with members of the mysterious Lungompa sect who were said to live in mountain caves and to have extraordinary powers. My encounter with these remarkable "saints" in isolated regions of Tibet was one of my most amazing experiences. I still wonder how those people manage to survive, clad only in felt blankets and threatened by bears and wolves. As for the yeti, however, it seems that some people are prepared to believe anything they are told. Desmond Doig, one of Hillary's collaborators, came to the following conclusion: "It is possible that somewhere in Tibet, which is more inaccessible than ever to the foreigner, this creature [the yeti] does exist. It is one of the enigmas of mankind still to be solved."

How long is man prepared to be taken in? Significantly enough, regions where the "tracks" of the yeti were discovered are the same as those inhabited by the Tibetan bear. These bears, however, are to be found only in districts which neither journalists nor mountaineers have penetrated during their necessarily limited expeditions. The legendary fearlessness of the animals, their complete indifference to man and their "demoniacal" strength are, to a great extent, characteristics also attributed to the hypothetical yeti. In northeastern Tibet, I hunted dozens and observed hundreds of these bears and I was repeatedly surprised by their "humanness."

The actual discovery of the abominable snowman was, however, somewhat prosaic. As we reached the upper Hoangho region in the winter of 1935, the leader of the Wata nomads told me the fantastic story of a monster covered with yellow hair, as big as a yak and notorious for the devastation it caused. At once I offered a reward for its capture. And, as we finally reached the cave of this yeti, 14,000 feet up under the glacier zone, there was no going back. The Watas accompanying me suddenly drew their swords, but remained petrified at the black mouth of the cave. I posted the faithful Wang above the cave with a loaded shotgun and I slowly made my way toward the entrance of the cave, my rifle ready. Suddenly I caught the penetrating smell of the bear! Then I saw a shaggy bundle of yellow hair and kicked a few stones into the cave, pointing my rifle at the cave entrance. Quick as lightning, a huge head appeared with gleaming eyes and many shining teeth. I fired and the gigantic creature collapsed.

Later, when I reached the source of the Yangtzekiang, I found myself in a veritable paradise for bears. Here the shaggy creatures were the sole rulers of the immeasurably vast, empty landscape. They often stood up on their hindlegs, looking for all the world like huge, hairy men, growling and snorting and instilling fear in the hearts of man and beast alike. Although members of my party knew perfectly well that these "dremu" were ordinary animals made of flesh and blood, and not supernatural beings, they were always filled with terror when the huge creatures seemed about to attack.

Hunting in Africa

Exhausting marches in long processions are rare in modern-day safaris in Africa. Sturdy cross-country vehicles are more commonly used to reach remote hunting grounds. In bush country rarely visited by hunters, animals are often not at all shy of vehicles. Hunters and tourists can often get very close to them. However, to give game a fair chance and for purposes of animal conservation shooting at animals from vehicles is banned in most African countries.

Despite its troubled recent history, wars of liberation and political and racial upheaval, Africa—with a surface area of almost twelve million square miles—remains the continent with the greatest quantity and widest variety of game. It is a paradise for zoologists, lovers of wilderness and hunters.

Many of the present-day survivors of Africa's original peoples have retained the hunting methods of their forebears, for whom hunting was exclusively a means of existing. But hunting procedures in some parts of the continent have been considerably altered by the impact of modern weapons and of practices imported during colonial times. Africans in some places substantially expanded their hunting catches beyond their immediate needs, with serious consequences for animal populations. The survival of various species of game became increasingly precarious. Questionable hunting practices—for example, the notorious use of fire to stampede animals toward their doom—became common. Whole village communities joined together to set fire to large areas of land, the outer limits of which were netted off to help hunters kill the panicking game. The resulting fires often exterminated all animal life in the region.

Many of the African governments are now fully aware of the danger such random slaughter posed to their natural heritage.

They became increasingly aware of the importance of wildlife conservation, stringently enforced hunting regulations and the study of animal life. Politicians and zoologists are agreed, however, that many of Africa's peoples, raised in the tradition of hunting for sustenance, may prove reluctant to accept the significance of protecting their animal reserves. That is one reason why so much emphasis has been placed on the continued existence of wildlife attractions as an international tourist attraction, contributing considerably to the wealth of the country in general, and to local people in particular.

Kenya and Tanzania, however, already have firmly established hunting regulations. In Sudan, Cameroon, Chad, Rhodesia, Angola and Mozambique, strict hunting regulations are also in force. Southwest Africa is an exception in that farmers of the region possess hunting rights for their lands and care for local game with great success, using animal conservation methods similar to those employed in Europe.

Gone are the days when hunters and scientists set out through African wildernesses on journeys which lasted for years and during which they risked their lives and were confronted with constant danger from poisoned arrows and rogue elephants. On those safaris, which explored what was then known the "dark" continent, hundreds of bearers, who made such protracted excursions possible, lived on game. Both they and the white hunters were subject to tropical disease and various other jungle and desert afflictions and dangers.

Today's big game hunters take airplanes from America or Europe and land a few hours later on the borders of the African wilderness, to be met by safari leaders and their assistants.

They can see, experience, hunt and shoot more in Africa in two weeks than during a whole year spent in deer and bear country at home. The skill of the professional hunter, however, should be matched by his sense of responsibility and a knowledge of zoology, to ensure that endangered species are not still further endangered by his African exploits.

In addition to various species of antelope and boar, hunters in Africa tend to be chiefly interested in the so-called "big five" species of African game: the elephant, rhinoceros, buffalo, lion and leopard. Each of these can be unpredictable and is potentially extremely dangerous. These days, however, most hunters are accompanied by experienced professionals armed with high-caliber rifles. Their duty is, among other things, to make certain that their clients' inexperience does not have tragic consequences.

Elephants

Which is the most dangerous animal to hunt is, of course, debatable. Individual experiences, often colored by special circumstances, will influence people's judgments. But many hunters who have been out on safari have no doubt that the elephant provides the greatest challenge, particularly in areas where there is little in the way of cover for the hunter when he suddenly becomes the hunted. This potential moment of extreme danger makes hunting the African elephant a gripping and adventurous activity.

There are differing views on how many elephants there are in Africa today. But it is reasonably certain that they number several hundred thousand. These huge pachyderms have multiplied, particularly in the various national parks, in some of which they have created problems of over-population. In some districts of Kenya, Tanzania, Uganda, the Central African Republic, Chad, Sudan, and North Cameroon, huge herds can still be found. The cost of safaris and their comparatively brief duration have contributed to the preservation of substantial elephant populations, which might otherwise have been seriously diminished by avid hunters.

The discovery of elephant tracks and the pursuit of the animal make for exciting experiences. A good elephant tracker often acts more out of instinct than from examining the actual tracks. It is relatively easy to track down an elephant in tall grass or bush country. But knowledge and skill bordering on the uncanny are required not to lose the tracks on hard ground. At normal pace, an African elephant walks about as fast as a man does. It can, however, maintain a trot at double that pace for long periods of time.

When setting off on his elephant hunt, the hunter seeks the tracks of a large bull elephant, an important discovery and the prelude to a hunt that could last several hours, or even days. When the elephant has been sighted, and if the wind is favorable, the actual stalk begins. There is no truth to the popular belief that elephants have bad eyesight. They can be what humans might consider scatter-brained or inattentive, largely because, aside from man, they have no enemies. But they are perfectly capable of seeing both movement and color and they can be easily alarmed by unusual sounds, even the click of a camera shutter.

A hunter who catches up with an elephant will have to act swiftly to kill it as painlessly as possible. The best means is a bullet through the brain. This requires extreme accuracy in aiming, though the elephant's brain is about as big as a basketball and is situated in the center of its skull. When the animal's head is in normal position, the hunter must aim for the eyes or ears, depending on his own position. Single bullets—not pellets—should be used, and it is important that the rifle is of high enough caliber.

It is also possible to kill an elephant with a bullet through the heart; for this a rifle of even bigger caliber is necessary. Despite its size, bringing down an elephant can be an extremely tricky undertaking, and even an experienced elephant hunter will not necessarily find it easy to pick off his prey in the midst of a herd.

The largest tusks ever brought back by a hunter weighed about 200 pounds each. An elephant with tusks weighing 150 pounds each was shot in the Central African Republic in 1971, and it is still possible to find such specimens not only there but also in parts of Kenya, Tanzania and Zaire.

Above: Trackers, bearers and hunter on safari on the plains of Chad.

Left: The tusks of this elephant, photographed in southwest Tanzania, weigh about 130 pounds each.

Right: An elephant on the attack.

Buffalo Hunting in Africa

Even the experienced hunter rarely fails to be astonished by the wide variety of African buffalo breeds. They include the red buffalo, the bulls of which can weigh up to 550 pounds, which is characterized by its light brown or reddish-brown coats and which lives in wooded terrain. They include also the so-called African buffalo, the bulls of which often weigh more than a ton, and which lives on the Masai plains and in a few districts of Uganda. There is also the West African buffalo with its large, crescent-shaped horns; those found in the Chad region are generally larger and heavier than those of eastern Zaire and Sudan. Many intermediate breeds between the huge plains buffalo and the smaller red buffalo have resulted from interbreeding. In extensive pasture land, however, many kinds of buffalo live together without interbreeding. There are, for example, no crossbreeds between the red buffalo of Ituri and the African buffalo of neighboring Uganda. Both types are, incidentally, examples of the well-known "jungle-plains rule," according to which forest dwellers tend to be smaller and more primitive than plains dwellers which tend to be larger and more highly developed.

Aside from man, the only real enemy of the buffalo is the lion. Lions do not hesitate to attack buffalo calves and older animals which have become separated from the herd. But often their victims are strong young buffalo and a confrontation can turn into a hard and bloody battle. In some districts, buffalo have contributed to decimating lion populations. It is not uncommon for the attacking predator to be killed by its intended victim. This happens most often in areas where antelope populations are small and the lions, deprived of more easily vanquished prey, are more readily tempted to take on animals which are less frail. The greatest danger to buffalo used to be epidemic disease: foot-and-mouth disease and, above all, cattle plague, which was rampant in parts of Africa at the end of the nineteenth century, destroying almost ninety percent of the buffalo population of East Africa in a very short period of time. That menace is now, for the most part, past history. In countries where it is not assiduously hunted and where enough fodder is available, buffalo populations have increased considerably.

Usually, the buffalo hunter pursues his prey by following its tracks. Only when the animal comes into view does the actual stalking begin. The animal has an extremely acute sense of smell: the hunter will be noticed immediately if he makes the mistake of approaching upwind. Buffalo also have exceptionally sharp eyes and are constantly on the alert. Older cows, who appear to be on perpetual sentry duty, prick up their ears at the slightest unusual sound and raise their heads. Once the herd is fleeing, it is virtually impossible to intercept.

A peaceful herd of buffalo, or one which has been alerted but is in flight, forms up into a square, with sentries on all sides. In this posture, it is practically impossible for the hunter to come anywhere near the animals. He is often obliged to exercise a considerable amount of patience before he is able to spot a strong bull—the only suitable object of h attention—in the midst of a large herd. T first bullet is all-important. It must be dead target. It is not an easy task under the circu stances. A shot from a rifle of sufficiently hi caliber, penetrating down behind the shoulde will result in the animal's death—if n immediately, then soon afterward. A shot the neck, however, is certain to kill at on But it requires a shorter range and is therefo difficult, if not often impossible. A shot in t breast, above the front legs, is also deadly.

A buffalo which breaks cover and attac frontally is regarded by many hunters as t most dangerous animal they can encounter. shield-like "helmet," the broad base of t widespread horns, provides effective prote tion against bullets. Others, however, co

...der the smaller red buffalo to be even more ...nister because the hunter often comes into ...lose contact with it while hunting in dense ...ungle undergrowth. When that happens, the ...ed buffalo frequently attacks immediately; ...is alarmed and the hunter's flight room is ...ready sharply restricted.

A wounded buffalo requires the greatest ...ution and respect from the hunter. An animal ...eakened by a bullet wound may suddenly ...nange its direction of flight to attack its ...ursuer in a totally unexpected fashion. ...hen that happens, only death will stop the ...ounded animal's onslaught. When an en-...ged animal lowers its horns and charges, ...ly lightning reflexes can save the hunter. In ...ch a situation, a shot in the animal's back-...one is the safest course of action. It is only ...ossible, however, if the hunter is positioned

slightly higher than the buffalo. If not, a bullet in the breast is the hunter's best option.

Experienced big game hunters know the tricks and wiles of buffalo in great detail. If the first bullet has hit but not killed the hunted animal, a bull is capable of enduring painful wounds after the first shock has passed — wounds which, it seemed reasonable to assume, would prove fatal.

Buffalo horns can reach a span of up to four feet. The horns of the red buffalo are much smaller but are also coveted by many hunters.

A totally different species is the Indian or water buffalo. Used in many parts of Asia as a beast of burden, this creature has long been domesticated, though some wild breeds can still be found in Borneo and other nearby regions. This animal measures almost six feet at the shoulder, can weigh almost a ton and in its wild state is extremely dangerous, capable of vanquishing the largest of tigers.

Safari

A hunter new to the wildlife of Africa is expected to learn local customs and local regulations at the start of his first safari. He can also pick up useful habits at the very beginning. If he manages, for example, to bring down a specimen of small game early on, it can be used as bait for more demanding targets such as lion and leopard.

The hunter new to Africa will soon realize that shimmering light and almost unbearable heat can be confusing and can complicate making accurate judgments on distance and aiming. Also, many hunters believe that African game is considerably more sturdy than corresponding species elsewhere and is more difficult to kill. For this reason, high-powered weapons are recommended, with high-caliber firearms suggested particularly for shooting elephant and buffalo at close quarters. To avoid unnecessary wounding of game and other unwelcome occurrences, newcomers on safari are advised to follow closely the instructions of their professional hunters. Only the benefit of experience, combined with patience and care, can lead to a successful hunt.

Arrangements can be made for hiring the services of authorized professional hunters in Nairobi and other major cities which are safari jumping-off points. With the increase in animal conservation regulations such professional assistance is more than merely advisable, it is obligatory. The professional hunter will know what special pre-safari arrangements have to be made (licenses, etc.), where to go to find the different species, what fees will have to be paid for the privilege of bringing down various kinds of game and what local hunting lore might be useful to the visiting hunter.

Sometimes, a visiting hunter is reluctantly obliged to shoot one of the zebras of the African plains, to be used as lion bait. Local inhabitants highly prize the zebra's tender meat and the hunter may find that the highly decorative zebra skin makes an attractive trophy. Even more treasured souvenirs of a safari hunt are the tusks of the African wart hog. These animals are fast on their feet and they flee with their long, tufted tails pointing up in the air. A herd of wart hogs fleeing through high grass can be detected by their erect tails. Lions and leopards kill a great many

of these animals and old wart hogs with large tusks are, therefore, comparatively rare. As with wild boars, it is usually a matter of luck for even the most skillful hunter to find a wart hog with impressive tusks.

Among the many kinds of antelope, the impala is the most abundant and lives in sun-baked countryside dotted with clumps of trees and bushes. The graceful red-brown and white males bear lyrated horns measuring almost three feet. These animals, which live in herds, are excellent jumpers and when alarmed they spring out of the undergrowth in elegant and powerful leaps which may be as high as nine feet and as long as ten yards.

Stalking from bush to bush, the hunter on safari will pursue waterbucks through dripping foliage. The females are so similar to the European red deer that they are also known as "deer antelopes." The sitatunga, or marsh antelope, the males of which bear lyrated horns, is particularly difficult to bring down.

In the Masai highlands of Kenya and Tanzania the hundred-pound Grant's gazelle and the deer-sized Thomson's gazelle are both present in large numbers. The male of the light gray to reddish-brown Grant's gazelle bears heavy horns held proudly on its strong head. The animal bringing up the rear in the herd usually stops during flight to sniff the air and assess the danger. That is the moment for the hunter to take aim.

The impressive and belligerent Thomson's gazelle, with its exceptionally acute senses, demands skill and stamina from its stalker—the hunter must come within about 250 feet on the blazing plains to be certain that his bullet has a chance of hitting this swift and sturdy creature. The lively springbok, which lives almost exclusively in Southwest Africa today, also demands the greatest skill and precision.

In the arid East African salt plains, the gnu is still evident in abundance. With its defiant stature, almost as if it was planted in the ground, the gnu may seem to be twice its actual size in the shimmering sunlight. It is often true, therefore, that the dazzled hunter thinks he has spotted a buffalo and realizes his mistake only after the animal takes to flight with gigantic leaps and bounds. Speed is essential if the hunter still intends to make it a target. Even if the bullet hits true, the bull may go a great distance before falling dead.

Equally difficult to kill is the oryx, which lives in dry regions and digs up roots and bulbs which contain water. Its long, dagger-shaped horns are protective weapons greatly feared both by animal and human predators. The eland is more peaceable by nature. It bears a bristly fringe and large dewlap and can weigh up to a ton.

Thornbush savannahs and lightly wooded plains are the home of various breeds of the strange-looking hartebeest, as well as the roan and the sable antelope. "Cow-antelopes," as the hartebeests are sometimes called, include several distinctive sub-species, including the sassaby and the topi, which lives near Lake Victoria. The topi is in the habit of standing on termite mounds and other elevations to obtain a clear view of its territory, thus offering the hunter an easy target.

In regions graced with ample cover live two animals which present hunters with particular problems: the reedbuck, which is found in damp, boggy thickets at dusk; and the gerenuk, which favors thick, thorny bush country.

Many hunters are particularly taken with the search for five species of antelope which have corkscrew-like horns. These include the bushbuck, which is fairly widespread; the sitatunga, which lives mainly in marshland or near water; the nyala, with its splendid mane; and the greater and lesser kudu, finely built antelopes which can leap over obstacles six feet high with ease. Hunting the greater kudu through stony, bushy hill country is without doubt one of the most exciting experiences to be had by the hunter on the African plains.

Hunting's Mystical Links

Although there have been vast changes in Africa in recent years, there are still corners of that once "dark" continent where communities of primitive hunters and food gatherers still exist. The bushmen, who live in small groups in the Kalahari Desert and nearby districts, once subsisted largely on small game. Now these people, who live in huts made of woven branches and twigs, or simply behind wind screens, have had to alter their dietary habits. The sharp decline in game has forced them increasingly to depend on roots, berries and leaves and, much more infrequently, on small animals.

Pygmies, who are distinct from both the yellow-skinned bushmen and more highly developed black Africans, also belong to an ancient food-gathering and hunting culture. The sprawling jungles of the Congo valley are their last refuge but, like the bushmen, these dwarf-like people have fully adapted to their environment. They live in tribal communities, each consisting of about a hundred men and women, and hunt with nets as well as bows and arrows. These primitive hunters regard the jungle as a sacred realm. According to their tribal magicians, the sun is obliged to share its overwhelming power with the rain which is created by the jungle, just as the jungle is created by the rain. Pygmies shy clear of doing anything that might damage the jungle and never hunt more animals than they require for sustenance.

Primitive hunters still believe in the power of hunting magic. Many of them believe certain animals—often the leopard—can be employed as a mediator between man and the animal world. During pre-hunt rituals, dancers paint themselves with white spots, not merely to imitate the coat of the leopard,

but actually to become the animal and thus be able to speak with other animals. In this way, they can determine which tracks it would be wise to follow. The giant pangolin, a scaly, termite-eating animal that rolls itself into a ball when attacked, also plays an important role in pygmy beliefs. It is revered as an incarnation of the great spirit of the jungle. It is thought to be the source of life and to have taught ancient jungle peoples how to build shingled leaf roofs over their huts to ward off the rain.

Pygmies, some groups of which have not yet reached the cultural level of Stone Age man, live in a state of permanent truce with their gorilla neighbors. They offer gorillas food as a gesture of friendship—in marked contrast to hunters who sometimes exterminate whole herds of apes to capture a few for zoos.

A pygmy hunting camp consists of temporary leaf huts. In the center of the camp is the largest of the huts, the symbolic focus of the camp, the baraza, which only male members of the tribe may enter. It is here that the pygmy oracle is consulted the evening before the hunt. To embark on their hunting expedition without fear and confident of success, the hunters symbolically kill the soul of animals magically conjured up by frenzied spear-brandishing leopard-men dancers. At the same time, the hunters, to whom the act of killing is a source of guilt, pray to the protective gods of the animals they expect to dispatch for pardon, so that harmony between forest, animal and man remains undisturbed. It is a remarkable example of surviving primitive game-management procedures.

The hunting practices of the pygmies are, however, uncompromising and their primitive weapons are sometimes brutal. For hours, days, and even weeks on end, groups of them may follow the trails of elephants, their mightiest prey. When these diminutive hunters finally surround an old bull, a battle of savage proportions begins.

They creep up behind the elephant and slash its Achilles tendons, thus rendering the colossus, which might weigh between two and three tons, virtually immobile and defenseless until it is finally slaughtered in a long and cruel struggle. Then the women and children rush up. Men and women slash at the dead animal with axes in a display which has been described as similar to an attack by ants. When they are finished, only the elephant's skull and a few bones are left for hyenas and vultures to finish off.

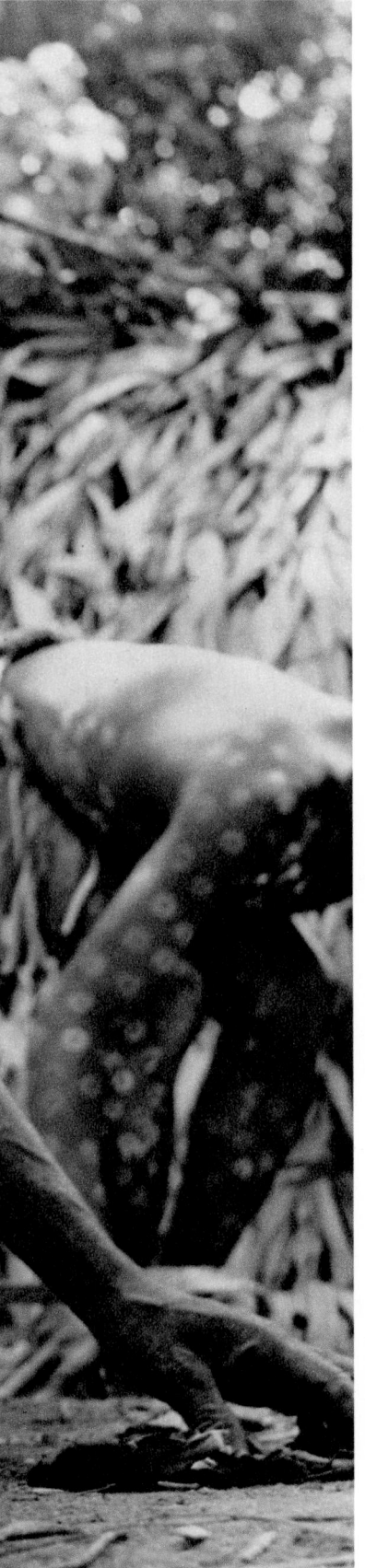

Beholden to Nature

Wildlife management existed long before it was really necessary. Now that it is essential, it is neither widespread nor intensive enough. A form of game conservation has been practiced since the time when the wide open spaces were divided up and marked off in various parts of the world as the exclusive preserves of privileged personages. In Europe, forest preserves have been set aside for protected game since the reign of Charlemagne (eighth century). The aim then, and for a long time afterward, was to provide the hunter with well-stocked hunting grounds. Little concern was felt for the animals. In the seventeenth century, mounted wardens patrolled and supervised European forest game preserves. By the eighteenth century, hunters in some places were obliged to observe close seasons, primarily still only to make certain there would be enough game to go around. Even earlier, hunters had voluntarily imposed restrictions on their hunting activities—vetos, still known in Spanish hunting jargon as *veda*. But not until the twentieth century did the concept of a game reserve, in which animals would be protected against the threat of extinction, gain wide currency, primarily in North America and western Europe. It involved degrees of responsibility and commitment in sharp contrast to previous patterns of game management in which the interests of the hunter rather than those of the hunted were the primary consideration. In those days, game wardens were humble servants of estate owners. Today they are instruments of the community, dedicated to the preservation of our natural heritage. Today also the code of behavior and practice for the hunter is clearly defined. He has assumed a function previously held by vanishing larger species of beasts of prey. He is a regulator of remaining species, culling their stocks to assist in perpetuation of the various surviving breeds. Hunting was initially a means of sustenance for the hunter; then it was a sport as well. Now it has taken on an added dimension of responsibility.

Feeding Wildlife

Winter snow storms often cut mountain deer off from their natural feeding grounds. Heavily laden with animal provisions, a group of game conservationists make their way on skis through a snow-covered forest to alleviate the distress of starving animals.

Only recently has wildlife biology gained recognition as a science in its own right, spilling over from such related specialties as ecology and ethology. Other fields of study also contributed to early efforts to comprehend animal life, but a comprehensive understanding of the animal world, individual species, and of the environmental influences upon animal development was slow to evolve. A calculated effective contribution by man to the perpetuation of animal life, and to the improvement of the conditions on which animals thrive, was correspondingly late in coming.

An early form of casual human destruction of animal environments was the clearance of many mixed woodland areas, which gave way to ever-spreading settlements. The greater the energy with which the ax was swung to bring down trees, the greater was the loss of natural plant life—often replaced with poor unvariegated pasture lands. The consequence was a sharp increase in animal starvation. As pasture land was divided into smaller, cultivatable plots, this process was accelerated. Particularly susceptible young game was destroyed, and without young specimens entire breeds were threatened with extinction. Recognition of this danger led conservation authorities, game wardens, communities and often individuals to try to compensate for the loss of natural fodder for the threatened animals. That is where some understanding of animal biology has been useful. In times of need, animals should have foodstuffs suitable to their needs. Nutritional factors have to be considered. This feeding process, now an integral part of game management, is particularly important during winter time in northern regions.

Feeding places should be chosen for their accessibility to animal grounds, even in elevated snow covered regions. But the establishment of summer grazing areas, screened by appropriate bushes and other cover, is also important. Diking sea inlets and artificial irrigation of barren land has been particularly successful in North America for promoting the survival of severely threatened water birds.

The Rifle as Game Regulator

No less important than the improvement of animal biotopes and grazing areas is the regulation of populations of hoofed game, or ungulates, in controlled landscapes. Culling a certain number of animals—a job which falls to the hunter—is a basic principle of well-calculated game management. Previously, nature's regulators—beasts of prey—ensured the preservation of healthy and sustainable populations of hoofed game by preying on young, sick and old animals. But with the near-extinction of the bear, wolf and lynx, sickness grew more prevalent among surviving game. Degenerative symptoms grew more evident. The process of natural selection was disturbed. An excess of many species of game was the result.

Alas, the hunter was an imperfect substitute for the predators which he had almost exterminated, especially when he entertained the erroneous notion that additional feeding for wild game could recreate the balance which had been lost. Experimentation along those lines did not place enough emphasis on the real object of the exercise—the long-term future of the animals in question. Protection was extended to weaker and older specimens. It was an ill-considered act of mercy: although it was hoped improvement of the quality of the herd would result from the culling of occasional poor specimens, the outcome proved otherwise. The random approach to culling simply could not do the job. There was an uninterrupted increase in the number of weak, unhealthy, sometimes deformed specimens. In effect, the symptoms of the problem were being dealt with; not its causes. Until the twentieth century, it was considered bad sportsmanship to shoot females or young animals—anything, in fact, which did not bear coveted antlers. It was a kind of hunting which totally ignored the long-term future of game herds. Instead of allowing stronger, more mature animals to live and procreate as long as possible, negative selection resulted in degeneration of the quality of the game.

However, around the turn of the century, conservationists in North America and Europe began thinking in terms of selective culling of sick and weak animals. Most were influenced by Darwin's concepts of natural selection which were then gathering wide acceptance in scientific circles. Some also thought in terms

Deer are "individualists" strongly attached to their habitats. Each deer requires its own specific area. Comparatively scant populations, ratios of the sexes of 1:1, and maintenance of social hierarchy are ideal conditions for the maintenance of healthy deer populations.

If a game population exceeds a certain density, the overcrowding factor produces negative results: the quality of the game decreases, body weight is reduced, does produce fewer young and bucks bear crippled antlers.

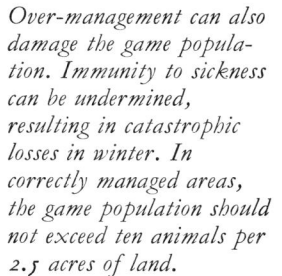

Over-management can also damage the game population. Immunity to sickness can be undermined, resulting in catastrophic losses in winter. In correctly managed areas, the game population should not exceed ten animals per 2.5 acres of land.

of conserving the wonders of nature for mankind. It became obvious to these conservationists that hunters had to begin thinking ecologically (though they used other words) and had to begin fulfilling the function previously undertaken by the vanishing predators. The rifle gradually came into its own as a game regulator as well as a hunting tool.

Many hunters today have learned to think in such terms although there is more use of the word "thinning"—borrowed from the world of forestry—than of the phrase "selective culling." In fact, "quantitative culling" is now more important than "selective culling," because the maintenance of game populations of a size the environment is able to support is more important these days than the mere elimination of isolated specimens. So appropriate thinning aims at both qualitative selection and, more significantly, at quantitative restriction of game population densities. Also of ongoing concern is the maintenance of a balance between the sexes and age groups. In short, the object is to correct any disproportion between the environment and the animal population.

Objection to human game management of this kind is answered by natural culling of animals in their original, natural state. Formerly, the environmental balance was established by predators; today it is the task of hunters. Shooting young or weak animals for environmental purposes is not an act of brutality but a result of biological knowledge and understanding. Killing is part of hunting, and there are people who utterly object to both on ethical grounds. Their objections are, however, based on one specific aspect of hunting and overlook the aim of maintaining the long-term general welfare and balance of wildlife. They forget that hunting is really only part of an ordered, natural system which predates the invention of firearms and even human existence. For criticism of hunting to be taken seriously, it must also take into account the intention of the hunter and the form his hunting takes.

It is consistent with the precepts of wildlife management to shoot, for example, all "surplus" specimens of hoofed game when they are still young. This keeps the base of the age pyramid—an important indicator of natural balance—as narrow as possible. By this means, the overcrowding of habitats can be prevented, making it easier to ensure a healthy environment for the species and enabling them to make best use of that environment. Selective culling is essential to improve the quality of game populations. If it is neglected, the natural order of the wildlife community will break down. The culling of female game is as important as any other "thinning" objective, to enable the population increase to be controlled and to help establish the desired sex ratio. Aside from damage to the future of the wildlife population, if the desired density of game suggested through environmental research is exceeded, considerable damage to grassland and woodland is also bound to result.

Substantial growth in game populations leads to mass distress which, in extreme cases, can even lead to extinction. Over-increase of isolated game populations leads to out-and-out battles for survival between species and specimens and can result in the total destruction of the basic biological balance.

An overly dense game population is characterized by the following physiological and ethological symptoms:
1 slackening of community structure, neurosis, migration;
2 reduced immunity to sickness, epidemic sickness, multiparasitism;
3 hormonal disturbances, disturbance in reproduction rhythm and development, increased rate of mortality;
4 pathological self-regulation (many embryos die before birth), decline in maternal instinct;
5 shorter life span; diminution of the size of antlers, premature ageing;
6 extreme reduction in body weight, extreme losses through increased natural mortality.

These are the most alarming symptoms. But wild game is threatened with a number of other dangers as well and it is the task of wildlife management to cope with them—by means of game regulations, the prevention of poaching, the protection of young animals, restrictions on populations of destructive and predatory game and control of other predators, particularly stray dogs and cats. Precautionary measures of this kind have led in many instances to the maintenance of larger, better and—above all—healthier game populations than ever before, or at least, as far back as detailed records are kept. This is true not only for certain species which have adapted to the intrusion of "civilization," but also for many which reached the brink of extinction—for example, the lynx, ibex, Spanish ibex, mountain hare, beaver, raven, black stork, graylag goose and many others.

The best way to ensure a harmonious relationship between the different interests of hunting, wildlife management and cultivation is the assignment of specific responsibilities to the hunter. In view of the fact that many regions are not really able to provide the wide open spaces required for the healthy development of many game herds, it is essential to establish a community of interest among all people involved with the animal world. These need not be confined to specific regions. Ecological units can, for example, be set up on as large a scale as possible, covering several broad hunting areas. These units should not be restricted in their studies by different jurisdictions over, or ownership of, land in the area under their purview.

Game management communities and all persons entrusted with game protection have the responsibility for keeping count of the animals in their regions, as well as improving the biotopes and feeding the animals in their times of need. One of the best ways of counting the total population of a biological habitat is through control throughout the year by as many expert observers as possible. It would thus be possible to establish a reasonably accurate census of animals by number, sex, age and quality. This census could serve as an instrument for controlling and supervising the sex ratio of the animals and the prospective number of young animals. The statistics would provide the responsible authorities and institutions with the basis for establishing what sort of culling process to sanction, thus ensuring a balance between the hunter's activities and the aims of nature conservation.

Wherever the task of maintaining the health and well-being of the game population, and the community of living creatures as a whole, is the main concern of both hunters and those responsible for wildlife management, the pursuit of sportsmanlike hunting is compatible with the aims of modern, comprehensive nature conservation.

International Conservation

Left: A game warden rescues a female key deer during one of the frequent floods in the Florida Everglades. Just a few hundred specimens of this dwarf species of the North American white-tailed deer still survive, all in the Everglades region.

Although little is known of Chinese methods it is common knowledge that unique animal species found only in the Sino-Tibetan region—such as the wild yak, orongo antelope, Thorold's deer, takin, golden monkey and giant panda—have been preserved from extinction through timely protective measures. The giant panda, which is found only in western China and eastern Tibet, is the world's rarest mammal and, as such, has been adopted as the emblem of the World Wildlife Fund.

Wildlife management in East European countries and the Soviet Union is also meticulously organized and extremely successful. In those countries, the regional conservation system has been developed to the point where hunters and hunting associations are responsible for the care of game populations over long periods of time. All of the Soviet Union is covered by a network of stations, research centers and management institutions related to the science of hunting. Expert planning commissions ensure the healthy development of ecological units for which they are responsible.

In the Soviet Union alone, over eighty game reserves have been created and the survival of nearly all the threatened species is ensured. The "rescue" of the thousand remaining saiga antelopes in 1919 has gone down in the history of hunting as the "Miracle of Kazakhstan." Today, about two million of these antelope exist; more than 100,000 of the animals are culled annually. Similar success has been achieved in breeding and freeing sable, the most valuable species of Siberian fur-bearing animals. The population of sable is now much larger than it was a century ago. Their fur, the "soft gold," has become a noteworthy source of income for the Soviet Union.

The utilization of game is based on careful planning. Populations of beaver, elk, maral deer, sika deer, reindeer, tiger, polar bear, otter and kulan have increased, as have those of the European bison in special reserves. Over 22,500,000 acres have been set aside for the preservation of these species alone and, in addition, numerous foreign species, including the raccoon, muskrat, American mink and nutria, have been introduced into the Soviet Union for fur production. Excellent results have also been achieved in the preser-

The development of theories of wildlife conservation was easy enough. In practice, however, the situation was more complicated. However carefully thought out, hunting regulations did not always conform to the environment for which they were designed and could not satisfactorily be implemented. It was also often the case that game laws, adequate if not always exemplary, were not altered to meet changing conditions in the regions for which they prescribed.

Appropriate game laws are absolutely essential today. In many places, however, their practical effect depends on international perspective and cooperation. Unfortunately, such cooperation does not exist in all areas of the world and, in many countries, game laws also leave much to be desired. In India and Malaysia, wild animals have been driven by the human population explosion into ever diminishing regions. Most of the larger animals have found final refuge in national parks. With the passing of the old era and its profligate rulers in India, the elaborate game conservation schemes they had devised to serve their own pleasure passed into history as well. Some of the praiseworthy game and

hunting administration procedures instigated by the former British colonial rulers of India also faded into oblivion.

In some countries of the Middle East, neither the authorities nor the populace recognize the importance of wildlife conservation—though it seems likely that they will have to devote attention to the problem in the not too distant future. On the other hand efforts in, for example, Iran and Israel in the field of game protection can be regarded as exemplary, though game laws and game management are practically non-existent in many Arab countries. But even in places where the overall picture is unclear, it has been possible to convince local governments to join in schemes to protect such threatened species as the atlas deer.

It is depressing that wildlife conservation programs are often introduced only when the situation has become so critical that measures, which would have been effective earlier, are hardly worthwhile any longer. Wildlife management and game protection do not always keep pace with general nature conservation. But it is known that China, for example, has achieved remarkable results in recent years.

ation of water birds; the population of wild
ack has increased more than seven times.

Hunting is a popular sport in the Soviet
nion. There are many hunting societies and
sociations. At the International Hunting
xhibition in Budapest in 1972, eight Soviet
ophies, including the antlers of the elk,
aral deer, markhor, Caucasian thur and
gali, were awarded international first prizes.
he 3,000,000 hunters in the Soviet Union
ave to pass examinations in hunting biology
well as hunting procedures, which clearly
dicates that hunting is considered part of the
mprehensive program of environmental
nservation.

The highest level of ecological research has,
owever, without doubt been attained in
orth America. The central Wildlife Man-
ement Institute is situated in Washington.
ut each state has its own regional research
nter which employs qualified wildlife bio-
gists. Inventions such as the narcotic gun
d the planting of tiny radio transmitters on
imals under observation (for gathering
formation on, for example, game trails,
rding habits, and the dynamics of capture)
ere first developed in North America.

These methods and techniques were later
adopted by wildlife biologists in other countries. The successful introduction of the lynx
into Switzerland made use of these "control"
techniques. Effective wildlife management in
North America is promoted by the refusal
there to regard wild animals as articles of
merchandise. In both the United States and
Canada, it is forbidden by law to deal in wild
game.

The worldwide national park movement
also originated in the United States. In 1872,
Yellowstone National Park was established,
the first of its kind in the world. During the
First World War, the National Park Service
came into existence in the United States as a
section of the Department of the Interior.
South Africa's Kruger National Park, founded
in 1898, and the Swiss National Park (1914)
were also models for many other nature and
animal reserves—large-scale conservation areas
for the preservation and scientific observation
of as wide as possible a range of native flora
and fauna, and for access to the public within
reasonable limits.

In many areas, advocates of wildlife conservation faced exhaustive problems before

they could begin to establish reserves, primarily related to the expansion and enrichment
of limited native game populations by the
introduction of specimens and species from
other continents. Although Australia and
New Zealand possessed no game animals in
the modern sense before the arrival of Europeans, they already had a varied selection of
game birds, especially geese and ducks.

Wildlife conditions in the Antipodes had
been brought about by the territorial isolation
of Australia and New Zealand for many
millions of years, during which time various
game animals developed in other parts of
the world. Thus the region became an excellent experimental area for introducing
breeds of European, North American and
Asian game, many of which increased mark-
edly in numbers to end one aspect of Australia's and New Zealand's ecological vacuum.
The best-known of these species are the tahr
and chamois in the New Zealand mountains—
a type of game distinguished by fine antlers.
The introduction of red deer from Europe,
however, was an example of bringing in game
without the necessary ecological and biological understanding of local conditions. The

David's deer, which are now again safe i[n] their native China, as well as in South Americ[a] stem from his game park at Woburn Abbey i[n] England.

The transfer of species from one continen[t] to another can, of course, be criticized a[s] "fauna falsification" when it takes plac[e] without any pressing need and when it alter[s] or endangers indigenous game population[s]. But it should not be forgotten that man[y] severely threatened species have been succes[s]fully preserved from extinction by this mean[s]. In many cases, there has been an enrichmen[t] of the local fauna. The efforts associated wit[h] game preservation and wildlife managemen[t] did not arise when game existed in grea[t] abundance, before the authorities or th[e] general public became aware of the threatene[d] disturbance to ecological balance.

This is true, not least of all, for Africa, sti[ll] the largest paradise for dedicated game hunter[s]. Out of the arguments for and against gam[e] protection and the establishment of gam[e] reserves emerged the realization that suc[h] reserves and national parks are profitabl[e] attractions for hunting and photo tourism. [It] was also generally recognized that on rela[tively] unfertile land, hunting edible game [is] far more worthwhile economically than tryin[g] to cultivate crops. Revenue produced b[y] hunting safaris and tourism, properly contro[l]led and directed, can prove beneficial to th[e] development of additional wildlife conserv[a]tion programs. For once, economic considera[tions] have made substantial contributions t[o] game management, for which there was reall[y] no need as recently as fifty years ago. Durin[g] colonial administrations, certain measures fo[r] wildlife conservation, related particularly t[o] hunting, were introduced. Some of them wer[e] adopted by African nations as they becam[e] independent, and a wide range of even mor[e] comprehensive methods and regulations wer[e] implemented in many African countries. Th[e] British, who have had longer experience i[n] this field, founded a college of wildlife man[a]gement, attended by students from man[y] of those nations. The dangers threatenin[g] African game populations derive from th[e] expansion of civilization into areas which u[p] to now have been exclusively the realm o[f] animals. This process includes the transfor[mation of animal territory into agricultur[al]

red deer's natural enemies are absent from the Australian scene and its numbers have increased beyond normal control. To restrict the damage to crops caused by these animals, red deer are subject to random hunting of a kind generally inconsistent with sportsmanship.

Contrary to the Australian experience, the introduction of red deer in high-altitude regions of southern Argentina at the beginning of this century proved successful. The animals were of impressive body weight and had fine antlers—two qualities missing in the smaller native deer of the country. It is natural enough for hunters to show more interest in foreign "exotic" species than in native deer, but the steady increase of the offspring of the imported animals nevertheless led to marked reduction in the number of indigenous species. In the southern Andes district, there are no longer any original South American deer to be found, only those of European origin.

In Patagonia's Parque Diana, fallow deer, white-tailed deer, chamois, ibex, wild sheep and even Chinese milu deer have been successfully introduced. The milu, known also as David's deer, was a strictly protected species in ancient imperial China but was virtually extinct by around the turn of this century due to natural catastrophes and political changes which permitted game protection regulations to lapse. Fortunately, however, a few specimens had earlier found their way into European zoos. The salvation of this species was the work of the Duke of Bedford, a dedicated conservationist. The

3elow: The brocket is threatened with extinction in ts North African and West Asian habitats. Here African game wardens use fast, cross-country ehicles to round up herds of these animals, to et them free in protected areas.

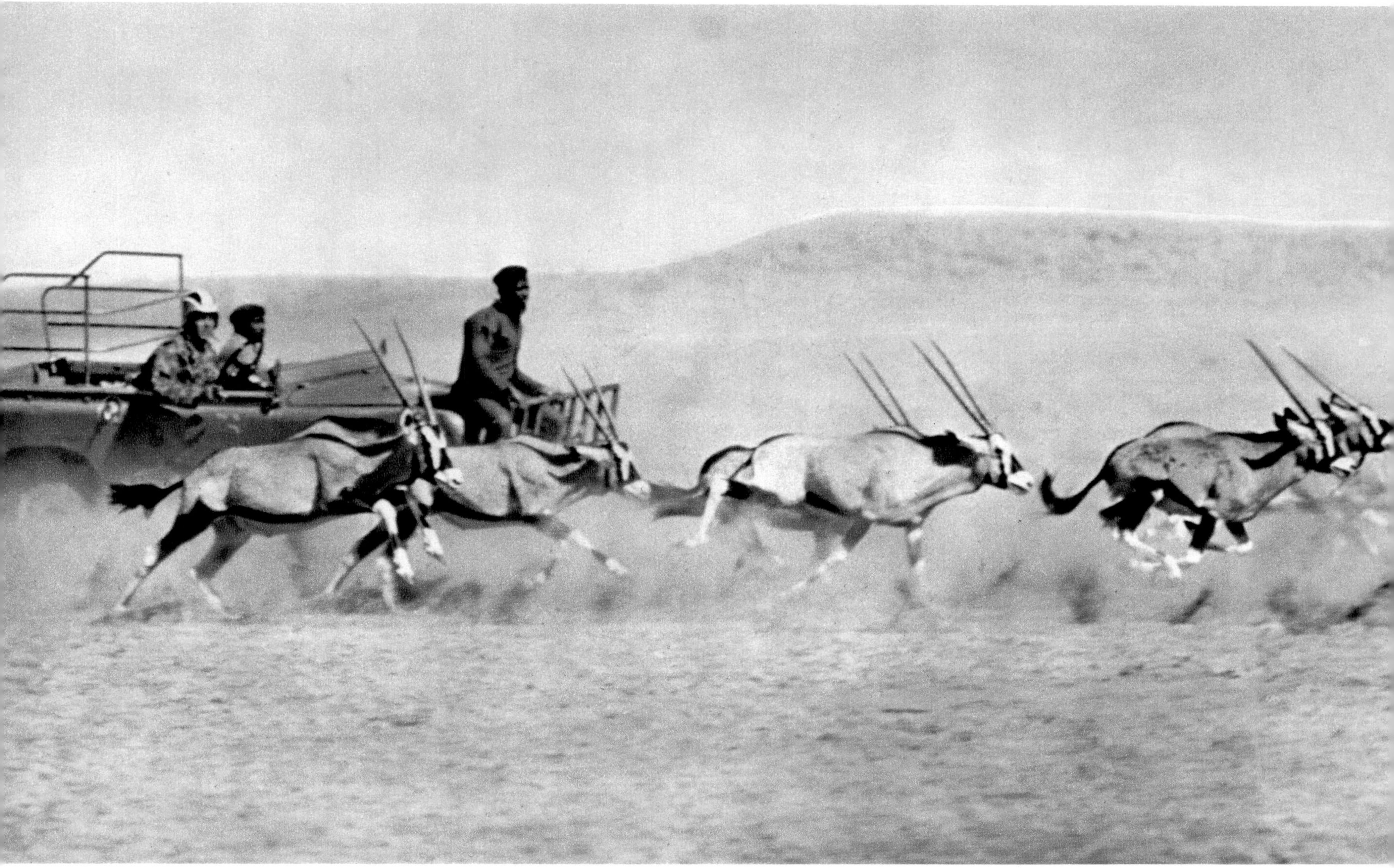

ind. But indiscriminate mass shooting of ame by "professional hunters" has been rohibited in most places and considerably educed. Planned reduction of game popula-ons through culling is less significant in Africa than in many other places. In many African countries, a regional hunting system, ot unlike that practiced in western Europe, revails for game management purposes.

Even in areas with the most abundant game opulations, the future of wild animals out-de reserves and national parks is the respon-bility of special game wardens who use nodern methods to fulfill their responsibilities -for example, counting game from the air o gather information on migration and opulation density. The earlier mistake of anning all hunting in large national parks had dire consequences and has now been corrected. The natural ground covering of vegetation was destroyed by elephants and hippopotamuses and this destruction upset the biological balance with disastrous effects on all species.

Despite the forebodings of pessimists, it can no longer be said, as was commonly believed a few years ago, that African big-game species were on the road to extinction. Recognition of the need for a healthy land-scape of flora and fauna, forming an indivis-ible whole, is now widespread.

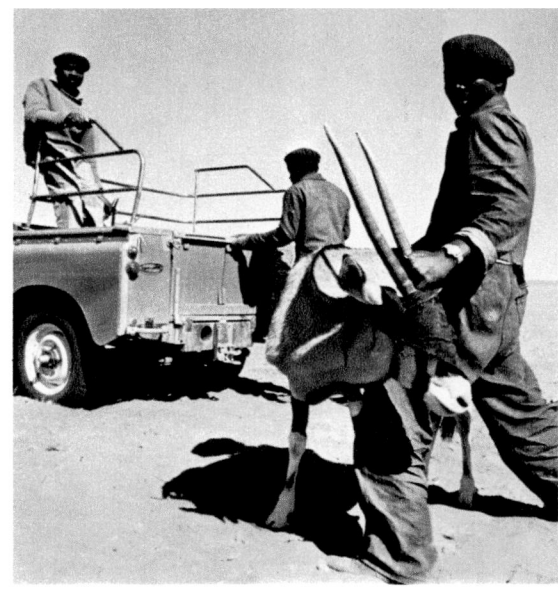

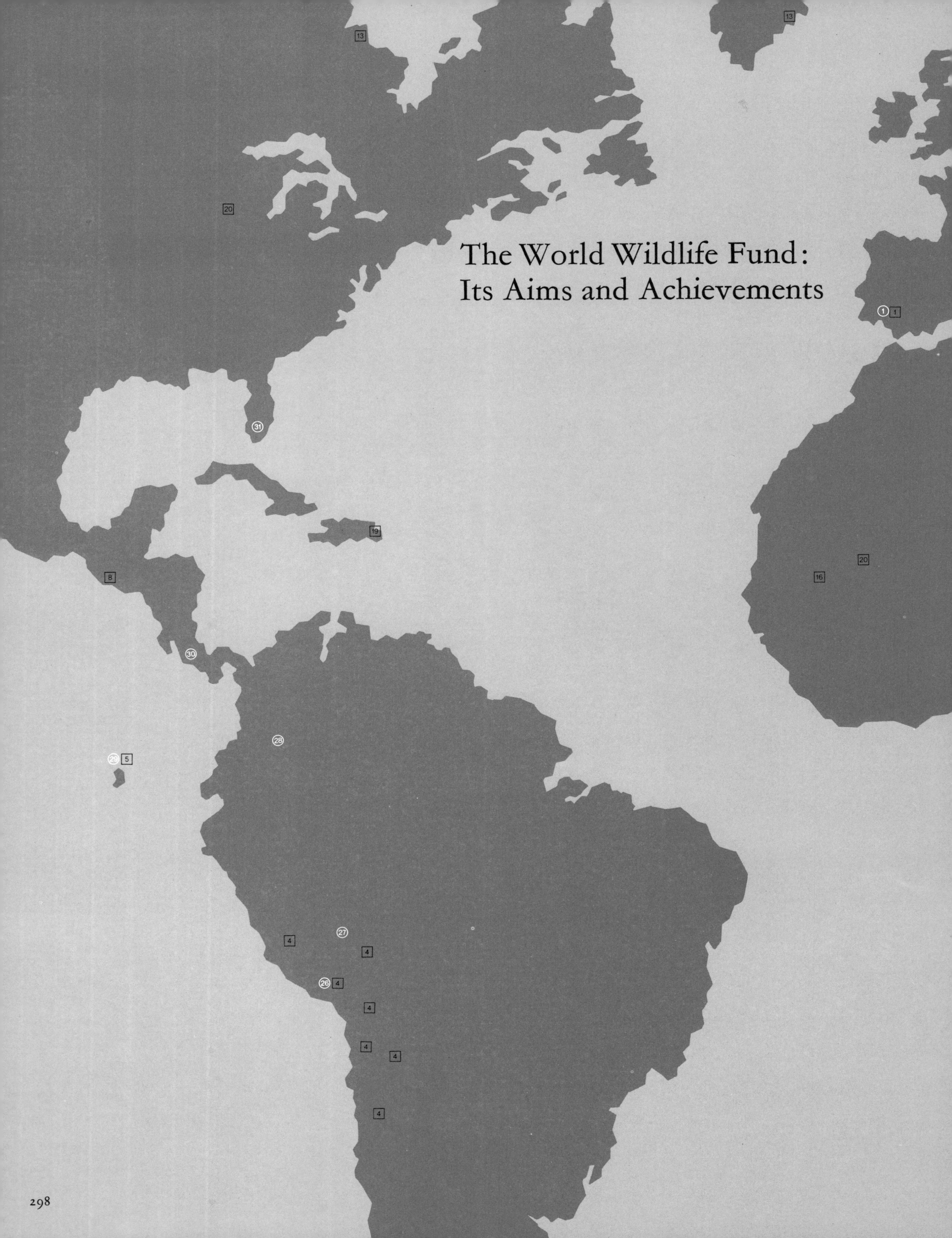

The World Wildlife Fund:
Its Aims and Achievements

9 The Somali wild ass *(Equus asinus somalicus)*. All species of wild ass are severely threatened.

10 The last Arabian oryxes *(Oryx leucoryx)* were saved by a rescue expedition.

11 Barasingha deer of the southern sub-species *(Cervus duvauceli duvauceli)* live only in the Kanha National Park.

12 The Ethiopian ibex *(Capra ibex walie)* is threatened by poachers and by erosion of its environment.

13 The polar bear *(Thalarctos maritimus)* is more severely threatened by hunting for sport than any other predator.

14 The tiger *(Panthera tigris)* is threatened by skin hunters wherever it exists.

15 The Asian lion *(Panthera leo persica)* is restricted to the Gir Reserve in India.

16 The cheetah *(Acinonyx jubatus)* is extinct in Asia, and endangered by skin traders and poachers in Africa.

17 There are only about fifty monkey-eating eagles *(Pithecophaga jefferyi)* still living in the Philippines.

18 Japanese crested ibis *(Nipponia nippon)*: it is doubtful if it will be possible to save the remaining population of about nine birds.

19 Puerto Rican parrot *(Amazona vittata)*. Its biotope has been destroyed, and only around fifteen birds still live free.

20 Peregrine falcon *(Falco peregrinus)*, one of the most severely threatened European birds, endangered by egg poachers, hunters and chemicals.

21 The destruction of vegetation by elephants. Population control is essential as part of environmental conservation.

22 Black rhinoceroses *(Diceros bicornis)*, Rhodesia, being transported over 900 miles to protect them from poachers.

23 Reintroduction is an important part of natural conservation: Mlilwane Reserve, Swaziland.

24 The Hawaiian goose *(Branta sandvicensis)*: Saved by successful breeding and reintroduction.

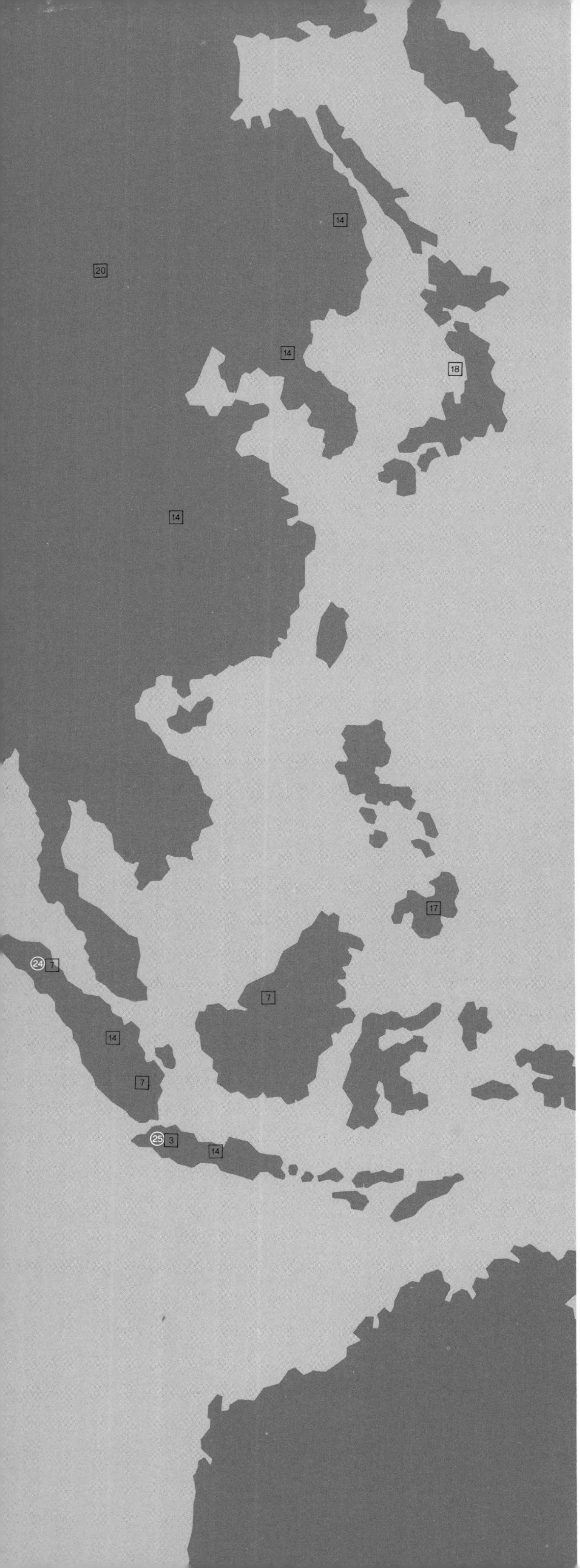

1 The emperor eagle *(Aquila heliaca adalberti)* in the Coto Doñana, one of the most important conservation areas in Europe.

2 The mountain gorilla *(Gorilla gorilla beringei)*. A successful fight is being waged against poaching and the devastation of its habitats in Africa.

3 The Java rhinoceros *(Rhinoceros sondaicus)* in Udjung Kulon; an examplary project in Indonesia.

4 The Vicuna *(Lama vicugna)*. Its populations have increased thanks to protective measures in South America.

5 The Galapagos tortoise *(Testudo elephantopus)*. Both the fauna and flora of the Galapagos are threatened by domestic animals.

6 The aye-aye *(Daubentonia madagasceriensis)*, one of the most severely threatened species of Madagascan fauna.

7 The orang-utan *(Pongo pygmaeus)*. Environmental destruction and trade in animals threaten its future.

8 Morelet's crocodile *(Crocodylus moreletii)* now exists only in captavity. The skin trade threatens all crocodiles.

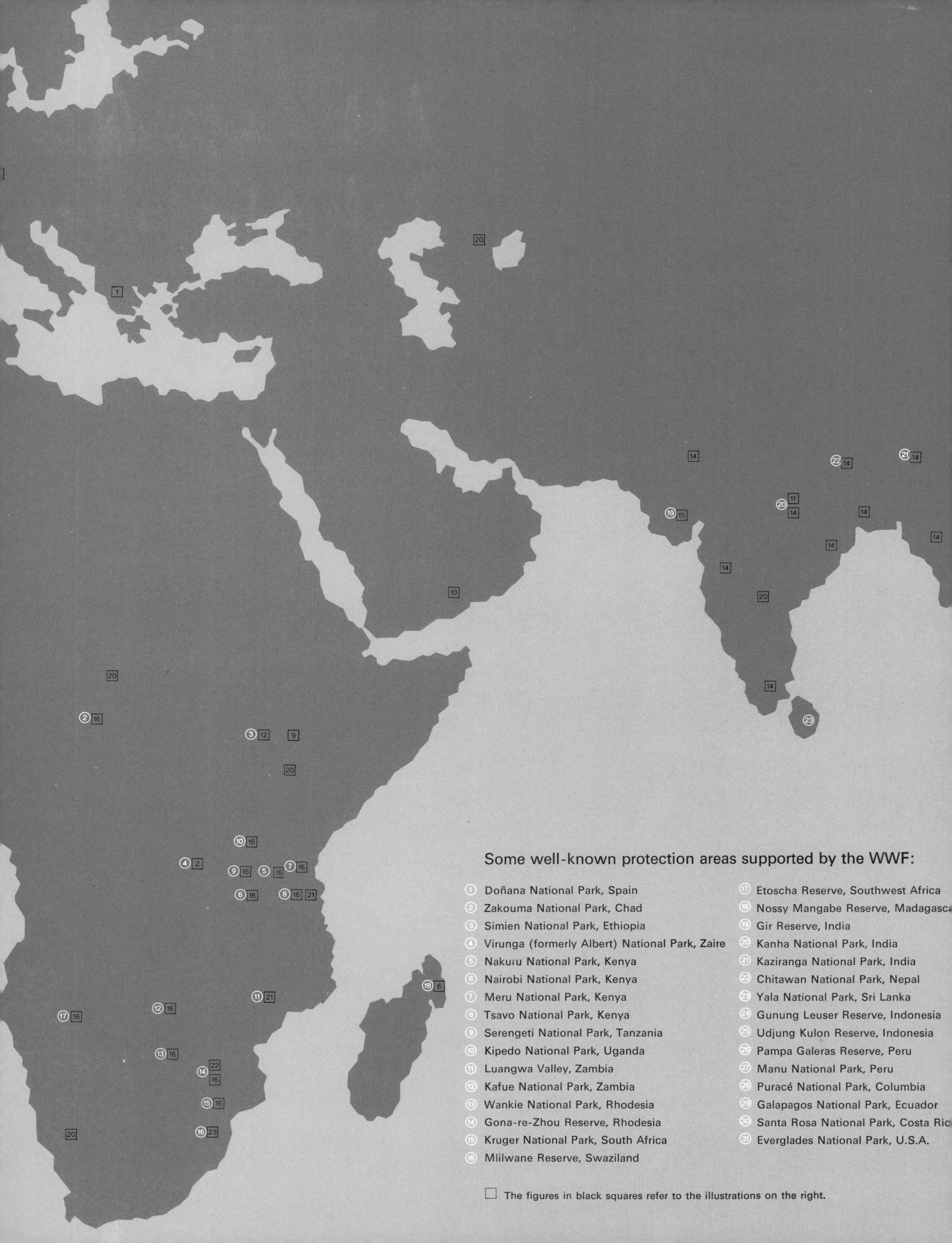

Some well-known protection areas supported by the WWF:

① Doñana National Park, Spain
② Zakouma National Park, Chad
③ Simien National Park, Ethiopia
④ Virunga (formerly Albert) National Park, Zaire
⑤ Nakuru National Park, Kenya
⑥ Nairobi National Park, Kenya
⑦ Meru National Park, Kenya
⑧ Tsavo National Park, Kenya
⑨ Serengeti National Park, Tanzania
⑩ Kipedo National Park, Uganda
⑪ Luangwa Valley, Zambia
⑫ Kafue National Park, Zambia
⑬ Wankie National Park, Rhodesia
⑭ Gona-re-Zhou Reserve, Rhodesia
⑮ Kruger National Park, South Africa
⑯ Mlilwane Reserve, Swaziland

⑰ Etoscha Reserve, Southwest Africa
⑱ Nossy Mangabe Reserve, Madagasca
⑲ Gir Reserve, India
⑳ Kanha National Park, India
㉑ Kaziranga National Park, India
㉒ Chitawan National Park, Nepal
㉓ Yala National Park, Sri Lanka
㉔ Gunung Leuser Reserve, Indonesia
㉕ Udjung Kulon Reserve, Indonesia
㉖ Pampa Galeras Reserve, Peru
㉗ Manu National Park, Peru
㉘ Puracé National Park, Columbia
㉙ Galapagos National Park, Ecuador
㉚ Santa Rosa National Park, Costa Ric
㉛ Everglades National Park, U.S.A.

☐ The figures in black squares refer to the illustrations on the right.

The Task of the World Wildlife Fund

To an ever-increasing extent, the hunter is seriously committed to the conservation of nature and the environment, and is someone actively concerned with the related problems. Despite popular misconceptions, hunting has up till now made an important contribution to the conservation of wildlife. It has done this particularly through the many preservation and close-season regulations which impose specific restrictions upon the hunter. It has also done this through wildlife management measures designed to preserve and increase wildlife populations. Nor should the educational value of hunting be underestimated, because the professional hunter is, as much as the naturalist, one of the first to become aware of the damaging effects of civilization by virtue of his constant contact with nature. Those concerned with conservation recognize this fact. But on closer consideration of the collaboration between the hunter and the conservationist, it becomes clear to today's thoughtful hunter that traditional hunting in the past did not always fulfill its obligations to conservation. This was true especially when it came to maintaining the biological balance and the preservation of the manifold kinds and categories of wildlife with which the hunter was entrusted.

Let us take a closer look at the various problems related to wildlife management. All efforts in this field have little effect when biologically misguided regulations stipulate special protection for female animals or the destruction of individual animals according to highly questionable criteria. Their effect is also diminished when ecologically mistaken cultivation plans are made.

From the conservationist's point of view, the division of animals into "useful" and "harmful" categories is absolutely untenable. It is wrong to protect species of interest to the hunter, such as game birds and ungulates, by biologically unjustifiable means while at the same time withholding protection from animals which threaten the hunter's personal interests by virtue of their natural enmity toward the former group. It is highly commendable that this traditional attitude of the hunter is slowly changing under the influence of wildlife biology; but how long will it be before most hunters realize that birds, wolves,

lynxes, bears and small mammalian predators (or "prey snatchers" as they were once called) should be considered helpers in maintaining the balance of life in the habitat, from which hunters can learn a great deal? The historical picture of indiscriminate slaughter by predators has long since been proved false by such biologists as Hornocker, Mech, Saunders and Haglund. We now know that predators are more selective in their killing than the most practiced hunters can ever hope to be. Lack of space prevents us from going into details in this area, and in any case the subject has been thoroughly treated by the above-mentioned scientists, as well as such others as Cowan, Crisler, Estes, Lack and Wright. It must, however, be emphasized that grave damage can be caused to wildlife communities when the "regulators" of the game cherished by the hunter are destroyed, when they are exterminated by the hunter, or when their justified reintroduction is prevented. Similar consequences occur when one-sided management produces large quantities of game without considering the effects on the other existing species of animal and plant life. It is only when the hunter is able to free himself from the "useful–harmful" concept and recognizes the biological importance and value of all the components of the ecological system with which he is concerned that he will be able to assume a meaningful role in the area of conservation. He can no longer think in terms of "species"—the basis of his concept and the aim of his conservation tactics must be a healthy, varied community of living organisms.

To meet this challenge is a basic task of modern conservation, and it has been the primary—although not the unique—concern of the World Wildlife Fund since its foundation in the autumn of 1961. As an independent international organization, the World Wildlife Fund's goal is to provide the means of protection for threatened habitats, animals and plants; to finance educational projects designed to arouse public interest and enthusiasm for conservation; and to animate politicians and authoritative organizations to initiate necessary protective measures on national and international levels. In order to ensure scientific objectivity for the projects

under its support, the WWF works in clo collaboration with its sister organization, th IUCN (International Union for the Conse vation of Nature and Natural Resources The acquisition of the necessary funds is base on the various activities of the WWF's pr motion societies in eighteen countries.

Up until the end of June 1972, the WW was able to support 710 projects in eighty-fo different countries. The outlay was $ 8,700,00

Due to economic and technical expansio and population increases, the burden impose by man upon the last remaining natur landscapes is weighing steadily heavier. Sin 1600 36 species and 64 sub-species of mamma have died out entirely, as well as 94 species ar 164 sub-species of birds. In the IUCN's "Re Data Book" of threatened species, species ar sub-species of 306 mammals, 281 birds, reptiles, 27 amphibians and 79 fishes are liste and one of the WWF's main goals is to preve the extinction of these species. Because of i restricted financial means, the WWF is oblige to give priority to areas threatened by imm diate danger to their species or environmen This is carried out chiefly by activities co nected with the preservation of biotopes an precautions against poaching. It is only whe all other measures have proved to be futi that breeding in captivity, with the eventu aim of subsequent reintroduction, is co sidered.

With the aid of technical assistance, th conservation of biotopes and research, th WWF has been successful in preventing th further decline of the Ethiopian ibex, th nilgiri thar, the vicuna and several su species of the red deer (barasingha, hangu Sardinian red deer). The preservation of th orang-utan and the mountain gorilla has als been promoted. In India, the WWF has helpe to build up the number of the last Asiatic lio in the Gir Reserve and the rhinoceroses Kaziranga. By means of an extensive progran it is hoped to prevent the extinction of th tiger. Irresponsible hunting of big game, suc as tiger and polar bear, as a sport has bee restricted or forbidden by numerous gover ments on the initiative of the WWF and th IUCN. Since 1962, the WWF has assisted th protection of the last Javanese rhinoceroses the Udjung Kulon Reserve, and their numb as increased to approximately forty. The WWF also supports a number of projects for the preservation of threatened species of birds, in particular birds of prey.

Because of unrestricted hunting and the destruction of natural habitats, breeding in captivity is the only possibility left for the preservation of many species. The WWF has financed a number of ventures of this kind with the aim of subsequent reintroduction when the chances of survival in free hunting territory have improved. Among the most spectacular undertakings are the preservation of the Arabian oryx and the breeding and successful reintroduction of the Hawaiian goose, the Hawaiian duck, Swinhoe's pheasant and several sub-species of the Galapagos tortoise. In the Mlilwane Reserve in Swaziland, numerous animals, many of which had ceased to exist there eighty years ago, have been successfully reintroduced. The same is true of the white and black rhinoceroses, both of which have resettled in Rhodesia and Mozambique thanks to the assistance of the WWF. At present a project is being carried out to save the griffon vulture in France—as yet unfortunately without success, since three of the four freed birds were shot shortly after reintroduction. Education of the public must thus form a substantial part of our work, not only in the developing countries, but also in the rest of the world.

In most cases, the purpose of these individual projects is more than just the protection of a threatened species. The species in question was often only the point of crystallization around which a comprehensive program was formed with the aim of introducing—after a thorough study of the situation and possibilities—the best means of protection and of stimulating state authorities into action. In many cases this resulted in the formation of reserves and national parks.

One of the first and most comprehensive projects of this kind was the establishment of the Coto-Doñana and Guadiamar nature reserves at the mouth of the Guadalquivir in Spain. It was there that the purchase of land was the only way of saving one of Europe's last unspoiled landscapes, with its unique animal life. In this undertaking, the Spanish government was induced by the WWF to acquire the surrounding areas so that they could be amalgamated with the WWF reserves to form the Doñana National Park. By means of similar measures, the WWF was able to assist in the preservation of parts of the Camargue in France, Marchau and Seewinkel in Austria, as well as numerous marshlands in England and the United States. In Africa, South America and Asia, the WWF's main activities are promoting existing national parks and ensuring their continued existence through

the service of experts and technical assistance in the management of areas and the fight against poaching. In particular, the East African national parks and reserves such as Serengeti and Arusha (Tanzania), Nakuru, Meru and Tsavo (Kenya) have profited from the WWF's continued assistance. Protected areas in Zaire, Ethiopia and southern Africa also belong to the promoted regions, and the protected areas in India such as Kaziranga (for the rhinoceros and tiger) and Kanha (for the remaining eighty-five swamp deer, otherwise known as Barasingha). In Latin America, the Santa Rosa National Park (Costa Rica) and the Manu National Park (Peru) also enjoy the assistance of the WWF.

Of particular interest is the preservation of the original animal and plant life of oceanic islands and large isolated areas of land which, due to their centuries-long seclusion, have formed a unique environment which may be regarded as a real textbook of evolution. After long isolation, these organisms lack the ability to compete with newly introduced modern forms of life; thus they are helpless when settlements, new species of plant life, animals and tourism take over the area without proper control. Galapagos, the Seychelles, Madagascar and New Guinea are a few examples of such well-known areas connected with the WWF. Apart from research on the institution of reserves, the WWF also finances practical work on the preservation or recreation of the biological balance in these areas. It is an erroneous assumption of over-conservative conservationists that human influence must be entirely absent from these natural oases, since without research and management effective conservation is impossible. The presence of scientifically qualified personnel is essential, and contemporary conservation can no longer shrink from taking unpopular steps. These could include, for example, the destruction of supernumerary ungulates which exist both in African and European national parks as a result of faulty management and which often disturb the natural balance in these areas. In this context it should be mentioned that hunting and the resulting availability of surplus game for human consumption is of exceptional value. The WWF, therefore, supports the education of local wildlife officers and game wardens. The Fund also sends qualified persons to many parts of the world to direct local projects, and to train the local personnel responsible not only for the management of the conservation areas but also for the arousal of the desperately needed interest in conservation among the local population.

The WWF achieved a great deal in the first ten years of its existence. Its success has been

attained through close collaboration between scientists, conservationists and a wide public which contributes the necessary financial means. The finances of the WWF are limited. But it is not the task of a private organization to take on long-term conservation jobs, since the preservation of wildlife is a basic responsibility of sovereign state governments. The aim of the WWF thus consists of drawing attention to deficiencies in existing conservation programs and remedying them by immediate action until the governments in question are in the position to take the necessary steps. In comparison with the demands which will be faced in the future, the WWF's achievements so far do not appear overwhelming. Worldwide destruction of nature is expanding. The last natural and unspoiled landscapes are becoming accessible and increasingly disturbed by faulty management. The natural landscape is disappearing, and with it countless species of plant and animal life.

When we look back on the considerable success of the WWF during this short period, however, it becomes clear that we are not helpless in trying to prevent the approaching catastrophe. Modern conservation, in collaboration with natural science, has effective methods at its disposal to restrict further destruction. The foundation stone has been laid by the IUCN and the WWF. From the collaboration between the two organizations over the years, a partnership has evolved which is thoroughly worthy and capable of further development.

The IUCN, through its worthwhile network of scientific collaborators, is in a position to construct well-founded conservation programs for which the WWF, together with other institutions, does all it can to produce the necessary resources. It is only through the concerted efforts of all conservationist circles that it will be possible to resolve the coming problems on the basis of scientific research.

The WWF, therefore, appeals to all hunters to consider the present critical situation carefully, to dispose of obsolete attitudes, and to proceed cautiously toward a new conception of hunting. It is no longer sufficient to direct wildlife management exclusively toward its effectiveness and usefulness to the hunter; it is now essential to reorganize the entire concept on the basis of modern, biological and ecological knowledge. The preservation of wildlife can, together with a knowledge of biology, enable the hunter to confirm his position as administrator of valuable natural treasures and to carry out his task more effectively than ever before in a constantly changing landscape and a constantly changing society.

Man can only return to nature when he temporarily revives the animal in himself. If we desire to profit from the pure and noble happiness of returning to nature, we must seek contact with the animals of the forest, meet them on their terms, accept their challenge, and pursue them.

This subtle rite is that which we call hunting because hunting is the imitation of animals. For those who give themselves up completely to nature, the air has a more delicious tingle on the skin and in the lungs, the rocks take on a more expressive form, and the vegetation gains in significance and meaning. All this can only happen, however, when the hunter feels an affinity with the animals he hunts during the stalk or while he crouches waiting for his prey. In this mystical link with the game, a deeper connection develops, and the hunter starts to be like the animal he hunts: he becomes one with nature.

JOSÉ ORTEGA Y GASSET

The Authors

XAVER AMMANN, PH. D.

His activities as a hunter led him early on to an intensive involvement with all aspects of dog breeding and training. He is the initiator of the amalgamation of various Swiss hunting- and working-dog associations. As member, judge and examiner of numerous clubs and associations devoted to canine matters, he has had considerable influence on the promotion of the science of hunting-dogs in Europe. He contributes to various publications on hunting and canine science.

Dr. Ammann wrote the chapters on pages 191–205.

RUTH BUCHER

She was educated early in nature observation and hunting by her father, a passionate hunter, and has hunted in Europe, the Near East and India. For many years co-tenant in large and small game estates in Germany, Austria and Switzerland, she also owned her own hunting estate for many years and was active as leader and keeper of her game. She is a passionate and successful conservationist.

Ruth Bucher wrote the chapters on pages 11, 13, 15, 78–9, 96, 100–3, 106–7, 110–120, 136–7, 143–4, 160–1, 165–6, 176–8, 180, 206, 238, 242–3.

CLAUDE HETTIER DE BOISLAMBERT

Spent twenty-five years of his life in Africa. Has hunted all over Africa, Asia, North America, the Arctic and all European countries. 1926–1939: numerous expeditions for studying zoological and ethnological situations in Central Africa. Educational journeys in Scandinavia, Central Europe and the Middle East. Was President of the International Advisory Committee of Hunting for ten years. As President of the "Haut Conseil pour la Chasse" in the former French overseas colonies, he created a well-functioning authoritative body and established reserves which are for the most part still in existence today.

Claude Hettier de Boislambert wrote the chapters on pages 280–3.

DR. HARTMUT JUNGIUS

1963: studied biology and geography at Kiel University. 1963: voluntary work in Winnipeg Zoo; visited the National Parks of Canada and the U.S.A. 1967–1968: matriculated at Pretoria University; studied the biology of the reedbuck in the Kruger National Park. 1969: engaged as UNESCO expert for nature protection and ecology in Bolivia. 1970: appointed by World Wildlife Fund as official expert on nature protection and conservation projects; travels in Peru, Chile, the Galapagos (including studies in the construction of game reserve areas). Is currently researching the possibility of the reintroduction of extinct animals.
Has published books on the biology of the reedbuck and problems relating to the conservation of the vicuna.

Dr. Jungius wrote the chapters on pages 298–303.

AUGUSTIN KRAMER, PH. D.

1957–1968: studies in zoology at Zurich University; period in Finland; worked at the bird sanctuary in Sempach. Thesis on the social organization and behavior of the chamois. 1968–1970: Postdoctoral Fellowship at the Department of Zoology, University of Alberta, Edmonton, Canada. Published works on the ecology and interspecific relationships of the American and roe deer, as well as on the habits of the Rocky Mountain goat. Since 1970: collaborator in the study group for game research at Zurich University.

Dr. Kramer wrote the chapters on pages 98–9 and 152–3.

DR. FRED KURT

Worked temporarily as an elephant keeper in a circus before commencing his studies. 1960: one-year expedition to eastern Ethiopia. 1967: thesis on the social behavior of the roe deer. Numerous research visits to Sri Lanka (1967–1969: elephant ecology); India (1969: nature protection problems); north Sumatra (1970: orang-utan, Sumatran rhinoceros). Since 1970 professor at Zurich University and director of various research projects in Switzerland (roe deer, red deer), and in Asia (Sumatran rhinoceros, orang-utan, marsh deer and tiger).

Dr. Kurt wrote the chapters on pages 73, 90–5, 127–132, 135, 138–141, 150–1, 155, 158–9, 170–5, 179, 182–4, 270–1.

WALTHER NIEDL

Studied in Prague. 1936: forestry official in southern Bohemia. 1939 and 1949: director of the Forestry Department of the City of Amberg. Currently working as graphic artist and portrait painter. Collaboration on various hunting publications (hunting, ecology, hunting ethics). Illustrator of numerous other works on hunting conservation and wild animals.

Walther Niedl wrote the chapters on pages 214–223, 230–7, 240.

KARL SÄLZLE, PH. D.

Graduated in zoology in 1932 at Heidelberg University. Since 1933 manager of the natural science collection of the German Hunting Museum in Munich, and since 1945 director of the same institute. Author of various publications on the history of hunting.

Dr. Sälzle wrote the chapters on pages 17–71.

DR. ERNST SCHÄFER

Previously chief curator at the State Museum of Lower Saxony; professor of biology and ecology at the Central University of Venezuela in Caracas. Director of the biological station of Rancho Grande. Four research and hunting expeditions to Tibet, China, India (1931–1939). Five-year stay in Venezuela as researcher and game biologist. Three hunting and research journeys to Alaska and Canada. Hunting journeys and studies in game biology in Zaire, Kenya, Tanzania, Southwest Africa and Rhodesia. Currently occupied with nature conservation and game biology all over the world. Author of numerous books and articles on hunting in professional journals.

Dr. Schäfer wrote the chapters on pages 74–82–8, 104–5, 108–9, 156–7, 168, 188–9, 208–218, 224–9, 244–69, 272–9, 284–7, 289–297.

NORMAN GELB

The English-language edition of this book was edited by Norman Gelb, who also wrote the Introduction on pages 8–9. He is author of Enemy in the Shadows, a history of espionage, and contributor to The Magnificent Continent, a textual pictorial study of North America. For many years a Europe correspondent for the Mutual Broadcasting System, he is a graduate of Brooklyn College and undertook postgraduate studies at the Universities of Minnesota and Vienna.

The chapter "The Study of Wildlife in North America" (pages 146–7) was written by Dr. W. Schröder, Institute of Game Research and Hunting of the Institute of Forestry in Munich.

cknowledgments

Adamson / Len Sirman Press, Geneva 181
mund Amstad / C. J. Bucher AG, Lucerne 90/91
ai Angermayer, Munich 132
rice Babey, Basel 35
Louise Baker 23
dhart Bakker-Hofbauer, Utrecht 203
vin A. Bauer, Jackson 160 161/162 247 250 256
us Behnke / Bavaria-Verlag, Gauting 95
nz Behrens / Bavaria-Verlag, Gauting 112 115
re Belzeaux / Zodiaque, Saint-Léger-Vauban 42
rid Bergman Sucksdorf, Lerdala 134 266/267 267 268
69
dré Bert / Jacana, Paris 166
liothèque nationale, Paris 44 45 57
rst Bielfeld / Bavaria-Verlag, Gauting 115
é-Pierre Bille, Siders 112
ck Star, London / Rapho, Paris 233
č Blahout, Tatranska Lomnica 221
ter Blum, Esslingen 185
British Museum, London 29
hel Brosselin / Jacana, Paris 241
Browning, Helena 157 257
ximilien Bruggmann, Yverdon 14/15 16/17 265
era Press (Africamera) / Len Sirman Press, Geneva 181
liano Cappeli, Florence 100/101
ge Chevallier / Jacana, Paris 161
nz Christ / Bavaria-Verlag, Gauting 56
mut Ctverak / Bavaria-Verlag, Gauting 94
rner Curth / Anthony Verlag, Starnberg 206/207
mitri Debabow / Erwin Buchholz, Lohmar 208/209 209
pendra Naryan Singh Deo, Bangalore 130
utsches Jagdmuseum, Munich 25 34 52 53 58 58/59
o 61 62 63 64 64/65 65 66 67 68 69 70 71 108
rre Didier / World Wildlife Fund, Morges 301
li Dolder, Düsseldorf 128 129 165 176 177 178 281 285
n Dominis / Life, New York 10/11 12/13
ns D. Dossenbach, Oberschlatt 165 167 170/171
72/173 182/183 184
mbarton Oaks, Washington D.C. 22
menic Feuerstein, Schuls 108/109
nneth W. Fink / Ardea, London 161
lene Fischer, Davos 244 252–253 258 258/259 259
78/279
drich Forman, Prague 30 31
nns Fugger, Schweiggers 120
né Gacond, Neuenburg 111 116
dré Gamet / Rapho, Paris 196
P. Gee / World Wildlife Fund, Morges 301
lerius Geist, Calgary 156
org Gerster, Zumikon 166 254/255
en Gillsäter, Stockholm 79 106 107 144
raudon, Paris 29
inrich Gohl, Basel 248 249
Gooders / Ardea, London 133
nneth W. Green / World Wildlife Fund, Morges 300
arles A. W. Guggisberg / World Wildlife Fund,
Morges 178 301
nst Haas, New York 2/3 6/7 183 304/305
rel Hájek, Prague 111 190/191 196 205 210 211 217 230
hn Hanks / World Wildlife Fund, Morges 301
b Hannah / Black Star, New York / Rapho, Paris 294
us Hansmann, Munich 46
lter Hege / Bavaria-Verlag, Gauting 4/5
uis Henri / Rapho, Paris 57
ude Hettier de Boislambert, Paris 278 280 282 283
ttfried Hinker / Bavaria-Verlag, Gauting 114
ns Hinz, Basel 19
rmer-Fotoarchiv, Munich 38 39 83
roslav Holeček, Prague 1 78 79 93 105 116 144 201 216
224/225 225 226 227 230 231 232 239
deněk Holeček, Prague 78 79 85 104 233

Andries Hoogerwerf / World Wildlife Fund, Morges 300
Thomas Höpker / Bavaria-Verlag, Gauting 212/213
Eric Hosking / World Wildlife Fund, Morges 300
Arnold Imhof / C. J. Bucher AG, Lucerne 74 75 94 94/95
95 98 231 237
Peter Jackson / World Wildlife Fund, Morges 301
Hartmut Jungius /World Wildlife Fund, Morges 300
Anton Kaiser, Oberwildflecken 79 114 228
Jürg Klages, Zürich 133
Hans Klingel / World Wildlife Fund, Morges 301
Knorr-Wedekind 214/215
Jan Kopec / Len Sirman Press, Geneva 180
M. Krishnan, Madras 140–141
Peter Krott, Stein 106 107
Kunsthistorisches Museum, Vienna 46
Fred Kurt, Zürich 270 271
György Lajos / Interfoto MTI, Budapest 223
Teppo Lampio, Helsinki 243
Frank Lane / Christiansen / Rapho, Paris 308/309,
front jacket
Harald Lange, Leipzig 166
Thor Larsen / World Wildlife Fund, Morges 295 301
Hans Lasswitz, Hanover 92 102
Bert Leidmann / Bavaria-Verlag, Gauting 115 211
Max Lenz, Berne 99 100 291
Walter Linsenmaier, Ebikon 84 85 114 115 118 119 125
126 130/131 131 136 138 139 274 275 276 277
A. Lobov / Agence de presse Novosti, Geneva 204
Karl-Henry Lundin, Stavsjöbruk 105 204 252 253
Werner Lüthy / Bavaria-Verlag, Gauting 246 246/247
Manfred Mackus / Bavaria-Verlag, Gauting 117
Aldo Margiocco, Campomorone 117
Lennart Mathiasson, Nyköping 103 114 121
Leonhard von Matt, Buochs 310/311
L. David Mech, Minneapolis 152/153
Max Meerkämpfer, Davos-Platz 235
Roland et Sabrina Michaud, Paris 32 33
Ministry of Information, Broadcasting and
Tourism, Uganda, Kampala 165
Alice Mommersteeg / Atlas Photo, Paris 200
Montana Fish and Game Department, Helena 143 144
160 161
Alessandro Mossotti, Milan 109
Horst Munzig, Mindelheim 188/189 189
Musée Cernuschi, Paris 24
Museum of Fine Arts, Boston (Francis Bartlett Donation)
39
Norman Myers / A.A.A. Photo, Paris 168/169 177
Norman Myers / Bruce Coleman Limited, Hillingdon 133
Norman Myers / Len Sirman Press, Geneva 180
Carl Näher / Bavaria-Verlag, Gauting 115
Jean Naud / A.A.A. Photo, Paris 178
Alexander Niestlé, Theesen 78 90 91 94 117 198 236
Alexander Niestlé / Bavaria-Verlag, Gauting 90 91 114
Bernhard Nievergelt / World Wildlife Fund, Morges 301
Ontario Ministry of Natural Resources, Toronto 143 152
244
Charlie Ott / National Audubon Society, New York
148/149 251
Jean-Jacques Petter / World Wildlife Fund, Morges 300
Pierre Pfeffer, Paris 140 141
Goetz Dieter Plage / Anglia TV, London 197
Hans Plattner, St. Moritz 96 97 99 290
Fritz Pölking, Greven 306/307, back jacket
Paul Popper Limited, London 208
James H. Powell jr. / World Wildlife Fund, Morges 300
Radio Times Hulton Picture Library, London 280
E. Hanumantha Rao, Bangalore 129
Albert Rastl, Bad Aussee 87
Hans Reinhard, Eiterbach 94 102 103 117
Hans Reinhard / Tierbilder Okapia, Frankfurt 234

Hans Peter Renner, Lucerne 15 18 83
Hans Retzlaff / Bavaria-Verlag, Gauting 56
Dick Robinson / Bruce Coleman Limited, Hillingdon
134 143
Josef Roedle, Pfrondorf 86 87
Roger-Viollet, Paris 47
Walther Rohdich, Münster 232
Leonard Lee Rue III, Blairstown 79 109 143 144 146/147
150 150/151 154 155 158 159 160 161 162/163 165 233
254 255 284/285
Satour, Frankfurt 165 166
Leszek Krzysztof Sawicki, Sulechów 222/223
Marlis Saxer / C. J. Bucher AG, Lucerne 40 78 79 142
143 144 164 165
Ernst Schäfer, Göhr 178 265 286/287 287
Adolf Schmidecker, Oberschleissheim 133 134
Arne Schmitz / Bruce Coleman Limited, Hillingdon 95
205
Horst Schröder, Waren 72/73
Emil Schulthess / Rapho, Paris 186/187
Emil Schulthess / World Wildlife Fund, Morges 300
Harald Schultz, Cardaillac 262 263 265
Hermann Schünemann / Bavaria-Verlag, Gauting 114 115
116
Marion Schuster, Pully 210 218
Schweizerisches Landesmuseum, Zürich 43
Blanka Šefl / C. J. Bucher AG, Lucerne 76/77 80/81
86/87 110 111 114/115 124
Fritz Siedel, Sande 79 88/89 215 231 236 240
Heinz Sielmann / World Wildlife Fund, Morges 300
South African Wildlife Foundation / World Wildlife Fund,
Morges 301
Werner Stangenberg / World Wildlife Fund, Morges 265
Statens Historiska Museum, Stockholm 43
State of Alaska, Dept. of Fish and Game / World
Wildlife Fund, Morges 295
Hans Steiner, St. Moritz 220
Edith Stolz / C. J. Bucher AG, Lucerne 82 179 298–300
136 292, jacket
Sunday Mail / World Wildlife Fund, Morges 301
Tokutaro Tanaka / Zanders Feinpapiere GmbH,
Bergisch Gladbach 122/123
John Tarlton, Christchurch 238
Onni Terävä, Tampere 197 235 242
Peter Thomas / Bavaria-Verlag, Gauting 210
S. A. Thompson / World Wildlife Fund, Morges 301
Three Lions / World Wildlife Fund, Morges 296
Tierbilder Okapia, Frankfurt 78 137 160 166
Walter Tilgner / Camera Photo Archives, Lucerne 78 79
84 220/221
Konrad Tönges, Grossfelden 92
Philippe Tourin / Atlas Photo, Paris 145
Uganda Tourist Board, Kampala 165
Walter Uhlig, Zürich 78 199 200
U.S. Fish and Wildlife Service, Washington D.C. 143 144
244/245 245
U.S. Forest Service / World Wildlife Fund, Morges 301
Jean-Philippe Varin / Jacana, Paris 133
Charles A. Vaucher, Presinge 219
Fritz Vollmar / World Wildlife Fund, Morges 301
Wangi / Jacana, Paris 134
Karl Weidmann, Los Teques 260/261 264 265
Hubert Weisbrod, Zürich 228/229 229 283 284 312/313
Åke Wintzell, Täby 202 203
Evert Woxberg, Borlänge 113
Yoshimaro Yamashina / World Wildlife Fund, Morges 301

All illustrations not acknowledged here come from the
archives of C. J. Bucher AG, Lucerne.

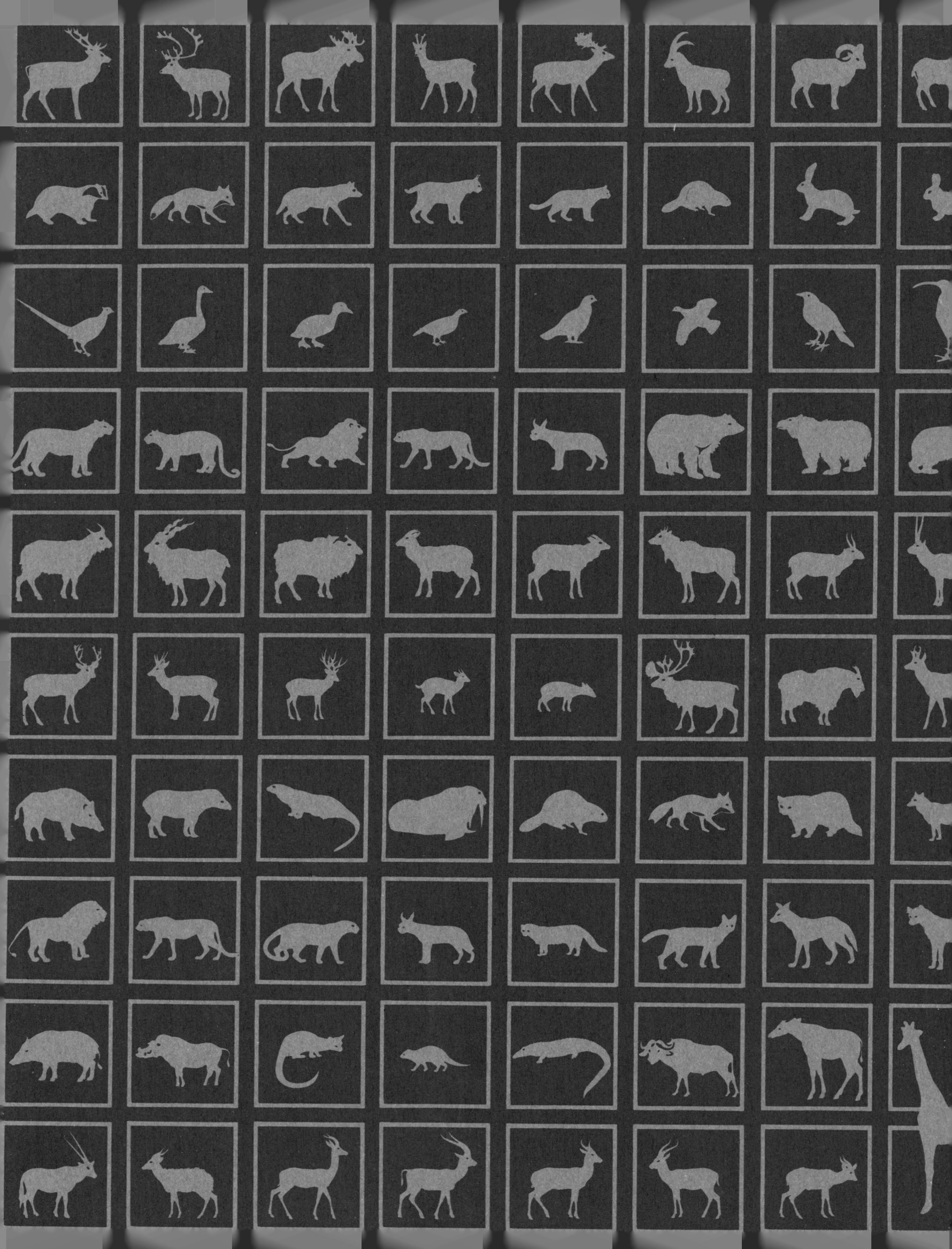